Introductio
American !

Introduction to American Studies

Third edition

Edited by

Malcolm Bradbury
and Howard Temperley

LONGMAN
LONDON AND NEW YORK

Addison Wesley Longman Limited
Edinburgh Gate
Harlow
Essex CM20 2JE
United Kingdom
and Associated Companies throughout the world

Published in the United States of America
by Addison Wesley Longman Inc., New York

First edition   1981
Second edition 1989
Third edition   1998

ISBN 0 582-30738-4

British Library Cataloguing-in-Publication Data

A catalogue record for this book is available from the British Library

Library of Congress Cataloging-in-Publication Data

Introduction to American studies / [edited by] Malcolm Bradbury and
    Howard Temperley. — 3rd ed.
        p.   cm.
    Includes bibliographical references (p.   ) and index.
    ISBN 0-582-30738-4 (pbk.)
    1. United States—Civilization.   I. Bradbury, Malcolm, 1932– .
II. Temperley, Howard.
E169.1.I68   1998
973—dc21   98–13563
                                                            CIP

Set by 35 in 10.5/12pt Baskerville
Produced through Longman Malaysia,

Contents

Chronology

1773	Boston Tea Party
1774	Coercive Acts
1775	Fighting at Lexington and Concord; Second Continental Congress assembles
1776	Thomas Paine, *Common Sense*; Declaration of Independence
1778	Franco-American alliance
1781	Articles of Confederation proclaimed; defeat of British at Yorktown
1782	H St John de Crèvecoeur, *Letters from an American Farmer*
1783	Articles of Peace ratified (Treaty of Paris); Noah Webster, *American Spelling Book*
1785	Ordinance passed for sale of western lands
1787	Constitutional Convention meets in Philadelphia; Northwest Ordinance provides for government of national domain
1787–88	Alexander Hamilton et al., *The Federalist*
1788	Constitution ratified
1789 ·	George Washington elected first US President
1790	First US Census shows population of 3.9 million
1791–96	Hamilton–Jefferson feud leads to emergence of first American party system (Federalists versus Democratic-Republicans)
1793	Eli Whitney invents cotton gin
1800	Thomas Jefferson (Democratic-Republican) elected third US President
1803	Louisiana Purchase extends US border to Rockies
1807	African slave trade to US abolished; Joel Barlow, *The Columbiad*
1812–14	War of 1812
1815–17	Collapse of Federalist Party
1819	Washington Irving, *Sketch Book of Geoffrey Crayon, Gent.*
1820	Missouri Compromise exludes slavery from Louisiana Purchase Lands north of 36° 31′
1823	Monroe Doctrine; James Fenimore Cooper, *The Pioneers*
1824	Election of John Quincy Adam as sixth US President heralds break-up of Republican Party
1825	Erie Canal links Hudson River and Great Lakes
1826	James Fenimore Cooper, *The Last of the Mohicans*
1828	Noah Webster, *An American Dictionary of the English Language*; Andrew Jackson elected seventh US President
1831	Nat Turner uprising in Virginia; Edgar Allan Poe, *Poems*
1832–33	Nullification Crisis leads to scaling-down of Tariffs on imported goods
1833	American Antislavery Society founded
1835–40	Alexis de Tocqueville, *Democracy in America*

1836	Colt pistol patented; Texas achieves independence from Mexico and becomes a sovereign republic
1837	Ralph Waldo Emerson, 'The American Scholar'
1840	Abolitionists launch Liberty Party; William Harrison (Whig) defeats Martin Van Buren (Democrat) in contest for US Presidency; Edgar Allan Poe, *Tales of the Grotesque*
1841	Horace Greeley launches *New York Tribune*
1843	W H Prescott, *History of the Conquest of Mexico*
1845	Annexation of Texas
1846	Introduction of McCormick reaper; by agreement with Britain, US acquired control of Pacific North-west up to the 49th parallel (Oregon Settlement)
1846–48	War with Mexico leads to acquisition of California and Pacific South-west
1849	California gold rush; Francis Parkman, *Oregon Trail*
1850	Nathaniel Hawthorne, *The Scarlet Letter*; Compromise of 1850; Seventh US Census shows a population of 23 million
1850–53	Collapse of Whig Party
1851	Herman Melville, *Moby-Dick*; *New York Times* launched
1852	Harriet Beecher Stowe, *Uncle Tom's Cabin*
1854	Kansas–Nebraska Act repeals Missouri Compromise; emergence of Republican Party; Henry David Thoreau, *Walden*
1855	First edition of Walt Whitman's *Leaves of Grass*
1857	Supreme Court's Dred Scott decision denies citizenship to US blacks and right of Congress to exclude slavery from territories
1859	John Brown's raid on arsenal at Harper's Ferry, Virginia
1860	Abraham Lincoln (Republican) elected sixteenth US President
1861	Secession of Southern states leads to outbreak of Civil War; Morrill Tariff inaugurates new high-tariff policy
1862	Homestead Act
1863	Emancipation Proclamation frees slaves in areas under rebel control
1865	Surrender of Confederate forces; slavery abolished by 13th Amendment; assassination of President Lincoln
1867	First Reconstruction Act; purchase of Alaska from Russia; Horatio Alger, *Ragged Dick*
1869	Mark Twain, *Innocents Abroad*; completion of first transcontinental railroad
1870	Bret Harte, *The Luck of Roaring Camp*
1875	Mary Baker Eddy, *Science and Health*
1875–76	Second Sioux War; defeat of Custer's cavalry in Battle of the Little Big Horn

1876	Invention of the telephone by Alexander Graham Bell
1877	Withdrawal of Federal troops from the South marks end of Reconstruction
1881	John D Rockefeller's Standard Oil Trust established; Henry James, *Portrait of a Lady*
1885	Mark Twain, *The Adventures of Huckleberry Finn*; William Dean Howells, *The Rise of Silas Lapham*
1887	Dawes Severalty Act provides for the settlement of Indians on homesteads
1888	Edward Bellamy, *Looking Backward*
1890	Sherman Antitrust Act; Eleventh US Census declares frontier closed
1891	Formation of the People's (Populist) Party
1893	Chicago World's Columbian Exposition
1895	J P Morgan and Co established; Stephen Crane, *The Red Badge of Courage*
1896	Supreme Court upholds legality of 'separate but equal' facilities for blacks
1898	Spanish–American War; annexation of Hawaii and Philippines
1899	Thornstein Verblen, *The Theory of the Leisure Class*; Frank Norris, *McTeague*
1900	Theodore Dreiser, *Sister Carrie*; Twelfth US Census shows population of 76 million
1901	US Steel Corporation established
1903	Henry James, *The Ambassadors*; Jack London, *Call of the Wild*; W E B Du Bois, *The Souls of Black Folk*
1906	Upton Sinclair, *The Jungle*
1907	Peak immigration year: 1,285,000 immigrants enter US; Henry Adams, *Education of Henry Adams*; William James, *Pragmatism*
1909	First Model T Ford; Gertrude Stein, *Three Lives*
1913	Armory Show exhibits modern art
1914	Eight-hour day with five-dollar minimum wage introduced in all Ford plants; President Wilson proclaims US neutrality
1915	British steamer *Lusitania* torpedoed with loss of over a hundred American lives; Germany restricts submarine warfare; D W Griffiths, *The Birth of a Nation*; Edgar Lee Masters, *Spoon River Anthology*
1917	German resumption of unrestricted submarine warfare; US declaration of war; T S Eliot, 'The Love Song of J Alfred Prufrock'
1918	Wilson outlines his Fourteen Points to Congress; Armistice ends war in Europe

1919	Prohibition Amendment ratified; Sherwood Anderson, *Winesburg, Ohio*; Senate votes down US membership of League of Nations
1920	Red Scare leads to mass arrests of labour agitators; Sinclair Lewis, *Main Street*; Ezra Pound, *Hugh Selwyn Mauberley*; Fourteenth US Census shows urban population exceeds rural
1921	Quota laws restrict immigration
1922	T S Eliot, *The Waste Land*; Eugene O'Neill, *Anna Christie*
1923	Henry R Luce launches *Time*; D H Lawrence, *Studies in Classic American Literature*; Wallace Stevens, *Harmonium*
1925	F Scott Fitzgerald, *The Great Gatsby*; Gertrude Stein, *The Making of Americans*; Scopes (evolution) trial in Dayton, Tennessee; Harold Ross launches *The New Yorker*
1926	Ernest Hemingway, *The Sun Also Rises*
1927	Execution of Sacco and Vanzetti; Charles Lindbergh flies Atlantic
1928	First full-length sound film; 26 million cars and 13 million radios in use in US
1929	William Faulkner, *The Sound and the Fury*; Ernest Hemingway, *A Farewell to Arms*; stock-market crash
1930	Hart Crane, *The Bridge*; Ezra Pound, *A Draft of XXX Cantos*
1932	William Faulkner, *Light in August*
1933	Inauguration of Franklin D Roosevelt; beginning of New Deal; end of prohibition
1934	Scott Fitzgerald, *Tender is the Night*; William Carlos Williams, *Collected Poems, 1921–31*
1935–37	Neutrality legislation passed in order to prevent US being drawn into future foreign wars
1936	John Dos Passos, *U.S.A.*
1939	John Steinbeck, *The Grapes of Wrath*; Nathanael West, *The Day of the Locust*; Britain and France declare war on Germany
1940	Richard Wright, *Native Son*
1941	Lend-Lease Act; Orson Welles's *Citizen Kane*; Japanese attack on Pearl Harbor leads to American entry into war
1942	American troops fighting in Pacific and North Africa; UN Declaration signed in Washington
1943	Rodgers and Hammerstein, *Oklahoma!*
1944	Allied invasion of Normandy; advance of Russian forces into Czechoslovakia, Hungary and Poland
1945	German capitulation; surrender of Japan following dropping of atomic bombs on Hiroshima and Nagasaki; UN Conference in San Francisco
1946	Robert Penn Warren, *All the King's Men*; William Carlos Williams, *Paterson, Book One*

1947	Truman Doctrine and Marshall Plan designed to counteract Soviet expansionism and provide for European reconstruction; Taft-Hartley Act restricts trade union power; Tennessee Williams, *A Streetcar Named Desire*
1948	Norman Mailer, *The Naked and the Dead*
1948–49	Berlin blockade and airlift
1949	NATO established; Arthur Miller, *Death of a Salesman*
1950–53	Korean War
1950	Alger Hiss convicted of perjury; McCarthy launches anticommunist crusade; Seventeenth US Census shows population of 151 million
1950–60	Advent of mass television
1951	J D Salinger, *The Catcher in the Rye*
1952	Ralph Ellison, *Invisible Man*
1953	James Baldwin, *Go Tell it on the Mountain*; execution of Rosenbergs for atomic espionage
1954	J Robert Oppenheimer denied security clearance; Senate censures McCarthy; Supreme Court rules against school segregation; Wallace Stevens, *Collected Poems*
1956	Suez crisis; Soviet invasion of Hungary; Eugene O'Neill, *Long Day's Journey into Night*
1957	Jack Kerouac, *On the Road*; Federal troops enforce school desegregation in Little Rock, Arkansas
1958	John Kenneth Galbraith, *The Affluent Society*
1959	Saul Bellow, *Henderson the Rain King*; Robert Lowell, *Life Studies*
1961	Inauguration of President Kennedy who calls for a 'New Frontier'; Bay of Pigs (Cuban invasion) fiasco
1961–68	Birth control pill comes into general use
1962	Cuban missile crisis; international live telecasts by satellite; Rachel Carson, *Silent Spring*; Edward Albee, *Who's Afraid of Virginia Woolf?*
1963	Assassination of President Kennedy; Betty Friedan, *The Feminine Mystique*
1964	President Johnson calls for a Great Society; Saul Bellow, *Herzog*; Gulf of Tonkin Resolution leads to build-up of US ground forces in South Vietnam
1965–67	Race riots in Los Angeles, Cleveland, Chicago, Newark, Detroit and other major cities
1968–72	Student protest on US campuses
1968	Assassination of Robert Kennedy and Martin Luther King; Norman Mailer, *Armies of the Night*; John Updike, *Couples*
1969	US astronauts land on moon
1970	US forces invade Cambodia; National Guard fire on students at Kent State University, Ohio; Saul Bellow, *Mr Sammler's Planet*

1971	Severing of historic link between the dollar and gold marks the end of the postwar international monetary system
1972	President Nixon visits China; SALT I agreement with Soviet Union
1973	US ground troops withdraw from Vietnam; Allende Government of Chile overthrown; OPEC quadruples price of oil; Thomas Pynchon, *Gravity's Rainbow*; *Roe* v. *Wade* gives women right to abortion
1974	Watergate scandals lead to resignation of President Nixon
1975	South Vietnam and Cambodia surrender to Communist forces
1976	Saul Bellow awarded Nobel Prize for Literature
1979	Egypt and Israel sign peace agreement at Camp David; President Carter launches national campaign to conserve energy; Shah of Iran overthrown; Soviet invasion of Afghanistan; Congress refuses to ratify SALT II
1980	Hostage crisis in Iran; Ronald Reagan elected President; Japan overtakes US in steel and automobile production
1981	President denounces Soviets and calls for massive increases in defence spending
1982	Administration adopts tax-cutting policies to promote economic growth; first evidence of AIDS epidemic in US
1983	President announces Strategic Defence (Star Wars) Initiative
1986	Iran–Contra revelations embarrass administration; US planes bomb Libya
1987	Alarm grows over trade and budget deficits; world stock markets fall
1988	Tom Wolfe, *The Bonfire of the Vanities*
1989	Fall of Berlin Wall
1990	Soviet troops begin withdrawal from Eastern Europe
1991	Collapse of Soviet Union; Russian Communist Party disbanded; UN force drives Iraq out of Kuwait
1992	Rodney King verdict sparks riots in Los Angeles
1993	Treaty links US, Canada and Mexico in free trade area; Toni Morrison receives Nobel Prize for Literature
1995	Right-wing terrorists bomb Federal building in Oklahoma City; Blacks and whites divided over O J Simpson acquittal
1997	Poland, Hungary and Czech Republic invited to join NATO

Introduction

Howard Temperley and Malcolm Bradbury

▶ I

E ver since its discovery, America – especially that part of North America that became, after the War of Independence, the United States – has been an object of perpetual fascination to outside observers. Initially this may be attributed to the wonder of its discovery; later it can be seen as a result of the sheer speed of its growth. What first presented itself to the Renaissance European gaze as a geographical wilderness, untouched by civilization, though settled by aboriginals, became, in course of time, a burgeoning democracy and then, as a result of the new nation's massive territorial expansion, a technological wonderland and a superpower, presiding over the affairs of half the human race. It is hardly surprising that these images and developments should stimulate the imagination, not just of those who settled in America, but those who saw it from elsewhere. But what has made these images – and the underlying realities of American development which, with various degrees of accuracy, they reflected – so compelling is the way in which they have been used, over the years, to throw light on the past, present and future of other societies. For, whatever observers made of this new phenomenon in the West, it was hard for people not to draw parallels and comparisons between what was happening there and what they hoped or feared would one day happen to their own societies. Since Sir Thomas More and before, America has been both Utopia and Dystopia for those in other lands. From its finding and founding, and even before, America has been a point of refraction – less an objective reality than a mirror, in which observers have seen their own reflections, sometimes curiously diminished, sometimes immensely enlarged.

This varied, multi-faceted view of America has also been shared by those who settled there. For many Americans, America has been a semi-mythical place, to which they or their ancestors were drawn from elsewhere, which has been open to multiple definition and interpretation. To be sure, just by living there Americans were freed of many of the more simplistic preconceptions held by those who never visited the country or the hemisphere. But 'there' in the case of America is apt to mean only one part of what is, after all, a very large continent, a geographically and ethnically

1

varied land-mass. In any case, there were always apt to be discrepancies between what America stood for in image or concept – the City on the Hill, the Land of the New Start, Democracy, Equality, Liberty, Opportunity – and the explicit realities Americans actually encountered in their everyday lives. It became conventional to note, in American life, a space between real and ideal, between fact and dream. A recognizable spirit of idealism in constant struggle with material fact pervades much American writing. Foreign visitors, immigrants, slaves and minorities have particularly noticed or experienced these discrepancies, which arise, in part, because all that is America – nationality, society, character, ideals, ideology – had to be invented. But what has been invented has spread its meanings back through the world. Similarly, Americans have also had to define the world beyond their shores, and just as the views of outside observers have always been influenced by what they wanted or needed to believe about America, so the beliefs of Americans about other parts of the world have often been based on what they, too, wanted or needed to believe about other countries.

Defining America, in short, has been both an American and a foreign preoccupation. It is part of a familiar triangulation process by which individuals and societies locate themselves, geographically, politically, culturally. This is a universal phenomenon, and examples occurred long before the discovery of America. Aristotle attributed the peculiar virtues of the Greeks to the geographical chance which placed them between the energetic but anarchic tribes of Europe and the ingenious but servile nations of Asia. In the same way, other peoples over the centuries attempted to define their identities by referring to the characteristics, real or imagined, of neighbouring societies. There are, however, clear historical reasons why, in more recent times, America should have featured so prominently in this process. One is that, as a new nation, which deliberately severed its political ties with the Old World (from which, nonetheless, it necessarily continued to draw much of its culture), Americans were particularly inclined to speculate on the nature of their nation's identity. And such doubts as they had on this score were exacerbated by the continuing influx of new and increasingly diverse groups of immigrants, as well as by the rapid and vast expansion of the United States itself, and the geographical mobility of its native-born. Thus Americans have been inclined to engage in these acts of triangulation more often than most peoples. At the same time, for outsiders, the primitiveness of the original state of the continent, the fascination of its novelties and wonders, the rapidity of its settlement, the distinctiveness of the cultures which developed there, and the nature of the causes which, over the years, the United States espoused, made her, for those who condemned as well as those who welcomed these developments, a necessary point of reference for their own acts of triangulation – a potent image in the modern world.

It is easy to see why America should have so fascinated the Europeans of the sixteenth century. Since Classical times, the sum of the world's known parts had remained much the same. Great migrations had occurred, empires risen and fallen, beliefs waxed and waned, but the boundaries within which these events occurred remained virtually unaltered. To the north lay the Arctic Circle, to the south Africa, to the east India, China and the legendary spice islands, to the west the Atlantic Ocean. The effect of the voyages of Columbus and his successors was to add a wholly new element to the equation. Here was a continent, enormous in area, rich in resources, peopled by exotic and diverse cultures, whose existence up to that time had been unknown. But above all – and this was what made it so peculiarly fascinating – it was a New World in the sense that it had developed in its own way, untouched by Christianity or indeed any other outside influences. All the wars, controversies and other perturbations of Europe had simply passed it by.

Although America had been unknown, it would not be true to say that it had been undreamt of. It existed in the European imagination long before the news of Columbus's discoveries in 1492. Since ancient times men had speculated about Atlantis and other mythical lands beyond the western horizon – much as people today imagine life on other planets. In a sense, as historians have argued, America was invented before it was discovered. This was, of course, one aspect of that process of mental trigonometry already mentioned, for when concrete examples are lacking there is a natural propensity to invent them. But the presence of a *terra incognita* provoked the European imagination to fantasy and speculation about every kind of alternative to familiar history and existence. This element of invention remained a fundamental part of the perception of America, leading, for example, to the many 'imaginary Americas' of the arts that existed from before discovery to the present day – such as books like Franz Kafka's *Amerika* (1927), written without a visit. One reason why the discoveries amazed and transformed the Renaissance world was that they raised the principle of an alternative history. They also created the need to relate fact to fantasy, to compare the reports of what life was like there with beliefs about what it theoretically ought to have been. So the discoveries constituted a profound challenge to existing ideas and assumptions. Did the peoples of the Americas constitute a separate creation? If so, did they have souls like other men? Were they susceptible to Christian conversion or were they, as some suspected, enthralled to the Devil? Answering such questions was not easy, particularly when the cultures of the native Americans proved to be so diverse, and reports about them often wildly inaccurate. Did they even have arms, legs and heads like other men? Most did; but others, it was widely rumoured, did not.

In other words, the initial response to the discovery of the Americas was not simply to collect and catalogue information, although there was a good deal of that. Mariners needed maps and were not prepared to depend on vague theories about where islands were situated or how various coastlines ran. So innovation was stimulated and, along with it, precision of measurement. Explorers were instructed to collect examples of the local flora and fauna, settlers told to experiment with various crops, artists despatched to draw pictures of the new land and its inhabitants. One result of the discoveries, therefore, was to encourage the development of a more scientific view of the world. At the same time, however, the discoveries inevitably gave rise to a great deal of speculation, as observers attempted to square what they saw, or were told, with what they previously believed, or now wished to believe, or which they felt they ought in faith to believe.

In a sense, the situation has not really changed. Though we no longer believe that there are races of people in the New World whose heads grow out of the middle of their chests, we are aware that life there differs from life in other parts of the world, and we are prone to regard these differences as constituting in some way a challenge to our own societies and systems of belief. It was not long before the wonderment inspired by Native Americans was transferred to those who took America as a place to settle. To be sure, they were not as exotic as the natives, but they were generating new institutions in a new world, and it soon became evident that the ways of life in the New World differed in important respects from those of the Old. There was even speculation that this was the result of some form of geographical determinism, so that in due course Europeans there would revert to the condition of the natives. Indeed, there was no lack of evidence that in many cases something very like this was happening. But, whatever the nature of the forces at work, it was plain that when people and institutions crossed the Atlantic they suffered a sea-change, and that, whatever their plans, however determined they might be to preserve European practices, they invariably ended up with something different.

These changes were particularly marked in the case of the English settlements in North America, above all those that became in time the United States. There had been an indigenous culture in the Americas from prehistory, a major pre-Columbian culture many aspects of which survive in parts of the Americas. The explorers and settlers found not the pure virgin land they sometimes mythicized, but a populated one. Yet in a sense they brought history with them. They came to the New World with European issues in their heads, and these issues, values, historical awarenesses came to be projected on America. They brought Europe's ideologies and technologies: the Bible, the Church, the city, the school, the seminary, the printing press. They thus linked America's history to the general development of the Western world; and they carried with them Europe's ways of writing, recording, ordering and celebrating the world they found. Even if they came in revolt or dissent, they still depended on the language, commerce and thought of England or, increasingly, other parts of Europe. Yet they became in some real sense indigenous. That process may in part be put down to the constraints which Parliament placed on the Royal Prerogative at home in England, and the fact that the early settlements were initially so unsuccessful, economically speaking, that it was scarcely worth anyone's while governing them. Thus the English colonies escaped those tight controls which other European settlers found imposed on them by their home governments. There were Royal Governors, and, from the middle of the seventeenth century on, carefully regulated patterns of trade. But each colony had its own assembly, responsible for raising taxes and framing laws. Thus, to a remarkable degree, they were free to go their own ways.

One consequence was that Britain's colonists enjoyed an unusual degree of liberty as compared with their fellow countrymen at home – or, for that matter, other settlers elsewhere in the New World. This meant they tended to be more flexible in their responses to their environment than would have been the case had they been continually required to regulate their behaviour in accordance with instructions from overseas. A further consequence was that, when eventually they did become more wealthy, the wealth they generated was remarkably evenly distributed throughout the population at large. There were exceptions. Native Americans were largely excluded; African slaves, of whom there were a great many in the southern colonies, were systematically denied the enjoyment of the fruits of their labour. There were rich men, mostly planters and merchants, whose wealth and prestige placed them well above the average. But there was no counterpart to the aristocracy of the mother country, and social distinctions, though they plainly existed, were in general less marked. Most settlers were farmers, and, as such, were as rich or poor as their own and their families' labour made them. This was not what the first settlers – many of whom had arrived with thoughts either of precious metals or else of Bible Commonwealths – intended. Nor was it what the English Government had in mind when it helped sponsor the early expeditions. In a sense, no one had *planned* it at all. It had simply grown up as a result of a *laissez-faire* policy, a superfluity of cultivable land, and a lack of more immediately attractive alternatives such as those which had drawn Spaniards to the mines and more readily exploitable indigenous populations of Mexico and Peru. For all that, it represented a new variant of Western culture, and as such it excited a good deal of interest overseas, even before the Revolution brought it so dramatically to the world's attention.

Curiously enough, what most impressed observers of the British North American settlements, before the Revolution and after, was much what had previously drawn their attention to the lives led by Native Americans: freedom from the constraints of European society. Of course, the colonists were by no means as free from such constraints as the natives had been. History had not passed them by, and they had brought European ideas, institutions and processes along with them and set them to work. Yet many of their achievements could be seen as working out processes which, first initiated in Europe, had, for historical reasons, failed to reach fruition there. To this extent, the societies of North America were *more* in touch with history, or at least with recent historical trends, than those from which they had broken away, and they evolved a historiography deriving from this perception. To an age in which an increasing number of Western thinkers were becoming converted to the idea of Progress, and the belief that necessary changes were being thwarted by the dominant powers of church and state, it was of no small significance that societies should exist which, European in origin, committed to the realization of European ideals, had begun to develop in circumstances which rendered them largely immune from such restrictions. These were post-Gutenberg societies, preoccupied with self-definition; a world with a ministry of learned men, where writing, the arts, science, law and philosophy established themselves; communities formulating modern historical ideas and institutions. It was hence gratifying to progressive minds that these societies were more committed to rational ideas of liberty and equality than those from which they had detached themselves, since these were the ideals the powers of Europe were most concerned to suppress.

Here was a test case, a laboratory experiment, showing how people in general, European as well as American, might order their affairs if only given the chance. The American Revolution was implicitly a transformation of Europe – more than an American event. And among other things it transformed the image of America from a static, paradisal Brave New World to a historically active power, a 'Beacon of Freedom' which, by the end of the eighteenth century and throughout the nineteenth, was a continuing source of inspiration to forward-looking people elsewhere.

▶ II

Needless to say, the reality was a good deal more complicated, as became evident when the French Revolutionaries set themselves the task of achieving similar ideals on European soil. Freedom from political constraints, it soon appeared, was not the only factor that made North America distinctive. There was a great difference between the immense, still largely unexplored continent across the Atlantic and the small, densely populated, historically rooted nations of Europe, with all their traditions and antagonisms. The attempt to impose on France the social values of Revolutionary America proved both bloody and futile. This became apparent to Americans themselves, now concerned to define the distinctiveness of American experience, and fulfil the aims of a romantic liberal nationalism. The problems of cultural formation and innovation were great. If politicians, writers and artists sought a declaration of intellectual, artistic and cultural independence as potent as the political one, they immediately found traces of their dependence on Europe. Lexicographers like Noah Webster sought after the Revolution to define a separate American language, distinct from British. Yet, though from the start books had appeared, historical records been kept, faith and experience registered in works of historical interpretation, theology, philosophy, politics and poetry, the modes of thought, the structures of feeling, the codes of discourse remained largely imitative. America had developed a literary and artistic class, yet the main cultural capitals and institutions stayed in Europe, whither many of those artists and writers expatriated themselves. The issue of the basic provincialism of American culture now became central. 'Who reads an American book?' asked Sydney Smith in *The Edinburgh Review* in 1820; Melville later prophesied that in the future everyone would, and that prophecy is now largely true.

But it took much time and raised essential problems of American identity: the theme with which so much American writing and art is concerned. The problem of inventing America continued. Without an indigenous historical past of sufficient strength to sustain a rooted folk tradition, forge a distinct language, or create fresh artistic genres, with only a sense of mission, often combined with a sense of cultural deprivation, and in a democratic social order suspicious of artistic élitism, the arts of the new nation seemed hard to originate, their very existence an ambiguity. Thus Americans found themselves mythologizing Europe in reverse: as past to America's future, as stasis to America's dynamic movement – and as culture to America's bare democratic space. In fact, the arts flourished in the American colonies, in travel-writing, sermons, theology, poetry. After the Revolution, in the era of Romanticism, they soon enriched themselves. By the 1840s there were signs of remarkable achievement, and what we call the 'American Renaissance' – the work of Poe, Emerson, Hawthorne, Melville, Whitman and others – gave a firm foundation to American literature. Yet a mixture of nationalism and uprooted uncertainty lay behind it. The reverse triangulation process became evident in American culture and the arts: it expressed hunger for self-definition, but equally looked to the world outside.

At the same time, the United States became, and to a degree remained, itself a romantic ideal to which reformers in other parts of the world looked for guidance and inspiration. To generations of British radicals, fed by the spirit of nineteenth-century liberalism, America was not only standing proof that the reforms they called for were practical; it represented in rough outline the kind of society they wanted in Britain itself. By the same token, the United States was also a potent, threatening symbol to those who felt that any shift towards a more democratic policy would threaten their positions in society, or otherwise jeopardize what they held to be the nation's best interests. In practice, most observers, on the Continent as well as in Britain, fell into neither category. They saw in a rapidly developing United States a mixture of elements, some of which invited emulation, others of which did not. Liberals could applaud America's democratic political system yet at the same time deplore the fact that the system was used to uphold a slave regime which, even to European conservatives, appeared unjust and anachronistic. European travellers reported on America: Chateaubriand, Tocqueville, Fanny Trollope, Charles Dickens, Harriet Martineau. Theirs were reports not unlike those that came from Russia after the Revolution: often they showed shock and disappointment, as with Dickens. Tocqueville went to see 'more than America'; his *Democracy in America* (1835–40) looked beyond America to a sociological view of the workings of democracy – noting the benefits, and the price – which included the problems of evolving a democratic art and literature.

Americans, too, explored their own contradictions – especially in literature. In the novels of James Fenimore Cooper, the Gothic, agonized stories of Poe, the transcendental essays of Emerson, the novel-romances of Hawthorne and Melville, we can sense a prevailing tension, a split between idealism and realism, individual and society, artist and culture, European heritage and American, between what Lionel Trilling called the 'yes' and the 'no' of the culture. It is there as a cultural stress, and as formal anxiety. 'Two bodies of modern literature seem to me to have come to the real verge: the Russian and the American . . .', wrote D H Lawrence in *Studies in Classic American Literature* (1923), a book that helped bring home to twentieth-century American writers, still concerned about the distinctiveness of American writing and culture, the usable past behind them. 'The furthest frenzies of French modernism or futurism', wrote Lawrence, 'have not yet reached the pitch of extreme consciousness that Poe, Melville, Hawthorne, and Whitman reached.'

As the nineteenth century developed, the images represented by the United States, internal and external, became more complex. For those abroad, this was partly because, thanks to newspapers and easier travel, people were becoming better informed. It was no longer so easy to confuse the idea with the reality. It also reflected the fact that America was becoming more diverse, and increasingly divided against itself. Even those radicals in England who supported the North in the Civil War, and rejoiced in the overthrow of slavery, were far from sure they liked the post-war society of massive corporations, home-grown plutocrats and downtrodden immigrant workers they saw emerging. Its elements were too much like those they objected to in their own societies, yet manifested on a more massive and terrifying scale. Many began to wonder whether, after all, freedom, equality and progress went together, as they appeared to in the past. If freedom meant the freedom of capitalist to exploit workers, it was hardly worth having. Of course there were aspects of American society that liberals still found attractive – its relative open-endedness, its capacity to accommodate change. But if what they sought was a way of reconciling change with the interests of society at large, in particular with those of its less advantaged members, it was plain they would have to look not to a diminution in the power of the state, something American Government up to that time symbolized, but to its increase.

The same complication of image was felt by Americans themselves. They saw the Jeffersonian America of the yeoman farmer giving way before industrial and corporate growth, and a whole image of Americanness fading with it. Writers grew realist, concerned with the detail and often the unpleasantness of American life. They responded to the fundamental transformation of American images, and allied themselves with reform and naturalism. In this, they were, as always, close to the movements of Europe – even though American realism had as one of its aims the reporting of the distinctively American. For now many Americans were beginning to see in the growth of capitalism the development of an irresponsible power. Yet, with the tradition of governmental non-intervention, it was often more difficult for them to achieve effective reforms than for Europeans, who, although they had often regretted it in the past, at least had governments capable of shaping social and economic affairs. On the whole, Europeans were quicker than Americans to recognize the problems of industrial society, less inhibited by libertarian traditions in advancing proposals for dealing with them. By the late nineteenth century, European radical thought, taken as a whole, was a good deal more trenchant and thoroughgoing than its American counterpart, with the result that Americans were as apt to look to Europeans for inspiration as vice versa.

III

This rebalancing of the refracting images of America and other nations has continued into the twentieth century, when, as a result of wars and revolutions or simply the problems of the modernizing process, governments all round the globe turned to radical expedients. Many of these proved to be a good deal more thoroughgoing in their efforts to bring about social change than anything attempted in the United States. In the world's political spectrum the United States ceased to be regarded, as for so long she had been, as pre-eminently the country of the Left. This is not, though, to say that America ceased to serve as a political model. Indeed, much of the political reconstruction which occurred after the Second World War – the policies leading up to the creation of the European Union for example – were undertaken with the American example specifically in mind. Others, however, chose to pursue more autocratic courses, justified, not infrequently, on the grounds that they represented the only way to catch up with and overtake the United States. Such governments claimed to be democratic by virtue of being *for*, albeit not *of* or *by*, the people. In the event, however, it is the American system as characterized by free elections and market capitalism that has tended to prevail, although which of its many versions works best is debatable. What is clear is that the United States is no longer the prime exemplar of democratic virtue it once appeared and that there are now many other nations whose claims to democratic credentials, while more recent, are equally valid.

Yet while America was ceasing to be the land of the future in one sense, she was rapidly acquiring a new kind of claim to that title. She had, of course, for long been regarded as a land of opportunity – largely because of the relative open-endedness of society and the possibilities it afforded for individual advancement. But until the mid-nineteenth century the United States was, economically speaking, an underdeveloped country. The dramatic rise of American industry in the latter half of the century, however, fundamentally transformed the nation, upset its inward image, and also opened up exciting new possibilities. By 1890, just as the frontier was closing, the United States had achieved primacy as an industrial producer; by 1900 her manufacturing output exceeded that of her two principal rivals, Britain and Germany, combined. This astonishing achievement, together with the associated growth of massive cities and new transportation systems, owed much to factors of scale, the immense natural resources of the continent, labour problems leading to capital-intensive industrialization, and the tradition of practical know-how and invention for which Americans had long been famous. Much of the basic technology was European. Americans had not invented machine technology any more than they had invented democracy. But their wholesale and skilful application of it, their willingness to innovate and invest, and the sheer speed of their rise to economic and industrial pre-eminence combined to capture the world's attention, just as surely as their early commitment to democratic values had done a century before. By the beginning of the twentieth century, the image America presented to the world, and Americans themselves, had become more or less what it is today: an image of modernization and modernity.

So the United States came to be seen, in writing, painting, and thought generally, as a modern technological and urban wonderland. There were those who remained haunted by the older American images – the West, the Big Country, the Land of New Starts – but these were in many ways receding into nostalgia, a nostalgia that nonetheless retained, and still retains, power in American politics and iconography. American cities, with their skyscrapers and drug stores, seemed modern in ways cities elsewhere were not. So did American roads, built to accommodate an automobile-owning citizenry at a time when few elsewhere had cars. American life-styles and American cultural expressions seemed no longer provincial but urbanely advanced. New mass media, like radio and cinema, seemed American technological marvels, and spread American images and influences internationally: images that bore testimony to the fact that in America ordinary people behaved in novel ways, and took for granted privileges – owning telephones, taking annual holidays – which in other countries were the prerogative of the rich and powerful. In the arts,

Gertrude Stein, settled in experimental Paris, looked on European modernism in writing and painting and pronounced it an American possession, appropriate to the new 'space-time continuum' only to be found in the United States.

As always, what fascinated observers was not just these phenomena in themselves, however remarkable they were. It was what they portended for their own societies, where similar tendencies were also evident. Often it was hard to distinguish what was specifically American from what was modern; usually the two went together, and Americanization and modernization appeared much the same thing. Nonetheless, it seemed to many that by looking at America it was possible to discern the shape of the future, and many Americans shared this futurist confidence. In matters of art and culture, Van Wyck Brooks in 1915 declared America's 'coming of age', and with justice. For an extraordinary creative generation in the arts, paralleling the energy and achievement of the 'American Renaissance' (Ezra Pound called it the 'American Risorgimento'), made its claims apparent with such power it became possible to suspect, especially after the cultural collapse of Europe during and after the First World War, that the centre of the arts was shifting across the Atlantic – a view further encouraged by the westward flight of refugee European intellectuals and artists in the Thirties. American arts had always been cosmopolitan, fed by European influence and by immigrant and expatriate elements; they evoked both the images and anxieties of a modernizing world. Increasingly, people did read an American book, watch an American movie, listen to American music – a reflection both of increased power and of the engaging yet ambiguous attraction of modern American mythologies.

After the Second World War, these notions and images became even more complicated as, with the new balance of nations and power, the United States found herself one of the two great 'superpowers', counterposing the essential principle of modernization and development through individualism and capitalism against the communist way of economic planning and the ideologically single state. Atomically armed and strategically powerful, the United States radiated its political and economic influence round the world. In business operations and merchandising patterns, on television and movie screens, in speech, clothes, life-styles, its international role and its capacity to offer an image of a modern, free-wheeling life, especially to young people, became increasingly evident.

The superpower had evolved a superculture. And if one reason for the claim of the United States on world attention came from its history, politics and power, another came from its cultural achievements and their evident importance. Even if, as the American novelist Gore Vidal once remarked, writers in powerful countries win more attention than they deserve, the fact remains that some of the best modern writers, painters and musicians are American, and America is a major capital of the contemporary arts. Another part of their significance, though, is that they display not so much the ideology as the persisting complexity of American culture: its tensions, its stresses, its wry, critical, often traumatic insight into modern experience. They also represent the internationalism of at least part of modern American culture – a culture that has increasingly opened out to the fundamental ethnic and ideological variety of American life, assimilated many modern thought-movements, shown remarkable qualities of eclecticism. The relationship between any society and its artistic achievements is never direct nor easy to analyse (as we shall see in this book). But one of the deductions we may make from contemporary American arts and writing is that they articulate the functional complexity of American culture, the refractability of its images, their eclectic variousness drawn in part from the American social order.

As for today, the issue has grown even more difficult, as the view that America represents the way the world is going has lost some plausibility. Partly this is a matter of other nations catching up – a process that in Europe would doubtless have occurred sooner but for the ravages of two world wars. The United States, thanks to its size, is still the richest country in the world, but its productivity relative to that of other countries has declined and its citizens are no longer necessarily the best paid. Since 1948 the United States has become a net importer of oil and manufactured goods. Many basic industries upon which she depended, like steel and rubber, have moved elsewhere with the result that the United States has become a debtor nation. This represents a profound change in the nature of her longstanding economic relationship with the rest of the world. From 1896 until the late Seventies she always sold more goods and services abroad than she bought in return. During the years after the Second World War, in particular, she was the principal source of world investment capital. Most of the large multinational companies which played such an important part in the economic expansion of the postwar years were American-based. From their subsidiaries and the loans advanced by American bankers she reaped large dividends. These were the years of Coca-colonization and the Almighty Dollar. Between 1950 and 1963, American companies invested $17 billion in the underdeveloped world and repatriated $29 billion in profits. But since the Seventies the flow of capital has been the other way as basic industries have shifted overseas and more and more American corporations have been taken over by Japanese and European companies. Increasingly the United States has become, as she was in the nineteenth century, an exporter of agricultural products. Yet despite the massive sales of agricultural surpluses, the goods and services bought from other nations amount to more than those she exports. At the same time government spending has created annual budget deficits which since the mid-Eighties have averaged almost $200 billion. In effect, foreign investors have been underwriting not only the dollar but American foreign policy. To those accustomed to regarding the United States as the guarantor of world economic and political stability the signs have not been entirely reassuring.

Since the end of the Cold War the pressure on the US government for military spending has eased and by the Clinton mid-Nineties, Americans were enjoying the benefits of rapid economic growth combined with low inflation and high levels of employment. This has contrasted with the experience of many European nations whose growth has been slower and where jobs have remained scarce. It is frequently pointed out, however, that this success has been achieved at a high social cost, evident in the growing disparity between the earnings of those at the top of the scale and those at the bottom. Where once the United States was notable for the relative equality of condition of its citizens, as remarked by Tocqueville in the 1830s, it is now exceptional by virtue of having the widest earnings differentials of any developed country. This is the result less of deliberate government policy than of market forces and Americans' dedication to the principles of free enterprise. It is a development many deplore. A system that assigns virtually all the benefits of economic growth to the highest-earning 10 per cent of the population and the largest proportion of that to the top 1 per cent is not easy to defend on either ethical or social grounds, but in an age of global capitalism it is the natural outcome of a set of principles which Americans believe have served them well in the past and to which they remain dedicated.

Whether others will follow down this same path remains to be seen. Some would argue that it represents the ultimate, post-Cold War triumph of the capitalist ethic. Be this as it may, the collapse of the Soviet Union and with it of a belief in the capacity of command economies and of socialist strategies generally to satisfy individual consumer needs has produced, not simply in the US but world-wide, a heightened awareness of the virtues of self-help, entrepreneurship and democracy for which America always stood. The international economic growth that led to the coming of the post-industrial age owes much of its drive and its ideology to the United States. That innovation in science, commerce, life-style and culture that has represented the American dynamic, the American temper, is in many ways more potent now than ever. Interest in America over the years ahead will undoubtedly have much to do with the way it continues to innovate and cope with the processes of post-modern change. Perhaps America is in the process of becoming a more 'ordinary' country – larger and more powerful than most, but rather less remarkable than it once seemed. In the Revolutionary period, Americans were drawn to theories of the Cycle of Empire – the curve of historical rise and fall that explained the decline of Europe and the 'rising glory' of the United States. It may be that the cycle has to some degree been run, and the special magic of the United States will turn into a network of great highways, franchise restaurants, gas stations, highrise cities and sprawling suburbs that looks and feels not greatly different from those to be found in many other parts of the world.

Yet it would be unwise to assume that the uncertain mood of the present represents the shape of the future. The capacity of the United States to alter and adapt to changing circumstances is historically famous. The jeremiad is an old American form of writing, and successive generations of Americans have similarly felt deep doubt about the nation's destiny. The rhythm of dream and nightmare, of boom and crash, are part of national self-awareness. And, despite the amazing consistency of American ideals – there were those who thought the Constitution would not last for more than twenty years – great changes of situation, world-role and cultural direction have occurred before in American history. Undoubtedly the process will continue. It is equally reasonable to suppose that whatever America will come to represent in the new millennium will be as different from its present character as that character is profoundly different from the America of two hundred years ago. Great recent changes – the demographic shifts of population towards the South-west, pluri-culturalism and rising consciousness of the ethnic minorities, the mixture of technological boom and economic uncertainty, new relationships on the Pacific Rim – are signs of this. But whatever the America of the next century becomes, it will remain – not just for Americans, but for the rest of the world – a culture and continent of compelling interest.

▶ IV

One sign of that interest is the enterprise of 'American Studies', with which this book is concerned. American Studies has been practised inside and outside America, and one way of explaining it is to say that it is a product as well as a study of this history of growth and change, image and reality, national dynamic and external radiation and influence. The term can mean many things, and has. It may simply mark out a geographical area for analysis – an area not clearly defined, since by the term we may mean the United States, the Northern American land mass, or the entire hemisphere. The analysis can be of many kinds, and use a wide variety of disciplines and methods. It can be a study arising from within the culture, a form of national self-understanding. It can be an approach from outside, guided by exterior viewpoints or ideologies. It can be a term describing the work of many people who have separately attempted to characterize the politics, constitution, sociology, culture, the entire texture of American life, using different approaches and methods. Or it can describe an attempt to bring these methods together through some form of inter-disciplinary endeavour, as different subjects and disciplines try to unite methods and interests. When a multi-disciplinary approach is tried, the methods can themselves either be plural and eclectic, or amalgamated into one single theory by which we can synthesize a notion of

American history, life and culture. But the term itself does not indicate how this is to be done, and certainly does not explain what methods, approaches, and disciplines are involved, or in what order of precedence.

It has been one of the marks of American history-writing that it has constantly revised its methods and interpretations. The same revisionist attitude has been apparent in the study of American culture, the changes often reflecting major changes taking place within it – recent emphasis on feminist interpretations of American culture is a good example. The same has been true of the writing of American literary history, where major changes of approach are frequent. For example, the canon of authors who represented the great tradition of nineteenth-century American writing a hundred years ago – Irving, Bryant, Longfellow, Whittier, Lowell – was largely overthrown by critics in the twentieth century, who found their 'usable past' in Emerson, Melville, Hawthorne, Whitman and Emily Dickinson, a poet virtually unpublished in her own lifetime.

The revision of the canon continues today, as Native American and African American, Hispanic and Caribbean traditions of myth-making and narrative alter our perspective on the past and the present. One reason for the constant revision is that the myths and images we have talked of are themselves part of the story, and those myths and images are themselves in constant process of change and reinterpretation. Nations and societies are not clear-cut entities; historical facts are also historical fictions. One mark of 'Americanness' – it undoubtedly has much to do with the relative modernity of settlement in America – is the constant search for an interpretation, an overview: an explanation of 'American' experience, the 'American' national character, the 'American' way. The same triangulations that have been so important a part of American self-awareness are themselves a key element in the notion of American Studies.

What has been striking about the study of America – and especially the United States – has been the way it has drawn commentators, scholars, analysts towards the notion of what has been called a 'holistic' – a systematically comprehensive – approach to the 'American gestalt'. The desire is always there in scholarship. It is also strongly American, part of Emerson's ideal of the 'American scholar' who would distil all systems, Whitman's notion of the American poet who could 'contain multitudes'. This inclusive aim has undoubtedly something to do with the relative lack of ideological division and contention in the tradition of American thought, and its tendency to abstractify, often idealize, the national concept. But the desire to develop inter-disciplinary study has been a crucial part of modern intellectual thought generally – a reaction against the 'balkanization' of knowledge inevitable in the increased specialism that came with the modern explosion of knowledge and discovery.

During the Fifties and Sixties there was a great growth of 'cultural studies', as people in a variety of disciplines – history, sociology, economics, politics, art, literature and popular culture – attempted common projects. That continued, and was to find a new centre in the Structuralist revolution in French philosophy. It was not surprising that the cultural-studies approaches of the Fifties and Sixties and the Structuralist and Post-Structuralist enterprises that followed from them, should take America as a key area of attention. America was a superpower with a wide cultural radiation, a classic case of the modernizing and post-modernizing process that was affecting the world. American popular culture dominated the new communications technologies – film, television, satellite, cassettes, CDs, PCs – on a worldwide basis. These processes and technologies, and the things associated with them – the rise of youth culture, street and ghetto culture, the whole modern revolution of expression – changed the very idea of the word 'culture' and led to its academic revaluation. As the French critic Jean Bandrillard said in his book *America* (1986), writing in a long tradition of European commentary, America was the new 'hyper-reality'.

This emphasized how little the American achievement in the arts, serious and popular, had been studied coherently in the past. Not until the appearance of F O Matthiessen's notable book *The American Renaissance*, a complex examination of the great literary explosion of the 1840s and 1850s in the work of Emerson, Thoreau, Hawthorne, Melville and Whitman, did a major enterprise in American literary and cultural history come to seem necessary. Matthiessen's book appeared in 1941, the year of American entry into the Second World War. It coincided with a sense of national urgency, and a more important international role for American culture. Outside as well as within the USA, America was becoming anew an object of attention and fascination. The American spirit and the American past demanded explanation. As America became a superpower during the Fifties, a number of major books appeared on fundamental American themes and myths, many attempts to break away from traditional and narrow types of historical and cultural study. Some of the most important were Henry Nash Smith's *Virgin Land: The American West as Symbol and Myth* (1950), David M Potter's *People of Plenty: Economic Abundance and the American Character* (1954), R W B Lewis's *The American Adam: Innocence, Tragedy and Tradition in the Nineteenth Century* (1955) and a little later Leo Marx's *The Machine in the Garden: Technology and the Pastoral Ideal in America* (1964). All were books of wide-ranging intention, by scholars who usually came from the disciplines of history or literature, but aimed to explore the fundamental themes of American culture. They were serious in their methods, relating historical, sociological, economic literary and artistic materials to basic cultural myths and issues. These were some of the central books of American Studies, and did much to shape its direction. They generally assumed that national cultures are distinctive, that all forms of expression in a culture share a certain common ground and certain governing principles, that cultures have dominant myths interpreting historical processes according to national ideals. In *Virgin Land*, Henry Nash Smith looked to literature to find 'collective representations', a body of symbols and myths that express the 'assumptions and aspirations of a whole society'. Together they suggested the broad aim of an inter-disciplinary enterprise in cultural studies, and foretold the broadening of academic and intellectual study of American culture.

Nonetheless they did not suggest a single method or an overriding synthesis that would show us (as, for instance, a Marxist theory might) how to analyse the fundamental inter-relationships of an entire society, relating substructure to superstructure. In an article of 1957 called 'Can "American Studies" Develop a Method?', Henry Nash Smith identified the growing field, and saw it would have problems defining its methods. He argued that the focus of attention was 'culture' – by this he meant the expressive, ideological and creative life of the nation – which could best be examined by combining the methods of history, sociology, and literary study:

> Why may we not say quite simply that the problem of method in American Studies can be solved by presupposing a value implicit in culture which includes and reconciles the apparently disparate values assumed in the disciplines of, say, literature and sociology?

This did not mean that a total merger was possible. Disciplines needed to sustain their own distinctive methods and insights, and he recommended a method of 'principled opportunism'. Roughly speaking, this is the method that has been pursued. But this pluralistic view has often been challenged, largely as a result of various endeavours since the Fifties to find a 'total' method of cultural study – based in Marxist theory, cultural anthropology, the various forms of Structuralism, Post-Structuralism and New Historicism. The aim of finding some systematic definition of the relation between literary, artistic and popular cultural forms of expression, myths and cultural themes, ideological directions and historical processes, and the total social structure has been widely explored – one reason why discussion of method is a recurrent aspect of American Studies.

It cannot be said there is, or will ever be, a single solution. In many respects the idea of 'culture' remains a chimera, even though it is a fundamental concept, and nothing is more necessary than the systematic endeavour to analyse historical processes, structures, myths, images, forms of folklore, communications systems, technologies and values as these construct a world for a whole society (and in America's case for other societies too). 'Culture' can be used as an objective term; it can also suggest a critical aim. The 'critics of culture' (to take the title of a book by Alan Trachtenberg) have played a key role in shaping modern American society and forming modern consciousness. The perspective will always vary – for instance, if one is within American culture, trying to explore (or change) its key values or motifs, or outside it, trying to perceive American cultural influence as a world force. What is plain is that American Studies have now become far more specific, more open to a wide variety of methods, interests, approaches, more informed by new scholarship, and much more international. There are nowadays Russian, French, German, Indian, Japanese, Chinese as well as American 'American Studies', and 'principled opportunism' has to be the only way for scanning or relating the massive amount of work in the field.

This cannot be deplored. Especially in multi-cultural times, when the triangulation of cultures is now replaced by their constant interaction with each other, either onscreen or by ease of travel, we would hardly expect total descriptions of the whole life of a people, a single mythic account, a perfect critique, an ideal deconstruction. American Studies have come to mean many more things, but above all a form of cultural studies where the problems of analysing the complexities and excitements of a post-modern, techtronic, multi-ethnic, ideologically plural, creatively energetic, constantly changing yet still coherent society arise. Most of the best work has come not from the application of single theories but from pre-emptive strikes by a variety of individuals employing the insights of different fields of study – drawing on new history, sociology, social psychology, international relations, economics, literary theory, philosophy, art history and iconography, film and media studies, and newer contributions have come from programmes in Women's Studies, African American Studies, and Native Indian Studies. Today there is no dominant reason why, according to Henry Nash Smith's notion, the core disciplines should be literature, history and sociology, though in practice they largely are. But all of those subjects have been through major changes since Smith wrote. History has been re-shaped by new forms of popular history, and by the 'New Historicism'. Literary criticism has turned into literary theory, and sociology has bred new forms of cultural studies. Despite the fact that, according to the theorists of Deconstruction, the Grand Narratives are over, Deconstruction itself has been a new Grand Narrative ('America *is* Deconstruction', claimed Jacques Derrida). What American Studies, a pioneer in 'Studies' generally, has done is to show how hard it is to study a literature without a sense of culture and history, or study national history without perceiving historical narratives as forms of literary expression, and cultural constructs.

This was itself made very evident in those postwar years when Americanists often developed theories of American exceptionalism, which emphasized the progressive and peaceable nature of American aspirations and the rectitude of her dealings with the world. It was not an inappropriate view; indeed, from the days of George Washington Americans had been reluctant participants in world affairs, and in the two modern world wars had been late and unwilling interveners. This was not because Americans were intrinsically more virtuous than other peoples, but because nature and territorial expansion favoured them with a broad continent and defensible frontiers. Still, these facts encouraged a view of the world, and the nation's role in it, that was notably different from that of most nations. (It is hard to imagine a Briton or a Frenchman assuring Krushchev, as Milton Eisenhower, the President's brother, did in 1959, that his nation had never started a war and all it wanted was for all nations to live in peace under their own chosen governments.) Today it is hard to recapture the confidence behind such statements, for America has been involved in a major way in world affairs. It has often been a disillusioning process – in Vietnam, for instance, the first war the United States actually lost. That too has led Americans, over the last two decades, to look ever more closely and sceptically at their own history and future. One effect of this and other failures and crises has been to bring American experience more in line with that of the rest of humankind. In the field of historical studies, that is reflected in an increasing recognition that America developed in interaction with other societies, and can often best be studied comparatively. It was not, after all, the only country to have a moving frontier, chattel slavery, massive immigration, world responsibilities, or even a sense of a special and unique destiny. That is not to deny the uniqueness of American experience, but to suggest its peculiar qualities may be different, more subtle, and more pervasive than had often been supposed.

 V

Why study America? Earlier in the introduction we suggested an answer. As the French observer Tocqueville in his famous book *Democracy in America* (1835) proposed, we study it because it is America, and because it is more than America. It has shown us much that we need to understand about modern (or post-modern) ideas, processes, experience, the workings of modern society and history. A society founded in historical daylight, it has passed through the great rhythms of modernizing change – from an agrarian, utopian form of liberal democracy to a post-techtronic, high-powered, market-based, post-modern society with supreme influence in the culture of the world. What has happened here often pre-dated or symbolized developments elsewhere. For good or bad, it has radiated influence, values, commodities and economic domination on a world scale. It has displayed many of the processes – technologizing, secularizing, urbanizing, materialistic, imperialistic – central in modern history. When America seemed more cut off by a vast Atlantic, set in a 'New World', such experiences once appeared distinct, the product of an 'exceptional' people with an 'exceptional' character in an 'exceptional' situation. It gave the Western world the prospect of a new start, and gave many citizens, most of them migrant, the sense they were freed from the grimness or depravity of history, oppressive institutions or poverty elsewhere.

For the international imagination, 'America' may often have been a vague geographical entity – indeed the same term served for a nation and an entire continent – but it soon became well-defined. In modern form it began as a group of small settlements on a continent populated by 'pre-Columbian' cultures of great variety. Though they have now won deserved importance in the record, they had small impact on the settlers. Not till the mid-nineteenth century did the nation become a true trans-continental power, reaching from coast to coast, coastal plain to prairie, desert, spinal mountains, temperate to semi-tropical zones. Yet what it imposed on this remarkably varied terrain was a pattern of social, cultural and political unity. Visitors to the USA still remark on the 'sameness' of America, from Maine to Miami, Wisconsin to Waikiki. This can be too much exaggerated; one important aspect of American Studies must be an understanding of regional, ethnic and multi-cultural variety. But it is a sign of the remarkable socio-cultural coherence and the effective spread of what were once East Coast ideas and systems across what many in the nineteenth century mistakenly assumed was a largely 'empty' continent. Here is a nation that is profoundly mixed – ethnically, geographically, socially – sustained and changed by constant waves of immigration from an ever-changing range of sources. Yet it still has, despite growing multi-plication and increasing cultural pluralism, essentially one single language and a continued concept of 'Americanness'. But 'Americanness' has never been a stable, fixed concept, and will never be one. The important thing to remember is thus that this is a nation in flux, remarkably mixed in peoples, culturally assimilative and plural, not least because of its geographical position between the Atlantic and Pacific rims, and socially of huge variety: all of this underlying its political life, its cultural expression, and its life-styles.

This double mixture – its cohesion, and its pluralism – gives another reason for its centrality. On one hand, we can see it as a single object of attention (in this book we have concentrated on the America of the United States), on the other we can explore it as a story of the evolution of most modern societies. Here are key themes of recent historical experience – modernizing, technologizing, urbanizing development, growing material prosperity and increasing psychological unease, the gains and losses of future-oriented or progressive cultures – which are matters of concern almost everywhere. The United States can be regarded as a parable of modern development: Hegel's 'land of the future, where the burden of the world's history shall reveal itself'. It focuses key questions of modern societies, modern materialism, modern social conflict, modern psychological expectations and alienations. Social mobility, ethnic variety, the constitutional goals ('life, liberty, the pursuit of happiness'), the 'second identity' of a society that feels it has consciously broken with the past: all this has encouraged pluralism, materialism, existential self-discovery, openness to change, and, often, rootlessness and alienation. After the Second World War, there was much concern in Europe and elsewhere over the impact of Americanization. The influence of American products, market and industrial practices, life-styles, fashions, social and psychological attitudes, preoccupations has been vast, and has fundamentally changed many traditional cultures. Much of this has been caused not by 'Americanization' as such, but by modernizing change which has followed American models and opened cultures to American access. Today, after the end of the Cold War, in the Russian republics, Central and Eastern Europe, and China, the same processes and anxieties are under way. America has not just been an economic and technological power that has helped steer modern change; it has also been an image of life, in an age overwhelmed by processes of historical acceleration. It has also come, through screen and travel, ever closer to us.

Here is another important reason for the growth of American Studies: the strength and vigour of American 'serious' and 'popular' culture. Interest is relatively recent. For a big part of American history it was assumed in and outside the USA that it was a land of natural and material sources largely bereft of what Europeans thought of as 'culture'. Yet the result of late settlement, its missionary intent and the fascination with American purposes was that it was always a highly expressive and articulate culture. From the start America has been a discourse: its annals were kept, its mission prophesied and recorded, its unwritten spaces put into writing. The sermon, the journal, the record of exploration, the travel-book, the declaration, the political polemic were always important. So was the hunger for self-definition, the exploration of sensations, ideals, aims and principles, American dreams. That has shaped both the amount of expression, and the material *of* the expression. This process – of writing down the record, creating the text, constructing the narrative, capturing the myth – is important to American Studies. Through it we see not just a modern people in process of development, but the shaping of new artistic forms for expressing this. To establish the word, or the picture, on the American shore was a feat in itself. It meant the founding of a new tradition, a process that has been increasingly recognized as important in the later twentieth century, as in the melting pot of the world arts, societies and groups within them articulate myths, images, forms of expression of their own.

As in the writing of American history, where historians like Francis Parkman, Henry Adams, Frederick Jackson Turner, Charles Beard and V L Parrington sought vast inclusive explanations of American history, character and experience, so American literature has often shown the same epical inclusiveness. This is clear in many already classic works – Cooper's Leatherstocking novels, Melville's *Moby-Dick*, Whitman's *Song of Myself*, Ezra Pound's *Cantos*, William Carlos Williams's *Paterson*, Gertrude Stein's *Making of Americans*, John Dos Passos's *USA*, Thomas Pynchon's *Mason & Dixon*. As Lawrence said, American literature is both a highly modern literature, with much of its achievement in the twentieth century, and a deeply historical one, a struggle with nature and the soul. As Americans came to dominate the great new twentieth-century medium, film, and to shape and control much of what is shown on the television screens of the world, the same mythologizing instincts and iconographies are evident. Here is a new commercial technology central to the information age, largely the product of American inventiveness. It too has become a window on American dreams, American nightmares, the American landscape and the American streetscape, and the plural, future-oriented social geography which imprints the processes of American culture on all of us.

▶ VI

All these are themes and problems we set out to explore when we constructed this book. It was first conceived in the Seventies, heavily revised in the Eighties, newly revised in the Nineties. In this edition we have asked the contributors to reassess their entries, and added a new final chapter on the Nineties. It is deliberately intended *as* an introduction, to a complex field, and it deliberately concentrates on relating American history to literature and expressive culture. Like many contemporary American Studies programmes, it thus emphasizes history and literature. It advances no single method, and does not bind the contributors (most from American Studies departments in Britain) to any one approach. The aim was always to produce a collaborative work, so most chapters have been written by two specialists (usually a historian and a literary or cultural critic or theorist) working together, with the aim of producing different kinds of exploration of organized study of the USA. The main plan is chronological, but also stresses key themes in American culture: the immigrant, African-American and Native American experience; the significance of the key regions and sections. We have asked contributors to incorporate many matters: political and legal institutions, geography, music, architecture, painting and film, the role of women, the rise of the city and of technology. We have put most weight on the modern period, and towards the end the distinctive experience of the modern decades – recognizing that an essential feature of modern America has been the speed of historical change, and the way fast-shifting responses to the 'present' have been essential to American politics, culture and psychology.

As contributors hint from time to time, much is not here, and a student will need to take many matters further. A parallel book – *Modern American Culture: An Introduction*, edited by Mick Gidley (Longman, 3rd impression, 1997) – goes more fully into many themes in modern American society, including architecture, media, music and performance arts, and ethnicity. Our contributors would wish us to add we have been active editors, making many suggestions and changes to make the book into a coherent survey. Our aim has been to encourage readers to see what it has meant or might mean to be American, and what it means to see

America in its own right and as a power in the wider world. It is an introduction which, we hope, will be of use to those in different disciplines, as well as those in programmes of American Studies, and to the general reader. For, in the fifty or so years since its real development, American Studies stays a key subject on the map of modern enquiry, just as the United States still remains a fundamental force in the world.

Norwich, 1997

▶ For further reading

Paul S Boyer et al., *The Enduring Vision: A History of the American People* (3rd edition, 1996).

Malcolm Bradbury, *Dangerous Pilgrimages: Trans-Atlantic Mythologies and the Novel* (1996).

Hugh Brogan, *The Penguin History of the United States of America* (1986).

Emory Elliot (ed.), *Columbia Literary History of the United States* (1988).

Mick Gidley (ed.), *Modern American Culture: An Introduction* (1997).

James D Hart (ed.), *The Oxford Companion to American Literature* (4th edition, 1965).

Seymour Martin Lipset, *American Exceptionalism: A Double-Edged Sword* (1996).

Jack Salzman (ed.), *American Studies: An Annotated Bibliography* (3 vols, 1986).

1

New Founde Land

Ellman Crasnow and Philip Haffenden

▶ Inventing America

America existed in the European imagination long before its official discovery by Columbus in 1492. The unknown world located at 'the end of the east' was a focus for Edenic and Utopian legend from classical times on. Plato speculated that the land outside of the Oikumene – the world known to the Greeks – contained Atlantis, a lost continent. In early Christian times, interest revived through the story of St Brendan, the Irish monk who journeyed among enchanted islands to the west of Ireland; closely related to this fable was the legend of the seven bishops who fled boldly into the Atlantic from Moorish Spain, to discover the beautiful island of Antilia, upon which they built seven cities. All these tales influenced the explorations of the fifteenth century, which brought legend into closer contact with fact. Columbus himself believed in the Antilia legend. The idea of the 'paradise terrestrial' was further developed by the *Travels of Sir John Mandeville* (1356), a late medieval fantastic work which had immense appeal in Western Europe. Sir John placed the location of this paradise east of the fabulous land of Prester John, which itself was held to contain the fountain of Youth and rivers that ran gold, silver and jewels; again, Columbus looked for many of these details on his voyage to 'Cathay', and so did the other early voyagers who transformed late medieval Europe with the impact of their discoveries.

To the late medieval idea of the paradise at 'the end of the east' there came to be added another fundamental myth: the Renaissance myth of Utopia, given form in the imaginative work of that title by Sir Thomas More, first printed in 1516. Ideal climate was an essential element: the air 'soft, gentle and temperate'. The urban environment – planned and aesthetically pleasing – was in accord with nature. Society was guided by free, compulsory education for the young, in adulthood extended to daily lectures. Free minds were exercised at town meetings, through which government took place. It has been said that every group of English pioneers from Maine to Georgia was influenced by More's ideas. So the travellers' eyes were raised to an unattainable peak; whatever bounties the land had to offer, whatever opportunities there were to reform the

Old World, had to fall short of the Utopian ideal. But the idea of an alternative world was crucial in the Renaissance imagination, charged as it was with the notion of freedom from existing institutions. It is important to note that these sanguine expectations were founded, in one important respect, on absence. They are an account of what is *not there*. Indeed they almost rely on a *lack* of empirical evidence to use the New World as a vehicle for the projective imagination. This 'imaginary America' has been an important meaning of the land. Writing about it preceded knowing it. And, despite the disconfirming experiences of history, this ambition has evolved in the mythopoeic attitude of many later writers, for example, Barlow and Whitman in the nineteenth century, Hart Crane, Charles Olson and Thomas Pynchon in the twentieth.

During the sixteenth century, encouraged by such ideas, explorers from every part of Western Europe probed the New World. Fishing prospects drew Englishmen into the North Atlantic, perhaps initially in the 1480s through voyages from Bristol in search of the mythical island of Hy-Brasil. The discovery of the 'New Founde Land' off present Canada by the Genoese John Cabot in 1497 focused English interest on the exploitation of its rich fishery. But the northern coasts lacked the drama of the Indies; it was not really until the search for a north-west passage to Cathay, in the second part of the sixteenth century, coincided with contentions with Spain over religion and trade that the British shared the broader Renaissance vision of 'the New World'. The major explorers were, of course, the Spanish and Portuguese. By 1550 Spain had extended its empire over Central and vast areas of South America. However, she showed less interest in the land north of Florida, where the rewards in gold and other readily exploitable resources appeared fewer. Portugal was over-extended in Asia as well as Africa and Brazil. In 1524 the Florentine Giovanni da Verrazzano, with royal backing from France, had sought a passage between Spanish Florida and Newfoundland to put France in contact with Asia. His landfall was at Cape Fear, North Carolina, and he then explored the coast northwards, visiting the Hudson estuary, stopping for two weeks in Narragansett Bay (Rhode Island), and making contact with the Indians of Casco Bay (Maine). Myths thus began to build up around the more northerly explorations, and there were hopes of finding a northerly empire as rich as that of the Aztecs and Incas. English taverns heard of 'the Glorious Kingdom of Norumbega' (on the Penobscot) from David Ingram, a silver-tongued English sailor who claimed to have walked there from the Gulf of Mexico, and to have found a huge city with gold-clad women.

However, for many years from 1550 the main preoccupation of the English propagandists with North America was the quest for a passage to the East. In 1566, Sir Humphrey Gilbert, half-brother of Sir Walter Raleigh and close acquaintance of the influential cartographer John Dee, produced the important *Discourse of a Discoverie for a New Passage to Cataia*, which circulated in manuscript for a decade before being printed. Like

Verrazzano, he was concerned with finding the northern passage to Cathay, but, swayed, probably, by More's *Utopia*, he added further ideas, seeing America as a place of refuge for religious dissidents and the poor of England. Yet all the colonizing ventures of the Elizabethans were underwritten by a complex web of exploitative aims, brought together by Richard Hakluyt in his *Discourse Concerning Westerne Planting* (1584), which elaborates the colonial ideal, though very much in the interests of what was later to be called mercantilism. Colonies – plantations – were intended to serve the purposes of the state, not to create an earthly paradise. The colonists' prime function was to improve the quality of life for those who remained behind in England. By emigrating, they reduced the numbers of unemployed and, if soldiers, reduced the dangers from demobilization. As planters, they could produce essential commodities for England's economy, and in due course offer markets for her goods. They could provide bases from which to counter the nation's enemies, especially Spain, and check the dangerous spread of Catholicism among the Indians. Colonists, whether in Ireland or North America, were considered servants of the nation, their interests regarded as subordinate. Not that they were to be victims. The expectation from the enterprise was private profit, at least for the leaders, and compensation for the rank and file in generous acres of land protected from European annexation by the might of the mother country.

Yet in nearly all these reports, practical as they were, the projective imagination exists; fantasy and fact shade together. America still retained mythical associations. Thus John Seelye, in *Prophetic Waters* (1977), offers us the apt phrase 'geophantasy' to describe how Verrazzano's supposed glimpse of an inland sea persisted as a graphic illusion in successive maps. In the South, of course, the Spaniards remained explicitly romantic. Ponce de Leon died searching for a fountain of eternal youth; the ill-fated expedition of Hernando de Soto was recounted as a tale of chivalric adventure. For the northern experience, the hard facts seemed more relevant. Still, Michael Drayton's 'Ode to the Virginian Voyage' (*c.* 1605), based on an expedition sponsored by Raleigh, freely celebrates 'Earth's onely Paradise' and seeks to fire the 'heroic minds' of Englishmen with romantic ambitions:

> And cheerfully at sea,
> Success you still entice,
> To get the pearl and gold,
> And ours to hold,
> Virginia,
> Earth's onely paradise.

Drayton transfers the tradition of Arcadian pastoral across the seas, as many other poets soon would, as Shakespeare would in *The Tempest*. And this naturally resulted in a degree of conflict between fact and fiction

– all too clear in Captain John Smith's *General History of Virginia* (1624), where William Simmons comments on the actuality of the foundation of Virginia after 1607:

> Nay, so great was our famine, that a Savage we slew and buried, the poorer sort took him up again and eat him; and so did divers one another boiled and stewed with roots and herbs: And one among the rest did kill his wife, powdered her, and had eaten part of her before it was known; for which he was executed, as he well deserved: now whether she was better roasted, boiled or carbonado'ed, I know not; but such a dish as powdered wife I never heard of.

Yet Smith's promotional – indeed self-promotional – work nonetheless shows expectations of the land of plenty persisting, even in this 'starving time':

> it were too vile to say, and scarce to be believed, what we endured: but the occasion was our own, for want of providence, industry, and government, and not the barrenness and defect of the Country, as is generally supposed.

Despite such travails, Britain's colonies survived. In Virginia there arose a society of tobacco cultivators; in New England small townships dotted the sea coast. In due course other colonies were founded: Maryland in 1634, Rhode Island in 1636, and New York (formerly a Dutch colony) and New Jersey in 1664. Gradually the British were taking possession. Yet America did not cease to be a place of wonders. It had to be promoted, and its life listed and recorded. Much of the writing now employed a device to become prominent in later American writing, notably in Whitman – the catalogue. William Wood's *New Englands Prospect* (1634), following on from further settlement, thus lists the land's resources, down to its shellfish, in prose and verse:

> The luscious Lobster, with the Crabfish raw,
> The Brinish Oister, Muscle, Periwigge,
> And Tortoise sought for by the Indian Squaw,
> Which to the flats daunce many a winters Jigge,
> To dive for Cocles, and to digge for Clamms,
> Whereby her lazie husbands gut shee cramms.

Indeed, as the New England colonies developed, the device of the catalogue became a complex Puritan form. Samuel Sewell (1652–1730), who held high office in Massachusetts, was author of a remarkable *Diary* recording his experiences, and writer of America's first anti-slavery pamphlet. He also produced various biblical and apocalyptic studies. One of these, the *Phaenomena* (1697), surveys the plenty of New England, mentioning Smith's *History*, and proceeds:

As long as *Plum Island* shall faithfully keep the commanded Post;
Notwithstanding all the hectoring Words, and hard Blows of the
proud and boisterous Ocean; as long as any Salmon, or Sturgeon
shall swim in the streams of Merrimack; or any Perch, or Pickeril,
in *Crane-Pond*...

But this is a *Puritan* catalogue, a catalogue with a difference. The condi-
tional clauses gesture forward through their syntax to the religious end:

...So long shall Christians be born there; and being first made
meet, shall from thence be Translated, to be made partakers of the
Inheritance of the Saints in Light.

The catalogue has now been transformed into a religious plot. For, with
the advent of settlement, a new type of mythification was taking place.
Legend and report alike gave way to the ascription of an intentional
pattern that was attached to America – a pattern more complex and
more purposeful than the earlier, more fantastic imaginative projections.

▶ Settling the colonies

This is logical enough; it was only with the establishment of permanent
settlements in the seventeenth century that the assertion of American
purposes and an American cultural identity could really begin. In recent
years, historians of note have stressed that there were created, by about
1700, four distinctive regional cultures that were extraordinarily durable
and remarkably resistant to change. These regions or 'zones' were the
Chesapeake, the Delaware and Hudson valleys, the disordered backcountry
– especially the Carolinas (termed 'marchland' by Bernard Bailyn) – and
a Massachusetts-dominated New England. This work, characterised in particular by the prolific writings of Jack P Greene, was initially regarded as
having virtually destroyed the concept of American exceptionalism for the
colonial period. It has directed attention to the successful transplanters
of the Chesapeake who forged a social order that would in time conquer
the American continent and who, by the second half of the eighteenth
century, significantly surpassed New England in their per capita wealth.
More recently, however, there has been renewed endeavour to counter the
role of the inheritance from the mother country by stressing the effects
of a common 'local screening process' in which many of the components
of the imported English culture were eliminated or simplified, in part by
interaction with other Europeans, Native Americans and African slaves.
Though it cannot be contested that in much of the colonial world there
was greater stress on action and the pursuit of wealth than on ideas and
the contemplation of one's position in God's universe, New England's
role as the formative section in the colonial era (as well as the primary

residence of the belief in American exceptionalism) rests on its claim to be the source of the American mind. Thus, in our comments, we emphasize the role of the Puritan colonies; this reflects the greater complexity and tension of Puritan culture, and its inescapable significance for later American history. For, with the Puritans, many of the essential 'American' themes emerge. Their culture was of course derived from Europe, but it is best seen and understood through the workings of its internal dynamics, an interplay of forces grouped in opposing functional categories, working as a 'doctrine of contraries', as in the logic of the French Protestant martyr Peter Ramus, who was so highly influential in Puritan America. The central categories for observing Puritan New England are those of location and dislocation, for this was a culture in which the sense of place was literally and figuratively crucial. Indeed, for the Puritans the primary experience was that of dislocation – doctrinal dislocation for many, geographical dislocation for all.

The Reformation had necessitated for all the English nation a dislocation with consequences both diverse and profound. The creation through Henry VIII of the Anglican Church encouraged questioning of the doctrine of apostolic succession; for some, this led to repudiation of the entire ecclesiastic hierarchy. God's will could be interpreted through Scriptures alone. The search for Purity brought forth a radical element under Robert Browne (the Brownists or Independents), for whom an autonomous church was a solitary congregation of 'visible saints'. The text came from St Paul, 2: Corinthians 6:17: 'Wherefore come out from among them, and be ye separate, saith the Lord, and touch not the unclean *thing*.' The unclean thing was the Church of England. However, though a congregation of Independents from Scrooby, Nottinghamshire, fled first to Holland and then ultimately in 1620 to Plymouth in the 'New World', the members did not aim to separate from the English nation as such, to which they were bonded by culture and economic interest. Nevertheless, their experience as an independent religious community, the tempering effect of the harsh New England environment, and the sense of fulfilling God's providence, had, by the spring of 1621, created in them a distinctive spirit. As one of them wrote: 'It is not with us as with other men whom small things can discourage.' Ten years later, New England settlers contrasted their ruddy vigour with the pallor of visiting Virginians: 'When they come trading in our part . . . we know them by their faces.'

But the intent behind the large-scale migration of Puritans to New England at the end of the 1620s is less easily defined. Their leaders disclaimed desire to separate from the Anglican Church (a stand maintained by Cotton Mather in the early eighteenth century); but Englishmen were unconvinced. And the relationship with the English state was equally equivocal. The General Court of Massachusetts – the colony's governing body – demanded an oath of allegiance which ignored Charles I. When Archbishop Laud tried to take away the charter of 1629, they erected fortifications and began military drill to defend the New England way. In fact their resolution was not tested – England was preoccupied with Scottish affairs and then the Civil War – but the defiance was evident enough. Prolonged civil strife in England in the 1640s further strengthened self-consciousness; and, in the absence of English protection against Catholic France or Spain (or their colonies), a Confederation of New England was formed, also to serve as a hedge against English interference, whether from King or Parliament. Large-scale migration also speeded the maturing of the Massachusetts Bay Colony, and congregations gathered to form churches first at Salem, then later at Boston, Roxbury and other coastal centres. Now the fear grew that complete religious autonomy would create discord and endanger the state: in 1637 a synod defined heresy, and introduced the principle of 'Brotherly counsel', and in 1648 another synod produced the Cambridge Platform of Church Discipline, explicitly granting the state power to enforce obedience 'in matters of godliness'. Thus location and state organization grew. Church attendance – for saints and sinners alike – was made compulsory in the early 1630s, and the upkeep of ministers was put on the rates.

These steps likened New to Old England, though in some respects New differed from Old in being more systematic. Novelty was not to be seen in the curriculum of Harvard College (founded 1636), though the speed of its creation indicated the urgent need to provide a native ministry independent of England's influence. The rapid spread of grammar schools, and the obligation by law (1647) that towns over a certain size should create them, had echoes of More's *Utopia*; it also helped create the 'bookishness' of New England culture, which in turn led to New England's predominance in the creation of an American literature. These policies reflected New England's desire to plant a better England on the American shore, and to use education to combat Satan, the old Deluder, who roamed the Edenic paradise. It was Massachusetts that established in 1639 the first printing press in the colonies, producing the famous *Bay Psalm Book* (1640). In one respect, however, Massachusetts did differ from England in that it extended the franchise only to 'visible saints': a contrariety that provoked opposition from the excluded on the grounds that it constituted a denial of English rights. Important critics of these theocratic tendencies were those merchants who supported Anne Hutchinson, who questioned the validity of the procedures used to identify visible saints, in the Antinomian crisis of 1636; though, ten years later, reconciled to church membership as the qualification for voting, they urged that it be broadened, not abolished. In general, the leaders of the Bay Colony, of whom John Winthrop – author of one of the two notable journals recording its foundation, the other being by William Bradford – was outstanding, sought to preserve their churches through strict and widespread regulation. Political dissent was tolerated no more readily than religious. However, attempts to regulate economic life by fixing prices and wages failed. But the social structure inherited from England was substantially preserved, though the range of ranks and classes was less various than in Old England.

The settlers' initial fears of interference from the authorities at home were not realized but, disappointingly, the successful Puritans in Old England did not move in the direction hoped for by those who had emigrated. During the Cromwellian period some eminent settlers, such as Hugh Peter and Sir George Downing, did return to serve the English state in high office. Meanwhile New England, like most of the colonial world, was largely left alone to mature on its own and at its own pace. However, under a restored Stuart monarchy, England, guided by Lord Clarendon, moved with cautious deliberation to impose the restraints of a purposeful economic policy on its New World settlements. The Navigation Laws of 1660 and 1663 sought the increase of English shipping and English seamen by regulating the export of all important colonial commodities and the import of European goods. Many of these restrictions benefited New England commerce, but those which did not were regarded as an intrusion. The tendency to ignore unpalatable imperial rules convinced Restoration statesmen that New England in general, and Massachusetts in particular, must be brought to a proper state of obedience.

By 1684 Massachusetts had lost its venerated charter of 1629, annulled by the English courts, and was about to be merged in a new and vast administrative domain, the Dominion of New England, stretching from the Delaware to the St Croix. Under the all-but vice-regal powers of a General Governor, Sir Edmund Andros, old landmarks such as the legislative assembly of the General Court disappeared, and others – for example, land titles, one of the major pillars of society – were threatened, as was the power of the Puritan theocracy. Other internal dislocations grew. After the Restoration, sights had to be lowered, and the disasters and uncertainties encountered raised doubts as to whether the Puritan experiment even in New England could succeed. By 1660 many young adults were failing to become church members, and in many churches the 'visible saints' were in the minority. What should be the fate of the children of those not full members of the church? To deny baptism would break the 'chain of godliness'; to admit children of unregenerate parents would flout the basic purposes of New England. A synod in 1662 compromised with the Half Way Covenant, permitting baptism but not communion or voting in church matters. Opposition to this in individual churches burdened New England with controversy and doubt.

Perry Miller (*The New England Mind from Colony to Province*, 1953) remains a major focus in any discussion of Puritanism, though many aspects of his thought, including the key issue of Declension, have been challenged by literary historians and by those described as seminary historians. Miller sought to penetrate the mind of the articulate, the speaking aristocracy, not the thought of the silent democracy. However, a new social history of New England concerned with the majority element has developed without reference to Miller. It has raised a vital question: were the ministers spokesmen for an élite or 'learned' culture that was different from the culture of the ordinary people? Though successful attempts have been made to narrow the gap between intellectual and social history, no major synthesis has yet emerged.

The seeds of dislocation were many, among them growth of commercial and economic wealth, through the West Indies trade. Merchants found membership of the British Empire important and were opposed to restrictive practices in the theocracy. But in theory Puritan culture could cope with all this. Indeed, it was so structured as to cope with any dislocation. Its strategy came from that ascription of intentional pattern to which we have referred; the Calvinist belief in the doctrine of Predestination, and the ubiquity and omnipotence of Providence, made everything meaningful. Urian Oakes, in a 1677 sermon on 'The Sovereign Efficacy of Divine Providence', could claim that, properly understood, chance does not exist: 'Truth is, Chance is something that falls out beside the Scope, Intention and foresight of *man*, the Reason and cause whereof may be hid from him; and so it excludes the counsel of *Men*; but it doth not exclude the Counsel and Providence of *God*; but is ordered and governed thereby.' For William Bradford – the leader and historian of the Plymouth Migration of 1620 – even the fact that 'sodomie and bugerie (things fearfull to name), have broak forth in this land' could be coped with and explained through the cosmic drama: 'One reason may be, that the Divell may carrie a greater spite against the churches of Christ and the gospell hear, by how much the more they indeaour to preserve holynes and puritie amongst them. . . .'

So the negative is turned into a positive; impurity is the evidence of purity, and the contingent a working of God's providence. In Puritan historiography there is the frequent device of the interpolated incident, as narratives break off to recount an apparently trivial happening that is in fact not trivial at all but an instance of divine intent. Bradford, recording the famous *Mayflower* voyage, writes of the first fatality on board not merely as an instance of 'greevous disease', but as 'a spetiall worke of Gods providence'. It is 'a proud and very profane yonge man' who dies: 'his curses light upon his own head; and it was an astonishment to all his fellows, for they noted it to be the just hand of God upon him'.

▶ Puritan typology

So stated, the providential order may seem to afford no more than an abstract, general sense of comfort and orientation. But its function was larger; it was brought to bear specifically on Puritan experience through the system of typology. Typology originated in early Christian times, a response to the problem of incorporating the Hebrew scriptures into a new biblical canon. A solution was found whereby 'types' – persons, places, events, institutions – in the Old Testament were seen as foreshadowing 'antitypes' in the New Testament. Thus Matthew 12:40 (NT) refers to Jonah 1:17 (OT): 'For as Jonas was three days and three nights in the whale's belly; so shall the Son of man be three days and three nights in the heart of the earth.' Jonah is no longer significant simply as Jonah, but as a type of Christ. Typology was extended to include not only correspondences between the Testaments but between sacred and secular history as well. So the great Puritan divine John Cotton, preaching a farewell sermon to the passengers of the *Arbella* in 1630, used 2 Samuel 7:10: 'Moreover I will appoint a place for my people Israel, and will plant them, that they may dwell in a place of their own, and move no more. . . .' Here God's intent is explained with reference to the community, and a key American myth stated. The settlers are the new chosen people, their land (New England) is divinely appointed, as was Israel's. The powerful sense of location in time and space, the establishment of identity and value, are obvious. The community is to enact an ordained destiny; 'a great hope and inward zeall they had' writes Bradford, 'of laying some good foundation . . . for the propagating and advancing the gospell of the kingdom of Christ in those remote parts of the world'.

Later generations emphasized this destiny; hence the title of an election sermon preached by Samuel Danforth in 1670: 'A Brief Recognition of New England's Errand into the Wilderness.' The sense of errand was to become a powerful prop for cultural identity, but it was not without its dangers. The first was ideological: the endorsement of national destiny could (and on occasion arguably has) become automatic, dissociated from its original context. The second was psychological: to act as a type is to act as an example, and the community may not maintain its standard. This anxiety was definitively conveyed to the *Arbella*'s passengers in the famous lay sermon preached during the voyage by their leader, John Winthrop:

> for wee must Consider that wee shall be as a Citty vpon a Hill, the eies of all people are vppon us; soe that if wee shall deale falsely with our god in this worke wee haue vndertaken and soe cause him to withdrawe his present help from vs, wee shall be made a story and a by-word through the world . . .

The City upon a Hill, as a type of Zion (and of the heavenly city), is positive; but, as an index of exposure to possible censure, it is negative. Sinners in the Puritan Church were placed on the mourner's bench for public admonition, and the backsliding community, whether a single congregation or entire New England, was always potentially in this role.

Yet backsliding itself could serve a purpose. It fitted into the typological pattern: Israel was a notorious backslider, attracting divine vengeance. Untoward events in the colonies could be made into vengeances, and turned to good effect for both explanation and remonstrance. The expressive form for such occasions was the jeremiad, an address which reviewed society's errand, stigmatized its declension, threatened (or identified) its punishments, and promised renewal for the repentant. Michael Wigglesworth took advantage of a drought in 1662 to produce a rhymed jeremiad, 'God's Controversy with New-England', which displayed 'New England planted, prospered, declining, threatened, punished'. The closing stanzas, however, are typically positive. God speaks in pentameter:

Ah dear New-England! dearest land to me;
Which unto God hath hitherto been dear,
And mayst still be more dear than formerlie,
If to his voice thou wilt incline thine ear . . .

The Puritans rested their strategies of location on the assimilation of human affairs to a total order, providential and predestined: the visible was located by reference to the invisible. Understandably, the linkage between these two worlds preoccupied them greatly. The scriptural figure of linkage is the covenant; and Puritan writing abounds accordingly with covenantal examples. But the degree of assurance with which linkage is asserted may vary. The most confident typological identifications are made: (*a*) communally – when the fortunes of a group can be made to accord with scriptural or apocalyptic patterns; or (*b*) after the event – when, in elegy, funeral address or biography, notables can be typified as Moses leading the people out of Egypt, or Nehemiah rebuilding the wall of Jerusalem.

It is in the present and future fortunes of the individual that least confidence can be shown. Thomas Shepard (1605–49), one of the ablest and most widely read of the first generation of Puritan preachers, offers 'exhortation to all confident people, that think they believe and say, they doubt not but to be saved, and hence do not much fear death', telling them that, on the contrary, they must learn 'to suspect and fear . . .'. Here we meet the problem of Puritan soteriology – that is, its doctrine of salvation. If everything is predestined, so is salvation. And, as Shepard remarks in the same sermon, 'those that are saved are very few; and . . . those that are saved, are saved with very much difficulty'. Add to this the view that no mere human activity can obtain salvation; it rests entirely on divine grace, and as Increase Mather (1639–1723) writes: 'God is not bound to give Sinners Grace: He is an absolute Sovereign, and may give Grace or deny Grace to whom he pleaseth.' So at the core of Puritan culture there is the crucial problem of identifying which individuals belong with the group of those who are to be saved: God's Elect. The problem is, strictly, insoluble. But one could accumulate evidence that must, in the nature of things, remain inconclusive; and an immense energy is poured into this accumulation. Journals, biographies and autobiographies sift individual lives for signs of 'justification', alert for symbolic moments. The problem of interpreting these signs is expressed in a prevailing rhetoric of vision, of proper 'seeing': the desire, as Shepard writes, 'that no man's Spectacles may deceive him'. But visible and behavioural signs are deceptive; as Samuel Willard (1640–1707) preached, 'Saints [are] not known by Externals'. The rhetoric of vision is accordingly introspective, as in Edward Taylor's adaptation of Shepard's spectacles:

> You want Cleare Spectacles: your eyes are dim:
> Turn inside out: and turn your Eyes within.

But even if it could never quite succeed in locating the individual within a predestined pattern, this habit of introspection left a rich heritage. For one thing, it occasioned the period's most moving human documents: its journals, memoirs, histories, apologetics and poetry. Thomas Shepard left an autobiography for the instruction of his son; at one point he traces the shifts in his attempted submission to providence on the death of his wife:

> this affliction was very heauy to me, for in it the Lord seemed to
> withdraw his tender care for me & mine, which he graciously
> manifested by my dear wife; . . . but I am the Lords, & he may
> doe with me what he will, he did teach me to prize a little grace
> gained by a crosse as a sufficient recompense for all outward losses;
> but this losse was very great . . . when her feuer first began (by taking
> some cold) shee told me soe, that we should loue exceedingly
> together because we should not liue long together . . . I haue euer
> found it a difficult thing to profit euer but a little by the sorest &
> sharpest afflictions.

Introspection also left its mark on the secularized 'New England mind' of later centuries, and greatly affected later literature. Characterization and symbolism in American fiction, in the line that runs through Hawthorne, is profoundly indebted to this Puritan habit. But it is important, especially from our modern standpoint, to realize that this subjective and in a sense symbolic experience is not valued for its own sake. It was to be *used* for evidence or instruction. The private often becomes public, and the individual is located in relation to the community as an exemplar; notably, in the public avowal of conversion which determined church membership (and in Massachusetts, enfranchisement). Conversion as regeneration was taken very literally as a cohesive device: a re-birthing, the taking on of a new identity as a visible saint, who (not without doubts) could join the Visible Church.

▶ Colonial culture

The antitheses of Puritan culture were never quite resolved. We cannot speak of synthesis when the individual cannot finally locate herself or himself in the total pattern, and when individual action is finally useless in establishing such location. As if in reaction to this irresolution, social and cultural structures tended to aspire towards order at all costs, as if to restore what Thomas Hooker (1586–1647) called 'the beautiful frame, and that sweet correspondence and orderly usefulness the Lord first implanted in the order of things'. The result was a hierarchically rigid social order in which toleration and democracy were excluded. The gulf between a tolerant and an intolerant colony was illustrated by the controversy between Roger Williams (1604–83), the radical Protestant who founded the settlement of Providence in Rhode Island, and John Cotton of Massachusetts. Williams argued in *The Bloudy Tenent of Persecution for the Cause of Conscience* (1644) that peace in the church and peace in the city were separate, that schism in the former need not affect the latter. Such an opinion was impossible in the Puritan theocracy.

Historically (and perhaps partly because of the portrait of Puritan Boston in Nathaniel Hawthorne's later evocation, *The Scarlet Letter* (1850)), the Puritans have become associated with intolerance, sexual control, witch-hunts. Intolerance was clearly present and functional, as a device of social coersion: a means of asserting identity by postulating an 'other' as the not-self, and so defining one's self against it. The 'other' in this period was sometimes savagely persecuted, sometimes strangely ignored, as if not there. Winthrop's *Journal* records a violent gale in 1643: 'It darkened the air with dust, yet through God's great mercy it did not hurt, but only killed one Indian with the fall of a tree.' (Mark Twain uses a like episode ironically in *Huckleberry Finn*: 'We blowed out a cylinder-head.' 'Good gracious! anybody hurt?' 'No'm. Killed a nigger.') Dehumanization of the Indian was neither immediate nor indiscriminate. In the early years of Massachusetts, the Indian's role was less crucial than it had been in Virginia or Plymouth, because of the experience gained. The relationship of natives to settlers at Jamestown in Virginia had been an uncertain one: white strength inclined them to generosity, while weakness encouraged attack. In the early days, English settlers imprudent enough to venture unarmed from the stockade risked sudden or slow death. But the advantages of political alignment with settlers against local enemies was evident to the Indians. And, though lacking a Pocahontas to show the way, the New England experiences were generally not dissimilar. A formal alliance between the English and King Massasoit of the Wampanoags lasted fifty years; and social contacts were often genial ('we use them kindly: they come to our houses sometimes by half a dozen or half a score at a time when we are at victuals'). In the 'strawberry time', as observers of the early process of settlement described it, the natives were treated as near-equals by many, and Indians were still regarded as white.

In Providence, Roger Williams's 'strange opinions' included friendship with the Indians, and a conviction that the Bay charter was worthless because the King could not give away land belonging to the natives. His enlightened relationship with those already indigenous in America (foreshadowing the policy of Quaker Pennsylvania in the eighteenth century) highlighted a fundamental issue facing all settlements in the New World. What should be the attitude to the native population? After the discoveries, Indians, like the New World itself, had been a thing of wonder. When Columbus visited Lisbon in 1492, the population flocked to see Indians as much as Columbus himself; and their physique, sexual behaviour, eating habits and warfare were exposed to inquiry and exaggeration. Yet the 'noble savage' became celebrated, while the marriage of Princess Pocahontas and John Rolfe overcame the hurdle of mixed marriages. After 1700, however, Massachusetts would forbid this by law.

For in New England, as elsewhere, the idyllic relation ceased with the first major conflict: here it was the Pequot War of 1637, when an entire tribe was virtually destroyed. The impact of this savage struggle was, however, lessened by the alliance of whites with Indian neighbours anxious to see the Pequot destroyed; and, though New Englanders acted often without mercy or compassion, they remained concerned with Christianizing the Indian. During the next forty years, aided by the missionary work of John Eliot and the views of Roger Williams and others, some 4,000 converts – 'praying Indians' – chose a European way of life and lived in or close to Puritan settlements. Not until King Philip's War in 1675–76 did New England experience the horrors of large-scale Indian massacres, such as had shattered confidence in Virginia in 1622. In the conflict, frontier posts were abandoned and battle came close to the doorstep of some of the larger seaboard communities. In time the unconverted Indians came to be seen as dogs to be hunted down, 'because they did not manage their war fairly'. And such were the dimensions of King Philip's War that it was seen as indicative of New England's declension, a focal point for jeremiad.

A more subtle, equally enduring and no less influential shock was administered by the Quakers, tolerated by Rhode Island, but regarded by Massachusetts as a threat. In the 1650s whipping preceded expulsion, and those who returned suffered extreme hardship and barbaric punishment. Finally, in 1658, in an unsuccessful endeavour to keep out these intruders who threatened 'the mission of Zion in the wilderness', the death penalty was made the punishment for re-entry. Next year two young men were hanged; in 1661 Mary Dyer received the martyrdom she so resolutely sought. Quaker sufferings did not pass unnoticed in England; the influence of Quaker leaders, especially Admiral Sir William Penn, Charles II and James, Duke of York, helped sharpen the resolve of the

Lords of Trade after 1675 to bring Massachusetts to heel. And, even after the Glorious Revolution of 1688, the Quakers – like the Abnaki Indians, who in war destroyed frontier settlements such as Wells, in Maine, and Deerfield, in the Connecticut Valley – long continued as a thorn in the Bay Colony's side. Indeed, a generation of almost continuous war after 1675 inhibited the growth of any firm sense of security. There was also the problem of New France, which grew, after successive campaigns against Quebec, to almost obsessive proportions (and was not stilled until the French citadel fell in 1759). The last major shudder of the seventeenth century for Massachusetts came with the Salem witches of 1692. It was a complex social and intellectual issue.

Witches, too, were the 'others'. The first enemy of the godly Commonwealth was, always, Satan. Unconverted Indians roaming the howling wilderness were his agents, as were those of other faiths. Women were identified with his worship – an indication of their weakness and inferiority. The witchcraft scandals, trials and hangings that struck Salem village came in time to disturb the entire province, evidence of Puritan unease and the terrifying power of Satan. But they were, as Perry Miller has noted, as much to be anticipated among the afflictions of New England as the Indian raids, and were equally intelligible to everyone concerned within the logic of the covenant, in a world where what Max Weber has called 'acting in accordance with God's pattern' was extended throughout all social, economic and political life.

How much, then, had Puritan Massachusetts in common with the other eleven colonies in being in 1713? (Georgia, the last of the thirteen colonies which were ultimately to break away from Britain, was not founded until 1733.) Excluding Connecticut, an early offshoot, Massachusetts presented in organization and structure a striking contrast with all her neighbours. The orderly creation of townships, the physical area in which a congregation resided (normally a village with attached lands) and the supporting educational system, had no parallel outside of New England save where New Englanders settled. Virginians aimed to re-create England – at least rural England – and operated with the minimum of institutional aids. Where precedents were unsuitable – as was the case with the regulation of Anglican clergy – old forms, such as the vestry, were adapted to suit the needs of an emergent planter class. But contrasts with Massachusetts are easier to find than parallels; Virginia was an economy based upon tobacco which, affecting the use of space and time, influenced the values of behaviour of the planters in a society increasingly dependent upon slavery. Nearer to Massachusetts in the dimensions of its conception, if not in its material purpose, were the ambitious social and political structures designed for the Carolinas by the political theorist John Locke and Anthony Ashley Cooper, later Earl of Shaftesbury. The Fundamental Constitutions influenced by James Harrington, author of the *Commonwealth of Oceana*, endeavoured to create a semi-feudal hierarchy with political and social influence determined by land-holding. The power of the nobility was to be restrained by that of the Commons or democratic element. The scheme for the Carolinas was utopian, while Virginia just grew. In neither was religion the driving force. But it was in Pennsylvania, the last of the seventeenth-century colonies to be formed. In many respects, the Quaker way in Pennsylvania contrasted sharply with that of godly Massachusetts, Quakerism was known for its contempt for forms and hierarchies, and for its hostility to dogma. Yet, just like the New England theocrats, the Quaker leaders found that the commercial life was not only a potent source of prosperity, but that it was also responsible for a shift in values which could discomfort them and undermine their ideals (though the practical religion of Benjamin Franklin was in due course to constitute a form of reconciliation). What is clear is that the priestly power achieved by the Congregational ministers in the seventeenth century was nowhere equalled outside of New England. And, though it declined thereafter, it remained a formidable force, and a power in the New England spirit.

▶ The Puritan arts

One consequence of Puritanism and its powerful ministry is often thought to be a hostility to the arts. Yet the paradox is that New England was perhaps the most significant centre of artistic creation in the colonial period. In the end, this is not surprising, given the bookishness of the Puritan colonies, the strength of an educated ministry, and the preoccupation with typology and with writing the providential record. Puritanism, certainly, had been a protest against elaboration in English Protestantism, and it maintained a similar standard in the matter of cultural expression: the important issue was 'use', the social and religious value of artistic expression. Yet this could be resolved: the typologizing disposition, and the concern with conscience and self-knowledge, led to a serious exploration of written forms. Indeed, even the criterion of 'use' sometimes seems perfunctory. It was a common Puritan practice to anagrammatize names, the intent being didactic and moral, an eliciting of providential meanings. But the anagrams were clearly enjoyed with a metaphysical and cryptogrammatic satisfaction. Similarly, Nathaniel Ward (1578–1652), the author of *The Simple Cobler of Aggawam* (1647), condemned, in the Puritan fashion, frivolous elaboration in women's dress, by which ladies 'disfigure themselves with such exotick garbes, as not only dismantles their native lovely lustre, but transclouts them into gant bar-geese, ill-shapen shotten shell-fish, Egyptian Hieroglyphicks, or at the best into French flurts of the pastery, which a proper Englishwoman should scorn with her heels . . .'. This sounds strict – but Ward evidently enjoys the elaboration of his own language. In an age of wit, he is conscious of wit, and he continues, charmingly: 'We have about five or six of them in our Colony: if I see any of them accidentally, I cannot cleanse my phansie of them for a month after. I have been a solitary widdower almost twelve years. . . .' The Puritan imagination could explore or generate many of the sensual riches it seemed to condemn.

Thus aesthetic satisfactions apparently denied in one area could freely emerge elsewhere. The theatre was proscribed; but theatricality is rife throughout Puritan expression. Edward Johnson (1598–1672) produced his *Wonder-Working Providence of Sion's Saviour in New England* during the 1650s; it is sometimes known as *A History of New England*, and it was meant to be, and was, a primary record of the founding of Plymouth, with a firm didactic intent to elicit God's marvellous purposes. But it is in fact an elaborately dramatized epic, in which the emigrants are directly addressed by Christ's voice, and the reader is specifically alerted to the symmetrical tableaux of the departure from England:

> Passe on and attend with teares, if thou hast any, the following
> discourse . . . both of them had their farther speech strangled
> from the depth of their inward dolor, with breast-breaking sobs,
> till leaning their heads on each others shoulders, they let fall the
> salt dropping dews of vehement affections, striving to exceed
> one another. . . .

Another kind of theatricality surely accounts for part of the success of New England's best-selling poem, Michael Wigglesworth's *The Day of Doom* (1662):

> So at the last, whilst Men sleep fast in their security
> Surpriz'd they are in such a snare as cometh suddenly.
> For at midnight brake forth a Light, which turn'd the night to day,
> And speedily and hideous cry did all the world dismay. . . .

The affective power that many Puritan writers display was not cultivated for its own sake – though it may have been appreciated as such. Its 'use' lay in the effect on an audience – particularly, the audience of that key form of Puritan expression, the sermon. Edward Johnson describes Thomas Shepard, with obvious approval, as a 'soule ravishing Minister'. The best sermons combine this eloquence with a highly determinate structure of doctrine and propositions, uses and applications. The experience intended by these preachers can be defined by contrast with their English contemporary Sir Thomas Browne, writing in *Religio Medici*: 'I love to lose myself in a mystery, to pursue my reason to an *O altitudo!*' The Puritan would not indulge the sublime, would not seek to lose himself. On the contrary, within the articulated form of the sermon, and the process of its argument, he was always placed. The animus against elaboration shows in comments on early Puritan writing. Cotton Mather (1663–1728) looked back to a sermon by John Cotton,

wherein sinning more to preach *Self* than *Christ*, he used such Florid
Strains, as extremely recommended him unto the *most*, who relished
the *Wisdom of Words* above the *Words of Wisdom*; Though the
pompous Eloquence of that Sermon, afterwards gave such a
distaste unto his own *Reverend Soul*, that with a Sacred
Indignation he threw his Notes into the Fire. . . .

But by the time this was written (1695) such a reaction was out of date.
Cotton Mather himself used a far more 'florid' style than his father
Increase or his grandfather Richard.

Verse was subject to much the same criteria as prose. It attracted no
special odium, but was widely practised as one among other forms of
expression. Edward Johnson, celebrating the death of a Puritan worthy,
can break into verse as a kind of mnemonic: 'For future Remembrance
of him mind this *Meeter*.' The major poets, Anne Bradstreet (*c.* 1612–72)
and Edward Taylor (*c.* 1642–1729), turned the procedures described to
their own advantage. Both attempted extended forms that correspond
with the rationally systematic structure of the sermons (and ultimately, by
analogy, with the providential order): Bradstreet's 'Contemplations', or
Taylor's 'Gods Determinations touching his Elect'. Bradstreet wrote charm-
ing personal poems on her husband or family which nevertheless manage
the exemplary transformation of private feeling into public type. Taylor,
too, could typify an intimate or trivial situation, as here, through a rhetoric of vision:

> Lord cleare my misted sight that I
> May hence view thy Divinity.
> Some sparkes whereof thou up dost hasp
> Within this little downy Wasp. . . .

Leaving England after the Restoration, Taylor continued the witty and
meditative tradition of English Metaphysical poetry in a Puritan context.
The Preface to 'Gods Determinations' shows some of his range, from
typically curious and intricate detail:

> Who Lac'd and Fillitted the earth so fine,
> With Rivers like green Ribbons Smaragdine? [emerald]
> Who made the Sea's its Selvedge [border], and its locks
> Like a Quilt Ball within a Silver Box?
> Who spread its Canopy? Or Curtains Spun?
> Who in this Bowling Alley bowled the Sun?

– to close verbal play on just two words, making it 'all' out of nearly
'nothing':

> Oh! what a might is this! Whose single frown
> Doth shake the world as it would shake it down?
> Which All from Nothing fet [fetched], from Nothing, All:
> Hath All on Nothing set, lets Nothing fall.

Gave All to Nothing Man indeed, whereby
Through Nothing man all might Him Glorify.

The complexity of the Puritan mind led, in actuality, not to a severe
denial of art, but to a set of complex typological, symbolistic and metaphysical usages which passed on into the American literature of later
times.

▶ The waning of Puritanism

In the event New England Puritanism could not stay pure amid the dislocations of American circumstances. It never recovered fully from the loss
of power occasioned by the creation of the Dominion of New England.
The accession of William III in 1689 gave the empire a constitutional
monarchy and a firm Protestant commitment, acceptable even to New
Englanders, though for most of their colonial history they were suspected
of republican tendencies. The colonial charters, most of them revoked by
James II, were restored by his successor, reassuring the colonists that their
political rights were secure. But there was one exception, and that was
Massachusetts. In 1691 it received a *new* charter; not only was the governor now appointed by the Crown, but the franchise was divorced from
church membership and related to property, as in England and the other
colonies. Puritanism was threatened, but it remained a potent force, still
capable of passing restrictive legislation. Indeed, as in the 1720s, Baptists,
Quakers and Anglicans paid taxes, under protest, to support Congregational ministers. The erosion of theocratic power was thus a slow one; so
was the transition from Puritan to Yankee. By the end of the seventeenth
century, latitudinarian forces, which were strong at Harvard, the very
citadel of Puritanism, had initiated, with the support of influential elements among the commercial classes, an abandonment of the old covenant ideal. Church membership widened, then declined numerically;
control of the churches by the General Court progressively weakened.

However, the principal mark of change was the 'Great Awakening',
the mass Evangelical movement which between 1720 and 1750 brought a
religious revival throughout the colonies. The new mood was represented
by Jonathan Edwards (1703–58), the last of the great Puritan preachers,
as gifted as any of his predecessors, and as concerned to search for evi-
dences, for 'distinguishing signs of truly gracious and holy affections'; but
these are now located in 'influences and operates on the heart'. There is
an increased subjective stress on his work, when compared with that of
the previous century. Edwards learned from Locke to 'exalt experience
over reason'; he incorporated some of Isaac Newton's beliefs into Calvinist thought; his account of consciousness in *Freedom of the Will* is the first
major contribution to American philosophy; his *Images or Shadows of*

Divine Things offers 'a new inward perception' that has some affinities with Transcendental symbolism in the nineteenth century. As the Great Awakening brought a revival of Calvinist vitality, a diminution of sectarian differences, and an increase in the millennial tendency of American religion, along with a weakening of authority and a declining respect for intellect, so the 'Moderate Enlightenment' and the 'Skeptical Enlightenment' of 1750 to 1789 opened the way to the spread of deism and the freeing of the individual from social constraints.

So, as the eighteenth century progressed, Massachusetts moved into the broader historical currents – political, ideological, intellectual, religious – that diminished the distinctions between colonies, and, in some respects, between colony and mother country. Perhaps of all the colonies Massachusetts seemed to move closer to the mother country, especially through the experiences of the Seven Years War, though this is open to argument. She has also been seen as assuming the important trappings of a European state through the forging house of Anglo-French conflict which had greater impact on her than any other colony. The Glorious Revolution of 1688 underwrote representative government in an empire generally seen as primarily inspired by commercial considerations – though prolonged periods of warfare thereafter, especially from 1739 onwards, may have encouraged the persistence from Stuart times of the concept of 'garrison government' (a kind of 'military rule over colonial people') originally nurtured in Scotland and Ireland. However, each settlement possessed a general assembly. The similarities between Parliament and the colonial assemblies encouraged the imitative process which, as Jack Greene has shown, was powerful in shaping colonial attitudes and aspirations. Certainly neither the instruments nor the situation were identical: colonial governors were not monarchs, and whether elected, appointed by proprietor or by the Crown, their influence was less than the King's in some spheres, greater in others, especially in time of war.

But the drive for greater parliamentary powers came, with some provinces like Virginia and Massachusetts having an early start, and others like Pennsylvania, and New York (acquired by conquest), rapidly forging to the front. The model of New England town government fed the quest towards political autonomy. And, though sometimes exaggerated, the influence of the frontier as a democratizing force was significant. It promoted some social changes, for instance in the role of women. It fostered the evangelical movement by preferring emotional over intellectual religion, and encouraged the rejection of the European-trained ministry. Often back-country areas, most of which were, thanks to population growth, under-represented in colonial assemblies demanded the same privileges as the communities to the east, appealing to the rights of Englishmen.

But, also drawn from England, a more radical ideology was emerging that transcended provincial boundaries. Colonists, alarmed at the spread of absolutism in Europe, sought a bulwark against political corruption and decay in republican ideas, the ideas of the 'commonwealthmen' popularized by John Trenchard and Thomas Gordon in the *Independent Whig* and *Cato's Letters*. In Massachusetts a Country Party, committed to local political rights lost in the charter of 1691, grew up; and three generations down to the Revolution (the mantle finally descended on Sam Adams) fought the 'Court' executive and its powerful instrument, patronage. Similar patterns appeared in other colonies like Pennsylvania and West Jersey. But in general colonial divisions had to do with local circumstances, and the ebb and flow of provincial politics did not before 1760 encourage a full-throttled drive for autonomy. As Governor Fauquier observed of the Virginia burgesses: 'Whoever charges them with acting upon a premeditated plan, don't know them, for they mean honestly, but are Expedient mongers in the highest degree!'

The dialectic of location and dislocation evolved into new forms. Whig ideology, leavened in the colonies by Commonwealth radicalism, owing something to European historians such as Paul de Rapin-Thoyras, the Huguenot exile, helped to create an American as distinct from an English identity. But American-born historians in the eighteenth century tended to strengthen rather a provincial than a wider identity. Robert Beverly's *History and Present State of Virginia* (1705) reflected a growing self-consciousness in the old dominion. Virginia had found other important writers in William Byrd, the Reverend Hugh Jones and later William Smith, and their often filiopietistic writing helped to generate self-esteem. William Smith's *History of New York* (1757), an important work, was designed to promote a better understanding of the colony in England. But, as Louis B Wright has observed, it was New England that produced more histories and other narratives than all the rest of British America combined. Much of this reflects the very powerful sense of identity which had been created in Massachusetts at an early stage. But part of it pointed forward to an identity as yet unformed, neither English nor New English. The vision preserved in Cotton Mather's *Magnalia Christi Americana* or the *Ecclesiastical History of New England* (1702) emerged in the nineteenth century. To Harriet Beecher Stowe and her generation, 'God's mercies to New England foreshadowed the glorious future of the United States of America . . . commissioned to bear the light of liberty and religion through all the earth and to bring in the great millennial day . . . The New England clergy . . . were children of the morning.'

▶ For further reading

Daniel Boorstin, *The Americans: The Colonial Experience* (1958).
Bernard Bailyn, *The Peopling of British North America: An Introduction* (1986).

Sacvan Bercovitch (ed.), *The Cambridge History of American Literature, 1590–1820* (1994).

John Carnup, *Out of the Wilderness: The Emergence of an American Identity in Colonial New England* (1990).

Jack P Greene, *The Intellectual Construction of America: Exceptionalism and Identity from 1492 to 1800* (1993).

Richard Middleton, *Colonial America: A History* (1992).

Larzer Ziff, *Puritanism in America: New Culture in a New World* (1973).

2 The first new nation

Peter Marshall and Ian Walker

▶ The making of the new Canaan

Until fairly recently the colonial period accounted, chronologically speaking, for more than half of American history. Between the establishment of the first permanent settlement at Jamestown in 1607 and the Declaration of Independence of 1776, 169 years elapsed. This was quite long enough, as the previous chapter has shown, for new variants of Western culture to develop. Britain's colonists might, and in practice frequently did, insist on their rights as Englishmen, but they were also aware that their own histories and traditions set them apart from Englishmen at home. In particular, they cherished their right to regulate their own affairs, through their elected assemblies, and not to have laws and taxes thrust on them by the mother country.

Viewed in this way, it is easy to assume that the colonies were naturally and automatically destined to break away. Yet up to 1763 there is little evidence that the colonists were eager for, or even prepared to contemplate, such a development. What altered the situation, and ultimately provoked the colonists into taking up arms, was the British government's determination, following the defeat of the French in the French and Indian War (1754–63), to impose closer controls over its imperial possessions. As the colonists saw it, this meant depriving them of their cherished liberties. To the British, on the other hand, these so-called liberties were without constitutional foundation; if the colonists had hitherto been left to regulate their own affairs as they saw fit, it was merely because the government in Britain had allowed them to do so, not because it lacked the constitutional authority. Faced with continued British intransigence, the colonists' sense of righteousness was reinforced by the conviction that it was not they but the British who were the aggressors in the conflict. Thus as the struggle escalated they resorted first to boycotts and protests, later to armed resistance, and ultimately to a military alliance with their former enemies the French as a means of preserving what they saw as their rightful liberties.

In a sense, then, the American Revolution was fundamentally conservative. It began as a colonial response to British policy. In retrospect it is plain that the colonists had misjudged Britain's aims no less than the British had misunderstood the concerns of the colonists. Yet once the fighting was over, Americans, as in the past, were quick to detect the hand of Providence in these events. On 8 May 1783, Dr Ezra Stiles, President of Yale College, preached an election sermon before the Governor and General Assembly of Connecticut, reflecting on what had happened. Later published under the title of *The United States elevated to Glory and Honour*, his address traced, with mingled awe, pride and astonishment, the process of American separation from the British Empire and the establishment of an independent nation distinguished, by the aid of divine guidance, for its unique civic virtue; it also faced the problem of giving an explanation *of* these events.

> How utopian it would have been [Stiles asserted] to have predicted at the battle of Lexington, that in less than eight years the independence and sovereignty of the United States should be acknowledged by four European sovereignties, one of which would be Britain herself. How wonderful the revolutions, the events of Providence! We live in an age of wonders; we have lived an age in a few years; we have seen more wonders accomplished in eight years than are usually unfolded in a century.

The liberty that Americans had secured for themselves would, before long, be extended throughout the world as their example became widely known:

> We shall have a communication with all nations in commerce, manners, and science, beyond anything heretofore known in the world . . . all the arts may be transplanted from Europe and Asia, and flourish in America with an augmented lustre, not to mention the augment of the sciences from American inventions and discoveries, of which there have been as capital ones here, the last century, as in all Europe.
> The rough sonorous diction of the English language may here take its Athenian polish, and receive its attic urbanity, as it will probably become the vernacular tongue of more numerous millions than ever yet spake one language on earth. . . .

A nation, Stiles concluded, whose Revolution had achieved so much so openly, was particularly committed to maintaining a purity of purpose: 'the United States are under peculiar obligations to become a holy people unto the Lord our God, on account of the late eminent deliverance, salvation, peace and glory with which he hath now crowned our new sovereignty'.

Stiles, not for the first time, had displayed an ability to develop, at a particularly apposite moment, a theme of both general and fundamental significance for Americans seeking to define their nation's purpose and

progress. Precedents for his claims had been established in both literature and life: so, earlier in the century, Bishop Berkeley's 'Verses on the
prospect of Planting Arts and Learning in America' had contrasted the
decay of Europe with the promise of the New World as

> Westward the course of empire takes its way;
> The four first acts already past,
> A fifth shall close the drama with the day;
> Time's noblest offspring is the last.

Half a century later, travellers encountered the sense of the poetry as
popular belief. Andrew Burnaby reported from Virginia in 1759–60 that

> An idea, strange as it is visionary, has entered into the minds of
> the generality of mankind, that empire is travelling westward; and
> every one is looking forward with eager and impatient expectation
> to that destined moment when America is to give law to the rest
> of the world.

Views differed on the form in which this was to be achieved. John Adams,
expressing in his *Dissertation on the Canon and Feudal Law* (1765) beliefs
whose sources in both secular political philosophy and the Book of Revelation have been declared by Ernest Lee Tuveson to constitute 'apocalyptic Whiggism', saw America as forming the centre of resistance to 'a
wicked confederacy' between the two systems of tyranny – ecclesiastical
and civil – that had subjected Europe to total ignorance until the Reformation, and had 'obscured true learning for long afterwards'. Youthful
opinions were no less emphatic: for the Commencement exercises of the
College of New Jersey in 1771, two of the graduating class, Philip Freneau
and Hugh Henry Brackenridge, offered Princetonians *A Poem on the Rising Glory of America*. The derivative quality of their verse did not lessen its
religious and visionary quality:

> And when a train of rolling years are past
> (so sung the exil'd seer in Patmos isle)
> A new Jerusalem, sent down from heaven,
> Shall grace our happy earth – perhaps this land,
> Whose ample breast shall then receive, tho' late,
> Myriads of saints, with their immortal king,
> To live and reign on earth a thousand years.
> Thence called Millennium. Paradise anew
> Shall flourish, by no second Adam lost.
> No dangerous tree with deadly fruit shall grow,
> No tempting serpent to allure the soul
> From native innocence – A Canaan here,

Another *Canaan* shall excel the old,
And from a fairer Pisgah's top be seen.

The idea of America as the new Canaan was examined at length by another author of much more exalted academic standing but perhaps even less poetic talent. Timothy Dwight (1752–1817), the 'Connecticut Wit' who became President of Yale, devoted fourteen years to the composition of *The Conquest of Canaan,* producing in 1785 an extraordinarily dull and noisy eleven-book epic in heroic couplets on the subject of Joshua's battles and entry into the Promised Land. The patriotic analogy intended was evident enough: Joshua was modelled on George Washington, while other American heroes were but lightly disguised. The Promised Land of Canaan was, of course, the United States:

Far o'er yon azure main thy view extend.
Where seas and skies in blue confusion blend:
Lo, there a mighty realm, by Heaven design'd
The last retreat for poor oppress'd mankind;
Form'd with that pomp which marks the land divine,
And clothes yon vault where worlds unnumber'd shine.
Here spacious plains in solemn grandeur spread,
Here cloudy forests cast eternal shade;
Rich valleys wind, the sky-tall mountains brave,
And inland seas for commerce spread the wave,
With nobler floods the sea-like rivers roll,
And fairer lustre purples round the pole.

Claims and expectations of this magnitude may have reflected individuals' optimism, but also gave rise to consequential difficulties: if America was so evidently superior to all other regions of the world, it had no cause to remain inferior in any respect. The achievement of political independence formed but a part of the whole acknowledgment of cultural distinctiveness, for as Noah Webster (1758–1843) proclaimed, in the 1783 preface to his 'Speller', 'America must be as independent in *literature* as she is in *politics*'. How this would be achieved was less clear, but authors and critics united to establish a national literature produced by worthy successors to the greatest authors of past civilizations. Freneau's view of the future was typical of these hopes:

I see a Homer and a Milton rise
In all the pomp and majesty of song, . . .
A second Pope, like that Arabian bird
Of which no age can boast but one, may yet
Awake the muse by Schuylkill's silent stream, . . .
And Susquehanna's rocky stream unsung, . . .

Shall yet remurmer to the magic sound
Of song heroic.

So widely spread was this ambition that even as prosaic a figure as a John
Adams permitted himself the hope that he should 'live to see our young
America in Possession of an Heroic Poem, equal to those most esteemed
in any Country'. Unfortunately, these eager expectations found all too
little satisfaction in the first outpouring of national literature, no matter
how idealistic the authors' intentions may have been.

In his preface to the *Vision of Columbus* (1787) – revised and reissued
as *The Columbiad* (1807) – Joel Barlow (1754–1812) was at pains to stress
his extra-literary purposes:

> My object is altogether of a moral and political nature. I wish to
> encourage and strengthen, in the rising generation, a sense of the
> importance of republican institutions; as being the great foundations
> of public and private happiness, the necessary aliment of future and
> permanent ameliorations in the condition of human nature.

Cast in the form of an imitative sub-Miltonic 'epic', the poem describes
how Columbus, now imprisoned, is visited by Hesper, the guardian Angel
of the New World, who reveals to him the future awaiting the land he has
discovered. The colonial years, the coming of the Revolution, the creation of the federal system, are unfolded in a visionary panorama, and
Columbus's prison despair turns to joy as he is shown the future glories
of a land where:

> Courageous Probity, with brow serene,
> And Temperance calm presents her placid mein.
> Contentment, Moderation, Labour, Art,
> Mould the new man and humanize his heart;
> To public plenty private ease dilates,
> Domestic peace to harmony of states,
> Protected industry, careening far,
> Detects the cause and curses the rage of war,
> And sweeps, with forceful arm, to their last graves,
> Kings from the earth and pirates from the waves.

Barlow's enterprise is a national republican epic, and a search for the
mythology of the new nation. Such epic intentions would persist through
much subsequent American writing. Yet it is noticeable that Barlow's revolutionary poem is cast in the forms of neo-classical eighteenth-century
English poetry; the spirit but not the form of romanticism which was sweeping Europe, and which to some extent the American Revolution itself
released, is visible. Behind idealist themes and the conviction of a vast
historical transition there lie hard facts of cultural dependence; in writing

as in social and political institutions, the struggle into nationhood was still just beginning.

▶ The growth of party

Literary figures might proclaim the presence of a faultless society, and the coming of a new imperial cycle. The political leaders of the new nation, proud as they were to have achieved independence, were more aware of the practical problems of its preservation than of the imminent attainment of some idealistic goal. Political realism invoked an altogether more prudent assessment of progress than that claimed by the authors of a national literature whose existence was hailed more frequently than it could be perceived. Many were alarmed by the growth of parties, a development not anticipated by the nation's founders. During the Revolutionary years much emphasis had been given to the need for solidarity. Yet once the war was over, it soon became clear that Americans were not all of one mind. This was evident during the period of the Articles of Confederation (1777–87) when, for a time, it looked as if the United States was not a nation at all, but a collection of states each intent on going its own way. These tendencies were arrested by the adoption (1787–88) of the new Constitution. Nevertheless, problems remained. In particular, the divisions in Washington's own cabinet between the Hamiltonians and the Jeffersonians, and their uninhibited use of rhetoric to castigate one another's policies, seemed to threaten the very foundations of the new state. If was out of these divisions that the first American party system arose, the Federalists (until their demise following the War of 1812) stressing the need for economic diversification, a governing élite and a strong central authority; and the Jeffersonian Republicans urging the need to protect the existing agrarian order and encourage a broad diffusion of wealth while viewing with distrust any growth in the powers of the central government. To a degree these same divisions are also evident in the struggles between Whigs and Democrats in the 1830s and 1840s.

Yet with the benefit of hindsight it can be concluded that there was little immediate likelihood of the destruction of the United States by either internal conflict or external attack in the decades after 1783, even though there is ample evidence to indicate that contemporaries thought otherwise. There were particular economic and political problems attributed to the aftermath of war and the deficiencies of the Articles of Confederation; there were general doubts as to the possibility of preserving stability in a state whose size far exceeded that considered compatible with the working of popular government; there were fears that the empires of the Old World, so recently deposed from the rule of North America, would not accept the outcome of the Revolution as a final decision. Although some of these alarms were reduced by the composition and ratification of the Constitution, the unanticipated emergence of political parties was viewed with disquiet. It has been suggested that those who chose to support parties did so out of uncertainty rather than from subscription to political beliefs. Richard Buel, Jr, in *Securing the Revolution* (1972), argues that 'Federalism was the choice of those who felt insecure as leaders because of changes wrought by the Revolution', and concludes of their opponents that until the War of 1812 seemed to prove otherwise:

> Many Republicans had defended the nation's unique institutions less because they were assured that this form of government was stable than because the alternatives were unacceptable. For most of the revolutionary generation, despite their brave words at the time of trial, republicanism had remained a faith still unproved by experience. (p. 85)

A political system so imperfectly defined might well seem unable to confront external dangers and liable to magnify their threats: to Federalists, the Revolution in France presaged universal upheaval and chaos, while to Republicans the fear of Britain's return as an imperial authority over North America could not be dispelled. Each party saw its adversary as a willing accomplice in the advancement of the aims of its alleged European ally. In these circumstances there was ample ground for many to maintain the belief that held, as Paul C Nagel has put it, in *Sacred Trust* (1971), that 'The political party from the start was considered the serpent in America's Garden' (p. 27).

Despite the undoubted partisan bitterness that distinguished Federalist from Republican, it is possible to attach too much significance to their differences: the two parties were not absolutely opposed and chose not to engage in mortal conflict on matters of fundamental importance. Thus, both accepted without question the fact of the Revolution and the emergence of the American nation: the form and purpose these events involved were grounds for deep disagreement, but any return to British rule was beyond consideration. Loyalism and Loyalists had no part to play in the politics of the United States. The first generation of American party leaders, no matter how greatly at variance, remained constant in their adhesion to a system whose novelty was compounded by its uncertain prospects.

Party arguments often turned on differing views of the purpose and limits of the Revolution. To a Federalist as vehement as Fisher Ames, 'The American Revolution was in fact, after 1776, a resistance to foreign government', and had no ground to engage in domestic change. The presence of democracy rendered this a constant danger, since the people were liable to fall under the sway of demagogues. 'To make the nation free', Ames declared, 'the crafty must be kept in awe, and the violent in restraint . . . it is only by the due restraint of others, that I am free.' Political turbulence sounded the alarm to others of a previously sanguine outlook: at the Constitutional Convention of 1787 Elbridge Gerry of Massachusetts gave vent to his fears. 'The evils we experience flow from the excess of democracy', he declared. 'The people do not want virtue, but are the dupes of pretended patriots. . . . He had', he said, 'been too republican heretofore; he was still however, republican, but had been taught by experience the danger of the leveling spirit. . . .' Federalists were continually exercised by the need to combat these tendencies and to maintain popular deference to their betters. Stephen Higginson insisted that 'The people must be *taught* to confide in and reverence their rulers', and it was generally agreed that restraint, obedience and subordination were popular qualities essential to the preservation of public order. Their Republican adversaries were certainly rendered more radical by Federalist description than by party intent: New England's fear, mistrust, and assertion of Southern, and particularly Virginian, political aims confirmed party differences throughout the quarter-century between the framing of the Constitution and the War of 1812. John Adams expressed a typical opinion when he asserted in 1805 that:

> The Southern Men have been actuated by an absolute hatred of New England. Nothing but their fears ever restrained them from discarding Us from their Union. Those Fears, as their population increases so much faster than ours, diminish every day; and were they not restrained by their Negroes they would reject us from their Union, within a year.

The threat of men rendered powerful and arrogant by the profits of slavery weighed heavily upon Federalists, to assume personal shape in their depiction of the malevolent character and purposes of Thomas Jefferson. Few Federalists seemed to have taken seriously the President's Inaugural assertion that all Americans were of both parties. As he left office in 1809, the precocious William Cullen Bryant could bid farewell to a 'wretch' whose intellectual pretensions, alleged sexual relations with a slave, and futile policies, had disgraced 'the presidential chair':

> Disclose thy secret measures, foul or fair,
> Go, search with curious eye, for horned frogs,
> Mid the wild wastes of Louisianan bogs;
> Or, where Ohio rolls his turbid stream,
> Dig for huge bones, thy glory and thy theme,
> Go, scan, Philosophist, thy Sally's charms,
> And sink supinely in her sable arms;
> But quit to abler hands the helm of state,
> Nor image ruin on thy country's fate!

If the violence of political conflicts was limited to words – Alexander Hamilton constituted the only untimely casualty of the revolutionary generation, and his death occurred on the duelling ground, not on the scaffold or the barricades – the uncertainty generated by the particular nature of the break with Britain would be very slow to disappear. It left, as Linda Kerber, in *Federalists in Dissent* (1970), has pointed out, an 'ambiguous legacy' to later generations, with the consequence that:

> In the years after the Revolution, the American walked a strange tightrope between optimism and pessimism. The Revolution had been both a radical break with the past and a conservative affirmation of it; that ambivalence persisted through the early years of the national experience. The Federalist characteristically searched the American social order to find the stability that would justify the Revolution; for the same purpose the Democrat searched it to find flexibility. (p. 212)

In the long run, the fact that the search was being undertaken within an American, not a colonial, social order would uncover a new national political and cultural structure, as de Tocqueville was so sharply to see in the 1830s. But, for the moment, efforts to achieve change appeared much more obvious than its successful provision.

▶ Declarations of literary independence?

There were some among the Founding Fathers who saw the development of the arts and cultural expression as a matter of small importance, given the practical problems; others looked with gravity at the task of proclaiming and defining the purposes of the new nation in the arts and culture. The proof of independence demanded not merely a distinctive literature; but also, according to some, a separate language in which it could be written: Noah Webster, the nation's first grammarian and lexicographer, was well aware of the implications of his interests. In 1807, looking back at over twenty years' work, he assured Joel Barlow that he had always

> had it in view to detach this country as much as possible from its dependence on the parent country. . . . Our people look to English books as the standard of truth on all subjects and this confidence in English opinions puts *an end to inquiry*.

Although, as he himself came to recognize, Webster's intentions of change always remained far larger than his achievements, his was a crucial contribution towards establishing the educational basis of the American nation.

Others shared the task. Webster believed that the creation of a common national loyalty could be fostered by the teaching of American history in the schools. Support in this endeavour was provided by the first generation of American historians, for whom the Revolution was the central episode of their accounts and to whom colonial differences were of far less significance than the national achievement of Independence.

Objectivity did not distinguish their narratives and if, to them, history was past politics, they themselves were present politicians. Despite this, however, partisan views were subordinate to common agreement on the national purpose. Although Mrs Warren's *History of the American Revolution* (1805) was a product of Republican sympathies and John Marshall's *Life of Washington* (1804–07) was a justification of Federalism rather than a biography, Arthur H Shaffer, in *The Politics of History* (1975), has concluded that:

> The division between Warren and Marshall was predominantly over specific policies and individual motives . . . these differences are minor compared to a common bias in favor of the national government as the expression of American nationality. . . . If Marshall had not been a prominent Federalist and Warren a known Republican, or if neither had dealt with the years after 1789, it would have been difficult to discover marked differences between them. In this they were characteristic of their fellow scholars; allegiance to national unity tended to minimize differences even among the most partisan of the historians. (p. 159)

The use of the Revolution as a principal source for an historical literature of national unity was fully and rapidly introduced: the story of Independence confirmed, rather than confused, the sense of communal identity.

Other forms of literature proved less suited to this purpose, though hopes and encouragement were continually being expressed. In part, as even those sympathetic to the new society had to admit, failure represented the inevitable absence of necessary elements, without which the achievements of Europe could not be matched. So, after his visit in 1793 and prior to his emigration to America, Thomas Cooper, Manchester radical and political admirer of the United States, had to admit that:

> With respect to literary men, it is to be observed that in America there is not as yet what may be called a *class* of society, to whom that denomination will apply; such, for instance, as is to be found in Great Britain, and indeed in most of the old countries of Europe. A class, whose profession is literature; and among whom the branches of knowledge are divided and subdivided with great minuteness, each individual taking and pursuing his separate department as regularly as the respective fabricators of a watch or a pin. Literature in America is an amusement only – collateral to the occupation of the person who attends (and but occasionally attends) to it. In Europe it is a trade – a means of livelihood.

Cooper did not believe that Americans were condemned to a permanent state of literary inferiority but acknowledged that, lacking libraries and limited almost entirely to modern books, with a land impoverished by war and where attention was naturally turned toward economic improvement, it would take time for an American literature to equal that of Europe. But Thomas Cooper's observations were scarcely original; indeed they were confirmed and elaborated many times over, then and for years into the future, by commentators on American culture (or the lack of it) from both sides of the Atlantic. For example, Cooper's eminent namesake, James Fenimore Cooper (1789–1851), complained bluntly in his *Notions of the Americans* (1828) of the many obstacles hindering the American writer, not least of which was the democratic dullness of the land:

> There is scarcely an ore which contributes to the wealth of the author that is found here in veins as rich as in Europe. There are no annals for the historian; no follies (beyond the most vulgar and commonplace) for the satirist; no manners for the dramatist; no obscure fictions for the writer of romance; no gross and hardy offences against decorum for the moralist; nor any of the rich artificial auxiliaries of poetry. The weakest hand can extract a spark from the flint, but it would baffle the strength of a giant to attempt kindling a flame with a pudding-stone.

This complaint about the absence of literary materials in the new land and the new nation would last on, up to Hawthorne and Henry James. It helps explain why early American writing is touched with a sense of displacement and doubt, even sometimes a sense of artistic alienation. This is clear in Washington Irving (1783–1859), usually taken as America's first professional writer. One of the New York 'Knickerbocker School', Irving tried to establish a native subject-matter; yet his famous *Sketch-Book of Geoffrey Crayon, Gent.* (2 vols, 1819, 1820), containing, among other things, 'Rip Van Winkle' and 'The Legend of Sleepy Hollow', was written just after the War of 1812 and in England, and aimed at an Anglo-American audience. To win the way to an American romanticism, cultural dependence was inevitable: even the famous folk-tales are adaptations of German sources on to American ground. Other essays dwell on the problems of establishing writing as an institution in the new nation – problems illustrated by the career and concerns of Hugh Henry Brackenridge (1748–1816), a generation older than Irving, who was a child of the Revolution. Brackenridge's composition, with Philip Freneau, of *The Rising Glory of America* initiated a commitment to patriotic literature that led him to the composition of verse dramas on *The Battle of Bunker's Hill* (1776) and *The Death of General Montgomery* (1777). In 1778 he established in Philadelphia the *United States Magazine,* from the belief that Americans 'are able to cultivate the *belles lettres,* even disconnected from Great Britain; and that liberty is of so noble and energetic a quality, as even from the bosom of war to call forth the powers of human genius'. He was unable, however, to prove his point, for the magazine failed within the year. Brackenridge, his savings lost, turned to law and politics in the frontier town of Pittsburgh.

In 1792 Brackenridge published in Philadelphia the first two volumes of *Modern Chivalry*; further volumes appeared at intervals and the edition was not complete until 1815. Although he had in the meantime pursued a successful judicial career, setbacks had also been encountered: *Modern Chivalry* may have been initially provoked by a failure to secure election to the Constitutional Convention in 1787 and defeat by an Irishman Brackenridge considered unfit to hold public office. This fictional work describes the wanderings and adventures of Captain Farrago, a sympathetic caricature of a Jeffersonian landed gentleman (perhaps of Brackenridge himself), well-mannered, well-read, sensible, kindly, conservative, always ready to lecture and instruct the populace, and his 'bog-trotter', 'redemptioner' servant, Teague O'Regan. Their quixotic adventures are designed to reveal the stupidities, crudities, and absurdities of their world through humour and satire, though Brackenridge, too, enters directly into the book in inter-chapters of 'Reflections'. His early idealism had been modified by experience: while seeing himself as a confirmed democrat, he now recognized that liberty was a matter of curtailment as well as expression, and had become fearful – as James Fenimore Cooper would – of populist excesses and a consequent diminution of standards. In the following extract Captain Farrago encounters an election: he is horrified to discover the populace about to elect one Traddle, an illiterate weaver, as their representative, and even more horrified when they turn their attention towards the 'menial' Irishman:

While they were thus discoursing, a bustle had taken place among the crowd. Teague hearing so much about elections, and serving the government, took it into his head, that he could be a legislator himself. The thing was not displeasing to the people, who seemed to favor his pretensions; owing, in some degree, to there being several of his countrymen among the crowd; but more especially to the fluctuation of the popular mind, and a disposition to what is new and ignoble. For though the weaver was not the most elevated object of choice, yet he was still preferable to this tatterdemalion, who was but a menial servant, and had so much of what is called the brogue on his tongue, as to fall far short of an elegant speaker.

The Captain coming up, and finding what was on the carpet, was greatly chagrined at not having been able to give the multitude a better idea of the importance of a legislative trust; alarmed also, from an apprehension of the loss of his servant. Under these impressions he resumed his address to the multitude. Said he: 'This is making the matter still worse, gentlemen; this servant of mine is but a bog-trotter; who can scarcely speak the dialect in which your laws ought to be written; but certainly has never read a single treatise on any political subject; for the truth is, he cannot read at all ... he is totally ignorant of the great principles of legislation; and more especially, the particular interests of the government.

'A free government is a noble possession to a people: and its freedom consists in an equal right to make laws, and to have the benefit of the laws when made. Though doubtless, in such a government, the lowest citizen may become chief magistrate; yet it is sufficient to possess the right; not absolutely necessary to exercise it . . . You are surely carrying the matter too far, in thinking to make a senator of this hostler; to take him away from an employment to which he has been bred, and put him to another, to which he has served no apprenticeship; to set those hands which have been lately employed in currying my horse, to the draughting-bills, and preparing business for the house.'

The people were tenacious of their choice, and insisted in giving Teague their suffrages; and by the frown upon their brows, seemed to indicate resentment at what had been said; as indirectly charging them with want of judgement; or calling in question their privilege to do what they thought proper. (Ch. 3)

▶ Problems of democracy

Brackenridge's unease resounds through early American writing. Americans were torn between stressing the promise or the problems created by a democratic society. If Federalists, with their more élitist view of government, had reached Brackenridge's view of popular elections with much greater speed and certainty, they possessed no clear alternative means of management. 'One of the central dilemmas of Federalism', James M Banner, Jr, has pointed out in *To the Hartford Convention* (1970), 'lay in the fact that the party never had any alternative but to accommodate itself to the ascendant democratic political mode.' Fearing the worst, Federalists strove assiduously to secure superiority within a constitutional system they could claim to have devised, no matter how alarming its political operation may have proved. In stark contrast, Jefferson declared himself happy to accept the people's choice: 'In general', he told John Adams in 1813, 'they will elect the real good and wise. In some instances, wealth may corrupt, and birth blind them, but not in sufficient degree to endanger the society. . . .' No Federalist could have subscribed to this belief.

For all his singular lack of moderation, Fisher Ames probably declared what many others thought when he asserted that:

The people, as a body, cannot deliberate. Nevertheless, they will feel an irresistible impulse to act, and their resolutions will be dictated to them by their demagogues. The consciousness, or the opinion, that they possess the supreme power, will inspire inordinate passions; and the violent men, who are the most forward to gratify those passions, will be their favourites. What is called the government of the people is in fact too often the arbitrary power of such men. Here, then, we have the faithful portrait of democracy.

Political fears were a consequence of beliefs in the inevitability of social degeneration. John Adams, for instance, held that the fruits of virtue would be vices. 'Will you tell me', he asked Jefferson in 1819

how to prevent riches from becoming the effects of temperance and industry? Will you tell me how to prevent riches from producing luxury? Will you tell me how to prevent luxury from producing effeminacy, intoxication, extravagance, vice and folly?

For his part, Jefferson's hopes for the future were far less bleak. In a letter to Pierre Samuel DuPont de Nemours in 1816 he pinned his faith to popular education:

Altho' I do not, with some enthusiasts, believe that the human condition will ever advance to such a state of perfection as that there shall no longer be pain or vice in the world, yet I believe it susceptible of much improvement, and, most of all, in matters of government and religion; and that the diffusion of knowledge among the people is to the instrument by which it is to be effected.

Neither proofs of progress nor of decay were to gain unqualified assent. If, after 1815, the cause of growth might seem to have prevailed, there were those who continued to offer criticisms in terms to which John Adams could have wholeheartedly subscribed. Lawyers in particular saw little but disaster in prospect: Chancellor Kent of New York assembled in 1836 a formidable array of social evils:

The rapidly increasing appetite for wealth; the inordinate taste for luxury which it engenders; the vehement spirit of speculation, and the selfish emulation which it creates; the contempt for slow and moderate gains; the ardent thirst for pleasure and amusement; the diminishing reverence for the wisdom of the past; the disregard of the lessons of experience, the authority of magistrates, and the venerable institutions of ancestral policy.

Differences on the question of the state of the nation were not, however, aligned after 1815 with party allegiance. The outcome of the War of 1812 appeared to have obliterated or relegated to permanent obscurity the issues, whether internal or external, that had sustained the Federalists. In political terms the optimism of Republicanism had prevailed decisively over the pessimism of their opponents after a war in which, or so Republicans liked to think, both the people and their symbolic representation, the nation, had demonstrated qualities of strength and certainty.

If a considered judgement on the military aspects of the War of 1812 might have reduced sharply the scale of American success, it would in no way have diminished the stature gained by the nation's first post-revolutionary hero, Andrew Jackson (1767–1845), who in 1815 had defeated the British at New Orleans. In many ways Jackson represented the same things Jefferson had stood for a generation earlier, but he was cast in a cruder mould. Jefferson, for all his democratic sympathies, had been a Virginian aristocrat. Jackson came from Tennessee, still a frontier area, and in his personal style as well as his politics he played up his frontier origins. In 1828 he decisively defeated John Quincy Adams in the election for the presidency, thus ending the period of single-party rule which had effectively existed since 1816. In contrast to Adams (the son of President John Adams), Jackson was able to present himself as a representative of the common people and, in particular, of the settlers in the growing and increasingly influential new states of the West. Thus in manner, as well as in fact, Jackson served notice that a new type of American had come to embody national characteristics. The Jacksonian epoch, characterized at the political level by its struggles between the Jacksonian Democrats and their Whig opponents, brought to the forefront of American awareness those problems of liberal evolution that were also preoccupying European radicals. With the 1830s, the sense of American direction grows stronger; but the sense of American conflict sharpens, especially in the realm of the imagination, where the ambiguous image of a self that either expresses the potential of society or transcends it altogether acquires a force in a period of intensified artistic creation.

▶ The path to the new arts

The decisive shifting of emphasis in Jacksonian America presented writers with new prospects and new problems. It offered the opportunity to new themes, yet it offered little likelihood that the new social exemplars would hold 'gentlemanly' authorship in high regard. These were the contrasts particularly felt by James Fenimore Cooper, America's first major novelist and fictional mythologist. Cooper's background in upper New York State gave him familiarity both with frontier conditions and the problems of landed ownership, with the idylls of freedom in the wilderness and the harsh specifics of agrarian conflict, apparent from the 1760s. It is not surprising that throughout Cooper's fiction there runs both a pastoral romantic myth and a fear of anarchy, mob-rule, and the consequent breakdown both of law and order and civilized standards of behaviour. Cooper was the novelist both of American pastoral and of underlying and deep-rooted social tension. Thus, in his first successful novel, *The Spy* (1821), the 'neutral ground' between the revolutionary forces and the British army is threatened by groups of irregulars and mercenaries known as 'Skinners' and 'Cow Boys': the 'Skinners' were republican 'gangs of marauders who infested the country with a semblance of patriotism, and were guilty of every grade of offence, from simple theft up to murder'. These 'fellows whose mouths are filled with liberty and equality, and whose hearts are overflowing with cupidity and gall' are in direct contrast to the heroic spy, Harvey Birch, solitary and dignified, motivated only by patriotic ardour and his honour as a gentleman. In *The Prairie* (1827), order and civilization on the frontier are threatened by the lawless Bush tribe led by the formidable Ishmael:

> At some little distance in front of the whole, marched the individual, who, by his position and air, appeared to be the leader of the band. He was a tall, sunburnt man, past the middle-age, of a dull countenance and listless manner. His frame appeared loose and flexible; but it was vast, and in reality of prodigious power. It was only at moments, however, as some slight impediment opposed itself to his loitering progress, that his person, which, in its ordinary gait, seemed so lounging and nerveless, displayed any of those energies which lay latent in his system, like the slumbering and unwieldy, but terrible, strength of the elephant. The inferior lineaments of his countenance were coarse, extended, and vacant; while the superior, or those nobler parts which are thought to affect the intellectual being, were low, receding, and mean. The dress of this individual was a mixture of the coarsest vestments of a husbandman, with the leathern garments that fashion, as well as use, had in some degree rendered necessary to one engaged in his present pursuits. There was, however, a singular and wild display of prodigal and ill-judged ornaments blended with his motley attire. In place of the usual deerskin belt, he wore around his body a tarnished silken sash of the most gaudy colors; the buck-horn haft of his knife was profusely decorated with plates of silver; the martin's fur of his cap was of a fineness and shadowing that a queen might covet; the buttons of his rude and soiled blanket-coat were of the glittering coinage of Mexico; the stock of his rifle was of beautiful mahogany, riveted and banded with the same precious metal; and the trinkets of no less than three worthless watches dangled from different parts of his person. In addition to the pack and the rifle which were slung at his back, together with the well-filled and carefully guarded pouch and horn, he had carelessly cast a keen and bright wood axe across his shoulder, sustaining the weight of the whole with as much apparent ease as if he moved unfettered in limb, and free from incumbrance. (Ch. 1)

Would the frontier be settled by brutish, uncivilized, disordered, landless people like Ishmael? Cooper certainly recognized, feared and was fascinated by his power and persistence; and though at the end of the fiction he and his band wander away leaving the stage and country to the gentry – Capt. Middleton and Inez – the solution is arbitrary and unconvincing, and the landless with sharp axes and few scruples would surely return. What Cooper realized was that in any society there must be firm laws governing relations between man and man and his environment, and in a frontier society these laws were often non-existent. Thus in *The Pioneers* (1823), Natty Bumppo and Indian John obeyed natural law before the settlements came: they killed only what they needed and ate only when they were hungry. But the new settlers have no relationship with the land and kill indiscriminately: for example, they slaughter great quantities of passenger pigeons (now extinct!) with anything they can lay their hands on, from long poles to artillery, until the ground is covered in bodies. Ironically, it is Natty (who later breaks the 'law' by killing a deer out of season) who points out to Judge Temple, the embodiment of Cooper's conservative, benevolent paternal democrat, the need to restrain human greed and weakness:

> 'It's much better to kill only such as you want, without wasting your powder and lead, than to be firing into God's creaters in such a wicked manner. But I come out for a bird, and you know the reason why I like small game, Mr. Oliver, and now I have got one I will go home, for I don't like to see these wasty ways that you are all practysing, as if the least thing was not made for use, and not to destroy.'
>
> 'Thou sayest well, Leather-Stocking', cried Marmaduke, 'and I begin to think it time to put an end to this work of destruction.'
>
> 'Put an end, Judge, to your clearings. An't the woods his work as well as the pigeons? Use, but don't waste. Wasn't the woods made for the beasts and birds to harbour in? and when man wanted their flesh, their skins, or their feathers, there's the place to seek them. But I'll go to the hut with my own game, for I wouldn't touch one of the harmless things that kiver the ground here, looking up with their eyes at me, as if they only wanted tongues to say their thoughts.'
>
> With this sentiment in his mouth, Leather-Stocking threw his rifle over his arm, and followed by his dogs, stepped across the clearing with great caution, taking care not to tread on one of the hundreds of the wounded birds that lay in his path. He soon entered the bushes on the margin of the lake, and was hid from view. (Ch. 22)

Cooper's criticisms of American society, when coupled with lengthy residence in Europe, from 1826 to 1833, led to his being attacked for his unpatriotic attitudes. He responded in *The American Democrat* (1838) with a definition of his stand:

The writer believes himself to be as good a democrat as there is
in America. But his democracy is not of the impracticable school.
He prefers a democracy to any other system, on account of its
comparative advantages, and not on account of its perfection.
He knows it has evils; great and increasing evils, and evils peculiar
to itself; but he believes that monarchy and aristocracy have more.
It will be very apparent to all who read this book, that he is not
a believer in the scheme of raising men very far above their
natural propensities.

It was not that doubters of the democratic system were so few but that
alternatives were quite absent. Even those whose mistrust of democracy
proved habitual believed that the destiny of the United States involved
unparalleled growth and expansion: as conservative a figure as Gouverneur
Morris could, in 1801, announce that 'The proudest empire in Europe is
but a bauble, compared to what the United States *will* be, *must* be, in the
course of two centuries; perhaps one!'

Proclamations of political power and significance, projects to create a
national literature, bore little relationship to American achievements in
the first decades of independence. Reviewing the condition of the United
States in 1820, Sydney Smith, writing in the *Edinburgh Review*, damned the
nation's qualities with the faintest of praises:

The Americans are a brave, industrious, and acute people; but
they have hitherto given no indications of genius, and made no
approaches to the heroic, either in their morality or character. . . .
During the thirty or forty years of their independence, they have
done absolutely nothing for the Sciences, for the Arts, for
Literature, or even for the statesman-like studies of Politics or
Political Economy. . . . In the four quarters of the globe, who
reads an American book? or goes to an American play? or looks
at an American picture or statue? What does the world yet owe to
American physicians or surgeons? What new substances have their
chemists discovered? or what old ones have they analyzed? What new
constellations have been discovered by the telescopes of Americans?
– what have they done in the mathematics? Who drinks out of
American glasses? or eats from American plates? or wears American
coats or gowns? or sleeps in American blankets? . . .

If such an estimate was unfair at the time of writing and totally inaccurate
as a prediction of the future, it served to point the distinction between
the ambitions of Americans and their actual realization. Recognition
abroad, whether of the nation's political standing or of its artistic and
literary contributions, was to be long delayed. The withholding of any
acknowledgements proved dispiriting to many who had so enthusiastically

greeted the appearance of specifically American qualities and then found their expectations dispelled. Yet some always persisted in the search, pursuing the task in a fashion which, for all the changes that had occurred in the meantime, Ezra Stiles would have found familiar. The Sermon of 1783 and Herman Melville's *White Jacket* of 1850 are linked by a common belief in the special mission of the United States; a process which, by mid-century, had begun to be defined and described in the nation's history and literature. It had much further to travel and to change in the process, but the society which could elicit Melville's description had developed in ways that would ensure a sense of uniqueness for at least a century to come:

> We Americans are the peculiar, chosen people – the Israel of our time; we bear the ark of the liberties of the world. Seventy years ago we escaped from thrall; and, besides our first birthright – embracing one continent of earth – God has given to us, for a future inheritance, the broad domains of the political pagans, that shall yet come and lie down under the shade of our ark, without bloody hands being lifted. God has predestined, mankind expects, great things from our race; and great things we feel in our souls. The rest of the nations must soon be in our rear. We are the pioneers of the world; the advance-guard, sent on through the wilderness of untried things, to break a new path in the New World that is ours. In our youth is our strength, in our inexperience, our wisdom. At a period when other nations have but lisped, our deep voice is heard afar. Long enough have we been sceptics with regard to ourselves, and doubted whether, indeed, the political Messiah had come. But he has come in *us*, if we would but give utterance to his promptings. And let us always remember that with ourselves, almost for the first time in the history of earth, national selfishness is unbounded philanthropy; for we cannot do a good to America, but we give alms to the world. (Ch. 36)

By 1850, in literature as in politics, the great themes of the American experience had been assembled. Yet we cannot miss in the range of Melville's work something of that sense of alienation and disturbance that tests and questions the note of American idealism which he also speaks to: expectation meshes with an anarchic doubt. Tempered through change, the hopes and fears of the revolutionary generation were now embodied in a distinctive national identity.

▶ For further reading

Richard Beeman et al. (eds), *Beyond Confederation: Origins of the Constitution and American National Identity* (1987).

Sacvan Bercovitch (ed.), *The Cambridge History of American Literature, Vol. 1, 1590–1820* (1986).

Lawrence Buell, *New England Literary Culture: From Revolution through Renaissance* (1986).

Michael Heale, *The Presidential Quest: Candidates and Images in American Political Culture, 1787–1852* (1982).

Ernest Lee Tuveson, *Redeemer Nation: The Idea of America's Millennial Role* (1968).

Gordan S Wood, *The Radicalism of the American Revolution* (1992).

3 New England in the nation

Christine Bolt and A Robert Lee

▶ Seeing 'New Englandly'

What has it meant to see – as Emily Dickinson said she did – 'New Englandly'? Probably more than any other region in American culture, New England evokes a body of quite specific associations – in founding intention and ideas. It calls to mind a landscape of settlement, of religious utopias, of stern 'theocracies', and also a later world of abolitionists and reformers, writers, thinkers and sages, men who, like Henry David Thoreau, 'travelled much in Concord' and explored the potentials of a significant part of American sensibility. In philosophy, religion, literature, it offers a starting place for perceiving a particular, and an American, way of regarding the mind and experience. It has been the focus of a number of key ideas – Puritanism, Zeal, Mission, Reform, Transcendentalism – that have fed the American sense of 'exceptional' personal and national destiny. New England ideas shaped national ideas in the deepest ways, and there has ever been in the New England mind a patrician bent, a confidence that New England's leading voices had a high and destined role to play in all the major debates and movements of their times: politics, humanitarianism, culture. There were, of course, many New Englanders whose lives were very different, but we can also sense in their less obvious and less patrician records something of the New England confidence. New Englanders were always fiercely self-aware and yet conscious of the need to look outside themselves for survival. The cultural symbol of their duality and their success is Boston, Massachusetts, that rich, central city receiving and dispatching the world's people, goods, ideas, and dominating not only the region but America in the first century of settlement. But to see 'New Englandly' is also to see in interrelated ways, to seek to ride, as Emerson would have it, several horses: of self and society, commerce and religion, science and imagination, realism and idealism. We too have an obligation to take, of New England, and the elements of its culture, the wider interpretative view.

▶ The Puritan mind

The most important single fact about New England was that it was settled in the seventeenth century by Puritans: its leaders clearly shaped the history of their section, and Puritanism was the most important formative influence on American culture. This influence came neither from the success with which the colonists realized their founding objective, nor from the welcoming climate and topography of New England. Despite celebration of the new promised land, the landscape the pilgrims found was daunting and its hardships severe. New England was cut off by the Green and White Mountains; there were few navigable rivers other than the Connecticut; the land was hilly and stony, winters prolonged and hard. The Puritans were thankful to find a country 'fruitful and fit for habitation', but primarily they journeyed there for 'advancement of the Christian faith': to practise their religion in communities that would inspire the wider world. Accordingly, they stamped their influence on a difficult land by zealous devotion to the details of social and religious organization. Even so, within thirty years of the Plymouth Landing in 1620, Puritanism was being challenged by forces of religious dissent and economic change. The former questioned Puritan respect for traditional authority and dislike of spiritual enthusiasm; the latter undermined the old distinction between the honest pursuit of a personal calling and what Cotton Mather denounced as 'the *Cursed Hunger of Riches* [which] will make men *break through* all the Laws of God'.

The legacy of Puritanism was paradoxical, but it was potent. The seventeenth-century Puritans had struggled to re-establish English ideas and social forms in the New World; in the process they opposed much that would later be regarded as quintessentially American – religious tolera- tion, the separation of church and state, 'progressive' education, rugged individualism. However, the tensions within and without Puritanism unin- tentionally moved its adherents towards new ideas and new ways. The Puri- tan Fathers favoured a stratified and regimented commonwealth, but in their autonomous congregations, with the considerable participation they allowed, there was a democratic tendency that would exert a powerful influence on nineteenth-century attitudes. Puritanism began with the abso- lute sovereignty of God and the institutionalization of religious enthusi- asm; but its elements eventually encouraged sectarian fragmentation and anarchic religious revivalism. Its emphasis on law was matched by a high respect for education: there was a lower level of illiteracy in New England than anywhere else in America, a system of elementary and grammar schools was established, and the region had more colleges than any other, a superiority it boasts to the present day. The static society that Puritans hoped to secure was undermined by the vigorous individual pursuit of 'calling', the stress on the moral dignity of work and profits, and the displacement of religious zeal into other realms. The social energies thus unleashed helped to transform the New England Puritan into the Yankee – that thrifty, pertinacious, ambitious, acquisitive, versatile and ingenious type whose commercial enterprise was to have its impact not only in America but around the world, and whose name would ultimately be applied by foreigners to Americans generally.

This ingenuity was not simply one of the unexpected consequences of Puritan teaching; it was essential for survival. Although New England quickly became the colonies' major shipping centre, most of its people remained dependent on agriculture. Diversification was hampered by a dearth of local markets, good river transport and commercial towns, while the Revolution destroyed the old triangular trade between New England, Europe and the West Indies. Fortunately, from the 1790s onwards, the credit of the New England states was improved by the federal assumption of state debts, the establishment of banks facilitated speculation of every kind, and shipping was assisted by bounties and protection. New trading opportunities were subsequently discovered throughout the world and new fortunes founded.

Yet there was much that was happening in the country that caused New Englanders disquiet. Rightly fearing that the rapid admission of new states would undermine their power in the Union, many successively opposed the purchase of Louisiana from France in 1803, Texas annexation and the Mexican War in the 1840s. Having constituted just over half the American population in 1650, they were reduced to a quarter in 1790, a fifth in 1810, a seventh in 1830, and a tenth in 1860. Whereas 4 of the original 13 states were New England states (Vermont declared its independence in 1777 and Maine, which was initially part of Massachusetts, in 1820), New England comprised 6 out of a total of 23 by 1820, and by 1860, 6 out of 33. The political consequences of minority status were felt both in the Senate, where individual states were equally represented, and in the House, where the size of a state's delegation depended on the size of its population, estimated by a decennial census.

This would not have mattered so much if New England had always seen eye to eye with other states on matters of importance. But such was far from being the case. Its leading citizens found difficulty in coming to terms with the rise of partisan politics after the Revolution and with the protection for its interests, including slavery, which the South managed to win under the new party system. New Englanders then supported the Federalists for their helpful economic programme, pro-British stance and respect for élitist government, voting solidly for that party in 1800 when most of the rest of the country favoured Jefferson and the Republicans. The election marked the beginning of the great Virginia Republican dynasty of Jefferson, Madison and Monroe. Yet New Englanders clung contrarily to the Federalists, despite the party's inability to change as society changed, thereby confirming their position as a minority section.

The War of 1812, 'Mr Madison's War', was strongly opposed in New England, where trade and shipping suffered, and secession from the nation was briefly considered. But in the end economic counter-pressures prevailed and New Englanders proved to be no more unanimous in outlook than citizens of other regions, or than they had ever been.

New England's hostility to the Union anticipated without matching the bitter sectionalism which developed in the South from the 1830s. The second party system which replaced the Virginia dynasty was much more to its liking, and the election of John Quincy Adams of Massachusetts as President in 1824 presented the New Englander as nationalist, not localist, and seemed to promise much. The promise did not last. By contrast with the emergent popular style of politics carefully personified by his opponent Andrew Jackson, Adams was presented by his critics as an over-refined aristocrat. Between the election of Adams in 1824 and the succession of Calvin Coolidge in 1923, only one New Englander, Franklin Pierce in 1853, became President of the United States. Of course the region continued to produce national leaders – Daniel Webster in the 1830s and 1840s and Charles Sumner in the 1850s and 1860s. But political power now lay elsewhere.

The influx of Irish immigrants into New England was another cause for concern. While the most enterprising of the native-born felt impelled to seek their fortunes in New York, the Ohio Valley and the Mid-West, hungry refugees from the potato famine crowded into the region to take their places. By 1860 a third of Boston's 168,000 inhabitants were Irish. The newcomers were poor, obliged to take any work they could get, and allegedly willing to sell their votes for favours even before they were eligible to cast them. They placed a strain on housing resources, social welfare and New England tolerance. Coming out of necessity rather than inclination into an ethnically homogenous part of America, they were soon disliked by the old stock as clannish, Catholic and an unhealthy element in 'the mass of ignorance and intemperance which disgraces our cities'. Such antipathies were emphatically mutual. Attempts to exclude them failed but, whatever their early impact on Democratic politics, the Irish remained before the Civil War an apparently unassimilable element in the population, at odds with both native whites and the small, still more despised black community. Moreover, the male migration westwards had increasingly upset the balance between the sexes in the New England states. There were 'some 20,000 "surplus" women' by 1850, a fact which contributed to the growing numbers of single women anxious to secure personal and economic independence in a far from encouraging world.

Surmounting these sources of unease, New England succeeded in making its distinctive voice heard in the nation. Often it was necessary to be content with cultural instead of economic influence, although as usual Yankee versatility imposed its mark. This was evident in the swift acceptance of technological innovation and the factory system. At first the operatives in such factories were mainly farm girls – as in the famous textile mills at Lowell, Massachusetts, which were remarked on by admiring foreign visitors alike for their cultivated workforce and employer paternalism. Spinning and weaving had always been household industries in New England, and with the development of new machines, together with the decline of farming due to competition from the Mid-West, it was natural for the women to move out to the factories. Later their places were taken by Irish immigrants, and conditions of employment generally declined. Without a tradition of collective action, workers could offer little resistance, despite the legalization of union activities by the Massachusetts Supreme Court in 1842. But when formal association failed, there was always the threat or reality of mass violence to alarm politicians and reformers, a tradition which was particularly strong in New England, with its long history of civic activism.

▶ Reform and New England

Reform, as a way of bridging political, religious and economic problems, became a central preoccupation of New England society in the nineteenth century; and to many, the region simply was, in Angelina Grimké's words, 'The moral lighthouse of our nation'. In the political realm, matters were greatly affected by the rise of the new party system from the 1820s, when Federalists and Republicans were superseded by Whigs and Democrats. New England proved to be the Whig stronghold, and the party recruited many former Federalist leaders and voters, notwithstanding the attractions of the Democrats. For Whiggery appeared to offer a positive antidote to what seemed the worst features of the administration of Andrew Jackson, the first Democratic President: limited government, ironically ensured through executive 'despotism', strident partisanship, demagogic appeals to the masses, and the replacement of enlightened political élites by second-rate professional placemen. Of course the two parties had similarities: both looked to the past as well as the future for inspiration – just as, according to the New England sage Ralph Waldo Emerson, each individual was affected by the 'opposition of Past and Future, of Memory and Hope'. Many Whigs, like the Federalists before them, supported a variety of benevolent organizations – the Bible Society, the American Temperance Society, the Sunday School Union, the Home Missionary Society – which aimed at keeping sin, secularism and disorder at bay. On the other hand, in the changing world of urbanization and industrialization, they took up new issues: the building of art galleries and libraries, educational and prison reform, campaigns for less acquisitive policies towards the Indians, improved provision for care of the handicapped and insane, women's rights, and pre-eminently, anti-slavery and abolition. In all these enterprises the emphasis on individual liberation and humanitarianism was important. Yet there were Whigs, notably in Massachusetts, who advocated harmony with the South and close ties with the Southern cotton producers (who provided business for the state's manufacturers and merchants, and who sent their sons to Harvard). There were, on the other hand, the 'Conscience' Whigs who distrusted this alliance with the Southern 'Cotton' Whigs, and some of them defected to the uncompromisingly abolitionist Liberty Party during the 1840s. Moreover, the Democratic Party also managed to exert considerable influence on Massachusetts politics, and was indeed popularly regarded as the party of progress, free-thinking and innovation; which may account for its attraction, in Harriet Martineau's judgement, to 'the men of genius'. And elsewhere, as in New Hampshire, where urbanization and industrialization were not so well advanced, the Democrats dominated.

There was thus no simple connection between politics and reform, and there were many who thought that reform should transcend politics altogether. Men of letters were repelled by the ultimate and deliberate blurring of party differences by party leaders, with a view to attracting the largest possible vote, while moral reformers often felt that efforts to improve American society should not be restrained by caution or the other imperfections of such institutions as political parties, believing that the individual's responsibilities were to God and his own conscience – an oblique derivation of Puritan principles. It is equally difficult to disentangle the religious roots of New England reform. Not only New England but the whole nation was affected by the religious revivals of the first half of the nineteenth century, in the course of which many sects came to place a fresh emphasis on the importance of religious enthusiasm, free will, and the immediate release of the individual from guilt through repentance and good works. However, New England did evolve its own distinctive forms of reaction against Calvinist doctrine, in the two great movements of Unitarianism and Transcendentalism. Transcendentalism, as we shall see later, was an essential part of the great intellectual 'flowering of New England', and its implications in philosophy and in literature are crucial. But it is also important to note that for many of its upper-class adherents the philosophy was essentially a spur towards reform, both individual and collective. Emerson reported that in the 1840s every reading man had the draft of a new community in his waistcoat pocket, and Transcendentalism united many prevailing reform interests, from feminism to socialism on the Fourierist model and to anxiety about the mechanical industrialism evolving in American life.

There are historians who believe that the Transcendentalists were primarily held together by their reformism and exercised a major influence on other reformers. This is to exaggerate their distinctiveness and practical significance. A belief in the perfectibility of man was central to the entire religious renaissance of these years, and was not confined to Transcendentalists. Like other Americans, Transcendentalists disagreed about the merits and methods, the appropriate pace and scope, of reform. They were more frequently the publicists than the organisers of reform efforts, and few found formal association appealing, even in the famous idealistic Massachusetts communes of Brook Farm, Hopedale and Fruitlands. These had a Transcendentalist involvement, but Emerson and Thoreau avoided them, preferring Concord and the path of Emerson's 'first-person singular'. To doubters – including Nathaniel Hawthorne, who went to Brook Farm but wrote ironically of it in *The Blithedale Romance* (1852), contrasting its pastoral images with the facts of the city – these foundations represented the extreme or eccentric wing of the new philosophies, though there was much that was admirable in Brook Farm's educational experiments and its attempts to reduce the division between manual and intellectual work. Communities with a religious and socialistic inspiration were certainly not confined to New England, although there were more there than elsewhere. Brook Farm was probably the best known, if one of the least enduring. As a contributor to *Harper's Monthly* noted: 'there were never such witty potato-patches and such sparkling cornfields before or since. The weeds were scratched out of the ground to the music of Tennyson and Browning, and the nooning was an hour as bright as any brilliant moonlight at Ambrose's.' But where the Transcendentalists did voice a widespread unease was in condemning the materialism of their day. Their faith in unfettered indi-vidualism was in accord with the ideology of the Democratic Party and of the contemporary entrepreneur, and they were the voice of as well as the critics of their age. Their dissatisfaction with existing institutions, among them the political parties, was the consequence rather than the cause of the weakness of these institutions as vehicles for reform, in times when old suspicions of organized parties had not entirely vanished, and in a country where the federal political system seemed to frustrate responsible government. Clearly Transcendentalism's attempt to look beyond the social order into a larger wholeness had its ideological roots.

The impetus given by New England to ante-bellum reform is striking. The South was restrained by distrust of modernizing forces which might undermine its defence of slavery, by the 1830s confined to that section. Pennsylvania and New York rivalled New England in enterprise; but New England's role was supported by its economic, demographic and cultural characteristics. A good transport network, a relatively dense population, a sound church and lyceum organization and a high level of literacy aided the work of protest's itinerant publicists. Equally, the large profits of the new industrial order and what Charles Francis Adams later called 'the terrible New England Conscience' demanded and facilitated the use of surplus wealth for public good. For such reasons, the efforts for anti-slavery, peace, educational improvement, women's rights and temperance were extremely strong there, and even though the section's political and economic power was weakening, the consequent threat to the influence of reformers in and beyond their own communities was not great before the Civil War. All these movements, and especially abolitionism, were national in scope and found vigorous support in the Middle States and the Mid-West. Yet, along with Philadelphia and New York, Boston was the key forum for the discussion and dissemination of reform, as indeed for the radiation of all important cultural trends.

▶ Boston as cultural capital

Although there never was in the United States an undisputed cultural capital comparable to Paris or London, nineteenth-century Boston re-joiced in its nickname 'the Athens of America'. Its citizens saw history made manifest in fine colonial buildings and all the prosperous vistas of Beacon Hill, and took pride not only in their city's thriving economy but also in its vast concentration of clubs, societies and improving establish-ments. In fact it was not until the 1880s, when William Dean Howells – the Ohio writer who had come East to continue the apostolic succession of Longfellow, Lowell and Holmes, and to edit the *Atlantic Monthly* – decided to move from Boston to New York, that the cultural pre-eminence of Boston in the nation seemed in dispute.

From the Puritan period onwards, Boston was active in education and ideas. Harvard College had been founded in 1636, only six years after the first settlement. By the mid-seventeenth century Boston had a flourishing book-trade and numerous booksellers. From Independence onwards, the region had produced a high proportion of the republic's writers and artists; and from the 1820s Boston led the way with a lyceum movement that aimed to improve educational facilities both in schools and society at large. During the winter of 1837–38, some twenty-six courses of lectures were mounted in Boston alone. Where the Puritan sermon had been the chief entertainment, now the public lecture and the political speech be-came prime attractions for godly audiences who feared the saloon but lacked alternative respectable forms of recreation. Reformers and evan-gelists, quick to see how converts might be made, wooed these audiences with a judicious blend of emotionalism, simplification, repetition and piety. 'The impassioned utterance of a common exhorter will often move a congregation beyond anything that . . . splendid exhibitions of rhetoric can effect', recollected the popular preacher Charles Grandison Finney. In William Channing, Lyman Beecher and Theodore Parker, Boston claimed the services of the three best preachers of the day, who between them represented the transition towards a more liberal theology. Nor was the printed work neglected in Boston: it produced the nation's best liter-ary periodical, the *North American Review*, the transient but impressive *Boston Quarterly Review*, and innumerable pamphlets, newspapers, reviews and reform journals, as well as many of the nation's books.

In addition Boston was the centre for historical scholarship, the most distinctive contribution of New England to the republic before the 'New England Renaissance' in poetry and fiction from the 1840s to the 1860s.

Among the historians who at various times lived there, we should note George Bancroft, Francis Parkman, William Prescott, Richard Hildreth, John Lothrop Motley, John Palfrey, Jared Sparks, George Ticknor and Samuel Eliot. Indeed, the great majority of eighteenth- and nineteenth-century American historians were New Englanders, and their work reflects the continuing Puritan preoccupation with the concrete and instructive, with glorifying the work of God in every aspect of men's lives, and with reaffirming the Puritan's sense of a special destiny in the New World. The bulk of the authors of local and school-book histories and many more eminent practitioners of the discipline were themselves clergymen, so that their biases were professional as well as regional. It was in Boston that the first American historical society was established (in 1791) and New England as a whole was notable for the number of town chronicles and other historical works it produced and which served as models for scholars in different parts of the country. Yet if pride in their forebears' formative role in the making of the country inspired New England historians, they were seldom parochial in outlook, seeing it as a patriotic as much as a religious duty to distil the essence of the unique national culture which was allegedly developing. In the process, they attached an importance the Puritans would not have appreciated to individual liberty and the idea of progress, and Francis Parkman, the aristocratic Bostonian, even delighted – in *The Oregon Trail* (1849) – in a Western movement which filled many New Englanders with jealous dread.

The reformers who made their homes in Boston were similarly influenced by a combination of local pride and large vision, an awareness of the heritage of the past and the exciting prospects for future change. Feminism and abolitionism in particular seemed to encourage the 'terrible propensities' which conservatives feared were being released as America approached democracy. It was in Boston that, in 1831, William Lloyd Garrison launched his *Liberator* with the intention of overcoming the apathy he found all around him on the questions of slavery and prejudice towards black people. If he was reassuringly pious and Whiggish in his politics, the relentless urgency of Garrison's message was alarming to many sections of New England opinion. 'I shall', he declared, 'strenuously contend for the immediate enfranchisement of our slave population . . . I *will be* as harsh as truth, and as uncompromising as justice. On this subject I do not wish to write, or speak, or think, with moderation . . . AND I WILL BE HEARD.' Although Garrison's main concern was slavery, his catholic approach to reform attracted many women to his banner and caused them, when they encountered hostility to their full participation in abolition activities, even from male co-workers, to consider the similarities between sexual and racial oppression and, by the 1840s, to begin organizing on their own account. Divided in ideas and aims, the women's movement nonetheless produced such genuine radicals as Margaret Fuller, the Boston Transcendentalist and feminist who declared that every woman should have the freedom 'as a nature to grow, as an intellect to discern, as a soul to live freely and unimpeded to unfold such powers as were given'. Not surprisingly, the contemporary press took a very jaundiced view of feminist endeavours, describing one Massachusetts women's rights convention as an 'Awful Combination of Socialism, Abolitionism, and infidelity'.

There was likewise some substance to the contemporary feeling that, whereas the agitators of the middle and western states generally displayed a practical approach to reform, whether this meant retaining good relations with the clergy or entertaining political compromise, the New England mind, however quick to see and seize new opportunities by the nineteenth century, still displayed a Puritan intolerance of opposition, compromise and popular opinion, which frequently doomed the region's zealots to disappointment, or at best to savouring the satisfaction they derived from each other's exacting company. New Englanders undoubtedly contributed to the break-up of the Whig coalition, the increasingly intransigent defence of slavery by Southern Democrats and, eventually, to the dissolution of the second party system and the rise of the Republicans, a party with an overtly sectional appeal. But that party, which owed so much to New England support and ideals, representing what Eric Foner has described as a 'profoundly successful fusion of value and interest', ironically secured the triumph of anti-slavery, the major cause of ante-bellum reformers, albeit only with the appalling sacrifices of war and of radical hopes that racial equality would be secured along with abolition. Moreover, while the influence of New England 'ultras' might be diminished after the Civil War in the more cautious atmosphere of Reconstruction politics, many of its reformers turned their attention then and in the following years to the challenges posed by mistreatment of the Indians and black freedmen, and by the maturing industrial revolution. The invasion of the South by Yankee schoolma'ams simultaneously able to find satisfying work among the ex-slaves and to make that region over in the New England image is, alone, a tribute to the enduring will of New England humanitarians. Something remarkable was indeed apparent, as the abolitionist Stephen Foster remarked, in 'the productions of this barren soil'.

▶ New England and the 'American Renaissance'

One consequence of New England's cultural hegemony was that when, between the 1830s and the Civil War, that extraordinary efflorescence of literature, art and ideas that we now call the American Renaissance occurred, New England was its clear centre. From the Revolution onwards Americans had been hungering for a declaration of literary and cultural independence as potent as their political one. By the 1820s, with the works of Washington Irving (1783–1859), turning European folklore into

American fable, with James Fenimore Cooper's (1789–1851) massive body of fiction, a vivid pageant of pioneer experience, and with the dark, interiorized writings of Edgar Allan Poe (1809–49), the stock of achievement had been accumulating. But it was over a few stunning years at mid-century, when American literature could suddenly count among its major achievements Melville's *Moby-Dick* (1851) and 'Benito Cereno' (1855), Hawthorne's *The Scarlet Letter* (1850) and *The House of the Seven Gables* (1851), Whitman's *Leaves of Grass* (first edition, 1855), Henry David Thoreau's *Walden* (1854), the 'hidden' poems of the Amherst genius Emily Dickinson, today brought into the light, and the poetry and essays of Ralph Waldo Emerson, that the high moment arose. Not all the figures of the Renaissance were Transcendentalists. Poe's inner landscape is a bleak and quite un-Emersonian world, and Hawthorne and Melville deeply questioned, with their 'NO! in Thunder', its note of Adamic optimism. Not all were New Englanders. Poe was from the South, Melville from New York, Whitman from Long Island. Yet, for all of them, Transcendentalist New England was a stimulus and a centre: it was, said Emerson, from New England's 'bar-rooms, Lyceums, committee rooms' that 'many words leap out alive' and 'fill the world with their thunder'. And it was Emerson's essay 'The American Scholar' (1837), which called for a specific American national culture ('We have listened too long to the courtly muses of Europe') shaped by American history, American democracy and American optimism, that was the starting cry of the Renaissance. A fellow Brahmin and Boston man of letters judged it precisely 'our intellectual Declaration of Independence'.

If the high culture of America sounded its aspirations through any one spokesman, it was Ralph Waldo Emerson (1803–82). His was the oracular voice of Transcendentalism, the shifting and often ethereal philosophy of human perfectibility and the belief in Nature as the ideal and outward show of benign Divinity that dominated the 'optative' spirit of American culture. He expressed the note of a time when the nation in general was on the move, when resources and space seemed vast, the bonds of the past no longer held the present, the virtues of individualism and self-reliance seemed proven, untried possibilities were being made real, America itself seemed imbued with spiritual and moral meanings. There was a New England legacy in Emerson's expression of this. None knew that legacy better, for his roots lay deep in the region's past, ministers to one side, astute Yankee businessmen to the other. For him, as for like-minded spirits throughout New England, in Boston and townships like Cambridge and Concord, the original theology of Election and Special Grace, in fact the whole Puritan vision of a punitive God and of Man as heir to a fallen and guilty human realm, was long defunct. Beliefs which compelled earlier New England luminaries like John Winthrop, Cotton and Increase Mather, and the redoubtable and evangelical Jonathan Edwards, now seemed a body of irrelevant Post-Reformation doctrine and liturgy. Indeed, by the 1830s, when Emerson was making his public bow, even Unitarianism, that liberal and humanist body of Christian ethics which had replaced Puritanism in the New England mind, and in which Emerson and many fellow-Transcendentalists had first trained, would itself no longer do. Emerson saw a new time – and found, in an America caught up in the westering impulse and the settlement of the continent, the prospect of a fresh liberation of self, an inward and exemplary regeneration of the human spirit.

Nowhere did he enunciate this more loftily than in 'Nature', a tract published anonymously in 1836, where he first struck his epochal note:

> Our age is retrospective. It builds the sepulchres of the fathers.
> It writes biographies, histories, and criticism. The foregoing
> generations beheld God and Nature face to face; we, through their
> eyes. Why should not we also enjoy an original relationship to the
> universe? Why should we not have a poetry and philosophy of
> insight, and not of tradition, and a religion by revelation to us, and
> not the history of theirs? . . . There are new lands, new men, new
> thoughts. Let us demand our own works and laws and worship.

By Transcendentalism, Emerson looked to the essence behind any one single cause – Abolition, Temperance, Reform – and sought to lay siege, as he said in his essay 'The Transcendentalist' (1842), to 'the whole connection of spiritual doctrine'. The world's essential meanings, he held, derived from spiritual 'laws' which 'transcended' all received dogma and institutions, and came to men through their intuitive faculties. Godhead lay within. So radical a confidence in the powers of individual vision, which Emerson called 'self-reliance', and in the benevolent God-principle he called 'The Over-Soul', struck the orthodox as 'the latest form of infidelity'.

And yet, paradoxically, Transcendentalist arguments owed much to older Puritan culture – the interpretation of Nature as 'God's hieroglyph', the commitment to the self's inner drama as part of a larger, 'exceptional' American destiny, the view of reality as the emblematic garment of the spirit. In one way, 'Nature' and the addresses and essays Transcendentalists subsequently sponsored belonged to a parochial New England debate: a dissident minister and his adherents repudiating the faith of their forefathers. But from a wider perspective, Emerson served notice of far deeper currents in his age and place – the belief in a hitherto unrecognized 'American' self and a new American way of seeing the world. What was affected, and reinvigorated, was a whole cultural vision. And this included a reconsideration of the place of the artist in American life, and of the very language and forms by which this 'American' perception of reality might be transposed into art.

But if Emerson knew himself by heritage to be a New Englander, he also belonged to the wider movement of nineteenth-century Romanticism.

His affinities lay with Plato and the neo-Platonists, and of his nearer philosophical contemporaries, with Kant (to whom he credited the term 'transcendental'), Berkeley, Hume and Locke, Swedenborg and his theories of 'correspondence'. He read closely in Coleridge, Wordsworth and Goethe, indeed in all the main figures of European Romanticism; he conducted a lifelong correspondence with his fellow sage and metaphysician Thomas Carlyle; he also looked East, to the Vedas and the *Bhagavadgita*. This eclectic reading had a deprovincializing aspect both for Emerson and those around him, and if sceptics like Nathaniel Hawthorne and Herman Melville judged Transcendentalism facile, a doctrine of American good cheer which ignored the human capacity for evil, or the place of war and pain in human affairs, they could not deny that it drew on reputable sources. Nor could it be denied that in seeking within the sovereign self rather than in society or tradition a sanction for individual vision, Emerson represented something fundamentally American, which Melville or Hawthorne would express in their own writing, and Thoreau in the literal conduct of a life. As he looked on the America before him, a culture of business, and frontier and aggressive materialist expansion, Emerson recognized that Puritanism had come to mean the Protestant ethic, that manifestation of 'grace' as entrepreneurial energy which Benjamin Franklin had cannily set forth in his *Autobiography* and *Poor Richard's Almanack*. 'Things' were too much in the saddle; he pitched his appeal to the idealist element in American experience, writing in 1844, in 'The Young American', 'I call upon you, young men, to obey your heart, and be the nobility of this land'. He re-evoked the image of the American as an Adam and a 'new man' that Crèvecoeur had fashioned in *Letters from an American Farmer* (1782), the note of an age of optimistic, pioneer individualism.

Above all, Emerson spoke to the need for poetic imagination, writing enticingly in 'The Poet' of the creative challenge offered by the New World:

> Our log-rollings, our stumps and their politics, our fisheries, our
> Negroes and Indians, our boats and our repudiations, the wrath of
> rogues and the pusillanimity of honest men, the northern trade, the
> southern planting, the western clearing, Oregon and Texas, are yet
> unsung. Yet America is a poem in our eyes; its ample geography
> dazzles the imagination, and it will not wait long for metres.

Indeed he was a major poet himself, and the power of his imagination is bared in the work-pages of his *Journals*, a rich quarry of aphorisms and notations on the awakening of his mind. To see the first draft of his central preoccupations – his trust in Nature's 'sanitive' powers, his regard for individual vision, his belief in a balanced and generous universal order – is to glimpse a spacious intelligence at work as it moves towards the dialectics of the major writings – 'Self-Reliance', 'The Over-Soul', the

Harvard 'Divinity School Address' which, together with his other *Essays* (first and second series, 1841 and 1844), his *Representative Men* (1850), his *English Traits* (1856) and his poems, represent him at his best. His larger work in the culture is represented by his part in *The Dial* (1840–44), which he edited from 1842.

Yet Transcendentalism was more than one voice. Most of the review's contributors belonged to the Transcendentalist Club, a forum for debate and the exchange of ideas. *The Dial*'s founding editor was Margaret Fuller (1810–50), a controversial thinker, prima donna and feminist – as she revealed in her *Woman in the Nineteenth Century* (1845) – on whom Hawthorne would model Zenobia in *The Blithedale Romance*. Others of the club's diverse lights included George Ripley (1802–80), the Unitarian minister who was main begetter of Brook Farm; Bronson Alcott (1799–88), a key influence on American pedagogy and child education; Orestes Brownson (1803–76), an obsessive son of the Puritans who converted to Catholicism, flirted with socialism, and whose autobiographies reveal the eccentric rim of self-reliance; the caricaturist Christopher Pearse Cranch (1813–92), whose line-drawings depict the main presence of Transcendentalism in a wry, irreverent light; Jones Very (1813–80), poet and ex-Unitarian minister, whose mystical sonnets deserve their recent revival; William Ellery Channing (1818–1901), poet and essayist, and nephew of the great Unitarian minister; and Elizabeth Peabody (1804–94), whose Boston bookshop served as a Transcendentalist meeting place, who provided America with its first kindergarten, whose sister Sophia married Hawthorne, and who is usually thought the model for Miss Birdseye in Henry James's retrospective look at New Englandism, *The Bostonians* (1886).

Among the Transcendentalist group themselves, there were signs that Emerson's plea for a literature of 'our own works' was being answered. Emerson, Thoreau and Very were all important poets. Around them, in New England, were others: John Greenleaf Whittier (1807–92), the author of powerful anti-slavery and pastoral verse; Henry Wadsworth Longfellow (1807–82), with his massive transatlantic popularity; James Russell Lowell (1819–91), versifier and satirist who followed Longfellow in the Smith Chair of Modern Languages at Harvard; Frederick Goddard Tuckerman (1821–73), a recently rediscovered New England Nature poet (and recluse) who in a poem like 'The Cricket' shows an extraordinary understanding of the non-human world. In Oliver Wendell Holmes (1809–94), yet another Harvard professor, but no admirer of Transcendentalism, New England vaunted a witty belletrist (*The Autocrat at the Breakfast Table*, 1858, etc.). His 'medicated' novels, as he called them, include his minor *tour de force*, *Elsie Venner* (1861), which in tackling the decidedly modern subject of schizophrenia attacked fundamental Calvinist assumptions about human behaviour. A New Englander more palpably responsive to Mission was Harriet Beecher Stowe (1811–96), born of Calvinist ministers' stock in Connecticut, internationally known for her world best-seller *Uncle Tom's Cabin* (1851–52) – a richer achievement than its reputation often admits, for it successfully blended purpose into art in creating the most famous and influential of all abolitionist works. But she also deserves to be known for her other fiction, especially *Dred: A Tale of the Great Dismal Swamp* (1856) and *The Minister's Wooing* (1859).

▶ Transcendentalist inheritors: Thoreau and Whitman

Of the major writers who answered Emerson's summons to the creative-Transcendentalist spirit, the nearest to hand was Henry David Thoreau (1817–62), Transcendentalism's most practical disciple, and a spirit almost martial in his emphatic individualism. When, after Harvard and a spell as handyman in Emerson's house and his editorial assistant on *The Dial*, Thoreau moved to a hut on Emerson's land at Walden Pond, near Concord, on 4 July 1845 – truly his Independence Day – he began a process which gave us, in his classic diary-narrative, *Walden* (1854), a deep mid-century account of a life lived inwardly to its existential limits. 'I went to the woods', Thoreau explained,

> because I wished to live deliberately, to front only the essential facts of life, and to see if I could not learn what it had to teach, and not, when I came to die, discover that I had not lived. I did not wish to live what was not life, living is so dear; nor did I wish to practise resignation, unless it was quite necessary. I wanted to live deep and to put to rout all that was not life . . . to drive life into a corner and reduce it to its lowest terms.

The economy of Thoreau's prose speaks perfectly for the economy of his purpose, the need to corner life, and arrest its overwhelming essence. That same fierce, independent energy animates nearly all his writing, and certainly the biographical pattern of his life. When he observes 'I have travelled much in Concord', he is speaking of Transcendental 'travel', the kind of 'home-cosmography' he alludes to in *Walden's* concluding chapter. Few American writers have pursued essence more tenaciously than Thoreau ('I love to come at my bearings' he confides at one point), or written a more engaging metaphoric idiom (his use of 'economy', 'expense', the 'cost' of things). More than any contemporary, Thoreau held Nature in the regard Emerson had described in 'The Young American':

> The land is the appointed remedy for whatever is false and fantastic in our culture. The continent we inhabit is to be physic and food for our mind, as well as our body.

In plumbing the depths of Walden Pond, Thoreau sought no less than the terms of his own innermost being, a Transcendentalist enquiry into his manifestly separate self and into Nature's subtler currents and significations. In observing with so responsive a curiosity each seasonal shift and turn, Nature's freezings and thaws, Thoreau detected a clue to the whole ecology of human personality, its resistances and higher possibilities. His attacks on the 'costs' of much contemporary capitalism, and of false wars and unacceptable taxes, he offers in the name of an utter commitment to the potential of his own, and every, sovereign self. As the Pond expresses Nature's 'eye', so Thoreau seeks to adapt his own 'eye', both to the natural surface of things and to a comprehension of their inward and shaping powers. With the arguable exception of John James Audubon (1785–1851), whose graphics gave to the world a magnificent view of American fauna and wildlife, nineteenth-century America knew no busier naturalist than Thoreau. But his was always a vision which sought to run deeper, the testimony of a radical New England seer and anarch.

This expansive spirit of 'exploration' marks Thoreau's other writings: *A Week On The Concord And Merrimack Rivers* (1849), composed while he lived in his pondside hut, and like *Walden* a journey (this time 'up-river') into self-illumination; 'Civil Disobedience' (1849), a widely influential testament of conscience against slavery and the State; his 'Plea for Captain John Brown' (1859), made in the name of the absolute claims of human liberty; and the journey pieces – *Excursions* (1863), *The Maine Woods* (1864), *Cape Cod* (1865) and *A Yankee in Canada* (1866) – collected after his premature death. More than any other Transcendentalist, Thoreau tried in life to make reality of precept. His insistence on the need to awaken buried consciousness and reach through to Nature's vital 'physic' led to a reputation still not entirely clear of eccentricity; but he saw with discomforting clarity, and his work shows an author who refused all complacency and unearned truth.

Still, the most full-blooded of all responses to Emerson's appeal came from a younger Long Islander who read his message at a certain distance. Born of a radical Jacksonian father and a Quaker mother, Walt Whitman (1819–92) began with several false starts – as journeyman printer, carpenter, real-estate dealer, journalist, bohemian – before he established his true *métier*. In 1855, in a slim and anonymous green volume, its type partly set by himself, he published his first version of *Leaves of Grass*, a verse sequence of twelve 'chants', which includes the earliest version of 'Song Of Myself'. The book would grow, over nine editions, by accretion and revision, into the Death-Bed Edition of 1891–92: an epic of more than 400 pages, working and re-working a lifetime's preoccupation with the 'single self' and Man 'en masse' and with Nature and the uniqueness of American destiny. From the outset, Whitman appropriated for himself the *persona* of 'Walt' – the bardic voice of democracy speaking at once for the quotidian and the 'divine afflatus'. It was an extravagant, bold, androgynous posture, 'unpoetic' in that it apparently offered catalogues and paragraphs of incantatory prose. But it represented a profound commitment to America as the theatre of the common man, a polity and geography in which all experience might be democratically confronted and declared. The poet, for Whitman, is no Shelleyian 'legislator'; rather he writes on behalf of, and to reveal the transcendent purpose of, the democratic human norm, as the custodian and mouthpiece of Emerson's 'each and all' (the text is from the 1891–92 edition):

> I am the poet of the Body and I am the poet of the Soul,
> The pleasures of heaven are with me and the pains of hell are
>   with me,
> The first I graft and increase upon myself, the latter I translate
>   into a new tongue.

The stance allows Whitman to speak also as the poet of Love ('a kelson of the creation is love'), of Orphic and natural sexual energy ('Urge and urge and urge, Always the procreant urge of the world'), of War ('I am the old artillerist, I tell of my fort's bombardment'), of Death and pain ('I am the man, I suffer'd, I was there'), and above all, of the 'divine' eternal purpose behind human existence which, at the close of 'Song Of Myself', he calls the 'form, union, plan'. Whitman's assumed *persona* is nothing if not confident, at once voluptuous and exploratory:

> I know perfectly well my own egotism,
> Know my own omniverous lines and must not write any less,
> And would fetch you whoever you are flush with myself.

In naming himself, he names a brother democrat, a Christly reconciler of warring opposites, assuming a voice of sensual caress which, for all its Emersonian affinities, speaks out unhampered by any New England reserve:

> Walt Whitman, of Manhattan the son,
> Turbulent, fleshy, sensual, eating, drinking, and breeding,
> No sentimentalist, no stander above men and women or apart
>   from them,
> No more modest than immodest.

On occasion, Whitman's rhetoric risks sounding operatic, intoxicated with its own ambition, a fault which has exposed him to harsh rebuke. But when read as an ordered and overall sequence, his poetry remains something wholly special. It draws on striking links of image and motif, a sureness of voice. Poems as fine as 'Crossing Brooklyn Ferry' or 'There Was A Child Went Forth' amply confirm his lyric powers of language. And the force of his commitment to his 'democratic' vision never flags:

> I speak the pass-word primeval, I give the sign of democracy,
> By God, I will accept nothing which all cannot have their
>   counterpart of on the same terms.

To read *Leaves of Grass* in its subsequent incarnations is to watch a poem – like Ezra Pound's later *Cantos*, or William Carlos Williams's *Paterson* – building on its own momentum. The 1856 edition, for instance, strikes a bolder sexual note than the first, and it reprints the letter Emerson sent privately to Whitman ('I greet you at the beginning of a great career'). In 1860, Whitman added his 'Children Of Adam' and 'Calamus' poems, sequences deeply taken up with sexual confession and observation. In 1867, he included *Drum Taps* (first published as a pamphlet), his sensitive and healing response to the Civil War and to Lincoln's murder, together with the exquisite elegy 'When Lilacs Last In The Dooryard Bloom'd'. The sixth edition (1876) included his most explicit 'transcendentalist' poem, 'Passage to India', and his major prose essay *Democratic Vistas*. Finally, in 1892, now the 'good grey poet' of national and international acclaim, Whitman offered his last edition of the 'book' ('who touches this touches a man') begun so inauspiciously thirty-five years earlier. Whitman's creation of the new audience ('you whoever you are'), the scale of his interpretation of Emerson's vision of man, and his role as a radical experimentalist in idiom and syntax, place him unambiguously at the centre of American literature. To a subsequent and central line of American poets – Carl Sandburg, William Carlos Williams, Hart Crane, Ezra Pound and Allen Ginsberg – his linear collage and self-appointed oracular role ('I am large, I contain multitudes') offered decisive imaginative points of depature. Whitman, if anyone, serves as Emerson's Arch-Transcendentalist, the sacramental and visionary poet-philosopher.

▶ The sceptic from Amherst

For Emily Dickinson (1830–86), circumstance dictated an inward, reclusive life as the daughter of the eminently respectable First Family of Amherst, a small market-town in western Massachusetts whose claims were its college (where Emily's father held the post of treasurer) and its Puritan orthodoxy and probity. For all that, of her nearly 2,000 poems only a handful saw print in her own lifetime, restitution has come posthumously, her life and work rightly acclaimed as that of a major New England poet, woman and personality. Though sometimes (and mischievously) dubbed 'The Nun of Amherst', her supposed style as recluse could not have masked a greater double existence. To immediates and neighbours, she might indeed have seemed the exemplary spinster, 'regulating' as she said her father's household, loyal, competent and 'domestic' – if at times moody and even rebellious as when she refused to accompany the family to Sunday communion. But to those who now read her through her elliptical, powerful, dash-laden poems, there can be no doubting that a more dramatic imagination would be hard to call to mind: a poet of Nature, of the great ceremonies of Life and Death, of religious doubt and dissent.

Whatever reservations she might have felt about Emersonianism, its general hopefulness and good cheer, she certainly derived a special impetus from its radical challenge to past orthodoxy.

'Tell all the truth but tell it slant' begins one of her best-known lyrics, a typically contrary turn of expression which might stand for all the paradox of her writing. Similarly if an answer were required for her celebrated 'I'm Nobody! Who are you?' it assuredly lies in the 'I' released through the poems, the 'I' behind each different inflexion – be it the domestic and playful persona ('I taste a liquor never brewed'), the self which contemplates Nature with so keen a relish ('A bird came down the walk'), the whimsical, irreverent speaker ('What is "Paradise," or "Faith" is a fine invention'), or the poet of Death and the Afterlife ('Because I could not stop for death', 'I heard a fly buzz when I died', 'I felt a funeral in my brain', or 'Safe in their alabaster chambers'). Circumscribed her life may have been in its outward show, but who could doubt that she found her truest existence in the drama of her poems, each a profound act of witness or challenge? The terms in which she expressed her measure of the world, whether as whimsy or anguished self-interrogation, could in one sense not have been more indelibly New England, right through to asking of the ex-Federal officer and literary critic Thomas Wentworth Higginson if her poems 'lived'. But in another sense New England was only her *donnée*. Hers was an art – and a scepticism – which reaches infinitely beyond Amherst, an art which places her in the foremost ranks of poetry.

▶ The nay-sayers: Hawthorne and Melville

In the warm account he gave of Nathaniel Hawthorne (1804–64), in 1879, for the English Men of Letters Series, Henry James judged him 'subtle and slender and unpretending', a nature 'strongest and keenest' when 'the dark Puritan tinge showed . . . most richly'. He also believed Hawthorne (and most American writers of prose narrative) to be dispossessed of the novelist's authentic subject – society, the play of manners. America – wrote the cosmopolitan James – could claim only a provincial social tradition, small pockets of consciousness which left the creative temper isolated and obliged to turn in on itself: only in Europe, where consciousness drew on infinitely richer grain, and society knew itself intricate, self-aware, old in institutions and habit, could the novelist find his best occasions.

But to his friend Herman Melville, Hawthorne had no need of a European stage. Deep amid the imagining of *Moby-Dick*, his own 'wicked book', as he once described it, Melville responded to Hawthorne with the deepest 'shock of recognition'. Here was no provincial New Englander, but 'the Portuguese diamond in our American literature', an immense and passionate imagination, in whom the world was 'mistaken' if it thought him less than the complete man of letters, a contemporary American master. And, above all, Melville confessed himself drawn by Hawthorne's 'blackness', his belief in a blighted and Calvinist fate to men's affairs, and to artifice whose subtleties called to mind the Shakespeare of the great problem plays and the tragedies:

> For spite of all the Indian-Summer sunlight on the hither side of Hawthorne's soul, the other side – like the dark half of the physical sphere – is shrouded in a blackness, ten times black . . . this great power of blackness in him derives its force from its appeals to that Calvinistic sense of Innate Depravity and Original Sin, from whose visitations, in some shape or other, no deeply thinking mind is always and wholly free. For, in certain moods, no man can weigh this world, without throwing in something, somehow like Original Sin, to strike the uneven balance. At all events, perhaps no writer has ever wielded this terrific thought with greater terror than this same harmless Hawthorne. . . . You may be witched by his sunlight, transported by the bright guildings in the skies he builds over you, but there is the blackness of darkness beyond. . . . In one word, the world is mistaken in this Nathaniel Hawthorne.

Melville's response undoubtedly tells as much about the axes of his own thought as of Hawthorne's. But the generosity of his esteem, and his insight into the duplicitous surfaces of Hawthorne's art, make his account as momentous a declaration as any in the history of American literary relationships.

Whether or not Hawthorne was truly the Promethean Melville believed, or more resembled James's great miniaturist of human foible and a fallen world, he assuredly wrote fiction different in texture from the great works of European realism. Hawthorne rightly defined his longer narratives as 'romances', a mode whose imaginative ground he describes in the Custom House sketch introducing *The Scarlet Letter* (1850) as 'neutral territory, somewhere between the real world and fairy land, where the Actual and the Imaginary may meet, and each imbue itself with the nature of the other'. Of all his fiction, *The Scarlet Letter* best brings his major themes to imaginative order, especially his play of emblem, allegory, figurative and perceptual ambiguity. Its ostensible tale of a Puritan adultery, and of a wronged husband's abuse of his intellectual powers to secure revenge, masks far wider enquiries. The book dramatizes the fundamental moral conflict between self-duty ('What we did had a consecration of its own' says Hester Prynne) and the community standard. Its other dialectics explore the conflict of 'science' and the values of the 'heart', the forest domain of sexual and creative energy as against the ordered world of society, daytime reality as against its night-time counterface. Both in 'The Custom House', an astute allegory of the American author's search for his subject and an appropriate form, and in the text proper, Hawthorne's equivocations are everywhere evident. He writes in a voice full of shades and hints, allowing the burden of interpretation to fall wholly, and unfailingly, upon his reader. As each object or person is defined, so equally is the definer: the scarlet 'A' itself, the triangle of Hester, Roger and Arthur, the elfin child Pearl, the forest realm, the scaffold and prison world of the Puritans. His seventeenth-century materials mask a nineteenth-century body of doubts, a brooding relativism. Behind this New England 'usable past', Hawthorne sought to project the perennial drama of human need and the will-to-power.

His other romances give further gloss to his aims. In *The House Of The Seven Gables* (1851), an emblematic dynastic legend, largely set in his home town of Salem, Massachusetts, he purports to seek 'a certain latitude' for his 'atmospherical medium'. In *The Blithedale Romance* (1852), re-working his Brook Farm experience, he rather coyly declares his tale to be 'a little removed from the highway of ordinary travel', and given over to 'an atmosphere of strange enchantments'. His last full-length work, *The Marble Faun* (1860), a fable of expatriate New Englanders faced with pagan and Catholic Italy, barely prevents his typical play of ambiguities from collapsing into mystification. Hawthorne sought his antecedents not in Fielding and realist literary convention, but essentially in Puritan typology and in the pictorial allegories of Spenser and Bunyan. Others helped to shape the American romance (James Fenimore Cooper, Charles Brockden Brown and William Gilmore Sims notably); but it was Hawthorne who first gave the form its distinctive identity.

The local effects of the romance equally mark out his principal collections of stories, *Twice-Told Tales* (1837), *Mosses From An Old Manse* (1846), *The Snow-Image And Other Twice-Told Tales* (1852). His touch is delicate, often genial, even if he himself thought them no more than 'attempts and very imperfectly successful ones, to open an intercourse with the world'. They are, in effect, 'story-mosses' meant to take root in the reader's gathering response; close-woven episodes which come at human experience obliquely. In 'Ethan Brand' and 'The Birthmark', two tales which depict 'The Unpardonable Sin', Hawthorne's phrase for the cool tyranny of egotism, he uses the Puritan emblematic language of wizardry and the fiery furnace to explore the contemporary spectacle of one human being exploiting great individual power over another, an iniquity that he calls in his *American Notebooks* 'the separation of the intellect from the heart'. In 'Young Goodman Brown', he makes his subject Puritanism itself, or rather its tyrannical and darker side, the process whereby a Puritan view of mankind can make sexual felicity a source of guilt and thus inhibit the creative energies of the human personality. This conflict of natural energy with authority, an old Puritan conflict, he dwells upon brilliantly in 'The Maypole of Merry Mount', a story appropriately set out as a confrontation between Elizabethan rout and Pilgrim law. And his characteristic doubts about Transcendentalism shape 'The Celestial Omnibus', a lively Bunyanesque parody.

In 1856 Hawthorne, now American consul in Liverpool, strolled with Herman Melville (1819–91) on the Southport sands, renewing their earlier encounters in the Berkshire hills of New England half a dozen years earlier. Hawthorne's entry in his *English Notebooks* yields a marvellous estimate of Melville's general disposition:

> Melville, as he always does, began to reason of Providence and futurity, and of everything that lies beyond human ken. . . . He can neither believe nor be comfortable in his unbelief; and he is too honest and courageous not to try to do one or the other.

The very qualities Melville had been drawn to in Hawthorne – his 'blackness', his covert disclosure of truth, his 'contemplative humor' – on this judgement, might equally have been his own. Similarly, the view Melville once gave out of Emerson – 'I love all men who *dive*' – testifies to the appetite for Truth he shared with the New Englander, for all that he doubted the Emersonian ethos, indeed pilloried it in *The Confidence-Man* (1857), as dark a portrait of American ruling illusions as any in the national literature. Unlike Emerson, Melville's searches led him to 'armed neutrality', a defensive scepticism in the face of an unknowable universe and man's inability, as he saw it, to resist evil. More than any of his contemporaries. Melville believed himself embattled, a seeker and 'diver' for whom almost all quests for Truth ended in circles and solipsism. The ground condition of his philosophy he expressed perfectly in 'Hawthorne And His Mosses':

> For in this world of lies, Truth is forced to fly like a scared white doe in the woodlands; and only by cunning glimpses will she reveal herself, as in Shakespeare and other masters of the great Art of Telling the Truth – even though it be covertly, and by snatches.

This impulsion to locate, and name, Truth, runs right through Melville's fiction, and indeed into his later, and still largely unread poetry, especially *Battle Pieces* (1866), his Civil War poems, and *Clarel* (1876), a formidable late-Victorian poem of religious doubt. Though not born in New England, Melville's whole inclination leant towards a transcendent and final view of Truth. The fiction he wrote, accordingly, is cast almost always in the form of the journey, as an impending *rendez-vous* with the true nature of things. He bequeathed a major body of writing, 'inside narratives' in the half-title of *Billy Budd*, whose depths, as Hawthorne observed of Melville's third book, *Mardi*, 'compel a man to swim for his life'.

Melville's first journey-fictions, *Typee* (1846), *Omoo* (1847) and *Mardi* (1849), which derive intimately from his ship and South Seas adventures as a common sailor, and *Redburn* (1849) and *White Jacket* (1850), based on two other sea-journeys (to Liverpool and back when he was eighteen and aboard a returning man-of-war in 1844), culminate in the imperial achieve-ment of *Moby-Dick* (1851). Each is told in the *persona* of a Melvilleian 'isolato', a solitary wanderer. In *Moby-Dick* it is Ishmael, the classic wan-derer and man of doubts. The *Pequod's* 'journey-out', a quest after ulti-mate 'transcendent' truths, and made as an apparently literal quest for whale oil, 'or 'light', Ishmael takes with Ahab, an emblematic captain of American industry and a crew-of-all-nations; the journey is profoundly mythic in dimension. Melville uses the *Pequod's* endeavour to confront and to catch the white whale, as a way of repudiating the illusion that any single register of truth can fix the world's ambiguous meanings – whether in language, systems of religious belief, folklore, categories of cetology, or simple naming of parts. The epic and adventurely scope of his story justifiably seizes the imagination; but so, too, should Melville's inventive topography, the playful and skilled doubleness of his telling.

With *Pierre, Or The Ambiguities* (1852), his imagination turned inland, to the spectacle of a heroic 'fool of truth' literally as well as morally incarcerated by the labyrinths of his quest. Melville's tales of the 1850s, five of which he selected as *The Piazza Tales* (1856), reveal his powers in closer focus. In 'Bartleby, The Scrivener' (1853), he wrote a parable of Wall Street, a diagram of liberal capitalism's deathly grip on the spirit. 'Benito Cereno' (1855) makes of a slave insurrection an enquiry into the metaphysics of evil and human blindness. In 'The Encantadas' (1854), sketches of the Galápagos Islands where Darwin found his inspiration for the theory of natural selection, Melville drew a map of earthly hell, a portrait of loss and unremitting human desolation. With the exception of *Israel Potter* (1855), an ironic fable about American national types and first published as a nine-part serial in *Harper's New Monthly Magazine* (1854–55), and the posthumous *Billy Budd* (1885–91), his last mythic tale of slaughtered innocence, Melville's only other full-length composition was *The Confidence-Man* (1857), a satire which gives no quarter to the gods of Progress and optimistic New World panaceas and which (in Chapters 14, 33 and 44) gives important bearings on his theories of fiction.

As he grew older, Melville's fiction became increasingly knottier, but his ambiguous and testing visions were hard-won and made in the face of an inattentive, and often uncomprehending, readership. He stood in uneasy relationship with the professed Transcendentalist good faith of the age, yet shared the taste for a view of man, and of America, which was at once cosmic and deeply sacramental. Melville's fiction thus represents a dissenting imagination, a conviction that far older and blacker forces than America commonly acknowledged gave shape to human destiny. It perhaps took Melville, a New Yorker and one-time Pacific whalerman, to 'see' most 'New Englandly' of all.

'This great allegory the world': Melville's phrase goes to the essence of the imaginative temperament of nineteenth-century New England. To the makers of the American Renaissance, the world was a realm to be decoded, unravelled. In this they were true heirs of their Puritan ances-tors. The same preoccupations are also to be found in the work of many later New England writers, among whom the habit has persisted, though to different effect as, for instance, in the poems of Robert Frost or Robert Lowell. The central phase of American literary culture, that remarkable efflorescence which occurred about the middle of the nineteenth cen-tury, is appropriately thought 'transcendental', a view of reality as but the show of the inward energies of the spirit. For many of their immediate successors, however, the faith in themselves and in their unique destiny was eroded as the long maturing forces of change – westward expansion, industrialization, immigration – convincingly augmented the power of the rest of America. Accordingly the Puritan conscience, though still active, lost something of its cutting edge, producing a merely genteel reform tradition. And for many New Englanders, self-confidence gave place to a defensive Anglo-Saxonism, mourning the loss of racial purity, the foreign threat to liberty, and the passing of the ancestral ways.

▶ For further reading

Daniel Boorstin, *The Americans: The National Experience* (1965).

Lawrence Buell, *New England Literary Culture: From Revolution through Renaissance* (1986).

Nancy F Cott, *The Bonds of Womanhood: Woman's Sphere in New England, 1780–1835* (1977).

A N Kaul, *The American Vision: Actual and Ideal Society in Nineteenth-Century Fiction* (1963).

Peter R Knight, *The Plain People of Boston, 1830–1860* (1971).

F O Matthiessen, *American Renaissance: Art and Expression in the Age of Emerson and Whitman* (1941).

4 The Old South

Edward Ranson and Andrew Hook

▶ Defining the South

We begin by assuming that there existed in the past, and that there still exists, a region of the United States known as 'The South', which, having undergone a peculiar historical experience, has evolved a variety of political, economic, social, religious, cultural, and even psychological characteristics distinguishing it from other sections of the country. Visitors to the South, whether American or foreign, carry with them similar expectations of difference, distinctiveness, otherness. And they are rarely disappointed. The South does appear different. Nevertheless, problems arise as soon as one tries to explain this difference either by analysing the experiences of the past, or by enumerating distinguishing characteristics – or even by trying to establish a definition of the South. The same difficulties emerge, perhaps even in heightened form, if the focus of one's attention is not the present-day South but the South of before the Civil War – what we know today as the Old or Ante-Bellum South.

Even these modern names create problems. Both are oddly attractive and appealing, in a way that, say, the 'Slave South' would not be. The 'Old South' contains a hint of sentiment and nostalgia, a regret for a world that is lost; the 'ante-bellum South' is redolent of that classical civilization so proudly claimed by the Old South as its model, not only for much of its architecture, but for its way of life. In fact, both names have clinging to them something of the South's enduring mythology. Promoted and promulgated by an enormous range of novels, plays, films, histories and pseudo-histories (the single best-known example is of course the novel and film *Gone With the Wind* (1936), written by Margaret Mitchell), the image of the heroic, romantic, legendary South continues to exercise a fascination which no reference to the complex realities of history seems able to dispel. Not even the counter-image, which has its chief source in Harriet Beecher Stowe's portrayal of Simon Legree in *Uncle Tom's Cabin* (1852), of the debauched and degenerate Southerner brutalized by his association with slavery, has been strong enough to drive out the romantic myth of an Old South populated by aristocratic, chivalrous planters and their beautiful, elegant womenfolk, living in serene white mansions, amid the fragrance of moonlit gardens, with slave gangs singing in the cotton fields. This romantic and glamorized vision can be traced fairly precisely to the 1830s and 1840s, and was given an enormous boost by the Southern defeat in the Civil War; it was then to be embellished in the popular culture of the late nineteenth and twentieth centuries. But it is now a major dimension of what the Old South has come to mean – and for the historian the mythology has become almost as important as the reality.

The historian's problem, though, is not just the relatively simple one of seeking to determine what degree of truth is contained in this elaborate stereotype. For, like nearly all stereotypes, it contains a limited or partial truth, but distorts much and leaves a great deal out of account. For example, it tells us little about the actual social, political, and ideological conservatism of the Old South; about the degree to which the region was in fact class and caste-ridden, insecure, xenophobic, racist and introverted; about the way in which a professed commitment to romantic and chivalrous ideals of honour and courage could, and did, coexist with barely suppressed currents of individual and collective violence. It is hoped that in the course of this essay a more accurate picture of the Old South will emerge than that provided by a set of popular images. But a useful beginning is to suggest how it was, in historical terms, that the romantic myth of the Old South came to be created, and why it has proved so enduring.

Perhaps the truth of the matter is that the mythology of the South is so powerful and tenacious because, deprived of it, the South would seem like the emperor without his clothes: that is, no longer clearly identifiable. In other words, at some specific point in its history, the Old South created and diffused a particular self-image in order to persuade itself, and the world outside, of its own distinct identity. Historical necessity required that the Old South should be seen to be different. Paradoxically, through the creation of images and myths, the Old South became a historical reality. Is it any wonder that the images and myths should have subsequently proved more tenacious and enduring than the reality?

▶ Was the South unique?

The Old South needed to create an identity for itself because, historically, it lacked any simple or straightforward means of self-definition. When, in the 1760s, two English surveyors named Charles Mason and Jeremiah Dixon ran a line between Maryland and Pennsylvania in an effort to settle a boundary dispute, no one imagined that the states to the north and south of that line had thereby any more or less in common with each other. Until as late as the early nineteenth century, the Southern states had in fact undergone much the same historical experience as the rest of the United States: fairly rapid geographical expansion, as new territories were acquired in the west and south, a moving frontier, and contact with European rivals and hostile Indians. As it grew in size, the South inevitably became increasingly diverse in topography, climate, soil and vegetation. There was no mountain range, no great river, no physical obstacle nor natural boundary separating it from the rest of the country. The South has therefore never been a single, monolithic region, easy to distinguish and describe. Rather it has always remained an ill-assorted collection of subregions, collectively known as 'The South' not because they were geographically similar, but despite the fact that they were geographically different. Nor is it geography alone that fails to provide a satisfactory definition of the South. In terms of its origins, language, law and religion, the South hardly differed from the rest of the nation; and those broad patterns of economic, political, and social change which affected the other regions of the United States produced parallel developments in the South. In the area of cultural history the story is the same. Even in the decades immediately prior to the Civil War, Northerners and Southerners by and large read the same books, responded to the same ideas, discussed and debated the same issues. Scott and Byron, Dickens and Bulwer Lytton were immensely popular writers in all sections of the United States. As thinkers, Emerson, Carlyle, and Macaulay were scorned or admired in both North and South. It is difficult to argue, therefore, that the cultural experience of North and South differed in any fundamental way, or that any Southern 'world view' had emerged even by 1860 that was wholly alien to that of the North.

Attempts to find factors common to the Southern states but absent elsewhere, which might be seen as creating a distinctive Southern identity, have not on the whole proved any more successful. The rural and agricultural nature of the South, its one-crop system, the widespread use of slave labour, the lack of urban and industrial development, the pre-bourgeois or pre-modern society, the poverty, the sense of failure, defeat or guilt: at different times all of these have been offered as explanations of the South's uniqueness. But none of them have commanded general agreement, and all have been subject to serious objection or qualification. Part of the problem is that few of these characteristics were peculiar to the American South; and most of them can be used to differentiate between the regions or sections of countries other than America. Not all of these countries, however, have had to endure the trauma of civil war; and, at least in the American context, the Civil War is the crucial factor. While it may be possible to demonstrate the extraordinary difficulty of discovering any set of facts, circumstances or characteristics which give the South a clear, separate and identifiable existence, while it may be possible, as it were, to argue the South out of existence, the fact of the American Civil War makes all such arguments academic. By 1861 the Old South not only existed; it was ready and willing to fight a long, bitter, and bloody war in a vain attempt to preserve its separate existence – though the process of secession was not as complete, smooth and unanimous as is popularly supposed, and the prospect of serious fighting must have seemed unlikely to many. The question is what were the forces and factors which created the Old South, and how, when and why did they do so?

▶ The early South

In the period before the American Revolution, the settlers in the Southern colonies – Virginia, Maryland, the Carolinas, and Georgia – did not think of themselves as 'Southerners': indeed, it is highly unlikely that many of them even regarded themselves as Americans. A sense of American nationality only began to grow in that period of unrest, discontent, and increasingly violent political argument and debate which preceded the outbreak of the Revolution itself, and in which the Southern states played a full part. The unity achieved by the opponents of the British administration in the different colonies, in fact, surprised the British and contributed to their defeat. The absence, during these years, of inter-colonial or sectional rivalries may be partly attributable to the skill with which the Southern political élite, particularly in Virginia, not unaware of the consequences of allowing Massachusetts and New York to dominate the revolutionary movement, used their position to lead and guide it. Nonetheless, the Revolutionary War itself, while forging an American identity, did not create a peculiarly Southern one, although the term 'the South' was beginning to be used at this time. Military campaigns were fought out in both Northern and Southern states; North and South both contributed to the patriotic army; and both sections contained sizeable Loyalist groups. The creation of the United States of America was thus in no way a sectional achievement.

In the political world of the new nation in the years after the Revolution, it is still difficult to identify any distinctive Southern point of view. It is clear that Virginia-born presidents like Washington, Jefferson, Madison and Monroe did not think of themselves as 'Southerners' in the way that politicians born in Virginia or elsewhere in the South a generation or so later were almost bound to do. Over such major political issues as the drafting and ratification of the new Federal Constitution, support and opposition did not divide along clear sectional lines. It is true that in the Federalist era from 1789 to 1801 the argument over the interpretation of the new Constitution did begin to assume a more sectionalist form. The North was inclined to favour a stronger form of central (Federal) government, while the South preferred a more restricted role for the central authority, with residual rights reserved to each individual state. There were also emerging differences over financial and foreign affairs, and different appreciations of the importance of navigation rights on the Mississippi. As a result George Washington felt impelled, in his Farewell Address of

1796, to warn his countrymen of the dangers of sectionalism and partisanship. Yet, despite this warning, sectional feelings continued to be manifested in such episodes as the Virginia and Kentucky Resolutions and in the voting patterns of the 1796 and 1800 elections. The demise of the Federalists after 1800 helped to create an appearance of renewed national unity, but latent sectional differences persisted – as the bitter divisions over the declaration and conduct of the War of 1812 revealed. Yet, even as late as the second decade of the nineteenth century, there is no clear evidence that the Southern states had achieved a well-defined and permanent group consciousness or identity, that they were aware of their distinctiveness. Indeed, the nationalist feelings that greeted the ending of the War of 1812, and the adoption by the Jeffersonian Republicans of the once despised Federalist policies, led to a short-lived period of apparent sectional harmony. The South that some fifty years later was to fight the Civil War was still waiting to be born. But however late it may have been in emerging, a Southern consciousness and a Southern identity had been potentially present from the early years of the colonial period. Despite all the varied arguments that have been adduced, attempting to assimilate the South into the rest of America, and denying it any distinct or special status, the possibility of a South radically and decisively unassimilated had always existed. It had existed in the form of the crucial figure in the history of the Old South: the African-American slave. It is only in terms of the slave and slavery, we believe, that the creation, existence, and demise of the Old South are finally to be understood. It was the very existence of the black slave in the tobacco- and cotton-growing states of the South which provided the one bond, the one shared interest, that could in time unify the South and create its identity. As a way of differentiating between one group of states and another, the presence or absence of slaves was always liable to be a crucial consideration, especially as slavery was disappearing in the North while at the same time it was becoming economically more important in the South, until a point was reached where slavery and the South were virtually synonymous.

▶ The South and slavery

Slavery in the South was of course a legacy of British rule. It had existed since the early seventeenth century, and was viewed as the only practical solution to the labour demands of plantation agriculture but had not occasioned a great deal of comment until the nineteenth. Many of the leaders of the American Revolution, including Washington and Jefferson, were slave-owners, and some at least were not unaware of the incongruity of their position: slavery was hardly compatible with the 'life, liberty and pursuit of happiness' that the new America promised its people, though, ironically, Southern whites as a group came to believe that their liberty within the Union was secured only by the maintenance of black slavery. Racial awareness also acted as a powerful unifying force within the South, while for individuals owning slaves promised prosperity, power, prominence and prestige. Although Southern touchiness on the subject made it necessary to omit any direct reference to slavery in the Declaration of Independence, the existence of slavery was recognized and accepted by the new American Constitution. Southern advocates of the Constitution argued for ratification on the grounds that slavery would be more, not less, secure under the new frame of government. When, in 1861, the Confederacy adopted a constitution remarkably similar in many ways to that of 1787, though it reinforced the defence of slavery, Southerners explained that they were returning to basics. One should not assume too readily, however, that America's Founding Fathers, when they created an allegedly democratic system, were either blind or cynical in the way they tried to deal with the slavery issue. Towards the end of the eighteenth century it was widely believed that slavery would gradually die out, and that the problem would thus solve itself.

It was Eli Whitney's invention of the cotton gin in 1793 which put an end to such expectations; the new efficient method of separating lint from seed made possible a vast expansion in the production of cotton. As a result, the economics of slavery were transformed and, rather than declining, the number of slaves in the South began rapidly to increase. Around 1820, there were $1^1/_2$ million slaves in America; in 1860, the figure was just under 4 million. Just how profitable the slave system was for the individual owner, for the South, and for the United States as a whole, remains a question of historical dispute. It does appear, however, that slavery was profitable in the 1850s and promised to remain so in the 1860s and beyond. It is also worth remembering that, on the eve of the Civil War, three-quarters of the cotton crop went for export, accounting for 60 per cent of the United States' foreign earnings. Thus, in strictly material terms, it is easy to understand why for much of the nineteenth century the South, rather than seeking ways to bring an end to the institution of slavery, was committed to its rapid extension into the new territories that America was now acquiring in the West and South-west.

The material benefits of slavery, whether real or imagined, were not enough in themselves to subdue doubts and misgivings in other directions. The enormous contradiction involved in the tolerance of a slave system by a nation whose whole political and social philosophy – indeed, whose very existence – centred on the concepts of freedom, self-determination and the rights of the individual, did not go unnoticed. From the earliest days of the republic, this paradox was picked on, in particular by those foreign observers (Charles Dickens, for example, in his *American Notes*, 1842) who believed it questioned the entire libertarian principle, or else were anxious that the American experiment in freedom and democracy should fail. Many Europeans saw in the continued existence of slavery within American society a potentially explosive issue which, as upholders of the traditional European power structures, they hoped and predicted would in the end bring America's democratic institutions crashing down.

▶ The failing compromise

The first major indication that these dire forebodings could be fulfilled came with the bitter controversy of 1819–21 surrounding the Missouri Compromise. Missouri territory had reached a stage in its development when it was in a position to apply for admission to the Union as a state. The point at issue was whether or not slavery should be permitted in the new state. The Southern states favoured the extension of slavery into that area; the Northern states opposed it. After a two-year struggle, a compromise was arrived at whereby Missouri was admitted as a slave state while simultaneously Maine was admitted as a free one; thus the balance of power between free and slave states in the United States Senate was preserved. At the same time, in the vast territory west of the Mississippi acquired from France in 1803 as the Louisiana Purchase, slavery was prohibited north of latitude 36° 30′, but permitted south of it. But, though a compromise had been agreed, the political and moral passions which had been roused were not easily subdued. The Missouri debates made it clear that anti-slavery sentiment was growing in the North, while the need to defend their interests produced a new sense of unity among the Southern slave-holding states. The doctrine of states' rights and the defence of slavery were becoming inextricably linked, and the slavery issue was at last shaping Southern sectionalism into a clear and definable form. To the ageing Thomas Jefferson, the whole affair was deeply alarming; the sectional nature of the struggle over Missouri was an ominous portent. 'This momentous question', he wrote, 'like a fire bell in the night, awakened and filled me with terror. I considered it at once the knell of the Union.' The compromise he saw as 'a reprieve only, not a final sentence'; the end could only be an 'irrepressible conflict'.

As we shall see, during the 1820s and 1830s the Old South's sense of its own distinctiveness, and of its separation from the rest of America, gradually increased. But in cementing Southern group identity, the catalyst was always the African slave. In January 1831 came the publication of the first number of William Lloyd Garrison's *Liberator* – a New England newspaper dedicated to the abolition of slavery. A few months later the South was horrified, and terrified, by the outbreak of the most serious slave insurrection it had ever faced: sixty whites had died before Nat Turner's revolt in Southampton County, Virginia, was finally suppressed. These two events electrified the South, and they did much to ensure that the spirit of sectional unity would continue to grow. In the face of enemies both without and within, what was needed was unity of purpose and attitude. The last open discussion in the South of the merits of slavery, and the possibility of emancipation, took place in the Virginia legislature in the 1831–32 session. When, by a surprisingly narrow margin in a body that over-represented slave-owning interests, Virginia decided to retain slavery, the time for discussion was over: in the view of the South, the issue was now settled. Hard on the heels of these events came the Nullification Crisis of 1832–33 when, in protest at alleged Northern economic exploitation of the South, South Carolina threatened to 'nullify' – or declare invalid – a contentious tariff act of the Federal Government. Admittedly the crisis over the tariff was primarily an economic one, but it centrally involved the issue of states' rights, and thus indirectly a crucial argument in the defence of slavery. It is in the 1830s, then, that the 'Old South' enters history as an undeniable reality, called into being by the need of the Southern states to unite in defence of the 'peculiar institution' – slavery.

Before the 1830s, Southern spokesmen had tended to apologize for the existence of slavery as a necessary evil. Under the pressure of Northern abolitionist propaganda, however, the South, as the 1830s went on, ceased to apologize. Rather, having allowed the abolitionists the great advantage of determining the nature and scope of the debate, it sought increasingly for ways of justifying slavery. From this period up to the outbreak of the Civil War, a great deal of the South's intellectual energy was expended in a fruitless attempt to win this debate. Pseudo-scientific arguments were produced to prove that black Africans were racially inferior, or specially suited for agricultural work. The sanction for slavery to be found both in the Bible and the Federal Constitution was constantly cited. History was searched for examples of civilizations that had made use of slaves. It was argued that paternalism was the guiding principle of Southern slave-holders, and that as a result slaves were better off and enjoyed better conditions than would have been the case had they remained in Africa. More aggressively, Southerners argued that there was little to choose between the chattel system of slavery in the South and the wage slavery that operated in the North. If anything, the oppressed and exploited workers in the mills and factories of the North were worse off than the plantation slaves in the South. While many Southerners were undoubtedly sincere in their defences of black slavery, the ambitious and unscrupulous soon seized the opportunity to forward their own careers by reaping the rewards of inflamed rhetoric.

Of course, the picture of slavery created by the Northern abolitionists was a very different one. Driven by the humanitarian and religious zeal which swept America in the 1820s and 1830s, the abolitionists were a heterogeneous group united only by the idealistic fervour with which they assailed slavery and the South. High-principled, as for the most part they were, there is no doubt that their crusading zeal exacerbated North–South feeling, encouraged the South to turn defensively upon itself, and so materially contributed to the coming of the Civil War. The abolitionists argued that slavery was working against the economic development of the South, and non-slave-holders in particular were disadvantaged by the system. More pointedly, they insisted that the existence of slavery was morally degrading in its effects upon those who owned slaves. But the main thrust of their onslaught came from the account they provided of the effects of the system on the slaves themselves: theirs was a life of degradation and brutal ill-treatment, economic, physical and sexual exploitation. Much emphasis was laid on the denial to the slave of the right to a stable family life: it was repeatedly insisted that not only were children taken away and sold at an early age, but that husbands and wives lived in constant fear of being sold to separate masters. Slaves were also denied both proper religious instruction and education of the most rudimentary kind. Defending slavery, the South was defending a monstrous social crime. At first the abolitionists believed that this great wrong could be righted by moral persuasion, or by the demonstration of the economic weakness they thought they perceived in the system; but by 1840 many saw the exercise of political pressure on the South as a more likely answer. In the end some did not shrink from violence as the only means of achieving the ideals they pursued.

Few historians today would accept as accurate either the abolitionists' nightmare vision, or the South's version of slavery as an early form of social security for the underprivileged. Equally, few would agree on what would constitute an accurate and truthful account. Perhaps there is no single truth about slavery. Certainly the fact that there were 4 million slaves and some 400,000 slave-owners on the eve of the Civil War should make us suspicious of broad generalizations. These figures allow us to question, for example, how far the Old South should even be described as a slave-holding society. There were some $1^1/_4$ million white families living in the Old South; thus only a minority of whites owned any slaves at all. And it is undoubtedly true that the large yeoman class of small farmers – who owned few if any slaves, but who constituted numerically the largest single group in Southern society – has traditionally been largely neglected by commentators and historians. Again, of the 400,000 Southerners who did own slaves, only a minority owned more than twenty, and the great majority fewer than five. The image of an Old South wholly composed of vast plantations with slave gangs toiling on their broad acres has no basis in reality. Some 50,000 slave-holders owned 20 slaves or more; 10,000 owned 50 or more; 2,300 owned 100 or more; a mere handful owned something approaching 500 slaves.

The conditions under which slaves were held must clearly have varied enormously from situation to situation, depending on such factors as the attitude of the owner or overseer, the size of the plantation, the number of slaves, the geographical location, and the nature of the crop. At worst, slaves could be regarded as renewable capital goods to be exploited to their maximum and then replaced; on the other hand, they could be seen as highly valuable investments to be prized accordingly. Certainly, slavery did not have the effect of making all slaves equal. Slave society was strictly hierarchical, running from the field hand at the bottom of the scale to the house servant or skilled blacksmith, wheelwright, or carpenter at the top. Slaves who lived in towns could form an even more privileged group; sometimes they were allowed to ply their own trades and simply remit a percentage of their earnings to their owners. Thus it is true that the day-by-day slave experience of several million human beings in the Old South was by no means a uniform one; the condition of slavery could and did vary enormously. And yet every slave, whatever his or her material situation, was still a slave. In a sense that the Old South could not or would not understand, slavery as an institution could not survive. Attempts to justify it were attempts to justify the unjustifiable. By the middle of the nineteenth century, at least in the Western world, slavery could only be an offence to every idea of progress and the growth of civilization. In attempting to cling on to its 'peculiar institution', the Old South was ultimately defying the movement of history itself.

▶ The South and secession

In the 1820s and 1830s the Old South's consciousness of its own existence continued to grow and began to assume highly significant new forms. It was under pressure of the knowledge that the United States was fundamentally and fatally divided by the slave economy of the Southern states that the South had at last become aware of its own existence as an historical entity. This knowledge in turn demanded that the South become aware of itself in areas remote from the institution of slavery. It had above all to recognize in itself a culture and a way of life that gave it both identity and a redeeming value. It was not enough that the Old South should define itself by its hatred of the Northern abolitionist; it needed to be seen to embody positive social characteristics that were worth preserving and maintaining at whatever cost. Precisely here it is possible to identify the source of what was to become the over-arching mythology of the South. It was the need to believe in itself, to identify its own value, that produced the most potent and enduring images of the South.

The mode of life possible on a handful of large plantations provided the basis for the self-identification the South needed and sought. Around the existence of such plantations there developed a whole set of theoretical assumptions about the South's way of life – and its absolute contrast with that of the North – which soon passed into general circulation. The South had created an aristocratic, agrarian civilization; the North, a democratic, commercial one. Totally different sets of attitudes and values animated the two sections. Essentially the North was a materialistic society given over to the pursuit of money; Southern society gave its allegiance to such values as honour and personal integrity. Hence, where Northern society was an aggregate of competing individuals, the South was an aggregate of communities. Northern society was rootless, changing, fluid, dominated by money-minded Yankees, while Southern society was conservative, upholding the values of a traditional way of life. In the end, the South found for itself even a satisfying myth of its historical origins: Southerners were descended from the stock of gallant, carefree, seventeenth-century Cavaliers, while Northerners derived from austere and frowning Puritan Roundheads. From the 1830s, what the South was defending was no longer simply the institution of slavery. It was an entire social structure, with a culture and way of life it passionately believed to be in every sense superior to those of the North.

So, as the opposition between North and South came to be seen not only as a collision of sectional interests, but as a confrontation between different cultures, the area of common political ground declined. After the Nullification Crisis in South Carolina, it came to seem that intersectional conflict was a permanent condition. From the mid-1840s it was no longer the case that one area of tension was followed by another; rather that a permanent crisis moved on from one phase to the next. The annexation of Texas (1845), the Mexican War (1846–48), the Compromise of 1850, the Kansas–Nebraska problem (1854–56), the Supreme Court's Dred Scott decision (1857), John Brown's raid on the Federal Arsenal at Harper's Ferry, Virginia (1859), the Presidential Election of 1860: these were no more than high points in a continuing crisis in North–South relations. There were, of course, many in North and South who refused to believe that the differences between the two sections of the United States were beyond resolution, and more who held that any attempt to break up the Union could lead only to disaster.

Even as late as 1860, when the Southern states saw in Abraham Lincoln's presidential victory their own final defeat in the national political arena, the movement for secession – though in most Southern states now too powerful to be denied – still encountered considerable opposition. Had the issues been debated purely on their political merits, the outcome might have been different. But extremists in both North and South had succeeded in raising the political temperature to so high a level that emotion rather than reason determined the actual course of action. Slavery excited the strongest emotions: for several decades it had been the flashpoint in North–South relations, and provided the ultimate occasion for all the major crises – from the annexation of Texas to John Brown's raid. Slavery, its precise status, its right to expand, had become the centre of every confrontation and the ghost at every political feast. The need to preserve and defend slavery may have brought the Old South into existence. But, as we have seen, to believe in itself the Old South needed to be persuaded that it possessed a society, culture and way of life crucially different from and superior to that of the North. And this in the end it did believe. In 1860, on the edge of the conflict that would bring the

'Old South' to an end and in the long run create it as a necessary memory, Mary Chesnut, a Southerner, wrote in her diary (*A Diary from Dixie*, published in 1949): 'We separated because of incompatibility of temper; we are divorced, North from South, because we have hated each other so.'

Thus for Mary Chesnut, who was writing in the dangerously exciting atmosphere of 1860, what we have been calling 'myth' was now incontestable reality. (We need here to remind ourselves that history is made just as much by what people *believe* as by what is actually the case.) So what North and South may or may not have had in common was now largely irrelevant: what mattered was the immense gulf of bitterness that now divided them. How far Mary Chesnut was right to believe that by 1860 North and South had in fact become two different worlds, two incompatible societies and cultures, is a question which modern historians and sociologists still debate. And there are those who argue that, even if the question of slavery is set aside, the society of the Old South can be seen as reflecting an awareness of traditional human values that indeed differentiates it from the progressive, thrusting, materialist society of the North. Honour, courage, generosity, amiability, courtesy may not be the kind of values to ensure success in the world of capitalistic economic competition; but they do provide the basis for an attractive and alternative way of life. The long conflict and the Southern defeat perpetuated the dichotomy, arresting the myth, turning it into a governing idea. In the later 1920s and 1930s, when there was much talk of a New South, urbanized and industrialized in the manner of the rest of the United States, these were exactly the kind of civilized, humane values that the group of major American writers who produced the Southern Literary Renaissance saw embodied in the culture of the Old South. Believing, like many other modern artists and writers, that the most powerful forces at work in twentieth-century society were hostile to human dignity and integrity, these modern Southern writers felt that the order and stability and sense of community traditionally present in Southern society provided a positive alternative to the 'waste-land' vision of the modern world, so powerfully projected in a great deal of twentieth-century writing.

▶ Writing in the Old South

However, even for the twentieth-century Southern writer most alienated from the modern industrialized life around him in America, and most eager to admire those dimensions of the society of the Old South which preserved the values he prized, there was, apart from slavery, another significant problem about the Old South which demanded recognition. Most mature cultures are preserved in the great works of the mind and imagination they produce. But the enduring creative achievements of nineteenth-century America were produced, not in the Old South, but in the New England heartland of the Yankee. As Allen Tate, writing in 1935 on 'The Profession of Letters in the South', put it: 'we had no Hawthorne, no Melville, no Emily Dickinson. We had William Gilmore Simms. We made it impossible for Poe to live south of the Potomac.' Tate is too honest a commentator not to put his finger squarely on the problem involved in the South's literary failure in the ante-bellum period: 'Yet the very merits of the Old South tend to confuse the issue: its comparative stability, its realistic limitation of the acquisitive impulse, its preference for human relations compared to relations economic, tempt the historian to defend the poor literature simply because he feels that the old society was a better place to live in than the new. It is a great temptation – if you do not read the literature.'

As a major poet, novelist, and critic, Tate's standards of literary excellence are high. Not all students of the Old South would agree the literature it did produce is quite as bad as Tate implies. None the less, by any standard the literary culture of the Old South is undistinguished. Why this was so exercised the minds of commentators from the early nineteenth century on, and remains a significant question. As early as 1816 George Tucker was explaining Virginia's backwardness in cultural matters in terms of the structure of its social life: the scattered plantations, the absence of cities, combined with a preoccupation with practical pursuits and a preference for foreign authors, had produced a situation in which a native literature could not be expected to flourish. Later writers tended mainly to develop Tucker's points. Towards the end of the nineteenth century, for example, Thomas Nelson Page argued in *The Old South* (1892) that the region's failure to produce a major literature resulted from its essentially non-urban, agricultural society, the consequent absence of publishing houses, and the failure to develop a reading public within the South for Southern authors. To these sociological explanations, Page added the equally conventional one that the literary powers of the Old South had been directed towards the worlds of politics and polemical controversy, and that the existence of slavery had led to 'the absorption of the intellectual forces of the people of the South in the solution of the vital problems it engendered'.

It is probably true that the political debate with the North did absorb a large share of the intellectual energies of the South. So it was natural that the way ahead for a talented young Southerner should lie in a career in politics or the related field of law; a career in the arts was scarcely a possibility. In 1842 Charles Dickens received a letter from Thomas Ritchie of the *Richmond Enquirer* which suggests that the cultural life of Virginia had remained much as it was when Tucker was writing in 1816: 'the *forte* of the Old Dominion is to be found in the masculine production of her statesmen, her Washington, her Jefferson, and her Madison, who have never indulged in works of imagination, in the charms of romance, or in the mere beauties of the *belles lettres*'. A still more dismissive view of the imaginative writer is evident in a story told by the minor Southern poet, Philip Pendleton Cooke. He reports how after he had gained some repute as an author, a friendly neighbour said to him: 'I wouldn't waste time on a damned thing like poetry; you might make yourself, with all your sense and judgement, a useful man in settling neighborhood disputes and difficulties. . . .' Equally revealing are the lives and careers of some of the better writers whom the Old South did produce. William Gilmore Simms, now hardly read, but in his own day the most important figure in the literature of the Old South, never felt that his native city – Charleston, South Carolina – adequately recognized and acknowledged his merits as a writer. Certainly until 1860, at least, his many novels – the most famous is *The Yemassee* (1835) – were much more widely read in the North than in the South. Early in his career, it was only by frequent visits to the North, and New York in particular, that he was able to meet other writers, editors, and publishers and so establish himself as an author. Again, John Pendleton Kennedy, whose novel *Swallow Barn* (1832), set in Virginia, played a crucial part in propagating the plantation myth of the Old South, wrote only two further novels before more or less abandoning literature for a political career. Then the wayward genius of Edgar Allan Poe could find no permanent home in the Old South. Poe's aim was to be a professional writer and live by his pen; but, in the society of the Old South, there was no way in which he, or any other imaginative writer, could fulfil such an ambition. For a year or two in the 1830s Poe made the *Southern Literary Messenger* in Richmond, Virginia, into a literary periodical of distinction; but his professionalism, and the seriousness of his commitment to art and literature, soon brought him into collision with the amateur, genteel tradition of Southern writing. Poe too was compelled to abandon the South.

The evidence all suggests that the society of the Old South was not one likely to foster a major literary talent. It is post-bellum Southern writing that we think of when we speak of the powerful Southern literary tradition. No doubt the cultural centres of America were in the North, but this still leaves us with the question of why such literature as the Old South did produce is of only indifferent quality: why is the work of the Simmses, the Kennedys, the Cookes, considered so unrewarding? Perhaps the answer is that the literature of the Old South is fundamentally dishonest, reflecting in its uneasy forms and structures the society in which it was produced. At one level, its hollowness is a question of the rhetoric in which it is couched: an ornate, pompous or weakly sentimental language conceals rather than reveals the reality it purports to describe. This is the high-flown Ciceronian style of the Southern orator – what Allen Tate describes as 'Confederate Prose', which he and his fellow writers of the later Southern Literary Renaissance strove above all to avoid. It is also the language of sham sentiment and empty attitudinizing that Mark Twain, a creative psyche in some ways divided between North and South, satirizes so devastatingly in several books, and associates with the unhappy influence of Sir Walter Scott on the South's feudal cultural mentality. In *The Adventures of Huckleberry Finn* (1885), both the successful frauds and deceptions of the King and the Duke and the meaningless massacres of the Grangerfords and Sheperdsons are products of Southern society's linguistic corruption. Southerners cannot, in Twain, distinguish between linguistic posturing and genuine expressions of feeling, and are eager to act out the shabby rhetoric they admire. Just how brilliantly Twain's book reveals the underlying flaws of the Old South is suggested by the way it also illuminates a second level of evasion which undermines much Southern writing: *Huckleberry Finn*, unlike most Southern writing, goes on to probe, at last, the truth about slavery. What Huck has to learn is that Jim, his companion on the raft on the Mississippi, is not an object, somebody else's property, a runaway slave, but a man, an individual with feelings and needs exactly like his own. But the essential humanity of the black was precisely what the institution of slavery formally denied. And this was the one simple truth that Southern society and Southern literature could not afford to recognize.

One of the most striking features of the cultural life of the Old South after the early 1830s is its intolerance of criticism. On such crucial subjects as slavery, state's rights, and relations with the North, freedom of debate was denied. Southern society had taken its stand on these issues; the time for argument was over. What was needed was the preservation of the South's ideological purity from the contamination of new or different ideas expressed either without or within. In this show of solidarity, Southern writers were expected to play their part. Critical social comment, the probing of accepted orthodoxies and values, the exploration of underlying social or ideological tensions, even the dramatizing of basic conflicts, ceased to be strategies a writer could adopt. Rather than challenge, the Southern writer had to conform to society. It is hardly surprising that in his work the great issues facing the ante-bellum South remain largely unexplored; the 'cordon sanitaire' the South had drawn around such a crucial issue as slavery was so tight that it could not be penetrated by the literary imagination – at least, not by the imagination of a writer who wished to remain a Southerner and be accepted by the South. (Black writing from the slave experience, which told a very different story, is discussed in Chapter 7.)

The world-wide success of *Uncle Tom's Cabin* (1852) perhaps suggests that the Old South was right to believe that the subject of slavery was best left alone. To write about the slave, whether well or badly, was inevitably to humanize him. Harriet Beecher Stowe's Northern abolitionist novel may have limitations in its portrayal of blacks, but its treatment of such themes as the economic basis of slavery, racial prejudice in the North as well as the South, and the predicament of the intelligent Southern slave-owner, lacks neither insight nor subtlety. Certainly *Uncle Tom's Cabin* remains a much more interesting book than the plantation romances of the Old South. And if Sir Walter Scott is not to be accused, as Twain did accuse him in *Life on the Mississippi* (1883), of having caused the Civil War by imbuing the Old South with a bogus sense of aristocratic values, medieval notions of chivalry and nobility, and romantic nationalism, he can be seen as responsible for the creation of the characteristic historical romance of the ante-bellum South.

Writing within a society reluctant to face squarely the major issues confronting it, Southern novelists such as William Gilmore Simms, John Pendleton Kennedy and William Alexander Caruthers began to turn increasingly towards the past for their subject and, modelling their work, often, on that of Walter Scott or James Fenimore Cooper, began an entire tradition of historical romances on such topics as the Southern frontier, the Indian wars, or the American Revolution. Most emerged during the 1830s, when indeed there appeared a notable promise of a Southern literary movement. Kennedy's *Swallow Barn* (1832) is undoubtedly influenced by Irving, and explores an idealized but recent Virginia plantation life in a series of delicate sketches. Caruthers's *The Cavaliers of Virginia* (1834–35) is a sentimental looking-back at the 'cavalier' connection and the South's 'feudal' origins. Simms's *The Yemassee* (1835), surely the best Southern work of fiction of the period, is about the impact of whites on the Indians of the South Carolina border, and compares favourably with Cooper's Indian novels. The historical novel was a fashionable genre, but in the South it became increasingly sentimental, as well as a way of turning to times when problems were less pressing. The difficulties of the Southern writer were expressed in the uncertainties and difficulties of the careers that followed. Kennedy became by the time of the war an anti-Southerner in Baltimore; Simms became a defender of the South's 'Greek democracy' and was ruined in the war.

▶ The South after 1865

In the Old South there were signs of a nascent literary impulse which finally grew evasive or stunted; there were those who later came to argue that the South lost the Civil War because of its lack of writers. This was the view of Thomas Nelson Page, one of several writers who emerged after the war to write the enlarging myth of the Old South, and explore the world of Reconstruction from a Southern standpoint. 'It was', Page wrote in *The Old South* in 1892, 'for lack of a literature' that the South 'was left behind in the great race for outside support, and that in the supreme moment of her existence she found herself arraigned at the bar of the world without an advocate and without a defence.' According to Page, the South 'was conquered by the pen rather than by the sword'; but he is honest enough to concede that the fault was the South's own: 'We denied and fought, but we did not argue. Be this, however, our justification, that slavery did not admit of argument. Argument meant destruction.' Page of course oversimplifies and overstates. The South did, as we have seen, argue and attempt to justify – though having allowed the Northern abolitionists to determine the area of debate it could only lose. But it is also true that the South lost the propaganda war for the hearts and minds of the outside world. *Uncle Tom's Cabin* dismayed and outraged the South, but the damage it did to the Southern cause was irreparable. In imaginative terms, the Old South could find no answer. On the other hand, even had she enjoyed the support of the finest writers imaginable, it is hard to see how the South could have survived once the North had demonstrated its determination to fight first to restore the Union and later to abolish slavery. Certainly the South believed in itself and the righteousness of its cause. Its soldiers fought well and bravely; its generals were often skilful; it had the advantage of defensive positions and internal lines of communication. But in most other ways the South was severely handicapped: eleven states against twenty-three, 9 million against nearly 23 million, and an equivalent Southern weakness in such crucial areas as iron and steel production, railroad mileage and equipment, shipping and naval power, mechanics and technicians, banking and finance. In government and diplomacy, too, the North's advantage proved overwhelming. Even in terms of political leadership the contest was an unequal one: Jefferson Davis, the head of the Confederacy, could not rival the charisma, moral authority, or unyielding determination of the Northern Lincoln. The longer the war continued, the more inevitable total Southern defeat became.

Yet there is a sense in which the weakness of the literature of the Old South is an index of the weakness and ultimate failure of the culture and civilization of the Old South itself. Literature and society were both fatally weakened by their unwillingness to face up to the reality of slavery. Not even the shock of defeat in the Civil War – how could the dare-devil, hard-riding, courageous, Cavalier South be conquered by the money-worshipping Federals, the corrupt employers, downtrodden artisans and meddling abolitionists of the North? – was sufficient to make the South face the truth about itself. The unavailing bravery and self-sacrifice of the Confederate armies served only to heighten Southern pride and sectional self-consciousness. In the period of Reconstruction, which occupied the last months of the Civil War and the years immediately subsequent to the ending of that conflict, a new chapter was added to the mythology of the South. A prostrate South was now the helpless victim of rapacious Northern politicians and businessmen ('carpet-baggers'), compliant white Southerners ('scalawags'), and their black allies. The romantic aura surrounding the Old South, and an idealized vision of a lost cause, a lost society, a lost way of life, increasingly obscured the historical realities.

And in the works of a new generation of post-war Southern novelists, such as Thomas Dixon and Thomas Nelson Page himself, the romance of the Old South was written and rewritten.

About 1870, John William De Forest, a Northern novelist – his excellent *Miss Ravenel's Conversion from Secession to Loyalty* (1867) is one of the few significant novels to emerge directly from the Civil War – identified the sources of the continuing weakness of Southern writing:

> Not until Southerners get rid of some of their social vanity, not until they cease talking of themselves in a spirit of self-adulation, not until they drop the idea that they are Romans and must write in the style of Cicero, will they be able to so paint life that the world shall crowd to see the picture.

In the twentieth century it has happened. Responding to the astonishing power of a revitalized Southern literary imagination, the world has crowded to see the picture painted by the writers of the modern South. From the mid-1920s, American fiction, poetry, drama, and literary criticism have received a massive Southern imprint, and Southern writers have everywhere demanded and received recognition and acclaim. The crowning achievement of the South's literary renaissance is the fiction of William Faulkner. But Faulkner's success has been brilliantly supported by that of other influential figures such as John Crowe Ransom, Allen Tate, and Robert Penn Warren, while the continuing vitality of Southern writing is abundantly evident in the work of a whole range of authors from Katherine Anne Porter, Eudora Welty and Carson McCullers, to Flannery O'Connor, Elizabeth Spencer, Shirley Ann Grau, Peter Taylor, William Styron and Reynolds Price. For all these writers the South and its history, the South and its society, the South and its identity or meaning, provide a major source of creative energy and stimulus. But when they turn, as they frequently do, to portray the living face of the South, what the world sees is not the moonlight and magnolia of the old romantic image of the South. Instead, what it sees is an image of itself. In the colourful, controversial, but inevitably tragic history of an Old South doomed by the burden of slavery, the twentieth century has come to recognize a powerful and compelling symbol of our flawed and fallible human condition.

▶ For further reading

Charles C Bolton, *Poor Whites of the Antebellum South* (1994).
Bruce Collins, *White Society in the Antebellum South* (1985).
Clement Eaton, *A History of the Old South: The Emergence of a Reluctant Nation* (1995).

Lawrence B Goodheart et al. (eds), *Slavery in American Society* (1993).
Jay B Hubbell, *The South in American Literature, 1607–1900* (1954).
Rollin G Osterweiss, *Romanticism and Nationalism in the Old South* (1949).
William R Taylor, *Cavalier and Yankee: The Old South and American National Character* (1957).

5 The Frontier West

R A Burchell and R J Gray

▶ What was the frontier?

A popular idea exists of the Frontier West of the United States as a vast and empty area where Nature dwarfs man and the only figures in the landscape are the cowboy and the Indian, with perhaps an occasional trapper, prospector or troop of United States cavalry filling a supportive role. A wagon-train may now and then cross from right to left, taking pioneers towards the sun, but it does not stop to deposit settlers, and the wagons disappear over the mountains on their way to a further land. There may be settlements within this wilderness – small forts, Indian villages and sickly cow-towns – but they do not appear to follow normal urban functions, seeming rather to stand and wait in silence, coming alive only when the cattle arrive from Texas or the cavalry ride out to mount a deserved counter-attack on fractious Indian tribes. There is, however, very little historical truth in this single static snapshot, which ignores all variety of time and space, and also excludes one of the great motifs of the Frontier West – that is, the continuous arrival and departure of people who connect it with, and make it part of, a much wider world.

The men and women who came to the Frontier West brought with them cultural preconceptions which they hastened to impose on their new homes. Their Frontier West was no limbo sitting outside the pattern of national development: it was rather an area of rapid change connected intimately with national expansion. The history of the Frontier West was ever one of defeat for difference, separation and individuality. The victory went continuously to the traditions of the East. One of the earliest and most powerful image-makers of the frontier, James Fenimore Cooper (1789–1851), portrays this paradox in the five novels of his 'Leatherstocking' sequence. Natty Bumppo, 'Leatherstocking', is the romantic borderer of early nineteenth-century historical fiction; he explores virgin land and space, but his actions are set firmly in a process of historical time, and 'civilization' comes in stages that finally overwhelm him.

The Frontier West requires careful definition. It was not equivalent to the wilderness: it was, rather, the intermediary between it and the developed East. Moreover, in the history of the United States, the frontier was not always synonymous with the West, nor was the West always the same as the frontier. In 1607, when the Virginia Company initiated the first successful English settlement, all the continent outside Jamestown was the new settlers' Frontier West. The frontier did not always lie *to* the west. In the 1850s parts of Maine, Florida and Georgia being opened to white settlement were certainly frontier areas. At the same time, however, newly settled parts of New York, Pennsylvania and western Virginia were not on the frontier, the essential difference being that the true frontier is not surrounded by civilization. None the less, from the 1840s, the nation had in fact *two* frontiers, one to the east and one to the west – for, with the acquisition of Oregon in 1846, and California in 1848, population – particularly drawn in by the gold discoveries of 1848 – began spreading from both coasts into the unsettled land between. But the most important fact about the frontier is that it was a historical process – the process whereby newcomers incorporated an area into the culture of the East, until the sum total of activity in it came so closely to resemble that of areas earlier settled that the frontier period can be said to have ended. 'Culture' here refers not to the schoolmaster from Boston, nor to the spread of music, art and ideas: it means all those patterns of behaviour that evince a society's values.

The idea of process involves the notion of time. The process did not go forward in uniform rhythm, decade by decade; it was affected by surrounding circumstances that altered themselves as time passed. Briefly, the history of the Frontier West can be divided into four phases. The first lies in the colonial period; the second in the pre-railway age of the early national period; the third falls in the decades between the spawning of the railways and the statement made by the Superintendent of the Census in 1890 that there was no longer any frontier line (that is, a single line marking off areas with less than two persons per square mile from those with more); and the fourth phase covers the period since the 1890 census, during which areas that could still be classified as frontier – parts of Oklahoma, Montana, Wyoming, New Mexico, Arizona, Nevada, Idaho and Alaska – have proceeded towards 'civilization'. On some frontiers this process was long and slow, particularly in the first two periods; on others, such as in northern California, the frontier could pass in half a decade. Most historians and literary critics too have regarded the second and third periods as having played the most significant and formative roles in the development of the American nation.

▶ The frontier as re-culturation

There has been much debate over how best to visualize what happened during the phase when an area was part of the Frontier West and underwent the process of cultural re-creation. Frederick Jackson Turner, in his famous paper on *The Significance of the Frontier in American History* (1893), suggested that the 'frontier was the line of most rapid and effective Americanization' and was responsible for creating 'a new product that is American, an American mind marked by restless, nervous energy'. Some have argued that significant change took place in the failure to re-create precisely what had formerly existed in the East, and that successive failures to reproduce identical cultural patterns are at the heart of the development of a separate American culture away from mainly British roots. We can hardly deny that the varieties of context in which the reconstitution took place affected the lives of those who experienced the process – to do so would be to say that man can remain impervious to his social and cultural environment. It was, however, clearly the case that the pioneers brought with them, if they were Anglo-American, or soon adopted, if they were foreign born, a fundamental and formative ideology of republicanism that in broad outline remained an unchanging guide to what they expected in the way of government and politics, in the control and distribution of resources, and in the general right to anticipate a certain level of socio-economic mobility.

The debate over the rate and quality of cultural change has often been concentrated on one point in particular: the question of whether the westward movement of peoples produced an increasing democratization of society. It has been claimed that, particularly in the period 1815–60, ruling groups and their institutions in the United States, previously able to maintain a deferential social order, found it more and more difficult to control affairs with the same success, because the rapid expansion of the settled area taxed and then overwhelmed their resources. Hence new élites emerged in frontier areas; however, these did not succeed in reconstituting the old conservative order, since they had no inherited power bases from which to work, and so they were vulnerable to challenges from other groups as eager to rise as they had been. At the same time, the democratic content of the republican ideology that had been adopted by the nation at the time of the Revolution was given ever more stress to legitimize the shifts in power that were taking place.

Inasmuch as these were times of poor communications, of scattered, largely rural communities concentrating on self-sufficient agriculture, of weak national government, and no national army through which a proto-aristocracy might seize or perpetuate power, the nation did indeed undergo cultural transformations that came through the weakening of institutions through expansion. Yet it is important to recognize that the eastern ruling groups received their major challenge at home, in the fast-growing areas of the East, which increasingly acquired groups of alien European immigrants who could not be peaceably incorporated into the power-structure, but whose entry into the system governing rewards could not be denied without doing great harm to the sentiments of the Declaration of Independence and the Constitution. The conservatism of both

Hamilton and Jefferson was undermined by every immigrant ship's arrival, as well as being slowly outdated by the creation of new societies to the west of the Appalachians.

▶ How the West was won

The conventional imagery of the westward movement includes ideas of simplicity and intimacy with Nature: the meeting with the 'virgin land'. Yet at all times, technology – especially the technology of communications – stood between Nature and man. Before the coming of the railways, communication was difficult, restricting economic growth and the total sense of social cohesion, and thus enhancing the impact of the wilderness and the frontier. In 1756, for instance, it took three days to go by coach from New York to Philadelphia, travelling eighteen hours a day across some of the most settled parts of the colonies. Before the Revolution there was only one hard-gravelled road: that leading out of Portsmouth, Maine. The first canal, from Middletown to Reading, Pennsylvania, was surveyed in 1762, but was not begun until after the Revolution. Consequently, if settlement had not been concentrated near the coast or along navigable rivers, for reasons of defence and marketing, and if the British Government had not provided a centripetal cultural force, then colonists might well have succumbed to isolation and experienced marked cultural change. Some observers of back-country society, especially in the western parts of the colonies running south from Pennsylvania, argued that this was already happening by 1776; but if it was, it was also occurring within a situation where both Colonial and British governments intended to control the pattern of settlement and its rewards.

A change did come with the Revolution; government control over expansion weakened. The new Federal Government tried to institute an ordered policy of land distribution, but largely failed, for want, among other things, of an efficient bureaucracy. Significantly, the Indian threat to white settlements east of the Mississippi was ended in a series of engagements, of which the most important were the Battles of Fallen Timbers in north-west Ohio, in 1794, Tippecanoe in Indiana in 1811, the Battle of the Thames in 1813 in Michigan, and of Horseshoe Bend in Alabama in 1814. Simultaneously, transportation improved, aiding the spread of population. By 1821, 4,000 miles of new turnpikes had been completed, although by then interest was turning towards canals. Further, the *Clermont* went from New York to Albany and back in August 1807, and inaugurated the age of the steamboat. The United States had secured title to the Mississippi Valley with the Louisiana Purchase in 1803, but it was the round-trip of the *Washington* in 1817, from Louisville, Kentucky, to New Orleans, that ensured the area's growth and development. In 1818, it still cost between 100 dollars and 125 dollars to travel between the two cities; but by the 1830s the price had fallen to between 25 dollars and 30 dollars. Fares on other routes fell proportionately, further easing the way west. The opening of the Erie Canal in 1825, linking the Hudson River with the Great Lakes, where steamships had also been lately introduced, gave yet another boost to westward expansion. By 1840 the population of the western states of Ohio, Indiana, Illinois and Michigan stood at 2,893,000; that of the southern states of Kentucky, Tennessee, Missouri, Arkansas, Louisiana, Mississippi and Alabama at 3,410,000. In 1800 the two areas had contained 51,000 and 336,000 people respectively.

Yet despite all these improvements, travel, even in long settled areas, remained slow. As late as 1833, it took $33^{1}/_{4}$ hours to travel from Boston to New York: the maximum speed of the fastest form of transport, the stagecoach, was only around $11^{1}/_{2}$ miles an hour on good roads. The canal boats taking migrants west along the Erie Canal travelled at about $1^{1}/_{2}$ to 2 miles an hour, while no boats anywhere appear to have been capable of exceeding 5 miles an hour. Such slow travel hindered communication, which in turn hampered the development of markets, and importantly, the communication of ideas and the control of government and institutions. Localism was very important in this period, while the level of technology in general made men dependent on climate, topography and local supplies, vulnerable to flood or blizzard, and conscious of their isolation. This was a Frontier West of a relatively low level of agricultural technology and, linked to it, of low agricultural productivity. At first farmers relied on wooden ploughs and then, between 1825 and 1840, on cast-iron ones. They were without Hussey's and McCormick's reapers until the mid-1840s, and without even the cradle (a frame attached to the scythe to lay the grain evenly) until about 1820. There was not much sense of a margin between man and Nature under these conditions. This period of the Frontier West was thus characterized by a sense of loosening social bonds, and a healthy respect for – if not a fear of – the face of Nature and the problems of expansion and development.

There has been debate over what shape the American economy might have taken had it been restricted to a transportation system based on canals, rivers and oceans. Whatever the economic consequences, the social and ecological results would have differed from what did take place, and would have extended the period of weak central control and cultural diffusion. The late 1820s, however, saw the introduction of railways, and thereby made it possible to construct a national transportation system to arrest some of the centrifugal tendencies that were at work. To judge by the American response, the railway met a deeply felt need: by 1840 the country had 3,328 miles, whereas the whole of Europe had only 1,818. There was no systematic plan behind this development: many lines were short and differed in gauge from their neighbours. Chicago was not linked to New York until 1855; and it was not possible to travel from the

Great Lakes to the Gulf of Mexico before the Civil War without at some point having to leave the train. Nevertheless, the railway was surpassing all other forms of transport, and grew by 28,000 miles between 1840 and 1860. In twenty years after 1851, the Federal Government granted over 150 million acres to railway companies to help them build into sparsely settled areas, as well as over 64 million dollars in loans to six companies to build transcontinental routes. Without the railways, and to a lesser extent the telegraph service, which first appeared in 1844 and connected the Pacific coast in 1861, a continental United States would have been far more difficult to integrate and control. Road conditions were very primitive throughout the nineteenth century: as late as 1905, the country had only 161,000 miles of surfaced roads.

It is arguable that it was national expansion before the Civil War that had the most important effects on the national culture, and yet the popularly held idea of the Frontier West would not seem to include the expansion over the humid, forested areas east of the Mississippi. By the Civil War, the tide of developers had reached the increasingly arid and treeless areas of the Great Plains, where low rainfall levels were particularly important in slowing down the pace of agricultural growth and, in the absence of costly schemes of irrigation, in turning men's minds towards cattle and sheep, which took far more room than wheat and corn. The Indian made his last stand in this West in the quarter-century after the ending of the war; but, although the classic period of white–Indian relations did not come to an end until the Battle of Wounded Knee in December 1890, the issue of which group would dominate was never in any real doubt. The Frontier West of the late nineteenth century came into being in a society that had already changed the balance between man and Nature through new technologies that were bound to give the whites the advantage. In general, pioneers now had steel ploughs and reapers; after 1874 they had barbed wire; and from 1863 it was possible to enjoy the benefits of a cheap Federal postal service. Although it was not possible to telephone from New York to San Francisco until 1915, no pioneer of the late nineteenth century ever experienced the isolation of the back-woodsman of seventy years before. This, of course, is the frontier of the 'Western' film.

Those who take their images from the movies find it difficult to imagine the West as dotted with mine-shafts. Yet mining played a very important part in opening the trans-Mississippi West, beginning with the Californian gold discoveries. Scarcely any Far-Western state went untouched by rumours of gold, while mining excitements brought gold-seekers as far east as the Black Hills of South Dakota in 1875. Although the first wave of prospectors would include a large number of unconnected individuals, each seeking a personal fortune, even early arrivals soon found that the race in which they had engaged went to the forces of organization and of capital, and that the individual prospector too soon became an archaic survival in an age of wage labour. Many refused to accept the conditions imposed by employers, and very recognizable forms of industrial unrest soon characterized the mining industry. Even in the Californian Gold Rush, the individual found little place within two or three seasons. The employers found it easy to retaliate against recalcitrant white labour by, for instance, bringing in Chinese, so that had it not been for vestigial unionism, and for the sense that the worker could leave the mines to try his fortune elsewhere, many 'argonauts' would have found themselves part of a proletariat, a sad reflection on the dreams with which they had started out for the West.

▶ Land policies

One of the most bloody Western mining strikes, at Coeur d'Alene in Idaho in 1892, is usually mentioned in any survey of the labour history of the United States. Less bloody, but more interesting in the way it highlights misconceptions, was the first big strike of cowboys, in the Texas Panhandle in 1883. Although the frontier was always seen as the home of economic opportunity, it generally obeyed the laws of capitalism very faithfully – apart from, perhaps, its earliest years, which were often so unlike what was to follow that they may be seen as no more than an aberration from the main line of development. Some men came with capital or credit, bought up land or prime urban sites, and remained to build fortunes on these foundations. Others came as wage labourers, and stayed no longer than three or four harvests. The frontier gave more to those that had than to those that had not, for no government intervened to use it as a site for social engineering to create a utopia of greater social and economic equality.

Land policies might have been used in this direction, especially the Homestead Act of 1862, which offered any citizen or intending citizen who was head of a family and over twenty-one years of age 160 acres of surveyed public land free, if he or she should reside there continuously for five years and pay a registration fee of from 26 dollars to 34 dollars. But there were at least four main reasons why the Act did not lead to an egalitarian society with uniformly rising living standards. These reasons were equally important whether the pioneer bought his land from the government or other agencies.

First, although the land might be 'free', its cultivation required capital. In the 1850s, in areas with fewer problems and costs of irrigation than the arid Far West, it could require 1,000 dollars to bring a farm into cultivation and 2,000 dollars on a 100-acre farm to maximize profits. Second, only a minority of even the farming population had sufficient skill and motivation for pioneering. It has been suggested that the United States shows not a stream of would-be farmers flowing from the cities to the West, but instead a flood of disgruntled farmers seeking their fortunes in the city. Possibly twenty farmers moved to town for every industrial labourer who moved to the land, and ten farmers' sons went to the city for each who became the owner of a farm anywhere in the nation. Consequently, it is quite possible to argue that, as this migration shows, the industrial, not the agricultural, frontiers were the areas of opportunity for the nineteenth-century American.

The effect of the Homestead Act was limited, thirdly, because the United States Government disposed of the majority of its land by other means: by auction; by grants to states for educational and other purposes; by grant to states and corporations for transportation improvement; and in return for military service during war. The government did try to control the amount of land going in to any individual's control in 1862 by distinguishing between offered land, available for private purchase in unlimited amounts, and unoffered land which could only be taken up in limited amounts under the Homestead Act and other land laws. Much of the land west of the states of Minnesota, Iowa, Missouri, Arkansas and Texas was defined as unoffered land, but those intent on large acquisitions could always buy from intermediaries like the railways or the states, or simply break a very loosely applied law. Between 1862 and 1904, only one-quarter of the public domain went to settlers under the Homestead Act, though it did have some success between 1863 and 1880 in the area that runs from Oklahoma through the Dakotas to Minnesota.

The fourth reason for the failure of land policies to provide general opportunity has to do with the increasing difficulties all farmers faced in the United States as the century progressed and a world market was produced for agricultural products in which there was a long-term decline in prices. Small units of production were inefficient, while it has been calculated that only 28 per cent of the total number of homesteads begun under the Act of 1862 were sited in areas suitable for 160-acre farming. There was no successful irrigation policy before the Newlands Act of 1902, and irrigated land was naturally expensive. California tried an Irrigation Law in 1887 and by 1889 unimproved land with water could cost between 100 dollars and 200 dollars an acre. In the Dakotas, a farmer needed to raise 20 bushels of wheat from 1 acre and receive 80 cents to 1 dollar a bushel for it if he was to do no more than stay out of debt. Between 1881 and 1914 he never received more than 1 dollar.

It was by no means totally impossible to overcome this list of difficulties and acquire a farm, bring it into cultivation and make a living, albeit a modest one in most cases. It has been calculated that between 1820 and 1850 it might take a careful saver, who was well paid and had continuous employment, ten years to acquire 500 dollars; and that after 1850, higher wages meant he might do it in five to seven years. The determined could usually rely on some credit and could begin by renting. A capital of 500 dollars in animals, equipment and cash could give a renter two-thirds of his product in the later nineteenth century. The likelihood was, however, of a long and probably unsuccessful struggle to make ends meet. In 1900 only 22 per cent of all farms were owner-operated, and increasing tenancy seemed inevitably to go hand in hand with the development of the frontier.

▶ The closing of the frontier

In fact, as the nineteenth century progressed, agriculture ceased to be the single dominant employer of labour even on the frontier. In 1890 no more than half the labour force in the states and territories west of the tier from the Dakotas to Texas was employed in agriculture. In most, fewer than one in three was. After the North-east, the West was, indeed, the most urbanized area of the nation. Despite the fact that there were only three cities west of St Louis in the list of the nation's fifty largest – namely San Francisco, Omaha and Denver – 30 per cent of the population of this area lived in settlements of more than 8,000 people. Altogether, there were twenty-four urban areas of over 8,000 people in the West in 1890.

The growth of urban areas occurred at the same time as the development of the surrounding countryside, so that in many cases there were, simultaneously, two frontiers: one urban, and one rural. In many ways, the urban West was of great value in the process of westward expansion, for the concentration of population permitted the exercise of some centralized cultural control. The fact that the first Beethoven symphony to be heard in the United States was performed not in Boston but in Lexington, Kentucky, showed how culture in the narrow sense emanated from urban centres as culture in the broader sense did more importantly, too.

The replacement of the Indian by the white man was one of the most important features of the cultural process that defined the Frontier West. This process began long before the final battle or the forced removal of tribes cleared an area of white settlement, for Indian cultures were deeply shaken by the technologies and diseases of the whites long before white men in any number appeared on the scene. There were many separate Indian cultures, so that the popular image of the Indian is no more than a careless agglomeration of characteristics taken from different tribes. Some Indians – the Pueblos are a striking example – were sedentary farmers, living in villages or small towns. One Pueblo tribe, the Hopi, was, as the name translates, pacifist – though more tribes resembled the warlike Apaches who did not, however, begin to take scalps until well into the nineteenth century, when they adopted the practice from whites. Only tribes like the Siouan-speaking Mandan and Hidasta of the northern plains wore the familiar feathered war-bonnets, but they lived in large dug-out lodges, usually half underground, and only took to teepees on hunting expeditions. The Indians of the north-west coast had the totem pole, for theirs was a culture that worked wood, but their cedar-bark loin cloths and mountain goats' wool blankets, together with their decorated hats of basket-work, gave them an appearance quite unlike that usually associated with the Indian. As so often in the construction of images of the Frontier West, that of the Indian has been reduced to a particular time and place, the post-Civil War High Plains, and then extended to all others.

The settlement of the Frontier West has been seen as a quintessential American experience, providing folk heroes and a central tradition. The winning of the West has necessarily been seen as the work of the spiritual descendants of the Plymouth and Jamestown settlers. Yet to uphold such a view it is necessary to ignore certain facts. For instance, about 25 per cent of the cowboys who ranged northward after the Civil War were black and perhaps another 10 per cent were Mexican. At the same time, probably three times as many foreign-born immigrants were being attracted to the trans-Mississippi West as native-born Easterners. Even in the colonial period it was the Germans and the Scotch-Irish who were prominent on the frontier.

But the story of the Frontier West has been seen as a single crucial American experience for important reasons. The United States necessarily suffered great problems in establishing a sense of its own identity after the Revolution, since independence could not mean the resumption of indigenous cultural patterns, while the constant flow of goods, ideas and people, from Europe in particular, made cultural isolation impossible, and hindered the development of distinctiveness. Even before 1776, the Indian and the black posed their cultural problem, for the decision to accord them an inferior status demanded a definition of American society. In the nineteenth century, the immigration of non-British, non-Protestant stocks posed a further challenge, increasing the possibility of cultural fragmentation. The ideology of republicanism helped prevent this, offering values that all immigrants could share, but equally as important a cohesive force was the experience of the developing Frontier West, where the challenges of distance, isolation, hardship and misfortune helped mould a common response that ignored national origin.

Thus the opening of the Frontier West and its acculturation was the result of a general commitment to a common future – even if the rewards of development were not equally distributed. By the end of the nineteenth century, a sense had grown that the steady incorporation of successive Frontiers West into the nation was of the utmost importance in maintaining a cultural identity. In a sense the new frontier was already there, in the city; still, the view of the Superintendent of the Census in 1890 that the frontier was fast disappearing was bound to introduce a period of anxious introspection, to be seen at one level in the emergence of very strong frontier themes in the national literature. At the same Chicago Columbian Exposition where in 1893 Turner enunciated his thesis on national identity, the novelist Hamlin Garland, who had grown up in the 'Middle Border' of Wisconsin, Iowa and South Dakota, called in effect for a new literary frontier of realism, or local colour, of Western writing – though only to find his audience from the railhead of the plains preferring a romantic gentility. But it was around this tension that the frontier began to stabilize its meaning. In the long run, the disappearance of a frontier line did not turn out to be culturally catastrophic: the nation survived, though one result of its sense of intrinsic connection between frontier and national identity was that the United States began to contemplate ending unrestricted immigration, in order to diminish the potential danger from the centrifugal forces of ethnic cultural diversity. This did not occur until the 1920s, but the frontier question underlay a number of issues in the intervening period; some, for instance, in foreign policy. During the previous 300 years the expansion of settlement and the extension of Eastern cultural forms westward had together been of the utmost importance in giving a particular meaning to the European experience in North America – turning Europeans into Americans and producing a central cultural tradition to hold the nation together. Though much of that tradition rested on myth, that very fact was a reason for its success in relieving some of the tensions of a culturally pluralistic society.

▶ The frontier in literature

Given the mythical force that came to be attached to the idea of the frontier in American culture, it is hardly surprising that it deeply affected the American literary imagination, and indeed the very nature and form of American writing. The idea of the new-found land to the West, the iconography of the wilderness, the fundamental encounter between man and Nature, the figure of the Indian: all these came to be, for the earliest American writers and their successors, among the most important motifs and themes in the national literature. Such themes, indeed, have extended beyond the boundaries of American writing to appear in European literature as well – in the pastorals of the Elizabethan and Renaissance period, for instance: in the romanticism of René de Chateaubriand's short Indian novel *Atala* (1801); in the ironic realism of Charles Dickens's venture to the American frontier's edge in *Martin Chuzzlewit* (1844); and in the 'Shatterhand' Western novels of the German Karl May set beyond the Mississippi by an author who did not even visit the United States until the end of his career. The sheer range of these images and myths is one of the obstacles facing those who try to define what we mean by 'the literature of the frontier'. It is, in effect, one of the reasons why the fictional form, like the historical fact, poses so many difficulties. And another reason for these difficulties is that, while the frontier has always been a central theme *in* American writing, it has also become, increasingly, an important source *of* American writing – as the cultural boundaries of the nation, and perhaps even its centre, have moved ever further westward. As a direct result of all this – the cultural shift to the West, that is, and the sheer complexity of the Western myth – the very term 'frontier literature' can be interpreted in a number of radically different ways. We could, for instance, take frontier literature to mean anything that was actually written or devised by the settlers – that is to say, literature that comes *from* the frontier. Then again, we could take it to embrace books and poems from elsewhere, which use the life of the pioneer or the Indian as their subject and setting – in other words, literature *about* the frontier. Beyond this, we could expand the term even further, to include any writing that bears the imprint of the pioneering experience and the westward movement; it could, to put it another way, also mean literature that has somehow been *inspired by* the frontier. This problem of definition is a serious one, the seriousness of which is indicated, not least, by the radical disagreements to be found among the many critics and scholars who have considered the subject.

Quite apart from these problems of form or definition, there is also the question of period. If, as the textbooks usually suggest, we identify the frontier period as being from 1607 to 1890, this might seem to mark the parameters of frontier literature: frontier literature, we could say, was written over the 300 years the frontier was actually there. But again, as in the historical discussion, there is the problem of emphasis. Was it, for example, as Turner insisted, the settlement in the middle region in the nineteenth century that provided the definitive frontier experience and, by extension, the true sources of frontier culture? Some critics have assumed this to be so; yet this does less than justice to the Puritans and the early settlers of the Virginia Tidewater region, and it leaves out of the picture the work of modern writers, like Willa Cather and William Faulkner, who were profoundly affected by the frontier past. The specifically literary problems are the greater because literature reaches across time and space: it mythicizes, re-creates, and incorporates structures from history. Indeed, if we accept the idea that literature *inspired by* the frontier is relevant, then no terminal date of any kind is possible. Even the heroes of contemporary novelists like, say, Jack Kerouac or Norman Mailer can be regarded as 'spiritual pioneers', trying to recover the frontier sense of possibility; even contemporary American literature can be seen – to quote one commentator, Van Wyck Brooks – as a 'sublimation of the frontier spirit'.

The last phrase suggests a third problem. In a sweeping and memorable passage in his essay on the significance of the westward movement, Turner suggests that the frontier was 'the line of most rapid and effective Americanization' and, as such, was almost entirely responsible for creating 'a new product that is American'. Literary critics have not been slow to take up Turner's suggestion and argue that what makes American *literature*, in turn, characteristically American is the consciousness of the frontier – or, more simply, that all American novels are really Westerns. The flaw in this argument is, of course, that it ignores the existence of other historical factors. It evades all the problems posed by the fact that what Turner calls, at one point, 'the American mind' was formed out of a dialectical interplay between various, and often quite separate, events and structures of belief. The frontier experience did not occur in a vacuum, historical or ideological. In fact, it was itself profoundly affected, even shaped, by certain distinctively European notions. For as Lewis Mumford puts it, in his classic study of American culture, *The Golden Day* (1921):

> in the episode of pioneering a new system of ideas wedded itself to a new set of experiences: the experiences were American, but the ideas themselves had been nurtured in Savoy, in the English lake country, and on the Scots moors.

These are the basic problems then: the ones of definition and period, and those created by the unavoidable recognition that other forces have been at work in American history. And the first step – to adopt a pioneering metaphor – in clearing a pathway to some solutions is to admit that no blanket definition of the term 'the literature of the frontier' is possible. There are, quite simply, different types and different periods of literature associated with the westward movement. The second step, perhaps, is to admit that, while this does necessarily complicate matters, the frontier as a fact and a myth *has* been a formative influence in American literature – and, as such, provides a useful framework both for studying that literature and for relating it to American history and culture.

▶ Types of frontier literature

Perhaps one indication of the sheer variety of frontier literature is that, at the most basic level, that of literature *from* the frontier, it is not even *writing* that we are talking about: a good deal of what the early pioneers actually created comes under the heading of folklore. The frontier heritage, some scholars have argued, has provided most of the peculiar experiences and culturally unifying memories which enable us to talk about an American folk culture in the first place. And, even if this is open to dispute, it is still clearly the case that certain things – like cowboy songs, ballads of the '49 Gold Rush, and early songs of pioneering – offer us some unique commentaries on the advance across the continent. So do the innumerable comic yarns, legends, and tall tales which helped make heroes out of the likes of Davy Crockett, Mike Fink, Paul Bunyan and Pecos Bill. The oral tradition also reminds us that there is a vast spoken tradition of Indian legends and poetry, much revived by the modern ethno-poets; but we can hardly identify that as frontier writing, however much we must root it in the classical experience of those whom the frontier displaced.

Moving away from the oral to the written, one might include in the category of literature issuing directly from the frontier certain reports and chronicles produced by the early settlers: the writings of the Puritan William Bradford, or of William Byrd the younger, in the colonial period, for instance, or of James Hall in the nineteenth century. But at this point the definitions begin to blur, if only because these reports were often produced for non-frontier audiences – in colonial times across the Atlantic, and later on in the East – which inevitably affected the way in which they were written. Besides that, many of those who provided them could be described, in a way, as agents of Eastern culture – set apart from their pioneering neighbours by their background, tastes, and literary pretensions. In short, literature *from* the frontier tends to merge with the literature *about* the frontier, being written either for those elsewhere, or in retrospect. A good deal of the actual folklore of the pioneer was indeed eventually 'civilized', taken up by writers and editors further east, where it became part of the national literary tradition.

The knockabout comic stories and tall tales of the frontier, for example, helped lay the foundations for South-western and vernacular humour, which in turn became nationally popular through figures like Mark Twain and Artemus Ward. Davy Crockett was transformed into a national hero, thanks to his autobiography, and other widely circulated narratives; and stories about Daniel Boone, Pecos Bill, and Kit Carson provided the staple diet of the late nineteenth-century 'dime-novel'. The distinction is still there, perhaps, between a cultural document and a literary version, but it is a shifting and occasionally elusive one. Mark Twain (Samuel Langhorne Clemens, 1835–1910) is a useful indication of this shift. Writing of the Mississippi Valley and the mining camps of the Sierras, he inherited the comic and vernacular traditions, but amended them and at the same time moved eastward. What further complicates matters is that after the Civil War, when American literature was less clearly identified with the New England establishment, the former pioneer areas became regional literary centres, producing a good deal of writing of their own. Usually, this writing is related in some way to the last stages of the frontier process. It offers a background record of 'local colour', for example; or it concentrates, as Hamlin Garland's *Main-Travelled Roads* (1891) and *Prairie Folks.* (1893) do, on the problems of declining homesteads, viewed from the standpoint of economic naturalism. But works about the experience of late-immigrant pioneers, like O E Rolvaag's *Giants in the Earth* (1927), which describes Norwegian homesteaders in the Dakotas, were still appearing in the early years of this century.

It is, however, when one turns from literature *from* the frontier to literature *about* the frontier that the floodgates begin to open, because the real impact of frontier life, as a myth or idea as well as a fact, was felt in the rest of American society, the culture of which the pioneering experience formed only one, separable part. Such literature is not only vast, it is also extraordinarily varied, ranging, as it does, from simple documentary through popular writing to imaginative work of the very first rank. First, and most obviously, there are the reports of exploration or conquest, which offer us fascinating versions of the various stages of the westward movement. From colonial times, there are the many exploration narratives collected by Richard Hakluyt and Samuel Purchas; while the works of James Adair (*The History of the American Indians*, 1775) and Jonathan Carver (*Three Years Travel Through the Interior Parts of North America*, 1778) provide two quite unique accounts of the frontier during the period immediately before the Revolution. The advance across the Alleghenies is vividly commemorated in the writings of John Filson (*The Discovery, Settlement and Present State of Kentucky*, 1784, which introduced Daniel Boone to the reading public) and in the work of Gilbert Imlay (*Topographical Description of the Western Territory of North America*, 1792). Exploration of the Louisiana Purchase territory, in turn, is the subject of the journals of Lewis and Clark, prepared for publication by Nicholas Biddle (1814); while Josiah Gregg's *Commerce of the Prairies* (1844) deals with the journey along the Santa Fe Trail into the Spanish outposts of the South-west. The migration across the plains and inter-mountain region to the Pacific coast is memorably registered in Lieutenant John C Frémont's account of his expedition to the Rockies (*Report of the Exploring Expedition to the Rocky Mountains* (1845) which, among other things, established Kit Carson as a national celebrity); and the settlement of the Great Plains, and absorption of the West into the nation, is described and interpreted in the narratives of the journalists Bayard Taylor (*El Dorado, Or Adventures in the Path of Empire*, 1850) and Horace Greeley (*An Overland Journey from New York to San Francisco*, 1860). This, however, is only the beginning.

Quite apart from these narratives (coloured, in most cases, by the imagination and frequently sprinkled with legend), there is a popular literature about the West, particularly in the nineteenth century. Mention has already been made of the South-western humorists, whose work grew out of the folk culture of the frontier. From about 1835 until 1861, a number of writers from such old South-western states as Georgia, Alabama, and Mississippi produced tall tales, scenes from provincial life, and sketches of backwoods rogues and eccentrics which were characterized by three things: broad humour, the use of dialect, and a tendency to emphasize the earthier aspects of frontier experience. Most of these writers – people like Augustus Baldwin Longstreet and George Washington Harris – liked to think of themselves as gentlemen of education and breeding. This, though, did not inhibit them when it came to recording the cruder side of pioneer life and character. Nor did it prevent them from reproducing the language of the frontier, bold, racy and idiosyncratic, and so preparing the way for the absorption of the vernacular into American literature as a whole.

At the other end of the spectrum from these humorists stand the popular romancers, creators of sentimental legends. These include such writers as Timothy Flint, author of *Nick of the Woods* (1837), and Robert Montgomery Bird, author of *Francis Berrian* (1826), in the earlier half of the nineteenth century, but above all the 'dime novelists' in the latter half. The 'dime novel' was devised by the editors of weekly story papers in the 1840s, and then exploited remorselessly by people like Erasmus Beadle (who manufactured millions of such books between 1860 and 1900). It was invariably written to a formula. Any exotic setting could be exploited, as the background to a series of thoroughly predictable adventures, but, for obvious reasons, the 'Wild West' was particularly favoured. The purveyors of this fiction (they can scarcely be called creators) helped to turn the Western adventurer, sometimes called Buffalo Bill or Deadwood Dick, sometimes given another name, into a popular hero. Strong, self-assured and self-reliant, he became a part of the newly emerging mass culture – and he has remained so, of course, ever since.

Finally, and perhaps most importantly, as far as writing *about* the frontier is concerned, there is the work of the major writers. It is they who incorporate the frontier into a fundamental thematic tradition. James Fenimore Cooper is of crucial significance here, since his five 'Leatherstocking' novels – *The Pioneers* (1823), *The Last of the Mohicans* (1826), *The Prairie* (1827), *The Pathfinder* (1840), *The Deerslayer* (1841) – are among the first American books to realize the epic potential of the westward movement. They are also the first to describe, however implicitly, the paradoxes on which the myth of the frontier depends. For Natty Bumppo, Cooper's hero, is at once uneducated and learned, simple and noble, practical and idealistic, innocent and experienced. He is a romantic hero, as Cooper's is a romantic perspective. And so, above all, he is at once a philosopher of primitivism, fleeing from the settlements, and an empire builder, helping to chart the wilderness and so spread those same settlements wherever he goes. This is suggested by the closing sentences of *The Pioneers*, the first of the 'Leatherstocking' novels:

> This was the last that they ever saw of the Leather-Stocking . . . He had gone far towards the setting sun – the foremost in that band of pioneers who are opening the way for the march of the nation across the continent.

Natty leaves Templeton, the setting of the novel, because he feels threatened by the growth of civil society, and yet he prepares the pathway for that society – indeed, he is in some senses a part of it. He exists, at best, in a neutral territory between the forest and the clearing, nature and culture, belonging wholly to neither: which is true not only of him, really, but of all major American heroes associated with some kind of pioneer territory. 'Between savagery and civilization.'

Turner's famous description of the American frontier area possesses a special poignancy – not only for Natty Bumppo, but for characters like Hester Prynne, who lives on the edge between the Puritan settlement and the forest in Nathaniel Hawthorne's *The Scarlet Letter* (1850), and Huckleberry Finn, Mark Twain's innocent hero in *The Adventures of Huckleberry Finn* (1885), who gravitates all the time between the freedom of the river and the riverbank communities of the old South-west. In a way, it has a similar poignancy for a figure like Ike McCaslin in William Faulkner's *The Bear* (1942), who cannot commit himself, finally, either to the beliefs learned in the wilderness or to the ideas instilled in him by Southern society – and for many other heroes in modern American literature, characters who are often, in fact, several generations removed from the actual, historical frontier.

At this point, of course, we are moving towards the third and most intractable of the types of frontier literature; that is, literature *inspired by* the frontier. The danger here is that virtually every American book can be said to reflect the pioneering experience in one way or another, if only because that experience has become an integral part of the national consciousness. A certain amount of tact is required, really, to distinguish between those works which have been affected, profoundly if circuitously, by awareness of the westward movement and those in which other influences are of greater significance. For example, it is surely correct to say that much of Thoreau's writing belongs in this category. For although Thoreau was not very interested in the actual frontier (and, indeed, often said that he felt repelled by the typical pioneer's excessive materialism), he was clearly fascinated by its potential as myth. As he saw it, using a characteristic pun, the real frontier was to be found wherever a person tried 'to front only the essential facts of life'. Thinking that 'it would be some advantage to live a primitive and frontier life' even 'in the midst of outward civilization', he turned himself into a pioneer of the imagination, constructing his own version of the Western experience at Walden Pond and in his books, *A Week on the Concord and Merrimack Rivers* (1849) and *Walden* (1854). Thoreau, we could say then, was writing a *kind* of frontier literature; as was Herman Melville in a work like *Moby-Dick* (1851), which describes the frontier of the sea, and Henry James, when he examined – in such novels as *The Portrait of a Lady* (1881) and *The Ambassadors* (1903) – the American frontier with Europe.

On the other hand, we would probably be wrong to claim, as at least one critic has, that Poe can be put in this category as well. Certainly, he was interested in the unknown and in dominion over nature, and many of his heroes can be described as explorers. But *his* unknown is totally inward and associated entirely with the past, while the realm his heroes explore has a heart of darkness. The burden of his imagery, in fact, and

the thrust of his narratives suggest that the Old South was more important to him, imaginatively, than the West was. Obviously, this is a contentious area, where the evidence has to be weighed very carefully; and it
becomes, finally, a matter of deciding at what stage an inheritance that all
Americans share, by the mere fact of being Americans, is crucial to the
understanding of an individual text.

▶ The periods of frontier literature

If frontier literature needs to be seen in terms of different types, it also
deserves to be looked at – just like the frontier process itself – in terms of
different periods: periods in which there were not only varying historical
forces at work in society but changing aesthetic assumptions at work
in art. The first of these periods, the colonial, was notable chiefly for
the establishment of certain crucial images of the frontier: images that
became deeply attached to the very idea of America itself. Seen from
the standpoint of Europe, or from the Atlantic seaboard, the newly discovered wilderness of America was transformed into what one enthusiastic
commentator – Edward Williams (*Virginia*, 1650) – called

> a Virgin Countrey, so preserved by Nature out of a desire to show
> mankinde fallen into the Old Age of the Creation, what a brow
> of fertility and beauty she was adorned with when the world was
> vigorous and youthfull . . .

The myth of the virgin land was born, or rather resurrected in a new
context, and with it the linked images of the pioneer and the good
farmer – the one of them a man who cleared a pathway into the wilderness, and the other a sturdy yeoman who transformed his surroundings
into a garden of the world.

The writers of the early national period developed these images and
several others associated with the frontier, bathing them in the light of
Romanticism and a burgeoning nationalism. In Crèvecoeur's *Letters from
an American Farmer* (1793), for example, the small farmer inhabiting the
'intermediate space' between sea and forest is presented as someone who
has experienced 'a sort of resurrection' and become, as a consequence,
'a new man'. He is another Adam, and the American wilderness offers
him the possibility of recovering Eden. The point is made, without embarrassment, over and over again in the literature of this era – and often
in ringing terms, as in these lines by Philip Freneau, from his epic poem
'The Rising Glory of America' (1771),

> . . . Paradise anew
> Shall flourish, by no second Adam lost,

No dangerous tree with deadly fruit shall grow
No tempting serpent to allure the soul from native innocence.

Utopianism and nostalgia are neatly combined in visions like this, as they are, of course, in the figure of Natty Bumppo. For the American West was by this time a focus for conflicting feelings; the longing for lost innocence, and a return to primal nature, was mixed with the emerging belief in some sort of manifest destiny for the nation, and the realization of a new imperial culture.

It was in the third period, however, that the belief in an imperial destiny was brought into full flower. As the westward movement accelerated with the help of the railways, and the Atlantic and Pacific seaboards were gradually bound together into one nation, so the association of the West with the idea, not merely of innocence, but of power grew steadily as well. This new assertiveness, growing out of the rapid advance of the pioneer across the entire continent, as well as a transcendental expectation of wholeness, is perhaps most noticeable in the work of Walt Whitman – as in 'A Broadway Pageant':

I chant the world on my Western sea . . .
I chant the new empire, grander than any before – As in a vision
 it comes to me;
I chant America, the Mistress – I chant a greater supremacy. . . .

The assertiveness is there, of course, not merely in what Whitman says but in how he says it. For while celebrating the westward movement, and the experiment in living it implied, Whitman was also conducting what he called his own 'language experiment' – developing new forms, a new line and a new vocabulary, which could adequately express the vitality of this 'new empire'.

In a sense, Whitman's equivalent in prose is Mark Twain, since Twain's best work is as formally innovative as Whitman's is: *The Adventures of Huckleberry Finn* (1885), for example, which grows directly out of the tradition of South-western humour, is a masterpiece of the American vernacular. But, in another way, Twain is very different from Whitman because the frontier Eden described in *Huckleberry Finn* is clearly a part of the past. The book was published, after all, only five years before the official closing of the frontier and it is set, significantly enough, in a prelapsarian, ante-bellum world. Utopianism is easily outweighed by nostalgia here; the pastoral, such as it is, has tragic implications. For Twain's audience must have realized, even as they read about Huck Finn lighting out for the Territory to escape being civilized, that America had come of age and the Territories were practically gone. Here, in fact, and in some of his other books – most notably, *Life on the Mississippi* (1883) – Twain is already moving towards that image of a lost pioneer world that would haunt Sherwood Anderson, in *Winesburg, Ohio* (1919), and which permeates the novels of Sinclair Lewis, such as *Main Street* (1920). Behind the main streets of Winesburg and Lewis's Gopher Prairie lie the last remnants of a pioneer past, a past that is now being trampled under by boosterism, commerce – and by young people beating a retreat to the big city.

All of this is by way of saying that Twain does, to some extent, anticipate the literature of the fourth of our periods: an era, including the present, when the frontier as a historical fact has disappeared and when its pastoral associations must be balanced against an awareness of those changes – that process of advance towards a modern urban society – which the frontier experience itself helped to bring about. To borrow a phrase from Leo Marx's study *The Machine in the Garden* (1964), the legend of the West and its accompanying imagery have acquired now the character of 'complex pastoral'. The virgin land and the pioneer, the small farmer and the garden of the world: the possibility of actually realizing these dreams in experience has more or less vanished – and yet, as dreams, they remain alive in American thought and writing. They survive as sources of inspiration, creative myths. And they survive not only in American thought: Franz Kafka's *Amerika* (1927), for instance, ends with its young hero joining 'The Great Nature Theatre of Oklahoma' and setting out westwards in the belief that 'All that he had done till now was ignored; it was not going to be made a reproach to him'. Of course, the forms this survival assumes are pretty various and often very subtle. The frontier and its legends may be located purely in memory, as they are in Twain's work and, more recently, in the novels of Willa Cather, like *O Pioneers!* (1913) and *My Ántonia* (1918). Alternatively, the legends themselves may assume parodic form, and so act as a measure of the distance between ideal and fact: the Joads in John Steinbeck's *The Grapes of Wrath* (1939), for instance, find themselves enacting a cruel parody of the pioneer experience, journeying westward from Oklahoma to California down Route 66 only to find a closed society and further oppression. A new setting may be sought for the imagery of pioneering – in the anonymity of the city, perhaps, where Fitzgerald's heroes, like the central figure in *The Great Gatsby* (1925), try to recreate themselves, turn themselves into sons of Adam, secreting a tale of the West in a tale of the East.

Or, then again, from disorderly modern experience the writer may look back into the space of primitivism, and the apparent coherence of past history; so Hemingway's heroes return to the rituals of hunting and fishing, while some of Faulkner's characters explore the possible implications of the destruction of the wilderness. The writer, and his hero, may favour a purely inner freedom: witness the protagonist in John Barth's *The End of the Road* (1958) or the private detective or space explorer of modern legend – characters who enjoy independence, and a sense of belonging to some world elsewhere, while nevertheless retaining a function within society. Or he may seek a kind of refuge in perpetual mobility – as Jack Kerouac's heroes do in, say, *On the Road* (1957) – conducting a journey without destination across the American continent, as an outward and visible sign of an inward quest. Finally, and even more subtly, the writer may take upon *himself* the role of pioneer, pursuing, as Hart Crane once put it, 'new thresholds, new anatomies'. He may try, in effect, as Crane tries in his epic poem, *The Bridge* (1930), to cross new frontiers of language and imagination, and so turn the actual text into a kind of neutral territory between the clearing and the wilderness, the familiar and the unknown.

At this point we have returned, by however circuitous a route, to the basic problem: where does 'the literature of the frontier' begin and where, if at all, does it end? What do we mean when we say a writer has been affected by the movement west? As this discussion has tried to show, there are ways of at least approaching answers to such questions, involving, among other things, a recognition of the sheer variety of frontier literature, and an acknowledgement of what is, in any case, part of the problem – the fact that the frontier (both as an experience and an ideology) has been involved in a dialectical relationship with many other forces and influences in American life. But even if these approaches were carried through in far more detail than is possible here, it is likely that many of the problems would remain. For the legacy of the pioneer is, in some ways, like a ghost, a familiar spirit haunting the national literature. It is there when we least expect it, and are perhaps not even prepared to see it; and very often the simple question of its presence or absence must remain open to debate.

▶ For further reading

Ray Allen Billington, *Westward Expansion* (1974).

Thomas J Lyon, *A Literary History of the American West* (1974).

Clyde A Milner et al. (eds), *The Oxford History of the American West* (1996).

Gerald D Nash and Richard W Etulain (eds), *The Twentieth Century West: Historical Interpretations* (1989).

Henry Nash Smith, *Virgin Land: The American West as Symbol and Myth* (1950).

Robert M Uttley, *The Indian Frontier of the American West, 1846–1890* (1984).

Richard C Wade, *The Urban Frontier: The Rise of Western Cities, 1790–1830* (1959).

6

The immigrant experience

R A Burchell and Eric Homberger

▶ A teeming of nations

It was not until the twentieth century that the United States came to celebrate the diverse origins of its population. It took roughly a century for Americans to adjust to the fact that, in Walt Whitman's words, they were 'not merely a nation but a teeming of nations'. Serious doubts about heterogeneity first arose in the 1840s and 1850s when the numbers of immigrants rose significantly due to economic change in Europe and America, famine and political and religious dissent. Americans had already discussed their diversity in the eighteenth century. In his *Letters from an American Farmer* (1782), St John de Crèvecoeur had explained to Europeans that from a 'promiscuous breed' of 'English, Scots, Irish, French, Dutch, Germans and Swedes' that 'race now called Americans' had arisen. His use then of the singular is instructive. It implies that he saw a single culture into which newcomers were blending. Crèvecoeur might well have assumed such a process, in a period when London could arguably be seen as the ultimate cultural centre of the American colonies. The lack of such an authority after Independence helped create the world of conflicting loyalties in which many immigrants of the nineteenth and twentieth centuries lived.

Immigrant experiences were very varied but all were shaped by a number of factors. These helped determine how easily the immigrant fitted into American society. First, there was what may be called the cultural distance to be travelled – least in the case of immigrants from the British Isles who spoke the same language as their new fellow inhabitants and who had common histories and traditions, including in most cases a common Protestantism. At the other extreme Chinese and Japanese immigrants did not share the alphabet, let alone the language and traditions of their new home. Their dislocation must therefore be the greater. It was also important how economically similar old and new homes were. If very dissimilar, the chances were that immigrants would be restricted to unskilled occupations with all that that entailed for future progress and status. It also mattered whether, like the Jews or the Irish, immigrants had come to settle or whether, like the Italians or Slavs in the early twentieth century, arrivals expected to be transients. It was also important when the immigrant arrived in the United States because this affected how and where they would fit into the American economy.

The date of arrival also affected the quality of reception. The immigrants of the 1840s and 1850s found a society that was unsure of itself and therefore particularly hostile. The groups that came immediately after the Civil War found less stress laid on religious differences, great demand for their labour and much less nativist hostility. But the size of migrations after 1900 frightened Americans once again and combined with contemporary views on race to reawaken anxiety and hostility to such an extent that by 1914 it appeared only a matter of time before the United States would turn its back on its traditional policy of largely unrestricted immigration.

Once this happened – in 1924 and 1929 – anxieties diminished, especially when the Great Depression of the Thirties made the United States an unattractive destination and immigration fell away. The fact that the United States continued to restrict immigration after the Second World War helped maintain the sense of confidence that immigrants could be assimilated without too much friction, but the Seventies and Eighties saw unease return. This was due to a growing realization that the Immigration Act of 1965 had strongly affected patterns of immigration. Asia and Latin America were now providing the vast bulk of immigrants, not Europe, from which the majority of the American population had previously come.

The period in which individuals migrated was important in further ways. Early immigrants sometimes had terrible experiences on the Atlantic in days when state supervision of ships, and their health hazards and provisioning, was lax or non-existent. Sailing ships could become becalmed and run out of supplies. Later immigrants benefited from the regularizing of schedules, ticket agencies, and improved ways of prepaying fares. Costs fell too: in 1816 a steerage to New York from Liverpool could cost £12, but by the 1890s it was possible to cross for less than £4. In very many cases later immigrants were able to join members of their own family or of their home community who helped to moderate the tensions of the uprooting. Knowledge of the United States grew with time, particularly as the number of letters from America received in Europe grew. If the following late-nineteenth-century Swedish 'American Ballad' is taken at face value, however, a level of ignorance could also remain.

Out there in the fields
There grows English money.
Ducks and chickens come raining down
Roasted geese, and others yet
Fly onto the table,
With knife and fork stuck in 'em.

Table 6.1 Total immigration by decade (in thousands)

1820–30	152	1881–90	5,247	1941–50	1,035
1831–40	599	1891–1900	3,688	1951–60	2,515
1841–50	1,713	1901–10	8,795	1961–70	3,322
1851–60	2,598	1911–20	5,736	1971–80	4,493
1861–70	2,315	1921–30	4,107	1981–90	7,338
1871–80	2,812	1931–40	528	1991–94	4,510

Table 6.1 shows the size of the flood of immigrants that has poured into the United States since figures were first collected in 1820. Immigration will be seen to have reached its first peak in the famine years of the 1850s; to have been comparatively low in the Civil War decade and in the 1870s and 1890s, decades in which the United States experienced economic recessions; and to have reached an all-time high in the decade 1901–10, when southern and eastern Europe in particular exported millions of emigrants, not merely to the United States. More accurately, immigration peaked in the decade 1905–14 when over 10 million people entered the country. Throughout the period 1841–1920 the annual rate of immigration never fell below 5.3 per thousand of the United Sates population, reaching close to 10 per thousand in the decades 1841–50, 1851–60, 1881–90 and peaking at 10.4 per thousand in 1901–10. Between 1931 and 1970 the ratio remained below 2.0 until the Seventies opened a period of accelerating legal and illegal immigration which took the ratio to 4.4 between 1991 and 1994.

Although immigrants have arrived in the United States from all over the world, some societies have provided a disproportionate share and there have recently been great changes in the composition of immigrants. Whereas Europe was the major source of immigrants before 1965, the Immigration Act of that year changed matters considerably. Between 1820 and 1965, 81.1 per cent of immigrants came from Europe; 2.8 per cent from Asia; 13.6 per cent from North America (including Mexico, Central America and the Caribbean); 1.5 per cent from South America; 0.05 per cent from Africa and 1.1 per cent from elsewhere. In stark contrast the figures for the period 1990–94 were 11.8, 28.2, 51.7, 5.3, 2.5 and 0.5 respectively.

Some parts of the nation have been more affected by immigration than others. Table 6.2 shows the position in 1890 on the eve of the massive immigration from south-eastern Europe and in 1920 on the eve of restriction. The South was the only section of the nation not to receive substantial numbers of immigrants around the turn of the century, though the South-west was to do so after 1945. Early-twentieth-century immigrants tended to remain on the east coast, drawn to the great cities and to the industrializing areas. The figures in Table 6.2 partly disguise the impact immigrants were having on the surrounding society in referring

Table 6.2 Percentage total population foreign-born, by region: 1890, 1920

	1890	1920
New England	47.2	61.0
Middle Atlantic	47.4	54.0
East North Central	44.5	42.6
West North Central	41.3	37.9
South Atlantic	5.9	6.2
East South Central	4.6	3.1
West South Central	11.6	11.3
Mountain	45.6	36.8
Pacific	51.0	46.6

only to the foreign-born. They do not include the children of the foreign-born who were very different from those whose ancestors had been in the United States for generations.

From the outset different immigrant groups preferred different areas. The 1880 census, for instance, revealed heavy concentrations of Irish-born in New York, Massachusetts and Pennsylvania, with a significant community in Illinois. Over 100,000 German-born were settled in New York, Illinois, Ohio, Wisconsin, Pennsylvania and Missouri. Over half the Norwegian-born in the country were in Minnesota and Wisconsin. Later groups showed similar tendencies to congregate, one consequence being that it is rare to find Italian-American literature set in the Mid-West or Jewish-American in the South. Willa Cather's Bohemians farmed in Nebraska, Abraham Cahan's David Levinsky created his rag-trade empire in New York, while Peter Finley Dunne's Irish philosopher sprang from the historic Irish community of Chicago.

▶ Uprooting and re-rooting

The United States has been in three minds about its immigrants. To begin with it preached and pursued Anglo-conformity, the desire to make the immigrant conform in every possible way to the host culture. Those who held the view of American nativists who supported bodies like the Know Nothings in the 1850s and the American Protective Association in the 1890s, clearly wanted immigrants to surrender all vestiges of their original culture. In 1909 in his play *The Melting Pot* Israel Zangwill, an English Jew, produced a second influential concept. The sense was given by the major character, David Quixano, in an exchange with his girlfriend:

> There she lies, the great melting-pot. Listen! Can't you hear the roaring and the bubbling? There gapes her mouth [points East], the harbour where a thousand mammoth feeders come from the

ends of the world to pour in their human freight. Ah, what a stirring and seething! Celt and Latin, Slav and Teuton, Greek and Syrian, black and yellow . . .

VERA [his girlfriend] Jews and Gentile –

DAVID Yes, East and West and North and South, the palm and the pine, the pole and the equator, the Crescent and the Cross, how the great Alchemist melts and fuses them with His purging flame. . . .

This was not quite Crèvecoeur's idea of amalgamation, as it suggested an equality among the ingredients and it reflected a progressive optimism that by melting something superior would emerge. More reflection, especially by emergent social scientists, called the idea into question and proposed a third version, known as cultural pluralism. The concept was largely the work of Horace Kallen and emerged from his experiences of immigrant Chicago, where he saw what later analysts would refer to as a salad bowl rather than a melting pot. This third view, now predominant, dealt with the fact that some immigrant values turned out to be more transient, more permeable than others, by differentiating between the public and private worlds, the more permeable belonging to the public. Such changes in public behaviour have been called behavioural assimilation, always easier to achieve than full or structural assimilation, especially if the immigrant arrived when young. The essence of these changes can be gathered from a passage in Mary Antin's autobiography *The Promised Land* (1912), where she recorded what happened to her and her family on arrival in the United States:

> We had to visit the stores and be dressed from head to foot in American clothing; we had to learn the mysteries of the iron stove, the washboard, and the speaking-tube; we had to learn to trade with the fruit peddler through the window, and not be afraid of the policeman; and above all we had to learn English . . . With our despised immigrant clothing we [had to] shed also our impossible Hebrew names.

Even such moderate changes in behaviour had their costs, however, in opening up a gap between generations. Older immigrants found it difficult and sometimes impossible to give up traditional ways. Antin did not list adjustment to the political system, but that was also vital. Since newcomers had to take an oath of allegiance if they wished to become citizens, they perforce had to adopt American political and constitutional values. It was not acceptable to be anything other than a liberal democrat. Thus in their attack on the Chinese in 1877 the California State Senate assumed it was reiterating what all knew were the minimum requirements for membership of American society when it charged:

During their entire settlement in California they have never adapted themselves to our habits, mode of dress, or our educational system, have never learned the sanctity of an oath, never discovered the difference between right and wrong, never ceased the worship of their idol gods, or advanced a step beyond the traditions of their native hide.

In point of fact most Chinese in California had arrived as contract labour and largely regarded themselves as sojourners – that is, transients who need not adjust since they lived apart and intended to return to China. They did not intend to attempt behavioural assimilation. But there was more to the matter than that for, when the Japanese did try, they were attacked on different grounds. A Los Angeles newspaper in 1910 reminded its readers that

Had the Japanese labourer throttled his ambition to progress along the lines of American citizenship and industrial development, he probably would have attracted small attention of the public mind. [But] Japanese ambition is to progress beyond mere servility to the place of the better class of American workman and to own a home with him. The moment that this position is exercised, the Japanese ceases to be an ideal labourer.

The level of assimilation was to be that of the contemporary black, very much short of the second level that sociologists have postulated, structural assimilation.

In reality it was very unlikely that immigrants could achieve full structural assimilation, defined as a full integration into the intimate, personal relationships of the host society. They were very unlikely to marry into it. Most immigrants could not make friends in childhood with members of the host community, either because they arrived too late or because they lived apart. Residential segregation had two aspects, both of which have to be considered. It was not merely the case that concentration spelled discrimination. Frequently members of ethnic groups chose to live close to one another in order to support the kinds of institutions which could survive only if there were a sufficient clientele. In some cases as with Orthodox Jews it was very necessary to live close to the synagogue; in others to live close to a café which sold familiar foods and drinks and took newspapers from the old country.

One of the most important reasons for living close to others of one's own kind was to belong to a burial society, which would ensure that the correct rites were followed and an appropriate funeral arranged even in the foreign land. These burial societies were extraordinary in their number and in the narrowness of their membership, sometimes including only persons from a single village in Europe. Thus 25 of the 35 Italian mutual benefit societies incorporated between 1903 and 1910 in Cleveland limited membership to persons born in a particular village, the Italian sense of localism being particularly strong. Many ethnic groups also chose to provide their members with a social focus in a city-wide association, as Romanians, Greeks and Slovaks did in Cleveland, Poles and Lithuanians did in several Massachusetts towns, and Irish, Germans and Scandinavians, among others, did, in San Francisco.

Relationships within these associations often merely continued ones that had existed in the old country and hardly needed to be supplanted. They often rested on the support members of groups gave each other in arranging passages, jobs and lodgings. Though the work of Oscar Handlin and others has argued that the immigrants were dangerously uprooted from their native lands, it is surprising how much soil they managed to take with them. Once a few migrants had pioneered the way others often followed in a 'chain migration'. For instance between 1887 and 1947 8,000 people followed the original emigrant Francesco Barone from Valledolmo in Sicily to Buffalo, New York. Once again Italians appear to have been particularly gregarious in the later nineteenth century. Among those settling in Cleveland around 1900, fully a quarter arrived in chains of 100 migrants or more, while only five Romanians and fewer than four Slovaks tended to come from the same village. In the earlier period the Irish very probably resorted to chain migration, earlier migrants very definitely providing a large percentage of the funds for those coming later. The same is probably the case for Jews. All this did mean that the uprooting was not quite as destructive as might be assumed; perhaps the metaphor should be one of transplanting.

Although it is proper to stress the interaction between the immigrant and the host community, that between immigrants of differing groups should not be forgotten. Indeed due to residential segregation it was often more likely that members of different ethnic groups would interact with each other than with the native stock, in school, at work and on the streets. From the mid-nineteenth century immigrants found the Catholic Irish in positions of authority, unacceptable to some groups, in two important fields: politics and the Roman Catholic Church. Consequently there were political riots in Philadelphia in 1844 which had their origins in traditional tensions between the Protestant and Catholic Irish. Some Polish signalled the level of their discontent with Irish control of the Catholic Church by seceding and founding their own, the Polish National Catholic Church. The Irish also came to dominate many labour unions which they used against other ethnic groups as well as against their employers, as the Chinese in California would testify. It was also true, however, that the Irish developed their political control partly by offering welfare services to other immigrant groups. As such rivalries suggest, the nineteenth-century immigrant world was one of sharp demarcations between ethnic groups with, for instance, little intermarriage. It took until the twentieth century, when some populations had been long established, for analysts to begin to see what they called a 'Triple Melting Pot', intermarriage between the three general Jewish, Catholic and Protestant groups, irrespective of national or linguistic origin. Marriage across the Jewish–Catholic divide, however, has remained rare even in the later twentieth century, suggesting that some cultural barriers cannot easily be broken down.

The virulence of ethnic conflicts has helped to explain the relative absence of class conflict in the European sense, for ethnicity in the United States warped traditional European class structures. Immigrants were more likely to identify with wealthier members of their own group than to fight them. Certain ethnic groups, the Protestant British, the Irish and the Jews, for instance, were attracted into the labour movement but not all went on into socialism, which developed independently. Immigrants came to the United States in order to rise in the world, not to defend hereditary positions, and largely failed to develop a consciousness of class. The immense variety of backgrounds, languages, religions, even skin colours, all militated against a blending of ethnic groups into a single class. Thus there were a variety of immigrant experiences making generalizations suspect. American society and culture, however, have always been partly the product of the demands, drives and experiences of immigrant groups.

▶ The immigrants and American culture

Paradoxes abound at every phase of the immigrants' experience of American culture. In the ante-bellum period, American scholars, scientists and doctors looked to German universities for training and inspiration, to Paris, London and Rome for culture; theirs was a provincial culture. 'No author', wrote Nathaniel Hawthorne in his preface to *The Marble Faun* (1859), '... can conceive of the difficulty of writing a Romance about a country where there is no shadow, no antiquity, no mystery, no picturesque and gloomy wrong, nor anything but a commonplace prosperity, in broad and simple daylight, as is happily the case with my dear native land.' Young American artists streamed across the Atlantic in search of antiquities, mysteries and culture. Those who travelled the other direction in search of commonplace prosperity, the poor immigrants Wellingborough Redburn observed in Herman Melville's *Redburn* (1847), seemed to be drawn from the lowliest class. The conditions they experienced in steerage were memorably described by Melville: 'In every corner, the females were huddled together, weeping and lamenting; children were asking bread from their mothers, who had none to give; and old men, seated upon the floor, were leaning back against the heads of the water-casks, with closed eyes and fetching their breath with a gasp.' When they arrived they were confronted with the daunting tasks of surviving in an alien culture, and often upon the slenderest means. In practice, what

Americans understood as their culture, and which we qualify as *high* culture, excluded the immigrants, devalued their national traditions, scorned their languages, and regarded variations from the Anglo-Saxon, Protestant norms as in every case inferior. They were often judged harshly:

> And the emigrants! They are horrible. They're not at all like those who made America. Today's emigrant is simply Europe's rubbish, its waste matter, a lazy, cowardly, impotent little manikin drained of energy without which there's no getting on here. A modern emigrant is incapable of making life, all he can do is look for a ready-made, safe and smug existence.

The irony behind this withering judgement – made by Maxim Gorky in 1906 – was that in it he was voicing prejudices which were already deeply ingrained in America. Despite his distaste for American materialism and hypocrisy, Gorky largely agreed with the nativists on this question. If, by the later nineteenth century, America was a nation of immigrants, there was a gap between the reality of immigrant life and the myths of the society which promised far-reaching opportunities and rewards for innovation and hard work. As immigrant communities grew in size, wealth and self-confidence, they sought to find a place in the national pantheon for their national heroes. In New York City parks there are statues of Beethoven, Simon Bolivar, Robert Burns, Columbus, Garibaldi, Goethe, Dante, Don Quixote, Alexander Humboldt, Louis Kossuth, José Marti, Mazzini, Albert Bertel Thorvaldsen (the Danish sculptor), Verdi and Giovanni da Verrazano (the Italian explorer who sighted New York eighty-five years before Henry Hudson, and for whom the bridge linking Staten Island and Brooklyn was named): virtually every city has similar statues, each a small monument to the efforts of immigrant communities to achieve recognition.

It could hardly be expected that immigrants would soon make a contribution to an American culture then dominated by Longfellow, Emerson and Irving. Even in provincial America the gap between Melville, from a very distinguished Knickerbocker family and married to the daughter of the Chief Justice of the Massachusetts Supreme Court, and the illiterate immigrants huddled in steerage was too great. Generations would be required. If the immigrants were remote from the great heights of culture, they were right in the middle of the festering problem of urbanization. 'We cannot shut our eyes', wrote Josiah Strong in *The Twentieth Century City* (1898), 'to the fact that the foreign population, as a whole, is depressing our average intelligence and morality in the direction of the dead-line of ignorance and vice.' Observers noted the links connecting the immigrants with big-city political machines and 'Bosses'. Try as they might, reformers met with little success in the effort to divide the immigrants from the corrupt machines. It was easy to blame the ignorance and venality of the new arrivals for the many ills of city life. The hostile contempt of Know Nothings, and their political heirs in the Republican Party in New York, was perhaps one of the reasons why the political bosses of Tammany Hall and the immigrants established such a quick and effective alliance. Instead of improving things for the immigrants, many feared that reform would make matters worse. Throughout the rest of the century immigrants remained at the heart of the problems raised by the cities.

It took Americans several generations to temper fears about immigrants. One of the crucial advances in understanding came through journalists, progressive reformers and sociologists who studied the city. The transition from village to metropolis was, according to the German sociologist Ferdinand Tönnies, accompanied by the collapse of *Gemeinschaft* relationships based upon tradition and communal authority. In the metropolis individuals acted only out of self-interest. Selfishness and naked competition would, it was feared, lead to a collapse of social discipline. New York, and other large American cities, seemed to contemporaries frightening illustrations of this new world of social pathology which Tönnies described as *Gesellschaft*. American sociologists who studied the city, and particularly those associated with Robert E Park (who had studied with Simmel in Berlin) and W I Thomas at the University of Chicago, argued that there was an abundance of intermediate structures created within urban slums and immigrant ghettos. Individuals belonged to groups, whether determined by nationality, region, locality, or even village; their religious and racial identities gave them a strong sense of difference from other groups. (The history of immigrant religious communities closely reflects these sectional tensions.) The idea that the immigrants arrived in America and found themselves in an undifferentiated environment, in which individuals were on their own – that they had gone directly from a world of village *Gemeinschaft* to urban *Gesellschaft* – was far from the truth. Immigrants often came with a relative's or countryman's address, and they in turn sent for others. Mutual aid at first took the most basic form of personal charity, a poor immigrant was helped by a richer one, and by fellow countrymen already in America. As the scale of immigration grew in the 1880s, charitable activities within the immigrant communities expanded.

The immigrant areas in most large American cities soon bristled with societies, fraternal associations, and businesses which served their needs. When they reached a certain size, immigrant communities created many of those mediating cultural structures which broke down the worst aspects of urban isolation and *anomie*. The immigrants in time published books in their native languages, and produced newspapers, magazines and, in larger cities, were able to support vaudeville and theatre. The German-American community in New York were enthusiastic Wagnerites, and pushed the Metropolitan Opera towards the new German music. Ethnic newspapers like the Jewish *Daily Forward* did much to sustain the sometimes tenuous cohesion within immigrant communities, and they provided a window upon the larger arena of American life. In turn, ghetto journalists like Abraham Cahan and Morris Winchevsky were able to present the sometimes exotic world of the ghetto to readers of the American press. The mediation they could achieve was limited, but their activities met with sympathetic responses from writers (like Hutchins Hapgood, whose splendid book, *The Spirit of the Ghetto* (1902) was written under the influence of Cahan), and from liberal and progressive social reformers like Jane Addams. Hull House, on Halstead Avenue in south Chicago, was founded by Addams and Ellen Gates Starr in 1889. It functioned as a centre for the educational development of the immigrant poor. Addams and Starr soon found that it was not enough to offer classes in citizenship and literacy to immigrants. The cultural missionary work soon led them to sympathetic involvement in trade union struggles, factory inspection, and the eight-hour day campaign. In a sense the immigrants were pawns in a struggle between the high-minded reformers and the corrupt bosses of the urban political machines. But with the appearance of Addams's *Forty Years at Hull House* (1910), and Lillian Wald's *The House on Henry Street* (1915), which described a similar project in New York, the immigrants were beginning to be perceived as subject as well as object.

It was no mere coincidence that at the time when the urban settlements were founded, and when the 'New Immigration' was dramatically increasing, immigrants become a real presence in literature. One of the earliest examples was Stephen Crane's *Maggie: A Girl of the Streets* (1893). Excited by the new possibilities for literature opened up by the naturalism of Zola, Crane portrayed the violence, drunkenness and corruption of slum life in New York. *Maggie*, which asked searching questions of the relations between moral codes and social conditions, gave a powerful portrait of the culture of the new immigrants. When Pete and Maggie go to the 'show', Crane beautifully captures the scene:

> As a final effort, the singer rendered some verses which described a vision of Britain annihilated by America, and Ireland bursting her bonds. A carefully prepared crisis was reached in the last line of the last verse, where the singer threw out her arms and cried, 'The star-spangled banner.' Instantly a great cheer swelled from the throats of this assemblage of the masses. . . . There was a heavy rumble of booted feet thumping the floor. Eyes gleamed with sudden fire, and calloused hands waved frantically in the air.

Upton Sinclair's powerful novel *The Jungle* (1906) contained an explosive account of the conditions in 'Packingtown' (Chicago). The Lithuanian immigrants who have been brought into the stockyards to depress wages are abused on a systematic basis. Sinclair records the weakening of traditional customs under the pressures of capitalism and dog-eat-dog individualism. His main concern was to make a case for socialism. No one could have been more surprised than Sinclair, the most famous socialist propagandist in America, when the public seized upon his portrayal of the insanitary conditions in the canning industry. Hoping to build the New Jerusalem, he created the Food and Drug Administration: 'I aimed at the public's heart and by accident I hit it in the stomach.'

But all too often the vaudeville caricatures of Wop, Polack, shanty Irish and Jew prevail in literary representation. The same sterotypes in fact appear within the ghetto, but serve rather different purposes: they enabled the partly assimilated to mock the greenhorn. The cultural life of the ghetto was richer than generally credited. There was, however, an undercurrent of sadness: the cultural achievements of the immigrants were self-extinguishing. Social mobility creamed off the cleverest and most adaptable. The inexorable pressure towards assimilation left a ghetto culture unable to believe in its own permanence. Its memorials are in diaries, letters, native-language newspapers and journals, and, supremely, in autobiographical memoirs.

The literary forms which lent themselves to immigrant writing were the realistic novel and fictive memoir. An important moment of recognition came when William Dean Howells welcomed Abraham Cahan's *Yekl: A Tale of the New York Ghetto*, when it appeared in 1896. The author was a recent immigrant from Russia who had established himself as a socialist and journalist. A disciple of Howells, Cahan wrote consciously within the modes of realism. Although *Yekl* is not the first book by an immigrant, it is the first to be seriously considered as literature. Howells noted that Cahan, like Stephen Crane in *Maggie*, has done his duty as an artist by having drawn aside the thick veil of ignorance which parts the comfortable few from the uncomfortable many in New York. Such books as *Yekl*, a bitter-sweet tale of love in the ghetto, and autobiographies like Mary Antin's *From Plotzk to Boston* (1899) and *The Promised Land* (1912), Jacob Riis's *The Making of an American* (1901), Edward Bok's *The Americanization of Edward Bok* (1920), and Ludwig Lewisohn's *Up Stream: An American Chronicle* (1926) now began to establish the dominant forms of immigrant writing. It was strongly autobiographical, and usually took the form of a success story, if often with an ironic twist. The immediate ancestry of this body of writing lay in the self-improving ideas of Samuel Smiles, the Horatio Alger books, and the underlying myth signified by the story of the man who rose 'from log cabin to White House'. In the late nineteenth century such ideas were the staple product of American popular culture, and they repeatedly enforced the message that, by hard work, perseverance, and quick wits, it was indeed possible to achieve an unimaginable success within American capitalism – an idea that had attracted many immigrants to the United States in the first place. The immigrant experience, despite the difficult adjustments which were required, reinforced this aspect of American ideology, and the immigrant autobiographies and memoirs became an addition to the genre.

The immigrant success story, however, had another side which was suggested by the titles of the now neglected novels of Anzia Yezierska: *Hungry Hearts* (1920) and *Children of Loneliness* (1923). Where for Mary Antin the immigrants' arrival in America was the beginning of a new life, for Yezierska, America was at best a mixed blessing. Promising so much, America cruelly frustrated those who came most open-heartedly. For Antin, 'America' was an idea which stood not only for a new society but also for the very possibility of human self-fulfilment. Inevitably, romantic dreams came into contact with the intractable and often harsh reality of life in the urban ghetto. This is the theme of Abraham Cahan's later, better-known novel, *The Rise of David Levinsky* (1917). It is a remarkable book which spoke directly to the romantic dreams of the immigrant, but contained many home truths about America and about immigrants themselves. Cahan was an ironic writer, and irony was a way to comprehend the sometimes harsh distance between dream and social reality that was so often characteristic of the immigrant experience of American life. Levinsky arrives in America from the Pale of Settlement in Russia, and gradually comes to terms with the new reality of American life. A crucial symbolic threshold is crossed when Levinsky, strongly advised that 'one must be presentable in America', has his fore-locks cut off. A scene follows which was enacted hundreds of thousands of times:

> I stood before him, necktie and collar in hand, not knowing what to do with them, till he showed me how to put them on.
> 'Don't worry, David', he consoled me, 'When I came here I, too, had to learn these things.' When he was through with the job he took me in front of a looking-glass. 'Quite an American, isn't he?' he said to the barber, beamingly. 'And a good-looking fellow, too.'
> When I took a look at the mirror I was bewildered. I scarcely recognized myself.
> I was mentally parading my 'modern' make-up before Matilda. A pang of yearning clutched my heart. It was a momentary feeling. For the rest, I was all in a flutter with embarrassment and a novel relish of existence. It was as though the hair-cut and the American clothes had changed my identity.

Levinsky went to school in the new land: he learned to deceive and cheat, to exploit workers, and how to make a fortune. His is a success story, and his narrative, related in the first person, is obviously modelled upon the autobiographies of figures like Riis and Bok. But at the end of the book Levinsky is a hollow, lonely man, more to be pitied than envied. Cahan is not trying to score a narrow or partisan point off the budding Levinskys of the lower East Side. Certainly his well-known sympathy for the unions and advocacy of democratic socialism provides a way of looking at Levinsky – as a 'fleecer of labor' and a 'cockroach manufacturer'. We are given other perspectives on Levinsky, especially those offered by the women he has met, which make it clear that Cahan's criticism of the dream of success has more than a political meaning; rather, Levinsky's failure is to be judged on an emotional and humane basis. Instead of cutthroat competition, through the portrait of Levinsky's emotional failure Cahan holds up an alternative image of selflessness, sacrifice and solidarity. Cahan's irony was based on a perceived gap between the intensity of the immigrant's aspiration and the reality of its fulfilment in America.

Although there was nothing like a uniform 'immigrant experience', the basic events of passage from the past and the familiar to the present and the new imposed a form on consciousness itself. The dichotomy between old world and new, and the division of identity (which Cahan so vividly captures), expressed a larger economic and social dilemma which all immigrants faced. The space between one world and another, or one generation and another, was often filled with irony. There are kind and affectionate ironies, as when Mike Gold in *Jews Without Money* (1930) describes his father as an 'upright conservative pauper'. There is a deeper irony, however, in the father's disillusionment and bitterness at his own failure in America:

> 'Look at me,' he said. 'Twenty years in America, and poorer than when I came. A suspender shop I had, and it was stolen from me by a villain. A house painter foreman I became, and fell off a scaffold. Now bananas I sell, and even at that I am a failure. It is all luck.'
>
> He sighed and puffed at his pipe.
>
> 'Ach, Gott, what a rich country America is! What an easy place to make one's fortune! Look at all the rich Jews! Why has it been so easy for them, so hard for me? I am just a poor little Jew without money.'
>
> 'Poppa, lots of Jews have no money', I said to comfort him.
>
> 'I know it, my son,' he said, 'but don't be one of them. It's better to be dead in this country than not to have money. Promise me you'll be rich when you grow up, Mikey!'
>
> 'Yes, poppa.'

Mikey, of course, has other ideas, which lead him to Max Eastman's *Masses* and *Liberator*, to the *New Masses*, and to the Communist Party. That we know all this adds yet another layer of irony to his father's words of advice. Gold's and Cahan's political irony is not characteristic of immigrant writing as a whole, but is a useful reminder that the seemingly straightforward autobiographies and realistic novels become, through their use and emendation of the structural irony in the immigrant experience, complex texts in their own right.

There were other points of tension which complicated the 'rags to riches' myth. In the nineteenth century, traditional religious cultures came into open conflict with the materialism and secular spirit of the modern world. This was to give yet another ironic tension to the immigrant experience. As Sarah Reznikoff writes in her 'Early History of a Seamstress', her desire for education (traditionally allowed only to men in Orthodox Jewish culture in the *shtetl*) initiated a conflict which could only be resolved by migration to America – but in America there was no time for education, only work. In Nathan Reznikoff's autobiographical narrative, a young boy in America finds the ritual fast more an endurance test than a meaningful religious observance. Religious faith itself becomes an unintended casualty of immigration. The conflicts within families and between sexes altered the way people viewed each other. Expectations long-sanctioned by tradition were undermined, and tradition itself became problematic. Irony became one of the great liberating tools in the struggle against the burden of tradition. But such ironies had an uncomfortable habit of cutting both ways. For the thoroughly Americanized second and third generation, modern America was ashes in the mouth, and tradition suddenly seemed more relevant. When asked to write about the Jewish experience in America, the hero of Joseph Heller's *Good as Gold* (1979) discovers that he knows nothing at all about it. That is the bitterest irony of all.

▶ Growing up in America

By the second and third generation, these ironies were sharpened and made more specific because America itself was more accessible. Literary life became visibly more plural as a German-Jewish generation of writers emerged (Hergesheimer, Hecht, Frank, Lewisohn – to say nothing of Dreiser, not Jewish of course, but close to his immigrant roots). Along with an emergence in literature, the sons and grandsons of immigrants began to appear in every area of American cultural life: popular entertainment, music, painting, photography, the theatre. So pronounced was their arrival that the conflicts facing second- and third-generation immigrants emerged in the popular culture. The struggle between tradition and the American way of life was exceptionally difficult in real life, but on the stage reconciliation was not too difficult to bring about. In the third act of Anne Nichol's *Abie's Irish Rose* (1924), gentile Rose keeps a kosher kitchen for her husband Abie, but makes ham for her non-Jewish friends. They have two babies: Patrick Joseph and Rebecca. Relations between Christians and Jews may have been uneasy in the real world, but on Broadway the priest and the rabbi shake hands and agree that love conquers all. *Abie's Irish Rose* is a 'melting pot' play, after Zangwill, in which the old heritage of distrust is wished away:

> What with all the shells bursting [on the Argonne], and the
> shrapnel flying, with no one knowing just what moment death

would come, Catholics, Hebrews and Protestants alike forgot
their prejudice and came to realize that all faiths and creeds have
about the same destination after all.

Sociologists might remind us that intermarriage between Jews and Catholics was uncommon. At the turn of the century the rate of Jewish 'in-marriage' was just under 99 per cent. By 1950 the figure was 96 per cent. (Since the 1950s the rate of exogamous marriages has vastly expanded, to the point where the survivability of the Jewish community in America has come – in the medium term – to look precarious.) How, then, can we explain the immense popularity of *Abie's Irish Rose*? Mainly in terms of the perfectly reasonable wish for some easing of ethnic tensions. The play symbolically enacts not so much the end of Jewish apartness as the beginning of Jewish integration, as Jews, into the community. It evades the reality of racial and religious tension, but not the underlying process, which was to bring Jews, and other ethnic groups, into fuller participation in American life. The price for that was a slice of ham.

The prosperity of the Twenties acted as a great solvent in the ghettos of New York. Business was good, and as immigrants prospered they moved into middle-class neighbourhoods. A decade later there was an explosion of interest in what it had been like to grow up in the ghetto. Mike Gold's *Jews Without Money* set the fashion in 1930, and was followed by a novel of substantially greater merit: Henry Roth's *Call It Sleep* (1934). Roth's re-creation of his childhood was heavily influenced by psychoanalytic thought, by then well established in New York, and by the techniques of stream-of-consciousness narrative and the use of symbols pre-eminently shown in the work of Joyce, Gertrude Stein and Virginia Woolf. *Call It Sleep* is, with Faulkner's *The Sound and the Fury*, one of the very few American books which belong to the period of high-European modernism between the wars. What may be Roth's greatest innovation is his treatment of one of the most fundamental of all immigrant dilemmas, the linguistic one. The Schearl family use Yiddish at home, which Roth represents by a clear, lean, standard English devoid of mannerisms. Roth counterpoints this with a close phonetic transcription of a grotesque Brooklyn-Yiddish-American-English as spoken on the streets of New York (Howells, writing of Cahan in 1896, prophetically wondered whether 'we shall have a New York jargon which shall be to English what the native Yiddish of his characters is to Hebrew, and it will be interlarded with Russian, Polish and German words, as their present jargon is with English vocables and with American slang.'):

> 'Aaa, dawn be a wise-guy! Hooz tuckin' f'om vinninn'! A dollar 'n' sexty-fife gestern! A thuler 'n'sompt 'n – ove hadee cends – Sonday! An' Monday night in back f'om Hymen's taileh-shop, rummy, *tuh* sevendy. Oy, yuh sh'd die. An' I sez if yuh ken give a good dill, Abe, yuh sheoll dill in jail auraddy!'

Which might be translated as:

> Oh, don't be a wise-guy! Who's taking [anything] from [the] winnings? A dollar and sixty-five yesterday! A thaler [?a half-dollar] and something-over eighty cents – on Sunday. And [on] Monday night in [the] back of Hyman's tailor shop, [we played] rummy, [and I won] two [dollars and] seventy [cents]. Well, you would have died to have seen it! And I said, if you can't give [me] a good deal, Abe, you'll surely [wind up] dealing in jail!

Roth helps us to see that within the ghetto it was *English* which was the bastard tongue.

Call it Sleep is an 'education' novel, if not a full-blown *bildungsroman*, and throughout the decade memoirists like Joseph Freeman (*An American Testament*, 1936) and novelists from immigrant families were busily at work on multi-volume novel sequences reconstructing the way ethnic children grew up. The most famous of these realistic narratives was James T Farrell's portrait of Irish-American life in Chicago (*Young Lonigan*, 1932; *The Young Manhood of Studs Lonigan*, 1934; *Judgment Day*, 1935). No less striking was Daniel Fuchs's trilogy describing Jewish life in the Williamsburg section of Brooklyn (*Summer in Williamsburg*, 1934; *Homage to Blenholt*, 1936; *Low Company*, 1937).

By this time mass immigration was over, and the tragedy of European Jewry was beginning to unfold. As the process of acculturation proceeded, many Jews, especially among the younger intellectuals, identified Jewishness itself with the restraints which foreignness imposed on their families. Lionel Trilling's rejection of a Jewish dimension to his criticism, and his lack of interest in Jewish culture, defines the situation with clarity. On the Left, the Communist Party offered a different path towards integration, but one which no less comprehensively demanded the abandonment of the traditional religious culture. Many Jewish and ethnic writers drifted into the Party orbit, and some, like the playwright Clifford Odets (*Waiting for Lefty*, 1935), actually learned from the experience. But for most the attempt to write proletarian literature was an unhappy and brief adventure before proceeding on their various ways. The Jewish presence in the Party was always strong, and throughout the Thirties influential. But the Stalin–Hitler pact and the war itself accelerated the process of integration by which ethnic intellectuals became simply Americans and joined the national consensus. The writers of Trilling's generation in New York had 'arrived' by the 1940s, and the New York family, as it was later called, emerged as the dominant voice of post-totalitarian humanism. Critics including Trilling, Meyer Schapiro, Harold Rosenberg, and Philip Rahv; the poets Delmore Schwartz and Howard Nemerov; and novelists such as Norman Mailer and Saul Bellow signalled the presence, on a massive scale, of writers from immigrant backgrounds. The arrival had taken approximately fifty years from Howell's review of *Yekl*. When, in 1951,

Trilling wrote a long piece rescuing Howells from neglect, no one seems to have caught the irony.

The temper of immigrant writing after the Second World War was almost exclusively set by Jewish writers. Few of them wrote from within the religious faith. Judaism, rather, was an embarrassment, to be mainly dealt with in terms of comedy and irony. Ethnic consciousness declined throughout the Fifties as assimilation proceeded apace. Inevitably a new round of ironies began. Philip Roth portrayed a comic confrontation between unworldly religious orthodoxy and the new, assimilated suburban Jew in 'Eli, The Fanatic' (*Goodbye, Columbus*, 1959). Not wholly free from nostalgia, Roth finds the fanatic more praiseworthy in the end than the surburbanites. The title of the volume is ironic, but it is an Americanized form of the knowing irony of Sholom Aleichem and Mendele Mocher Sforim rather than the specific form of structural irony which had been so characteristic of immigrant writing. The preoccupations of immigrant literature lost some of their uniqueness in this period, when the living experience of immigration passed on to other ethnic groups. The urban ghetto now belonged to the blacks, and to their literature, and soon they too felt displaced by the arrival of new Hispanic and Asian immigrants. It was mainly through nostalgia and humour that this experience was recalled by Jews (the numerous books by Harry Golden and the H*Y*M*A*N K*A*P*L*A*N novels of Leo Rosten). There were important exceptions, such as Bernard Malamud's *The Assistant* (1957), but for most Jewish writers their roots in the immigrant experience was less significant than their awareness of the travails and complexity of contemporary American life. Characteristic tones of Jewish writing in the Sixties were either grossly self-indulgent (Roth's *Portnoy's Complaint*, 1969), blackly comic (Joseph Heller's *Catch-22*, 1961) or else painfully introspective (Saul Bellow's *Herzog*, 1964): in each case the novels transcended the specific historic experiences of Jews in America and spoke to the common experience.

Something of that aspiration for universality within specificity has ebbed with the much-puffed return to ethnicity over the past two decades. The great renewal of interest in ethnic foods, dress and music were marketing opportunities. With the retrieval of Yiddish as a field for academic research, if not yet for cultural expression, there are signs of a deeper, more systemic interest in previously submerged cultural identities. Many groups, previously content to ignore their roots in the immigration experience, sought to rediscover their own, and their family's origins. It is a phenomenon of considerable interest, but it is not, yet, possible to say that the rediscovery of ethnicity has deep-seated implications for our understanding of the immigrant experience.

For 'ethnic attachments' are not at all the same thing as adhesion to a faith. Perhaps ethnicity may come to stand in American culture as an alternative to religious doctrine and observance. In the Jewish community the growing interest in ethnicity has come at the same time that endogamous marriage has sharply declined. The figures are disputed, but they point toward a steady decline in the number of Jews who marry other Jews and identify themselves with the institutions (from Hadassah to the Jewish Community Centers) which have for generations been in the vanguard of communal life. Being wealthier, and less threatened by anti-Semitism, has meant being less 'Jewish'. The gap between the traditionalists in the Hassidic community and the Jews of suburban America has never been deeper; religious extremism does not play very well in the suburbs. Perhaps in the end it was Saks and Bloomingdale's which undid the Jews in America.

The achievement of Isaac Bashevis Singer, whose books have all been written in Yiddish, inevitably stands to one side of the general movement of Jewish and ethnic writing in America. Singer is an undoubted genius, and, since Heine, the greatest of all Jewish writers. But he can never truly be part of an American literature (the same point might hold true for Nabokov) in that the exile and *émigré*, as opposed to the immigrant, only reluctantly if at all consciously accept a new identity for themselves. Those of Singer's stories and novels which have been set in America do not constitute the most important part of his work. Perhaps Singer's reputation was helped by the rebirth of ethnicity, but that is purely fortuitous and accidental; in any culture 'Gimpel the Fool' and *The Slave* would be acknowledged as the masterpieces they undoubtedly are. (Except, that is, in his native Poland where Singer's books are wholly unknown.)

It is no small irony that the run-down slums of the lower East Side in New York, and similar ghettos elsewhere, have come to stand for values which for many people are now under threat. The ghetto was remembered in the Sixties as the place where one's hopes for America survived intact. It was a symbol of an unalienated way of life, at once warm and human. And thus it joined the great procession of popular myths and fantasies feeding American culture. The ghetto and its immigrants have been transformed from the tense and ironic locale of Abraham Cahan to the chic sepia-tinted Little Italy of Mario Puzo's Don Corleone (*The Godfather*, 1969). Nostalgia, like other commodities, is now packaged and promoted. Even in such an implausible guise, the ghetto retains its power to remind us of a world we have now lost.

▶ For further reading

William Boelhower, *Through a Glass Darkly: Ethnic Semiosis in American Literature* (1987).

Matthew Frye Jacobson, *Special Sorrows: The Diasporic Imagination of Irish, Polish, and Jewish Immigrants in the United States* (1995).

Milton M Gordon, *Human Nature, Class, and Ethnicity* (1978).

Maldwyn Allen Jones, *American Immigration* (2nd edition, 1960).

Silva Pedraza, *Origins and Destinies: Immigration, Race, and Ethnicity in America* (1995).

Werner Sollors, *Beyond Ethnicity: Consent and Descent in American Culture* (1986).

Stephan Thernstrom (ed.), *Harvard Encyclopedia of American Ethnic Groups* (1980).

7 The black experience

C W E Bigsby and Roger Thompson

▶ Blacks and slavery

Between 1619 and 1860 some 400,000 blacks were transported from Africa to what is now the United States. This was not a large number as compared with the total Atlantic slave trade which carried around 9.5 million from Africa to the New World, most of them to the sugar plantations of Brazil and the Caribbean. Whether slaves were transported direct to North America or by way of the Caribbean made little or no difference to the blacks themselves; torn from their families and villages, marched to the coast, confined in Barracoons to await a passing ship, then crammed below decks for upwards of two months, they were finally brought ashore to be auctioned off. How many enslaved blacks perished in Africa it is impossible to say, but on average (depending on period) between 6 and 16 per cent died during the voyage and perhaps as many again during the subsequent period of seasoning.

In one respect, however, those Africans who found themselves in North America may be deemed to have fared better than those who went elsewhere; they became part of a population which was not only self-sustaining, but which actually grew at more or less the same rate as the surrounding white population. Thus, the abolition of the slave trade of the United States in 1807 did not bring about a decline in slave numbers, as was the case in Britain's West Indian colonies. The great westward advance of the cotton empire of the early nineteenth century depended on ever-increasing numbers of American-born slaves. In fact, the original 400,000 black slaves transported to North America had, by the time of the Civil War, increased ten-fold to more than 4 million.

One consequence of the natural increase of slaves in America was that among them little in the way of specific African practices, institutions, customs or beliefs survived. Except in the very earliest years, blacks born in Africa were always outnumbered by the American-born; and probably less than one in a hundred of the slaves emancipated by Lincoln had actually seen Africa. Even in the eighteenth century, when recently arrived African captives, recognizable by their tribal scars and wild appearance, were to be found in sizeable numbers, their ability to communicate with one another, on account of differences in language and culture, was strictly limited. For them, as for the native-born, the only common language and institutions available were those provided by their white masters.

And yet it would be hasty to assume that, because it is difficult to trace specific linguistic and institutional links, nothing from the African past survived. It is hard to imagine, for example, that slave songs, slave stories and, closely associated with both, slave religion, were entirely the product of their American experiences – that *any* group, consigned to slavery, whatever its previous history, would have produced the same songs, stories and beliefs. Altogether it makes much more sense to suppose that, as with other immigrants, something survived, even though it is definable only as a style of music or a way of seeing things. Culture, as Lawrence Levine has argued, is 'not a fixed condition but a process: the product of the interaction between the past and the present'. This was, of course, true of white American culture no less than of black; the difference was that blacks looked back on *two* pasts – their own, dimly remembered, African past, and the Euro-American past from which the dominant culture drew its strength, and to which they themselves owed not only their language but also many of their beliefs.

This mixed and ambiguous heritage is evident in the work of the first black American poets emerging, surprisingly enough, in the eighteenth century. Phyllis Wheatley (1753–84), the young slave of a Bostonian family, celebrated in verse the enforced move from Africa to America as a liberation from paganism, a redemption of the soul consequent upon an enslavement of the body. Yet, despite the patent prejudices of her audience, she was equally capable of observing the ironies of her situation, linking a conventional opposition to tyranny with her own circumstances. In her poem to the Right Honourable William Earl of Dartmouth she observes:

> Should you, my lord, while you peruse my song,
> Wonder from whence my love of *Freedom* sprung,
> Whence flow these wishes for the common good,
> By feeling hearts alone best understood,
> I, young in life, by seeming cruel fate
> Was snatched from *Afric's* fancied happy seat:
> What pangs excruciating must molest,
> What sorrows labor in my parents' breast!
> Steel'd was the soul and by no misery mov'd
> That from a father seiz'd his babe belov'd.
> Such, such my case. And can I then but pray
> Others may never feel tyrannic sway?

The mere fact of her ability to intrude her own racial perspective into the orthodoxies of English poetics stood as a challenge as well as an apparent, if inevitable, act of capitulation. Her ability to learn was itself a social as well as a literary fact at a time when the presumption of incorrigible ignorance in blacks was uneasily bolstered by laws prohibiting their education. And her command of literary form was potentially a subversion of the intricate balance of social and political as much as aesthetic structure.

Much the same could be said of the slave narrative, which was intended to do much more than narrate a history of injustice. It was a declaration of literary and social independence. It was simultaneously an assertion of selfhood and a set of political propositions. By definition, such narratives celebrated an achieved freedom but they were also agents of that freedom in offering paradigms of social action and in constituting evidence of an achieved selfhood. The person who narrates his or her own experience thereby possesses it, reclaims it from those who had asserted rights over all aspects of that experience. The narrative changes the passive into the active voice. For the most part these narratives were unsentimental, if naïve. Sentimentality was displaced into fiction, into works like William Wells Brown's *Clotel* (1853), the first novel written by an American black. But this, in turn, generated a series of stereotypes which, in seeking to liberate the black from enslavement, entrapped him in a myth which proved more enduring than slavery and which, primarily through popular culture, constituted a sustained assault on the black American's identity. Indeed, the patronizing caricatures of plantation literature (Thomas Nelson Page's *Red Rock*, 1898; Margaret Mitchell's *Gone with the Wind*, 1936), the vicious distortion of Thomas Dixon's *The Clansman* (1905), and the casual stereotypes of Hollywood films, generated social fictions which were all too easily transmuted into social fact by those seeking a single model of political, economic and metaphysical reality.

But the emergence of black culture was itself not simply a matter of asserting command over the written word. The work songs, hollers, and chants of the field slave were both sustaining a heritage with roots elsewhere than the soil of Alabama and Tennessee, and laying down the material out of which black folk culture would itself grow. Ironically, one consequence of imbibing white culture was to strengthen blacks' awareness of the contradictory nature of their own bondage. How to justify holding some people in slavery while permitting freedom to others had been a perennial problem for pro-slavery apologists, but it created particular problems for Americans on account of their country's proclaimed dedication to the principles of freedom, equality and democracy. How could a nation which valued such ideals hold 4 million of its inhabitants in bondage? This was a troubling question because the obvious answer – that the two could not be reconciled and that the slaves should be freed – carried with it the implication not only of bloodshed but of the possible destruction of the nation itself. In the event, the Civil War came and the nation survived, although only after half a million soldiers from North and South – one for each eight slaves emancipated and more than the original number of blacks imported – died in the struggle. Yet it was only when the war was over and the slaves had been emancipated that it became clear that this was merely a first step – and that, if ever blacks were to achieve equality in the fullest sense, much more would be required.

▶ The black experience and radical reconstruction

It was in 1865, with the South's defeat in the Civil War, that the black American entered history, in the sense of being able to control his or her own experience and, at least potentially, deflect the course of the social and political system which was now required to take cognizance of that freedom, even to the extent of legislating against its too effective utilization. Slavery may have fed, clothed and sheltered him adequately, organized his work, trained him in artisan and agrarian skills, even treated him less cruelly than Harriet Beecher Stowe, in her abolitionist novel *Uncle Tom's Cabin* (1852), had imagined. But the 'peculiar institution' had systematically denied literacy, freedom of movement, and any sense of racial pride or personal autonomy to blacks; they were pitched unprepared into the world of freedom. As Union armies rampaged across the South, blacks, automatically emancipated by Northern conquest, stopped work, walked off plantations, to follow Sherman's marauders or to revel in unfettered movement. The task that followed – that of social and personal reconstruction, the reconstruction of a selfhood harrowed by slavery and denied by patronizing and proprietorial whites, who had imposed on them the twin images of 'sambo' or the 'uppity nigger' – was complicated by the fact that the South, where most blacks lived, was ravaged, pauperized and bitter in defeat. Its immense investment in slavery had been liquidated, its manhood decimated, its cotton-based economy dislocated. The underdeveloped section of ante-bellum America had become a post-bellum disaster area. But some Southern institutions survived. One was the belief in white supremacy; the most degraded 'poor white trash' knew themselves superior to the most elevated 'nigger'. The immediate Southern answer to emancipation – symptomatic of what the black could expect in the South for a century – was the Black Code, which continued the restrictions of slavery and reduced African-American constitutional rights to a mockery.

Blacks looked to the North, especially to the radical abolitionist wing of the young and still insecure Republican Party, led by Thaddeus Stevens, Charles Sumner, and others. But Republicans were partly distracted by partisan considerations: confrontation with Lincoln's successor Andrew Johnson, the prospect of a revived Democratic Party based on increased Southern representation arising from emancipation, the fear that politically innocent blacks could be used by their ex-masters as voting-fodder. It was these conflicts and apprehensions that conditioned the policy of

'Radical Reconstruction', which sought to disfranchise rebel leadership and also to politicize blacks and make them supporters of the Republican Party. This policy was effected by the passage of the Fourteenth (1868) and Fifteenth (1870) Amendments to the Constitution, guaranteeing blacks 'equal protection of the laws', and forbidding states from disfranchising any person because of 'race, color, or previous condition of servitude'.

The result of 'Radical Reconstruction' was that the South, deemed now to be a territory, was placed under military rule. General O O Howard organized the Freedman's Bureau, initially for welfare assistance to unsupported blacks, later as a facility for their education, legal protection and economic aid. By 1868 adult males had the vote. This they used, under protection of Northern bayonets and prompted by Republican Union League agents, to return not only scalawags (white Southern Republican sympathizers) and carpetbaggers (Northern migrants into the South) but also significant numbers of their own race to county, state and federal offices. The lower house of the South Carolina legislature had a majority of African-American members: 87 blacks to 69 whites; South Carolina, Mississippi, Louisiana and Florida all had blacks in high executive and judicial posts; 14 Negroes sat in the House of Representatives, 2 in the Senate. They took part in the state constitutional conventions, which guaranteed freedmen full political and civil rights. South Carolina and Louisiana even forbade educational segregation in their public schools. Such blacks were rarely newly freed slaves. Many had lived in the antebellum North; some were ministers or teachers by profession; a few, like Senator Hiram Revels of Mississippi, had college educations, or, like Jonathan J Wright, Supreme Court Justice of South Carolina, had been members of the Bar in the North.

Reconstruction has had a bad record, and indeed there was corruption, embezzlement and incompetence, especially from carpetbaggers in several Southern states. But there was a serious attempt to replace the shattered economic infrastructure, and to spread educational opportunities. Blacks eagerly grasped the educational chances offered by state, religious and philanthropic organizations. 'It was a whole race trying to go to school', Booker T Washington later recalled. 'Few were too young and none too old to make the attempt to learn. As fast as any kind of teachers could be secured, not only were day-schools filled, but night-schools as well.' In office, some inexperienced and malleable blacks were certainly guilty of excesses, but the record of black leaders in Reconstruction states and counties merits James G Blaine's praise of their federal colleagues: 'The colored men who took their seats in both Senate and House did not appear ignorant or helpless. They were as a rule studious, earnest, ambitious men, whose public conduct would be honourable to any race.'

But if every black office-holder had been a paragon, the days of Radical Reconstruction would still have been numbered. As the Republican

Party strengthened itself, and its radical spokesmen died or retired, the cost of administering the defeated South came more and more in question. By the 1870s most Northerners were convinced of the need to let the South return to home rule. The Reconstruction regimes were weakened by factionalism, and the mass of the white population repudiated them. White intimidation and racial demagoguery had grown, as secret organizations – the Ku Klux Klan, the Knights of the White Camelia, the White Brotherhood, the '76 Association – terrorized blacks and their allies, murdering, lynching, raping, beating. What ended Reconstruction was the cliffhanging presidential election of 1876, when the Republican candidate, Rutherford B Hayes, conceded the removal of the last federal troops from the South in return for disputed electoral-college votes that put him in office. The South was returned to the South, and the blacks abandoned to 'the party of the fathers'.

Their position was not strong. Radical Reconstruction had shakily provided the vote, and educational opportunities. But it had not brought economic independence. Wartime plans for confiscating rebel plantations to provide each ex-slave with 40 acres and a mule had foundered. Many abolitionists had seen emancipation as a moral victory, not an economic and social challenge. The business wing of the Republican Party emphasized the sanctity of property rights, and was not averse to having a cheap, landless black labour force in the South. But blacks could not eat votes, and book learning did not nourish the body. The Southern economy was in disorder; despite an increase in the area of land under cotton after the Civil War, production did not recover to 1860 figures until the end of the 1870s. In any case, the last three decades of the nineteenth century were no time to try small-scale cotton farming. Thanks to world overproduction and the tight money policy of the American government, the price of cotton fell from 17 cents a pound in 1871 to 4.6 cents per pound in 1894. The freed black was trying to make his way in circumstances of long-term agricultural depression.

Some blacks managed, through homesteading, accumulated savings, or Northern philanthropic contributions, to acquire their own land; most, however, engaged in sharecropping, 'the planter', as Edward King explained, 'taking out the expenses of the crop, and, when it is sold, dividing the net proceeds with the negroes who have produced it'. Other systems, like the crop lien or mortgage, existed, but most of them exposed blacks, and poor whites too, to problems of capitalizing their next crop. Sharecropper farmers fell under the sway of the furnishing merchant who supplied seed, food, fertilizer, implements and mules against notes pledging the cotton crop as security. Local merchants charged exorbitantly for supplies and conventionally undervalued the crop. Monopolistic trusts came to control vital supplies – ploughs and fertilizer, for example – and, because the value of the dollar was appreciating, interest rates spiralled. The Depression reduced the value of Southern land to a level where it was virtually unmortgageable and unsaleable. Blacks shared, and suffered with, the decline of the South.

▶ The rise of black protest, 1890–1918

In 1895, thirty years after the end of the Civil War, the black leader Booker T Washington was asked to speak at the Atlanta Cotton States Exposition – designed as a shop-window for 'The New South', now rapidly industrializing with ramshackle cotton mills and factories. The son of a slave and a white man, born in West Virginia shortly before the Civil War, Washington had worked as a miner and house-servant in his youth before walking and riding the 500 miles to the Hampton Institute, a Northern-financed agricultural school, where he gained an education while working as a caretaker. By 1881 he was appointed principal of the Tuskegee Institute in Alabama, which he raised, through a policy of strict discipline, self-help, and successful approaches to Northern philanthropic institutions, into the leading centre of black industrial education in the country. The story of his own development he would tell in *Up from Slavery* (1901), an autobiography that was to become the first classic of black writing since Emancipation; his achievement at Tuskegee, where he inculcated in successive generations of bricklayers, carpenters and mechanics the protestant virtues of thrift, providence, politeness and hard work, he would record in *Tuskegee and Its People* (1905). Washington's address at Atlanta expressed his racial pride in black achievements; it called for legal protection for his people, and it asserted his philosophy of gradual Negro self-improvement. Yet there is no mistaking an obsequious tone in his biblically inspired rhetoric, a tone that was soon to be attacked. He recalled the loyalty of slaves, he accepted social segregation and inequality, and questioned African-American political ambitions. His message was a plea for, in essence, mutual co-operation between unequal partners.

At this time most blacks accepted Washington's message and his leadership, especially if, like him, they remained loyal to the Republican Party. The period was one of political tension, racial violence and economic depression, exacerbated by the Great Crash of 1893. From 1887 some black farmers had been attempting to solve their economic problems by joining Colored Farmers Alliances, based on white models. But these attempts at co-operative buying and marketing had largely failed under the combined hostility of plantation owners, merchants and financiers; they had, however, raised the political consciousness of white and black members, and led to the formation of the People's Party. Populism called for a third party of masses against classes; in some areas of the South, blacks did align with the People's Party, and were even elected to offices in it. But the ruling Democrats reacted predictably: terrorism, electoral fraud and economic threats were used mercilessly. The decade of the 1890s holds the record for the frequency of lynchings. In such a conflict, where white landlords controlled the political and economic system and would stop at nothing to maintain their rule, where white alliances with blacks were fragile and the chances of success frail, the 'uppity nigger' became an inevitable scapegoat. Humility and accommodationism were at this time perhaps the only policies which could have secured the continuance of Northern philanthropy and safeguarded the Southern blacks.

Booker T Washington's personal reputation burgeoned after Atlanta; he became the acknowledged leader and the recognized voice of black aspirations until his death in 1915. He published books, like *Sowing and Reaping* (1900) and *Character Building* (1902), expressing his gradualist philosophy. The 'Tuskegee Machine' became not only the channel for all philanthropy to black causes, but also the clearing house for Republican Party and federal patronage. Washington was consulted by President Theodore Roosevelt between 1901 and 1909, and unprecedentedly bidden to breakfast at the White House. Yet, politically, Washington had sadly miscalculated. Lynching continued unabated, the frustration of poor whites at the collapse of Populism in 1896 adding to the violence. Worse, quasi-legal disfranchisement and segregation deprived blacks of what little political power they still had in the South. Ever since Redemption, disfranchisement had been a danger to the blacks. When and where it happened depended more on the white political factions in the different states than on such 'trivial' matters as constitutional rights. In the 1880s, for instance, black voters were useful to black-belt conservatives. However, in South Carolina, where blacks were in the majority, various stratagems like the Registration Law of 1882 gave white electoral officials wide discretion to prevent blacks from voting. The first wholesale exclusion of blacks from the polls occurred in Mississippi in 1890, after the failure of Henry Cabot Lodge's so-called Force Bill, which would have given them federal protection. Through poll taxes, residence requirements, literacy tests and the 'understanding clause', the new Mississippi constitution effectively removed blacks from political life. After 1896 and the Populist débâcle, disfranchisement came everywhere, and often disqualified poor whites as well. The decision rested with the Electoral Registrar, who ensured that the South was a White Man's Land. The 'solid South' was effectively one-party; the Democratic nominating primary was more important than actual elections. To make assurance doubly sure, primaries were limited to white delegates.

Booker T Washington resisted disfranchisement, and used the funds he had to challenge the new constitutional arrangements in legal battles that went to the Supreme Court. But the hostile judgement in *William* v. *Mississippi* (1898) doomed such efforts to failure, while in *Plessey* v. *Ferguson* (1896) the Supreme Court (over the famous dissent of Mr Justice Harlan, who described the constitution as 'color-blind') sanctioned the concept of 'separate but equal' facilities for blacks and whites, in this case on transportation in Louisiana. This condemned blacks not only to inferior, money-starved school systems but also to wide-ranging 'Jim Crow Laws' segregating buses, railroads, schools, hotels, hospitals, restaurants, lavatories, theatres, trade unions, and many other institutions and facilities. This move to institutionalize the colour-line had also been spurred by the growing urbanization of the South, which brought blacks to Birmingham, Roanoke, Raleigh, Natchez, Atlanta and New Orleans in search of work in new industries; it was estimated that one-third of the black population of the South lived in urban areas by 1890, and whites sought new 'rules' to protect themselves.

Thus the two decades from 1890 to 1910 were disastrous for black Americans. Political and civil rights were sacrificed; education, which between 1865 and 1900 had reduced black illiteracy from 90 per cent to 30 per cent, was now at the whim of whites. Economically, the black farmer was reduced to peonage, or else driven to the lowest-paid jobs in southern industry. Moreover, despite Theodore Roosevelt's tentative overtures, Progressivism offered little to African-Americans. In North and South, consciences were salved by popular pseudo-scientific versions of Darwinism and genetics, which proposed fundamental racial differences. A syrupy romanticization of an aristocratic Old South, in fiction and folklore, pulled a veil over its contemporary shortcomings: political stagnation and corruption, cultural and economic backwardness, violence, illiteracy, ignorance.

Yet the 1890s were a decade that both raised and suppressed many hopes in American life, not least those of blacks. It saw the rising promise of a new black writing, for instance in the work of Paul Laurence Dunbar, the first black poet with a national reputation. The son of a slave, he was best known for his dialect poetry, a style which he himself resisted but which was popular with white publishers. Ironically, such experiments were efforts towards establishing that kind of cultural distinctiveness which a century later would be *de rigueur* with many black writers. Dunbar also wrote a fascinating novel about a black Christian who loses his faith in the naturalist wilderness, *The Uncalled* (1898). Charles W Chesnutt published black fiction, notably *The Marrow of Tradition* (1901), in which a black doctor, abused and ill-treated, eventually wins the support of the better element in a white community as a result of his selfless treatment of a white child. But at the same time there is a sympathetic portrait of a black rebel who is willing to die rather than accept a subservient role. Chesnutt touches here on the ambiguity of the black man, but also of the black writer, forced to mediate his expression through white publishers to a white audience, and so half-compelled to conceal the self he wishes to express. Most early black literature – from Phyllis Wheatley on – tends to be imitative of white modes, and to display some of the servility felt to be the necessary price of success. Yet, often, the subversive spirit survives, and the act of articulation itself becomes a kind of political assertion.

Two long-term reactions now began to make themselves felt. One was protest, epitomized in the career of W E B Du Bois (pronounced 'Boys'). A Northern black from a family of ante-bellum freedmen, he grew up in Massachusetts, experiencing only mild racial prejudice. It was when he visited the South in his vacations from Fisk University that he discovered the force of the colour-line. After studying in Berlin, he gained his doctorate at Harvard for a dissertation on the slave trade and became a professor of sociology, first at Wilberforce and then at Atlanta University. His first strategy for helping his race was typical of the prevailing Progressive muckraking mentality: disseminating information about African-American suffering by pioneering sociological studies of Atlanta and the black belt of Georgia. But as he witnessed his people's decline, and growing racial violence (there were serious race riots in Atlanta, Boston, Brownsville, New York, and Springfield, Lincoln's home-town, in the first decade of the twentieth century), he grew more outraged and outspoken. In 1903 he published his classical collection of historical, socio-economic, political, mystical and fictional essays, *The Souls of Black Folk*. Its most famous passage expressed the idea that the blacks were blessed and cursed with a double consciousness:

> The Negro is a sort of seventh son born with a veil and gifted with second sight in this American world – a world which yields him no true self-consciousness, but only lets him see himself through the revelation of the other world. It is a peculiar sensation, this double consciousness, this sense of always looking at oneself through the eyes of others, of measuring one's soul by the tape of a world that looks on in amused contempt and pity. One ever feels his twoness – an American, a Negro; two warring souls, two thoughts, two unreconcilable strivings, two warring ideals in one dark body, whose dogged strength alone keeps it from being torn asunder.

'The History of the Negro', he concluded, 'is the history of this strife', and it is this strife and sense of doubleness that much African-American expression in the arts and music has gone on to express.

In one essay in the book, Du Bois implicitly attacked Washington; in another, propounding the idea of 'The Talented Tenth', élitist, intellectual spokesmen and leaders of the black race, he offered alternative policies. Now the gap began to widen between Du Bois, like-minded black leaders such as Kelly Miller, Dean of Howard University, or Charles Chesnutt, and the 'Washington camp'. In 1905 the 'Niagara Movement' promoted a journal, *Horizon*, to protest against disfranchisement and racial inequality, but it was poorly organized and suffered Washington's hostility. Du Bois attacked Washington with increased bitterness and turned to the Progressive wing of the Democrats, but was soon disillusioned;

Woodrow Wilson, elected President in 1912, was a Southerner, one of whose first executive orders segregated the federal civil service. Du Bois, now the leader of the militant wing of blacks, had in 1909 become a founder of the National Association for the Advancement of Colored People (NAACP). He edited the NAACP journal, *Crisis*, and directed research, publicizing the injustices and discrimination suffered by blacks, to arouse the moral outrage of the American people. In his turbulent relations with his white progressive backers, Du Bois oscillated between calls for the complete integration of the races and the idea that black Americans, in alliance with black Africa, must go it alone. As an editor, he encouraged young black writers, assured his position as a leading voice of black protest in America, and led the way into the black intellectual revival that followed the war.

The second response to the triumph of Southern racism was also a form of protest: black migration to Northern cities. From emancipation onward, there had been much migration by blacks, westward into Texas, townward into the fledgling mills, factories and mines of the New South. But from the 1890s onward, increasing numbers, initially often young males, began the movement northward. The Great Migration in little more than a generation changed the black from predominantly a Southern farm labourer into predominantly a Northern city-dweller. The factors behind the 'push' from the South have been indicated, though the spread of the boll weevil between 1910 and 1920 added to them. The 'pull' of the Northern cities – Chicago, St Louis, Pittsburgh, Cleveland, Detroit, New York, Philadelphia, Boston – was aided, in classic immigrant fashion, by descriptions in letters and the propaganda of Northern black newspapers (like Robert S Abbott's Chicago *Defender*). Du Bois's *Crisis* also favoured migration. The First World War turned a steady stream into a flood. Northern factories geared to production were starved of labour by the drop in European immigration and by conscription. The South was flooded with job advertisements; labour touts offered cheap fares to the North. Southern industrialists used intimidation to stop the flight of labour, though the poor whites were doubtless less sorry to see their competitors pack train after train to 'The Promised Land'. Between 1890 and 1920 some 2 million migrated to Northern cities, a flow that was destined to continue until the 1970s.

Some migrants had already experienced urban life in the South, but the cultural shock of arrival in the North's great cities for field-hands or sharecroppers has rightly been compared to the trauma of enslavement. City life, as for all new immigrants, meant ghetto life. White residential blocks had been 'busted' by realtors intruding black families. After white flight, family homes had been divided, subdivided and sub-subdivided, to pack the black tenants in at exorbitant rents. Surrounding white neighbourhoods adopted restrictive convenants, formed 'improvement associations', or, as in Chicago, resorted to bombings and terrorism, to prevent black ghetto expansion. As more and more migrants arrived, overcrowding reached suffocating levels. It has been estimated that by 1940, had population density in the rest of Manhattan borough equalled that of Harlem, all the population of the USA would be contained in the one borough. Household and civic services could not cope, and neglect by landlords and municipalities made an appalling situation even worse. Inadequate plumbing, bad ventilation, poor hygiene, spasmodic refuse collection and malnourishment all helped to push infant mortality figures to two and three times the white level. Bad schooling, working mothers, lack of social amenities and of parental authority brought high crime rates and generational conflict. The ghetto became a magnet for exploiters and racketeers: the patent medicine man, the pimp, the storefront church and numbers racket became ghetto institutions. Even job prospects, which had drawn hopeful blacks from the South, began to collapse with the postwar recession and the return of demobilized whites to the labour market. 'Last hired, first fired' was the rule for blacks.

▶ Black arts and black politics between the wars

President Wilson's 'War to Save Democracy' proved a hollow slogan for American blacks. Encouraged by such leaders as Du Bois, and by government propaganda, African-Americans flocked to the colours, only to find that Jim Crow ruled the armed services. Black regiments were customarily assigned demeaning fatigue duties. They were forbidden to fraternize in France, though they could not fail to notice the relaxed racial attitudes there. When they returned home, they were attacked by white mobs if they had the effrontery to wear their uniforms in public. Veterans who returned to Northern ghettos likewise found claims to racial liberalism exposed as hypocritical cant. In 1917, East St Louis suffered a terrifying outburst of racial violence: 39 blacks were killed by rampaging white mobs, 500 were injured, and 312 buildings were destroyed. 1919 was, in James Weldon Johnson's words, the bloody 'Red Summer', with a major four-day race-riot in Chicago which killed 23 blacks and injured 342, and brought outbreaks of racial violence in a dozen other cities. The Twenties were not to be a tolerant decade, but the changed social situation, and black migration, had some advantages. Compared with scattered settlements in the rural South, the ghetto created a black community, homogenized by shared suffering, which quickly established its own institutions and began to recognize its own potential strength. Urbanized, the black was near to the centres of national cultural activity. He began to be celebrated in some white literature, as in the fiction of Sherwood Anderson, Carl Van Vechten, William Faulkner, Du Bois and Dorothy Heyward's *Porgy* (1925). Black writers, black singers and black music were in vogue.

Fashionable whites invaded Harlem nightclubs, catering to exclusively white clientele. White playwrights, like Eugene O'Neill and Paul Green, wrote on Negro themes; artists found inspiration in not-so-primitive African primitive art.

The spirit of the decade was summed up by Alain Locke in his 1925 anthology, *The New Negro*. A powerful collection of essays, verse and prose, this proposed the emergence of a new breed of writers who wrote 'as Negroes' rather than necessarily 'for the Negro'. In other words, cultural identity was no longer problematic; it was an assumed fact. For Locke, indeed, this charged American blacks with a responsibility to liberate their African brothers. But in fact the 'New Negro' was less interested in black Africa, except as an image of lyric innocence, than he was with examining his own environment, defining his own identity and announcing his own new-found sense of cultural independence. He may have been in vogue with the whites, who tried to promote an image of the black as a spontaneous, unrepressed sexual being – an image which served their own psychic and mythological needs – but his own concern lay elsewhere. It lay in a process of personal and group discovery which could express itself equally in defiant poems like Claude McKay's 'If We Must Die' (quoted by Winston Churchill in the House of Commons during the Second World War), or lyrical celebrations of the black past.

The mood of black writers was one of celebration. Where white literature of the period tended to dwell on images of sterility, unfulfilled hopes, unrealized dreams or disappointed aspirations, black literature tended to assert the sensual vitality and lyric potential of life. With the exception of Langston Hughes's poetry and Jean Toomer's *Cane* (1923), it was a literature to one side of the modernist concerns of Stein, Hemingway, Pound and Eliot. The imagination was not to be a last desperate resource; it was a key to shared experience, part of the process of liberation. No wonder, perhaps, that they shared so little with the whites who fondly imagined that their interest in jazz implied an understanding of the experience from which it derived. At a time when whites were deploring the collapse of community, identifying the alienation and social dislocations of urban life, black Americans saw in the city a cultural and political potential which was cause for hope.

The black writers were not blind to the debilitating nature of their physical environment but for the most part they chose to emphasize the complex cultural resources of a black community in the process of creating its own values, images and myths. And if this was expressed in poetry, prose, dance and, to a lesser extent, drama, it was also centrally expressed through jazz. A major influence on twentieth-century American music, this was an art which expressed a specific cultural experience. For F Scott Fitzgerald, the Twenties were the 'jazz age'. But he was simply appropriating what he took to be its apoliticism, its sensuality, its antinomianism. Its buried history was a cipher he was not inclined or equipped to decode.

But it was central to the black experience. For Hughes, its rhythms were those of black life. For Ralph Ellison, its subtle combinations of improvisation and fixed form, the dialectical relationship between individual and group, stood as an image of the individual black's relationship to his community. Where the blues offered a lyric sublimation of suffering, jazz proposed a more active and complex model. Jazz was folk, rather than popular, culture in that it was embedded in a shared experience. It was never simply social anodyne. The spaces in the music demanded collaboration not only by the soloists but also by those whose experience was the material out of which the music was made.

In the Twenties black writers, especially poets and novelists, found it relatively easy to publish and for a decade the 'First Black Renaissance', more usually known as the 'Harlem Renaissance' or the 'Negro Renaissance', flourished. Yet there was still a radical disagreement as to the objective of black writing. Claude McKay announced that he did not regard himself as a Negro poet, wishing to transcend 'the narrow confined limits of one people and its problems', Zora Neale Hurston emphasized her dependence on black folk culture, and Countee Cullen confessed to a race-consciousness which grew stronger and stronger. Partly, of course, it was still a question of audience. James Weldon Johnson suggested, indeed, that in many ways this was the primary problem for the black American writer – for whom does he write, for blacks or for whites? This was a dilemma felt every bit as strongly half a century later.

This emphasis on the nature of black identity, this desire to make a declaration of cultural independence, was reflected on a social level by Marcus Garvey's Universal Negro Improvement Association (1916). A West Indian, one of many 'black Jews' who migrated to Harlem in the early twentieth century, Garvey headed a back-to-Africa movement: indeed, though he never set foot on the continent, he declared himself Provisional President of Africa. In many ways, his organization was touched with farce, with its ostentatious uniforms and mass parades. He established a Black Star Shipping Line, but because of incompetence his ships either sank or were impounded; he himself was indicted for fraud in 1924, and eventually died in London. But it would be a mistake to see him simply as a clown or charlatan – though Du Bois moved from cautious support to indicting him as 'the most dangerous enemy of the Negro race in America and in the world'. For he instilled in individual blacks a sense of pride and dignity, suggested the need for black Americans to control their economic destiny, and demonstrated the possibility of creating a mass movement among blacks, indicating a political potential that could be mobilized to win advancement. He himself despaired of this in America, seeing the black future as a return to Africa. Thus there was an atavistic dimension both in the First Black Renaissance and in Garvey's economic and political plans. Yet, though this was a period in which Northern black communities became a demonstrable fact of urban and cultural life, the political lessons were not yet drawn, and Garvey's predominantly working-class movement was hardly reflected in the largely middle-class black writing of the period.

The 1930s brought an abrupt change of mood. The 1929 Stock Market crash and the Great Depression of the Thirties were, in Villard's words, 'an unparalleled disaster' for 'the great masses of colored people'. In the South, a further fall in cotton prices deepened the persistent agrarian depression of the 1920s. In many areas, lien farmers and share-croppers were evicted wholesale as credit dried up; livestock, implements, foodcrops and household furniture were seized by creditor landlords and merchants. In the cities, North and South, black unemployment rose to 50 per cent or higher, far above the level for whites. Established black organizations like the NAACP – which now concentrated on legal actions and legislative lobbying against lynching, segregation, and inequality of pay – and the Urban League, founded in 1910 to foster educational and economic opportunities for ghetto blacks, were overwhelmed by the scale of the disaster. In this near-revolutionary situation, the American Communist Party, on orders from Moscow, made determined efforts to win black support. Its interracial Southern Tenant Farmers' Union enrolled 31,000 members in the South for its labour-union tactics against landlords, who often responded with bullets. In 1931, the party's International Labor Defense grabbed the limelight from the NAACP in the trial of the Scottsboro boys, nine young blacks accused of raping two white women in Alabama, and Southern 'justice' was exposed in a carefully orches-trated international propaganda campaign in which the pathetic defend-ants often seemed forgotten. The Communist Party also fostered black unionization among miners and textile workers, and Tenants' Leagues among ghetto-dwellers. The difficulty was that the party was itself unde-cided about the nature of the African-American dilemma. Hence it tried simultaneously to present blacks as colonial peoples fighting for freedom, seeking independence in their own socialist republic in the black belt, and as simple victims of class warfare with common interests with the white working class.

It is this ambiguity that is reflected in such works as *Uncle Tom's Chil-dren* (1938) and *Native Son* (1940), by the period's most famous black writer, Richard Wright. Wright was, like many intellectuals of the time, a party member, but became increasingly disillusioned as he came to feel that the party's deterministic theories, hostility to bourgeois individualism, and cynical Comintern-ordained shifts of policy were inimical to his own liberal and existentialist views. *Native Son*, the story of Bigger Thomas, a Chicago ghetto black, has a naturalist theme, but his move is towards selfhood, an existential redemption; a theme that would return in Wright's later novel, *The Outsider* (1953), written in Paris. Like Ralph Ellison, whose portrayal of the Harlem 'Brotherhood' in *Invisible Man* (1952) stems from similar Depression experiences, Wright and other perceptive black intellectuals found themselves being used as pawns for the political ambitions of others, and moved towards a separate path. To Wright, the black artist had a crucial role: to create the values by which the black American was to survive, to 'furnish moral sanctions for action, to give a meaning to blighted lives, and to supply motives for mass movements of millions of people'. Many black writers would tread this anxious path, for the black writer – an example of Du Bois's 'talented tenth' – felt charged with forging the myths, creating the symbols, the heroes and animating fantasies of a people constructing their own self-definition: a task all the more difficult when menaced by public myths and dominant stereotypes which demeaned him, made him invisible, or distorted his nature through cultural and political prejudices.

The Thirties brought new political awareness into American life in general. Even so, the response of the Roosevelt administration to the plight of blacks was ambivalent. On the one hand, the President's reliance on electoral and legislative support from Southern conservatives and demagogues meant that he could show blacks no overt favour. On the other hand, leading New Dealers like Harold Ickes and Eleanor Roosevelt were outspoken enemies of racism, and helped ensure that blacks benefited from relief and social security measures. Black sharecroppers found New Deal farm policies raised their pitiful incomes; the galaxy of work projects brought some hope to the mass of black unemployed; and the newly formed Congress of Industrial Organizations welcomed black support in unionizing traditionally unorganized industries. The first great spokesman for black labour emerged in A Philip Randolph, of the Brotherhood of Sleeping Car Porters. The Federal Theater Project encouraged black playwrights and expressed black problems. Looking back on the Thirties, Du Bois declared that 'Negro Americans made more progress toward their goal of full citizenship' then than since Emancipation. Blacks responded with massive support for the Democratic Party; and their growing importance to its new urban power-base was reflected in federal appointments.

Yet Roosevelt had to be forced into his major concession: the Committee on Fair Employment Practises. As the United States took on its role as 'the Arsenal of Democracy' in 1940, shaking off its Depression malaise, it soon appeared that those blacks who had been first fired a decade before would be last hired, or not hired at all, by wartime industry. Randolph threatened to march 100,000 blacks on Washington to demand the end of Jim Crowism in the war-machine, the services, and federal government. The threat of direct non-violent action was sufficient: on 25 June 1941, the President signed the Executive Order 8802 'to provide for full and equitable participation of all workers in defense industry, without discrimination'. The limited victory of the March on Washington Movement served as a pregnant example for the future. Immediately, though, the gradual integration of munitions factories produced widespread racial tension. In Detroit the worst of several wartime race-riots broke out in June 1943. Blacks were attacked by white mobs in the ghetto and elsewhere; twenty-five were killed, hundreds injured, and much property destroyed. Moreover, Order 8802 neglected the armed services. Black officers and other ranks met white hostility, insults and violence. African-American troops were forced to eat separately on Southern trains; meanwhile German prisoners of war dined in the white restaurant car. Randolph bitterly described black troops as 'Jim Crow slaves in the army', and a black soldier serving in the Pacific suggested the disillusioned epitaph: 'Here lies a black man killed fighting a yellow man for the protection of the white man.'

▶ Black experience: 1945–70

It has been in the decades since the Second World War that the biggest revolution in the status of African-Americans and in the articulation of black consciousness has occurred. A major engine of change was black leadership, political and cultural, and the heroism, sometimes turning to rage, of many ordinary blacks reacting against oppression. American liberal and radical opinion was aroused, partly through the impact of television reporting. The independence of Black Africa represented at the UN in New York City and the growth of international anti-racist ideology put American racism in a new embarrassing perspective. Was America to be classed with South Africa as an international pariah? The new Democratic Party strategy stressed the importance of the black vote, as changes in the Senate undermined Southern political power in Washington. Liberal Democratic nominations altered the formerly conservative balance of the Supreme Court. Emergence from the Cold War mentality and the growth of radical idealism and activism by a new generation of white Americans brought a new attitude to domestic issues. Massive black achievements in literature, the arts, theatre and scholarship undermined assumptions of racial inferiority. So, too, did dominant theories in social science and psychology. From the early Sixties, the role of the black in America became a fundamental issue in American life.

Moreover, the growing role of the federal government in giving positive protection and assistance to oppressed minorities led to a cumulatively interventionist mentality in Washington. Truman, in 1946, appointed a Presidential Committee on Civil Rights which presented a blueprint for action for the executive, the Congress, and the states. It would, painfully and exhaustingly, have to be forced on to the statute books over the next twenty years against a determined Southern resistance. One positive achievement of the Truman era was the gradual desegregation of the armed forces from 1949 onward, effected by presidential executive order. But other initiatives ran on to the sandbanks of Southern control of congressional committees, and filibustering by Dixieland senators.

A second crucial breakthrough for black civil rights was judicial. On 17 May 1954 – 'Black Monday', to recalcitrant Southerners – Chief Justice Earl Warren delivered the unanimous opinion of the Supreme Court in the case of *Brown* v. *Topeka Board of Education* that 'in the field of public education the doctrine of "separate but equal" has no place. Separate educational facilities are inherently unequal.' Significantly, the court's decision completing sixteen years' erosion of *Plessey* v. *Ferguson*, cited findings by psychologists and social scientists. Subsequently the court ordered educational desegregation 'with all deliberate speed'.

But whatever the Supreme Court might order, it relied on the executive branch to enforce. President Eisenhower, who had made considerable Republican inroads into the South, showed no eagerness for the task. He did break a tradition going back to Redemption by sending federal troops to Little Rock, Arkansas, in 1957 when black parents sought to register their children in an all-white school. Television viewers across the world saw Governor Orville Faubus vainly try to block the school entrance – an oft-repeated sight, for Southern racists now girded themselves to thwart the Court decision. White Citizens' Councils, pioneered in Mississippi, and Klan-like organizations spread race hatred and anti-integrationism across the South. The familiar weapons of intimidation – bombings, burnings, stabbings, mob-violence, murders – were reactivated against 'niggers' and 'nigger-lovers'. Every kind of subterfuge to circumvent school integration was used: private white academies sprang up, sometimes helped by state subsidies; Virginia even closed down its entire public school system.

But the struggle was spreading to other areas. Within eighteen months of *Brown* v. *Topeka*, another sacred cow of Southern segregation, transportation, was attacked through the Montgomery Bus Boycott, sparked off by the arrest of Mrs Rosa Parks, in December 1955, for refusing to give up her seat to a white passenger. For over a year the boycotters organized by the Southern Christian Leadership Conference (SCLC) endured massive white intimidation before desegregation was conceded. Victory led to national recognition for its black organizer, the Rev. Martin Luther King, Jr. King fitted the traditional mould of Southern black leadership. A minister, and son of a minister, he used the evangelistic rhetoric employed by black preachers for generations. He also brought less familiar qualities to his mission. Travelled and well-educated (he had a doctorate from Boston University), he was in touch with world opinion on race, specifically with the Gandhian doctrine of non-violent resistance, which gave a cutting edge to his Christian commitment to love as an all-conquering power. A man of surpassing charity, courage, dignity, the articulate author of *Stride Toward Freedom* (1958) and *Why We Can't Wait* (1964), quickly came to symbolize blacks' new-found purpose and integrationist ambition.

There were other expressions of a new mood. The Fifties saw the emergence of a new generation of black writers of great influence. In 1950 the poet Gwendolyn Brooks became the first black writer to win a Pulitzer Prize. A conscious innovator, she drew upon folk ballads and experimental modes alike. It was a double tradition which lay at the heart of her literary strategy. Yet the social pressure created by her racial identity constantly informs her work. She is not a polemical writer, but she expressed accurately enough the shifting mood of the black community in the second half of the century, proving remarkably sympathetic to, and supportive of, the poetic rhetoricians of the Sixties, writers whose urgent politics left little room for the ambiguities so precisely located by her own verse.

The Sixties did, indeed, have little room for ambiguity, and the thrust of LeRoi Jones's poetry moved from a Beat-derived 'soft' metaphysics to a conscious mythicization of black experience. Poetry was, for a time, blunted into a weapon of crude but effective force. It became a kind of political and cultural mantra, a chant from the soul, a reiterated invocation of racial spirits. It was a poetry designed for the voice, for public performance – at its best in the work of Sonia Sanchez, at its weakest, perhaps, in the work of Nikki Giovanni, who, however, proposed the collapse of poetic structure as a correlative of the collapse of personal and public illusion.

As far as the novel was concerned, the Fifties began with Ellison's brilliant parable *Invisible Man*, the story of a faceless, identityless black whose anguish is as much social as metaphysical. But it *is* both; that is, it is an account of a racially derived sense of alienation and a metaphor of alienation. The literature of victimization sounds through the Fifties: Ellison suggests that the alienated plight of blacks matches that of all modern sufferers of disorientation and persecution, and urges the need for the individual to accept a private and public responsibility for reality. In *Invisible Man*, imaginatively, at least, the black American was already insinuated into the realm of American moral concern – a fact which later made Ellison a target for some abuse by certain black critics. For the novel takes as its central strategy the need to infuse life into those very liberal principles enshrined in the Constitution but systematically denied in relation to blacks.

In 1953 another liberal voice was heard, in the person of James Baldwin. His first novel, *Go Tell it on the Mountain* (1953), was a sensitive account of a young boy's initiation into the realities of racial, sexual and religious life. With *Giovanni's Room* (1956) he linked this theme of black identity with that of homosexual love. But it was as an essayist that he made the greatest impact, with *Notes of a Native Son* (1955), *Nobody Knows My Name* (1961) and *The Fire Next Time* (1963), the latter a controlled polemic which expressed the apocalyptic anger that the moral failure of Americans to deal with race had generated in him. But his was an ambiguous voice. When he used the pronoun 'we' it frequently meant 'we Americans' rather than 'we blacks', and his retreat to France seemed to many blacks evidence of a failure of commitment, a failure which bred a guilt which expressed itself in fictions which became less controlled as they became more shrill. By the mid-Sixties there were other voices which seemed to speak more clearly for the younger generation which now set the tone of racial revolt. Baldwin now found himself the target for attack, more especially by Eldridge Cleaver. Divided in his own mind between indicting white society for the 'unforgivable sin' of racism and proposing a sentimental synthesis in the form of 'love', he eventually allowed ambiguity to collapse into simple contradiction.

For all Baldwin's denunciation of liberals, his work can scarcely be characterized by any other word. His belief in the integrity and reality of the individual, his model of a society of socially responsive individuals, his stance as moral teacher, his 'devotion to the human being, his freedom and fulfilment' is liberal in origin and intent. And, despite an apocalyptic imagination, much the same could be said of John A Williams (*Journey Out of Anger*, 1963), William Melvin Kelley (*A Different Drummer*, 1962), Alice Walker (*The Third Life of Grange Copeland*, 1970), and Toni Morrison (*Song of Solomon*, 1977). Indeed, freed of some of the social pressures of the Sixties, black writers have expanded into a commitment to experimentation which would earlier have been regarded with intense suspicion (see Ishmael Reed, *The Free-Lance Pall Bearers*, 1967, and much African-American writing since).

In theatre, Lorraine Hansberry's liberal drama about a black family's desire to integrate itself in a white community, *A Raisin in the Sun* (1959), quickly gave way to more aggressive accounts of racial conflict in the form of James Baldwin's *Blues for Mr Charlie* (1964), and LeRoi Jones's *Dutchman* (1964) and *The Slave* (1964). Indeed, the Black Power movement had its cultural wing in the form of the Black Arts movement, whose focus was LeRoi Jones.

Formerly an avant-garde writer in New York, Jones moved his activities to Harlem, where he founded the Black Arts Repertory Theatre, an organization which served as a model for many other ventures in urban centres across America. Jones's plays, which proved so successful downtown, when transferred to the ghetto were seen as menacing revolutionary tracts. It was a logic which he accepted, writing, now, 'black revolutionary plays' whose declared intention was to create new black myths, to identify heroes and villains, to denounce the white man as the source of evil and to raise the consciousness of the black masses. He divorced his white wife and changed his name to Imamu Amiri Baraka. Throughout the Sixties and early Seventies he was the dominant and defining influence on the Black Arts movement. Ed Bullins in particular was inspired by his example, though his own plays were sensitive examinations of the black community rather than agit-prop sketches or revolutionary rituals.

The Sixties also witnessed the creation of a number of significant black drama groups, in particular the Free Southern Theatre, designed to take theatre to Southern rural communities, and the Negro Ensemble Company, founded in New York by Douglas Turner Ward and funded by the Ford Foundation. Both survived into the Eighties, though undergoing certain changes which reflected the shifting orthodoxies of racial opinion.

The Sixties were indeed dominated by discussions of those orthodoxies, more especially by the propounding of the notion that the black writer should celebrate and define an experience distinct from that of the white American. Literature and criticism alike were to conform to an orthodoxy vigorously if imprecisely announced by critics like Addison Gayle Jr (ed. *The Black Aesthetic*), by social historians such as Harold Cruse (*The Crisis of the Negro Intellectual*) and by writers such as Amiri Baraka. White critics were warned off. White writers, such as William Styron, who attempted to 'appropriate' black experience (*The Confessions of Nat Turner*), were denounced. Black writers and historians like Lerone Bennett (*Before the Mayflower*) re-examined, and in some cases re-invented, their past, deliberately subverting a view of history and black identity which had been defined by whites. Literature was to be part of the process of re-definition, not simply a reflection of reality.

During the Sixties blacks won even more social and political advances. Martin Luther King's widely acclaimed achievement sparked off a range of attacks on segregation. Young blacks in 1960 began sit-ins and picketing of segregated lunch-counters in the South. In 1961, the Congress of Racial Equality organized 'freedom rides' through the South to highlight segregation on interstate transportation. After savage reprisals by Southerners, the Interstate Commerce Commission outlawed discrimination on interstate travel. In the same year, the interracial Student Non-violent Coordinating Committee began its assault on the basis of white political power with its campaign to register blacks as voters. Campaigners were beaten up and buses burned. Northern liberals were seeing Southern violence at first hand.

The continued shift of the Democratic Party towards support for black aspirations was symbolized during the close-run 1960 election campaign by John F Kennedy's widely publicized telephone call to Coretta King, whose husband was in gaol. The new President, and his brother Robert, the Attorney-General, were faced with a rising tide of racial confrontation, reported almost nightly on television. In 1962 tanks and hundreds of federal troops and marshals had to be sent to the University of Mississippi to enforce the admission of James Meredith, a black freshman. In June 1963 the President mobilized the Alabama National Guard to ensure the enrolment of two black students at the state university when Governor George Wallace physically attempted to prevent it. In the same month,

Kennedy's civil rights proposals, hastened by the revulsion of the public at the savage over-reaction of Southern policemen, politicians and thugs to unarmed, unresisting black and white protesters, were put before Congress. They covered both voting and segregation, involved the Attorney-General in the enforcement process, and threatened sanctions by withdrawal of federal financial aid. In the summer, Martin Luther King delivered his 'I have a dream' speech to an estimated quarter of a million people who had converged on Washington. By the time of the President's assassination that autumn in Dallas, Southern politicians had already organized a dogged and time-consuming resistance. The following year, 1964, President Johnson, a liberal Texan and brilliant congressional strategist, helped by emotional reaction to Kennedy's assassination and to the bombing of a Negro church in Birmingham, Alabama, which killed four young black girls, was able to force the Civil Rights Bill through the Senate after 534 hours of filibuster.

Johnson's triumph was short-lived. Southern registration officials continued to use literacy tests and poll-tax requirements in a blatantly discriminatory way. King and other civil rights leaders organized renewed registration drives and marches. In March 1965, Alabama police attacked peaceful demonstrators *en route* for Montgomery on the bridge at Selma, using tear-gas, electrified cattle prods, night-sticks and savage dogs. James Meredith was wounded while leading another such march. The administration introduced a new Voting Rights Bill to throw the full weight of federal power behind black civil rights. In still resistant areas of the South, the federal government would take over voter registration and would police the polling stations; the literacy test would be abolished, and poll-tax requirements nullified. The Bill became law in record time in August 1965, and thereafter in the South, after a century of struggle, blacks at last had that basic political right 'without which all others are meaningless'.

The revolution of rising expectations had not escaped the attention of Northern ghetto blacks. The disadvantages under which they struggled had been articulated by President Kennedy in 1963:

The Negro baby born in America today, regardless of the section or the state in which he is born, has about one-half as much chance of completing high school as a white baby, born in the same place, on the same day; one-third as much chance of becoming a professional man; twice as much chance of becoming unemployed; about one-seventh as much chance of earning $10,000 a year; a life expectancy which is seven years shorter and the prospects of earning only half as much.

Five days after Johnson signed the Voting Rights Act of 1965, the Los Angeles ghetto of Watts exploded into a week of black rioting, looting, shooting and burning. The pattern was repeated in ghetto after ghetto in the next two 'long hot summers'. Few major Northern cities escaped outbursts of black frustration and anger. In 1968, the murder of Martin Luther King in Memphis triggered a new phase of outraged destruction. Parts of Washington DC resembled a blitzed city.

Meanwhile, young blacks in the North had become increasingly disillusioned with King's insistence on integration and Christian charity, which they found inadequate or irrelevant to their needs. The cry of 'Black Power', the title of one of Richard Wright's books, but first used by Stokely Carmichael (like Garvey, a West Indian) on a voter registration drive in the South in 1965, was enthusiastically taken up. The Black Muslim movement, dominated since the 1930s by Elijah Mohammed in Chicago, recruited many disillusioned young blacks, among them Malcolm X and the young heavyweight boxing champion Cassius Clay. Its celebration of the non-white world, its programme for forming a separate black nation in America, its contemptuous reversal of Christian myths – a white devil, for instance – and its insistence on Islamic asceticism and self-discipline, gave a new purpose to many young ghetto blacks lost in a chaos of drug addiction, crime, unemployment, truancy or vice. In 1966, as a protest against pervasive police harassment and brutality, Huey Newton and Bobby Seale formed the Black Panther Party in Oakland, California: a militant organization, visibly armed and rhetorically violent. Elsewhere, ghetto communities agitated for community control of education and welfare services. Black students demanded lenient admissions procedures to universities and vocational training and the mounting of black studies programmes in schools and colleges.

Increasingly, emphasis was placed on separate black identity. The word 'Negro' now became a term of abuse, betokening racial appeasement. Where Du Bois had once waged a battle to ensure that the word was written with a capital 'N', now Baraka insisted on using the word 'black', and more latterly African-American has become the key term – part of a strong and culturally powerful assertion of cultural identity and self-empowerment.

Ironically, the Johnson anti-poverty programme strengthened this movement by channelling money directly into the ghettos, thereby bypassing the conventional civil-rights leadership. Initially the new generation of young black leaders who emerged with heightened polemical styles concentrated on consciousness-raising, on a distinctive life-style, on confronting the black American with the question of his own authenticity. Du Bois's double-consciousness was to be resolved in favour of blackness; 'Black is Beautiful' was the early rallying cry. Yet, as ideas developed, the essence of the message came to emphasize racial separation less than radical revolt. People like Eldridge Cleaver (*Soul on Ice*, 1968), Malcolm X (*The Autobiography of Malcolm X*, 1966), Bobby Seale (*Seize the Time*, 1970), Huey Newton (*Revolutionary Suicide*, 1973), George Jackson (*The Prison Letters of George Jackson*, 1969), and Angela Davis (*Angela Davis: An Autobiography*,

1974), moved towards a class-critique of black problems and programmes, stressing the need for black and white equally to perceive their deprived state.

▶ Since the Seventies

Paradoxically, while these radical ideas were mulling, the black stake in the established political and educational system increased over the Seventies. The percentage of Southern blacks in all-black schools dropped, from 58 per cent in 1968 to 9.2 per cent in 1972. Some 2,200 Southern blacks held political office in 1978; there were less than 100 before 1965. Though significant discrepancies remained in employment (13 per cent black unemployment, 7 per cent white in 1977) and income, equal rights legislation made employers justify non-hiring of minorities. By 1976 black families had a median income of $9,252, a 105 per cent increase over a decade – though $6,000 below the white median. Some 30 per cent of black families earned $15,000 or more, compared with 2 per cent in 1966. The rise of a black middle class – most in white enterprises, but others thanks to black entrepreneurship – came despite a time of economic recession. In the South, more than half eligible African-Americans were registered to vote by 1978. Not only did cities like Los Angeles, Cleveland, Detroit and Washington have black mayors; so did key cities in the South, like Atlanta and New Orleans. African-American students were now a larger proportion of the student body at the southern University of Alabama than on most northern campuses. The police force of McComb, Mississippi – known in the Sixties as 'The Bombing Capital of the World' – was now fully integrated; Selma, Georgia, had a Dr Martin Luther King Street.

Many of these real gains, founded on liberal Sixties measures, came when racial conflict had shifted from the limelight. President Nixon's policy was of benign neglect. The double trauma of the Vietnam War and Watergate distracted liberal consciences from the unfinished business of racial equality. Though the thesis of racial inferiority, which seemed to gain new life from Arthur Jensen's experiments with IQ, won northern-liberal scorn, problems of social integration intensified in Northern cities, where whites left for the non-metropolitan suburbs, leading to more ghettoization and urban decline. Legal enforcement of bussing to achieve racial balance in the public schools brought public protests, not least, in 1974, in abolitionist Boston. Recession and financial crisis in city budgets threatened welfare programmes for Northern blacks. Meantime more fortunate African-Americans were joining the American middle classes in ever-increasing numbers. The Conservative revival of the 1980s extended into the black community. The Black Panthers were in effect destroyed by police bullets; Bobby Seale was a Washington lobbyist, Eldridge Cleaver converted to Christianity. Though a powerful tale of African origins, Alex Haley's *Roots* (1976) could scarcely be described as revolutionary. And other writers followed Zora Neale Hurston – an influential and now revived precursor – in looking back towards folk-history and cultural origins. The most notable was Toni Morrison, who returned to Southern folk-tale and slave narrative for her novels, and whose *Song of Solomon* won the prestigious National Book Award in 1977. There were even signs of black re-migration to the South.

The 1980s saw the beginnings of a major reinterpretation of black problems – and no less the realization that their solution might take decades rather than years. Reinterpretation took several forms. One striking element was the encouragement of black women writers by the burgeoning feminist movement. Writers like Paule Marshall (*Brown Girl, Brownstones*, 1959; *The Timeless People*, 1969; and *Praisesong for the Widow*, 1983), Maya Angelou (*I Know Why the Caged Bird Sings*, 1969), Alice Walker (*Meridian*, 1976; *The Color Purple*, 1982, made into an influential movie; *The Temple of My Familar*, 1988) or the poet-playwright Ntozake Shange (*for colored girls who have considered suicide*, 1976) and Morrison herself opened new territory which is still of great influence and power. Their accounts of black female oppression often shifted the chief indictment from white racism to black male brutality, improvidence or inconstancy, overlaying and complicating the problems of race, ethnicity and colour with those of gender.

The rise of Reaganomics, and the resultant defensiveness of liberalism, also produced a new slant on racial matters. Recently arrived American Hispanics and Asian immigrants often overtook black averages in the statistics of wealth, income and achievement. Some black academics – like Thomas Sowell, William J. Wilson, Anne Wortham and Walter Williams – began asking if liberal policies such as affirmative action in school bussing, welfare, food stamps, cheap housing and employment might be sapping the enterprise and demeaning the dignity of blacks in the urban ghettos. The hoped-for gains had appeared only patchily. It is now estimated that some one-third of African-Americans are genuinely middle class, with bourgeois values, life-styles and incomes comparable to whites. But a large remainder are members of a vulnerable working class, if not underclass, with mobile, one-parent, welfare-dependent families whose youth can be as deprived, ill-educated, liable to or vulnerable to crime, exposed to gang life or drug culture, with the attendant AIDS menace, as at the start of the civil rights movement. Preferential treatment has faced other challenges. White challenges to reverse discrimination brought, in the Supreme Court, the *Bakke* (1978) and *Weber* (1979) opinions, which outlawed rigid entry quotas in professional training, though accepting affirmative action in principle; the issue has continued to be contested throughout Clinton's two presidencies.

The sense of injustice in the ghettos continued, generating incidents of racial violence or conflict in the South, Northern cities, and California. In 1987 on the new national holiday, Martin Luther King Day, the Ku Klux Klan rallied in north Georgia. A threatened commuter who shot four black youths in New York City became a local hero; Mayor Koch of New York described the running down of a black youth by a white gang as a 'racial lynching'. Such conflicts continued into the Nineties, and racially sensitive events like the Rodney King trial or the murder trial of O J Simpson in California revealed the difference in culture, values and perception between white and African-American communities. Meanwhile the diminishing of school bussing, the flight of whites from inner cities, their resort to private or parochial schools and guarded neighbourhoods, and other key shifts in social pattern have reduced the sense of a common society.

Back in 1981, a southern black banker predicted that 'what comes next is going to be rather slow'. None the less there have been signs of sustained improvement, especially in education. Since the Sixties, blacks have gained on average four years more schooling. On university campuses they are in greater numbers than ever before, often benefiting from affirmative action programmes. As a result, the black middle class has tripled in size. The 1990 census showed that of 30 million black Americans, over 9 million lived in households with an annual income of $35,000 or more, the usual definition of middle class. Many of these had abandoned the inner city for the better schools and safer streets of the suburbs, just as whites had done. In film and television, in the age of Eddie Murphy and Whoopie Goldberg, blacks no longer find themselves confined to previous stereotypical roles. In nearly all walks of life there is real evidence they have entered the mainstream – as lawyers, news presenters, city mayors, fashion models, university professors, police chiefs, sports and film celebrities on a scale that once in America would have been thought inconceivable. Few in 1960 would have imagined a black governor of Virginia (Douglas Wilder), a black mayor of New York (David Dinkins), a black Chairman of the Joint Chiefs of Staff (Colin Powell), a series about a black bourgeois family topping TV ratings (*The Cosby Show*), a Southern black banker. For all the surviving tensions, the past forty years have seen more genuine gains and opportunities for blacks than the whole of the previous century of emancipation.

Yet these advances, and these role-models, equally point up the misery of those left behind in ghettos – whose lack of skills and employment, high illegitimacy rates, involvement in crime and drugs, and high representation in the prison population show problems with no easy solutions. Black anti-Semitism, and growing awareness of the anomalies surrounding affirmative action, have alienated many whites on whose support blacks once used to rely. By the late 1990s, America was dropping many of the programmes giving groups or individuals preferential treatment on racial grounds, while President Clinton saw signs of a new, self-imposed African-American segregation, symbolized by the Nation of Islam's all-male, all-black march on Washington in 1996 – a striking contrast to Martin Luther King's inter-racial march of three decades before. Yet if black politicians like Louis Farrakhan seemed intent on sharpening the racial divide, the overall social picture was growing ever more blurred. During the 1990s, with a booming economy and demand for labour, some of the wealth was reaching the less advantaged. Meantime the growing acceptance of America as a multi-cultural and multi-racial society, and the growing influx of other races and ethnicities (not just from Asia and Latin America but blacks from the Caribbean and Africa), has reduced the historic distinction of black and white. The rise of American Asians is one of the great success stories of the second half of the later twentieth century; less noticed has been the striking achievements of black migrants (Ethiopans, for example) who have kept a sense of ethnic distinctiveness yet displayed an entrepreneurialism traditionally associated with newcomers to the USA.

In the last fifty years, a vast but partial revolution has occurred. Legal barriers have gone, racial attitudes have changed deeply. Culturally blacks are closer to the centre. August Wilson's plays can dominate Broadway, Spike Jones's films the movie house. Samuel Delaney can be recognized as one of America's leading writers of science fiction, Walter Mosley of crime fiction. The poet Rita Dove has been national Poet Laureate, Toni Morrison was awarded the Nobel Prize for Literature in 1993, Maya Angelou became the first woman poet asked to read her work at a presidential inauguration, at the start of Clinton's first term. The appearance in 1997 of a major (Norton) student anthology of African-American literature – which traced its tradition not simply to parallel white texts but to the more complex heritage of the spiritual, gospel, the folktale, jazz, blues and rap – has made the black literary canon feel newly central to American and indeed all post-colonial writing.

Yet in terms of the lives led by most African-Americans, the dawn of the twenty-first century has not ushered in the economic, social and educational equality for which they yearned. Some part of Martin Luther King's 'dream' has been achieved, but not all. The American Dream remains less accessible to many African-Americans – still labouring under the accumulated burdens of history and slavery – than to the waves of immigrants still arriving in pluri-cultural America from poverty, oppression or displacement elsewhere.

▶ For further reading

Edward L Ayers, *The Promise of the New South: Life After Reconstruction* (1992).
Eric Foner, *Reconstruction: America's Unfinished Revolution, 1863–1877* (1988).

Henry Louis Gates, *Loose Canons: Notes on the Culture Wars* (1995).

Hugh David Graham, *The Civil Rights Era: Origins and Development of National Policy* (1990).

Andrew Hacker, *Two Nations: Black and White, Separate, Hostile, Unequal* (1992).

Nicholas Lemann, *The Great Black Migration and How It Changed America* (1991).

Lawrence W Levine, *Black Culture and Black Consciousness: Afro-American Folk Thought From Slavery to Freedom* (1977).

Harvard Sitkoff, *The Struggle for Black Equality, 1954–1992* (1993).

Thomas Sowell, *Ethnic America: A History* (1981).

The loss of innocence: 1880–1914

Brian Lee and Robert Reinders

▶ Forces of change: the machine and the city

Innocence, it could be argued, is a state of mind which prefigures dual feelings of loss and guilt. Thus childhood is a period of innocence; to become adult is to sin and lose innocence. Primitives are often considered innocents dwelling in a pre-lapsarian Eden close to the divinity of Nature, but Western man with his sense of collective guilt can only yearn for and never attain the innocence of the primitive. There is, however, another sense of loss of innocence that arises in many people when the values, *mores*, even physical qualities of the lives they have inherited and take for granted appear to collapse in a world undergoing change with a rapidity that to many signifies chaos and catastrophe. The thirty-seven years after 1880 produced deep changes in the quality of American life which seriously tested older value systems and behavioural patterns. These changes – chiefly associated with industrialization and urbanization – required new disciplines, new goals and a new kind of consciousness from a predominantly rural folk. The value system based on the existential realities of an agrarian society had to be adapted and partly transformed to meet the new realities. As relations between people and their surroundings altered, new methods of description and new forms of observation had to be devised. Of course, old ways of living, thinking and seeing persisted, or at best were reluctantly accepted, and to some the new times were times of crisis and despair. But after 1900 there are indications that others saw in the new urban-industrial structures the potential for a society which was logically ordered and humanely satisfying.

If one speaks of a loss of innocence in this period it may be measured – assuming one can quantify a feeling as tenuous as innocence – in statistics which reveal a society undergoing a process of industrialization and urbanization unprecedented in New World history. If, in Wilbur Cash's words, 'Men who, as children, had heard the war-whoops of the Cherokee in the Carolina backwoods lived to hear the guns at Vicksburg', then the teenage Illinois soldier who faced Confederate artillery at Chancellorsville would live to see the miracle of man's flight, and his

Cook County cornfields consumed by the steel furnaces, stockyards and apartment houses of Chicago, and

> A midnight bounded by the bright carnival of the
>   boulevards and the dark girders of the El.
> Where once the marshland came to flower.
> Where once the deer came down to water. (Nelson Algren)

Industry had begun in America long before 1880, and technological principles had been governing many areas of American society from well before the Civil War – a war that further accelerated industrialization and commerce, and which was followed by a period of massive entrepreneurial activity. Yet the presence of the open frontier still helped sustain an image of a rural, agrarian, unmechanical America. However, once the Depression of the 1870s had ended, the United States entered on a period of unprecedented technological expansion. The indices of growth from the end of the 1870s to the advent of the First World War were unparalleled. Gross national production (in five-year averages) far outstripped population increases, and more than tripled in 1882–86 ($11.3 billion) and 1912–16 ($38.9 billion). Capital in manufacturing industries (in 1929 dollars) rose from $2.7 billion in 1879 to $20.8 billion in 1914. The goods turned out by industry increased at the same level: the index of manufacturing production (1899 = 100) rose from 42 in 1880 to 192 in 1914. America was now competing with the great industrial nations, Britain and Germany, and was outstripping both combined. The result was a change in the landscape, a change in the direction of American energy, and a change in consciousness. Americans, said the historian Henry Adams – contemplating the American industrial marvels on display at the World's Columbian Exposition, held in 1893 in the massively expanding city of Chicago, where skyscrapers rose and new commercial enterprises flourished – needed a new kind of education, a new type of awareness, to confront the world of proliferating energy now surrounding them. As Americans looked forward into the twentieth century, they began to sense a futuristic, industrial world ahead.

At the heart of this industrial transformation, touching almost all aspects of American growth, was steel. With the coming of the Bessemer and Open Hearth processes, raw steel production (in units of 1,000 short tons) grew from 597 in 1876, to 6,785 in 1895, to 35,180 in 1915. By 1990 – the year when, according to Henry Adams, the machine had turned America into a modern pluriverse – the American steel industry was outproducing Great Britain and Germany combined. Nor was it just in steel production that the US achieved primacy. The signs of industrial growth were everywhere. Although by 1880 the United States already had the longest railroad network in the world, this continued to expand from 115,547 miles of track in that year to 394,944 in 1915, while the number of passengers more than doubled between 1890 and 1912. Oil production, literally and figuratively the lubricant of an industrial society, leaped (in thousands of 42-gallon barrels) from 5,261 in 1870 to 26,286 in 1880, tripled by 1900, and more than quadrupled again by 1915. The output of coal, which remained the basic energy source throughout the period, more than doubled each decade, rising from 50 million tons in 1880 to 443 million tons in 1915. When Henry Adams felt that new laws of history were needed, based on theories of exponential energy, he was expressing the sense of change and acceleration these developments brought.

Steel, railroads, oil and coal were industries that had their inception before 1880; more revealing was the growth of industries almost totally created in the period. From Frank Sprague's first commercial electric railway in Richmond, Virginia (1887), the electrical industry mushroomed: in 1890 there were 789 electric street railways with 8,123 miles of track and carrying 2 billion passengers; and twenty-two years later, 1,260 companies operating 41,065 miles of track and carrying 9.5 billion passengers. Electric light and power, unknown in 1880, and with a total value in plant and equipment of only $34 million in 1890, took off in the 1890s as plant and equipment values grew to $234 million in 1900, $964 million in 1910, and $1,500 million in 1914. If the growth of the electric industry aroused the enthusiasm of financiers and manufacturers, it also increasingly provided light and electric services to an expanding population. In 1907, 8 per cent of all dwelling units had electricity, a figure that had doubled by 1912 and tripled by 1917. Net production of electrical energy (in millions of kilowatts) rose from 2,507 in 1902 to 11,569 in 1912. The telephone, a curiosity at the Philadelphia Exposition of 1876, and still a rarity in 1890, when only 3.6 persons per 1,000 enjoyed the dubious honour of owning these primitive implements, increased so rapidly that by 1915 the ratio of telephones to population was one to ten. All of this growth – the above figures are only selective – meant an outpouring of goods available to a consuming public. The value of semi-durables (in current producer's prices) more than tripled between 1879 and 1915 ($828.2 million to $2,636 million) and consumer durables increased nearly 600 per cent ($304.3 million to $1,700 million).

Attendant on the growth of industry was the expansion of urban centres. The urban population (measured as communities of 2,500 and over) grew from 14,130,000 in 1880 to 41,999,000 in 1910, and although it was not until 1920 that the census indicated the urban population exceeded the rural population, it is likely that such a figure had been reached by 1914. In 1880, 28 per cent of the population lived in urban areas; by 1910, 44 per cent did so. Established cities grew at an unprecedented pace. The ten largest cities in America in 1910 – New York (including Brooklyn), Chicago, Philadelphia, St Louis, Boston, Cleveland, Baltimore, Pittsburgh (including Alleghany), Detroit and Buffalo – had had an almost three-fold population increase in the preceding thirty years: 4,835,688 to

Table 8.1 Population of newly created cities

	1880	1910
Los Angeles	11,183	319,198
Minneapolis	46,887	301,408
Kansas City	55,785	248,381
Seattle	3,533	237,194
St Paul	41,473	214,744
Denver	35,629	213,381
Portland, Ore.	17,577	207,214
Atlanta	37,409	154,839
Oakland	34,555	150,174

Table 8.2 Numbers of urban centres

Population ('000s)	50–100	25–50	10–25	5–10	2.5–5	1–2.5
1880	15	42	146	249	467	–
1890	30	66	230	340	654	1,603
1900	40	82	280	465	832	2,128
1910	59	119	309	605	1,060	2,717

12,631,602. New York alone increased its population from, 1,772,962 to 4,766,883; Chicago, the Topsy of American major cities, doubled its 1880 population in a decade (503,185 to 1,099,850) and had nearly doubled that figure again by 1910 (2,185,283). In the same thirty years, St Louis, Boston, Baltimore, San Francisco, Washington, Jersey City, Pittsburgh and Providence doubled their populations, while Cleveland, Buffalo, Milwaukee, Detroit and Newark more than tripled theirs.

All of these cities had, of course, been urban centres before 1880. More dramatic still, perhaps, was the growth of cities which were almost totally created in the period. It is in these cities that the sense of rural to urban change must have appeared most challenging and, to some, most traumatic, as the figures in Table 8.1 indicate.

But perhaps the main agency for diffusing urban life-styles and values were smaller cities. Their numbers grew rapidly between 1880 and 1910, as shown in Table 8.2.

In the period 1880–1910, thousands of sleepy little townships, with their few services for the surrounding agricultural population, were transformed into 'cities'. Where once had been a few false-fronted stores, a blacksmith's shop and a church or two, now there would be a bank, a weekly or even a daily newspaper, paved streets, a YMCA, a Masonic Hall, an Odd Fellows Hall, perhaps an armoury, speciality stores, a department store, an expanded railroad station, a street railway line, a hospital, uniformed police, and a scattering of small factories and warehouses. Small as some of these communities were, each had its own sense of urban identity, and the citizenry was increasingly conscious of itself in contrast to the rural folk that invaded the town on Saturday nights, 'whiskered adults self-conscious in their Sunday "best", young swains beauing bashful sweethearts, thin-chested mothers herding restless broods'.

Improvements in medical care helped urban areas to grow by natural increase, but this alone could never have accounted for the dramatic rate of development experienced by cities after 1880. The largest immigration to urban areas came from farms and villages. Thanks to mechanization, agriculture required fewer workers: in 1880, one farm worker could supply 5.6 persons and by 1920 he could feed 8.3; the number of man-hours required to cultivate an acre of wheat or corn dropped by one-third between 1880 and 1914. Agricultural areas, with their high birth-rates, provided a surplus labour supply which could not be absorbed by the opening of new agricultural lands in the Great Plains. The 'Buckwheats' drifted into cities, often by way of a few years spent in a village or township. New England, where rural depopulation had begun before the Civil War, saw a continuous farm-to-city migration. In the decade 1880–90, 932 of 1,502 townships in New England lost population as people moved to the cities. In 1880 the urban and rural populations of the north-eastern states almost balanced, but while the rural population thereafter remained constant at 7 million, the urban population had risen to 18.5 million by 1910. By the 1880s, rural depopulation had spread to the Mid-West; over half of the townships in Ohio and Illinois declined in population during the decade. Blake McKelvey estimated that 11 million urbanites in 1910 had moved from rural homes after 1880, and that one-third of all urban residents in 1910 were of rural American origin.

Urban centres were also swollen by large numbers of foreign-born citizens, chiefly from southern and eastern Europe. (In 1910 over half of all foreign-born originated in southern and eastern Europe.) Between 1880 and 1914, over 13 million immigrants entered America's portals. Some were temporary residents and eventually returned to their native countries; others took up agricultural occupations, often after a sojourn in a major city, but the majority of the foreign-born settled in US cities. In 1910 there were 9,635,900 foreign-born in America's cities, and an additional 12,346,900 native-born of foreign or mixed parentage. The European immigrants were concentrated particularly in large urban centres. According to the 1910 census, of the ten largest cities in America, 3,183,116 residents were of white native American parentage, 4,605,860 were of foreign or mixed parentage, 4,706,117 were foreign-born, and 336,493 were African-Americans. In only four cities – Philadelphia, St Louis, Baltimore and Buffalo – did those of native American parentage outnumber the foreign-born; and only in Baltimore did the native population exceed the foreign-born and American-born population of foreign or mixed parentage. Thus 75 per cent of the population of America's ten largest cities were either foreign-born or only a generation removed from foreign-born parents. The memory of Europe hung heavily over the American city.

▶ Looking backward

Yet these new experiences and those immigrant forces found little direct reflection in the expressive culture, little presence in literature. Life in the new American city, whether for the immigrant or the in-migrant, did not, it seemed, transmute easily into art. Indeed, in the face of change, American writing seemed generally slow to react. Since the Civil War, the dominant movement had been realism, a realism that explored some of the new communities and settings of American life, that looked for inspiration and 'local colour' to the life of the Plains or the Mississippi Valley. The three major novelists were Mark Twain, writing his vernacular, deflationary realism from roots in South-west humour; William Dean Howells, arguing the case for realism as the discourse of democratic ordinariness and 'smiling' American values; and Henry James, refining realism to aesthetic precision in Europe. Howells's best novel, *The Rise of Silas Lapham* (1885), brings a self-made paint manufacturer forward from the 'day of small things' before the Civil War into the new world of trusts and mergers. The corruptions of the system defeat him financially, but his morality remains. Howells imposes on the new landscape of commerce and industry the old, domestic, moral image of the family. Enthusiasts now began to proclaim in the last decades of the century that new literary movements and centres were emerging; but their proclamations remained no more than brave acts of faith as long as they were issued – like Hamlin Garland's statements on behalf of the movement of 'veritism', in *Crumbling Idols* (1890) – from the traditional literary capital, Boston. There were perceptible signs of shift. In 1889 Howells moved from Boston to New York, celebrating the new venture with a book in a fresh manner, *A Hazard of New Fortunes* (1890), which indicates within itself that a new language of fiction must be found. Garland would attend the Chicago Columbian Exposition to proclaim the need for a new Middle-Western literature, but it is not really until after 1900, with Theodore Dreiser's *Sister Carrie*, that we see the signs of this, and the real outcome had to wait for the 'Chicago Renaissance' of twenty years later, when writers like Carl Sandburg, Sherwood Anderson and Vachel Lindsay distilled the experience of the 'Second City' and the 'Hogbutcher of the World' into poetry and prose.

In 1887, Eleanor and Edward Marx Aveling, in their book *The Working-Class Movement in America*, complained that American literature had so far produced no studies of factory hands or dwellers in tenement houses: no

Uncle Tom's Cabin of capitalism. By 1906 Jack London would be proclaiming that Upton Sinclair's *The Jungle* had done this, but in the 1880s the promise seemed slim. That American culture at that time was backward-looking, more aware of lost innocence than future power, is nicely demonstrated by Larzer Ziff in his *The American 1890s*, where he describes a benefit reading given in 1887 for the American Copyright League by the day's major writers, including John Greenleaf Whittier, Oliver Wendell Holmes, James Russell Lowell, Mark Twain, Edward Eggleston, George Washington Cable and James Whitcomb Riley. Some of these were realists, but all were writers whose talents had been nourished in a different America and whose best literary efforts were employed to chronicle its passing. Others, like Henry James and Henry Adams, also felt themselves to be lone survivors from a golden past, but they elected to recapture it in Europe rather than America. And when they did turn their attention to contemporary America – in James's *The American Scene* (1907), Adams's *Education of Henry Adams* (1907) – it was to express a sense of void and despair at the chaos and ugliness or the mental disorder created out of the 'large and noble sanities' of the past. Thus the excitement generated by a society transforming itself within a generation did little to affect their gloomy conviction that there 'cannot really be any substitute for round-about experience, for troublesome history, for the long, unmitigable process of time'. All, perhaps, sensed the need for a new language, but it was slow to come, though gradually the 1890s made the great formal transition from moral realism to a deterministic, process-centred naturalism: a writing that increasingly found its centre in the new urban and industrial America.

But perhaps this slowness is understandable. Certainly now many native-born Americans could claim two or more generations of urban dwelling; moreover, many foreign-born, especially Jews, now came to America from European urban centres. Yet, though exact statistics are not available, indirect evidence indicates that the bulk of the native- and foreign-born who moved into the American cities after 1880 came from rural and village backgrounds. They were, as Herbert G Gutman contends, a pre-industrial folk 'who brought into industrial society ways of work and other habits and values not associated with industrial necessities and the industrial ethos'. Under the conditions of urbanization and industrialization, their folk behaviour and values were seriously challenged and transformed. Rural traditions and localism, linchpins of identity, broke down in urban anonymity. The Polish peasant came from a society where 'Every tree, every large stone, every pit, meadow, field, has an individuality of its own and often a name. The same tendency shows itself in the individualization, often even anthropomorphization of time . . . time becomes part of nature, and individualized periods of time become natural objects.' Whereas in America time takes on a different character: 'I long terribly for my country', Aleksander Wolski wrote home to Poland, 'nothing gives me pleasure in America. We must be very attentive in our work, every hour, because if anything is bad we are without work.' In Europe the peasant's social environment was bounded and determined by primary groups. 'The Sicilian peasant's interests are literally limited by the skyline. His only interests are the local interests of his village ... The spirit of *campanilismo*, of dwelling under one's church tower, of jealous loyalty to *Paesani*, to his fellow villagers, circumscribes the Sicilian's social, religious, and business life' (Harvey Zorbaugh, *The Gold Coast and the Slum*, 1950).

Industrialization imposed on the immigrant and native American of rural backgrounds a novel discipline which required conformity and routinized behaviour rare in rural society. The wage system separated the individual from ritual duties and obligations. Factories and mills required regularized, clock-based attendance, and a repetitive and constant work pattern. What was expected of the immigrant worker is found in a booklet to teach English to Polish labourers of the International Harvester Corporation:

Lesson One. I hear the whistle. I must hurry. I hear the five minute whistle. It is time to go into the shop. I take my check from the gate board and hang it on the department board. I change my clothes and get ready to work. The starting whistle blows. I eat my lunch. It is forbidden to eat until then. The whistle blows at five minutes of starting time. I get ready to go to work. I work until the whistle blows to quit. I leave my place nice and clean. I put all my clothes in the locker. I must go home.

Discipline was imposed on workers by men who themselves were part of a hierarchical system. In industry, unlike rural society, there existed a separation of ownership, direction and labour.

In the rural mind, accommodation was interwoven with land, and, without land, the family 'cannot act as a unit with regard to the rest of the community; it ceases to count as a social power' (W Thomas and F Znaniecki, *The Polish Peasant in Europe and America*, 1927). Even where rural dwellers were tenants, they had certain 'rights' to property by law or custom, and they were normally closely associated with property owners. In the city, dwellings were separated from land. The individualized, if often substandard, character of the rural home became in the city the tenement, and with the tenement block come an enforced and unnatural community. The relationship between the individual and his dwelling-place was casual and contractual – the contract often being made with an owner several agents removed from the tenant. Throughout the period, two-thirds of all housing was tenant-occupied: in 1900 in New York 87.9 per cent and in Chicago 74.9 per cent of all housing units were rented. Chicago was notorious for its railroad flats and New York for its tenements. In 1893, the year in which Stephen Crane published *Maggie*, over half of New York's population lived in tenement houses. The conditions of such lives have never been better described than by the twenty-one-year-old protégé of Garland and Howells:

> Eventually they entered a dark region where, from a careening building, a dozen gruesome doorways gave up loads of babies to the street and the gutter. A wind of early autumn raised yellow dust from cobbles and swirled it against a hundred windows. Long streamers of garments fluttered from fire-escapes. In all unhandy places there were buckets, brooms, rags, and bottles. In the street infants played or fought with other infants or sat stupidly in the way of vehicles. Formidable women, with uncombed hair and disordered dress, gossiped while leaning on railings, or screamed in frantic quarrels. Withered persons, in curious postures of submission to something, sat smoking pipes in obscure corners. A thousand odours of cooking food came forth to the street. The building quivered and creaked from the weight of humanity stamping about in its bowels.

Indeed, Crane's *Maggie* would begin to fulfil the Avelings' appeal for a literature of the American tenement, just as in 1899 Frank Norris's *McTeague* and in 1900 Dreiser's *Sister Carrie* would help fulfil Garland's prophecy of a Western literary movement based on the new realism: not, as H L Mencken said, 'the old, flabby, kittenish realism of Howell's imitators', but a new vision that got under the surface of things. Where James, Adams and Howells himself emphasized the chaos amid the crumbling eighteenth-century and nineteenth-century principles, their successors now began to chart the powerful forces that were to shape twentieth-century America. *Maggie* works by an observant indifference, noting inexorable processes at work, refusing moralistic conclusions. *McTeague* applies a naturalistic system to the story of a brutish San Francisco dentist and his thrifty Swiss immigrant wife. *Sister Carrie* explores the almost biological ascent of Carrie Meeber through the world of goods and cities from poverty to dominance. The older realism, morally concerned, was now giving way to new languages and codes for charting the new order of things. It explored the detail of city life, the workings of heredity and environment, the sense of social struggle. Even fiction about rural America – Frank Norris's *The Octopus* (1901), for example, set in California's San Fernando valley – is about the impact on farmers of the pressures of the monopolistic railroad. In the world of pastoral, machine and the system prevail.

The same shift was evident in other areas. Before the Civil War, opportunity had been defined in largely agrarian terms, in the spirit of Horace Greeley's advice: 'Go west, young man.' But now it was increasingly described in an urban context. Thus, in the novels of Horatio Alger – the most popular novelist in American history – the hero, with a few variations, comes from a farm or village, and with luck and pluck succeeds in the city. Or to use another example: in a famous lithograph of the period, a young man resting on a rural hillside, plough beside him, looks upon an idealized industrial city, aglow and challenging, which in its complexity contrasts with the simplicity of the rural setting. The picture is called 'The Lure of the City'. Dreiser, who first saw Chicago in 1884, never forgot the 'urge and sting' of his first days there, and used the experience to write the opening chapters of *Sister Carrie*. He also recalled his feelings directly in *Dawn*:

> I washed my face and brushed my clothes, then knelt down by the window – because I could hang farther out by doing so – and looked out. East and west, for miles, as it seemed to me, was a double row of gas lamps already flaring in the dusk, and behind them the lighted faces of shops and, as they seemed to me, very brightly lighted, glowing in fact. And again, there were those Madison Street horsecars, yellow in color, jingling to and fro, their horses' feet plop-plopping as they came and went, and just as they had when I sold papers here four years before. And the scores and scores of pedestrians walking in the rain, some with umbrellas, some not, some hurrying, some not. New land, new life, was what my heart was singing! Inside the street cars, like toy men and women, were the acclimated Chicagoans, those who had been here long before I came, no doubt. Beautiful! Like a scene in a play: an Aladdin view in the Arabian nights. Cars, people, lights, shops! The odor and flavor of the city, the vastness of its reaches, seemed to speak or sing or tinkle like a living, breathing thing. It came to me again with inexpressible variety and richness, as if to say: 'I am the soul of a million people! I am their joys, their prides, their loves, their appetites, their hungers, their sorrows! I am their good clothes and their poor ones, their light, their food, their lusts, their industries, their enthusiasms, their dreams! In me are all the pulses and wonders and tastes and loves of life itself! I am life! This is Paradise! This is the mirage of the heart and brain and blood of which people dream. I am the pulsing urge of the universe! You are a part of me, I of you! All that life or hope is or can be or do, this I am, and it is here before you! Take of it! Live, live, satisfy your heart! Strive to be what you wish to be you now while you are young and of it! Reflect its fire, its tang, its color, its greatness! Be, be, wonderful or strong or great, if you will but be!'

The cultural dominance of the city led to a changing image of the farmer. Before the Civil War the farmer was deemed an ideal type: the noble yeoman, the horny-handed son of toil, a man of nature, a Cincinnatus. But after the war the farmer became, in urban parlance, a 'hayseed', 'rube' or 'hick'. Where once his nobility was extolled, the farmer became a comic figure on the stage, dressed in overalls and sporting a goatee. One of the earliest Edison records was entitled 'Moving Day in Pumpkin Center' and reinforced the stereotype of the humbling, backward farmer already common on the stage. By the 1880s a literature about rural degeneracy appeared which would have been inexplicable before the Civil War. 'My people are degenerates; the people all through my district are degenerates', a New England rural pastor wrote to a Boston newspaper. Robert Dugdale's 'Jukes' of New York, Frank Blackmuir's 'Smoky Pilgrims' of Kansas and Henry Goddard's 'Kallikaks' of New Jersey, all came to symbolize a drama of rural decay.

Farm protest in the nineteenth century had its roots in real, economic grievances. The farmer was exploited by industrialists and businessmen who represented an urban-based elite. Adding fuel to farm bitterness was the knowledge that the urban exploiter also attracted their children. The city was the symbolic Babylon which lured the rural children of Israel. And as the city ways dominated, so rural inferiority increased. In Will Carlton's *Farm Ballads* the mother – soon to be sent 'Over the hill to the poor house' – rails at her daughter-in-law who had come from town: 'She was quite conciety, and carried a heap o' style.' The rural hostility is poignantly captured in Hamlin Garland's story, 'Up the Coulé', in *Main Travelled Roads* (1891), where the city and farm brothers face each other:

> They stood and looked at each other. Howard's cuffs, collar and shirt, alien in their elegance, showed through the dusk, and a glint of light shot out from the jewel of his necktie . . . As they gazed in silence at each other, Howard divined something of the hard, bitter feeling which came into Grant's heart as he stood there, ragged, ankle-deep in muck, his sleeves rolled up, a shapeless old straw hat on his head.

This sense of bitterness, combined with inferiority feelings, was a persistent strain running through farm protest movements before 1900. Richard Hofstadter, in his *The Age of Reform* (1955), contends that 'The agrarian myth encouraged farmers to believe that they were not themselves an organic part of the whole order of business enterprise and speculation that flourished in the city, partaking of its character and sharing in its risks, but rather the innocent pastoral victims of a conspiracy hatched in the distance. The notion of an innocent and victimized population colors the whole history of agrarian controversy. . .'.

The farmers mourned for their children in the cities; equally important was the fact that the children bemoaned the lost innocence of a rural past. In 1910 over half of the city population had an American or European past rooted in the land or in a local rural community. It was almost inevitable, therefore, that a literature of rural nostalgia would appeal to their collective memory. Indeed the school of local-colour writing, an important phenomenon of this period, must be considered in the context of an urban nostalgia for a rural past. Unlike much of the literature of the 1920s, with its acerbic views of village and country life, pre-First World War writing is almost elegiac in re-creating rural joys. This is true of Mark Twain's Hannibal, Zona Gale's Friendship Village, Sara Orne Jewett's Maine Villages, Edward Eggleston's Flat Creek, and Hamlin Garland's Wisconsin and Iowa farmers. Nowhere is this sense of rural nostalgia more vividly portrayed than by the popular and commercially successful poet James Whitcomb Riley. Born in the small Indiana town of Greenfield, he moved to Indianapolis, and lived there until his death in 1916. His poems are a paean to rural Indiana, with Doc Sifers, Little Orphan Annie, Old Aunt Mary, Squire Hawkins, Tradin' Joe, and Uncle Sifers offering sage rural advice from the front porches of Griggsby Junction. In the country, Riley saw man close to Nature. There was a different time scale, different sounds, colours, and smells:

> The husky, rusty, russel of the tassels of the corn,
> And the raspin' of the tangled leaves, as golden as the morn.

The city, by contrast, was artificial:

> My son-in-law said, when he lived in town,
> He jest natchurly pined, night and day
> For a sight of the woods, er a acre of ground
> Where the trees wasent all cleared away!

The contrast between the country (natural) and city (artificial) is a common theme in Riley's poems. Rural nostalgia is probably a less common theme in ethnic literature because much of it was written by relatively assimilated second- and third-generation Americans. That it existed on an intimate and personal level is indicated in the letters of Polish peasants collected by W I Thomas and Florian Znaniencki. Letters from Poland are filled with references to rural concerns, and from urban America came letters enquiring about crops, livestock, and the village community.

For other writers, rural values and country scenes were beyond recapture, and nostalgia, however comforting, was an unsatisfactory emotion. Yet the rural memories remained, as they would through into twentieth-century literature, in Anderson, Hemingway and Faulkner; and the lure of the city never quite obliterated the sense of loss which the move from the country entailed. One simple escape from this dilemma was into an untroubled and unconditioned future; and it is significant that, with the decline of Utopian communities during the third quarter of the nineteenth century, Utopian literature simultaneously increased in volume in works like Edward Bellamy's *Looking Backward* (1888) or Ignatius Donnelly's *Caesar's' Column* (1891). Often reformist and populist in spirit, these works expressed, in the form of romantic pastoral, a fear and hatred of modern technological and industrial society. Essentially it derived from the same impulses that lay behind another popular form, the historical novel, and it mattered little whether the authors looked backwards or forwards; it was always away from immediately contemporary America. One of the exceptions was Mark Twain's *A Connecticut Yankee in King Arthur's Court* (1889), a parody of this type of yearning romance, which squarely confronts the complex issues of primitivism and progress. Out of ambivalent feelings towards past and present, he creates a complex ironic pastoral which ends with his Yankee mechanic in sixth-century Camelot trapped behind an electric fence, surrounded by corpses. When one of his characters laments in the postscript 'We had conquered; in turn we were conquered', this sums up not only Twain's ambiguity about industrial innovation, but what many sensitive Americans felt about the progress or otherwise of the Gilded Age.

The image of the new America, industrial and urban, proved in fact hard to grasp. One way of measuring it was in its changing relationship with Europe: a theme, of course, in the novels of Henry James. America had once stood, to itself and others, for innocence (one need only recall the vogue for James Fenimore Cooper in Britain and Germany) and a predominantly agricultural America had been seen by many as, in Jefferson's words, 'the last best hope of mankind'. By contrast, Europe was old, class-ridden, wise (or at least sly): mobs roamed its cities, and its poor filled its prisons, workhouses, mines and mills. In President Monroe's words, the European political system was 'essentially different . . . from that of America'. Europe was beyond redemption. But what of an America which filled its sky with acrid smoke, sent its children down mine-shafts or into textile mills, and created its own chaotic and formless cities? Old ideals seemed lost; perhaps the simplest answer was to follow Marx and state that the United States was no exception to the contradictions of capitalism and class struggle, nor immune to a proletarian revolution. Or one might ignore differences, and fall back on belief in a community of interests, as in the cult of Anglo-Saxonia popular among upper-class Americans and North Europeans, but also present in the writings of Frank Norris and the socialist Jack London. Others argued that America had now become corrupt: that the world of Henry Adams's Arcadian boyhood in Quincy had, in a short time, become the world of banks and trusts, dominated by J P Morgan, John D Rockefeller, and other business predators. To such people, Europe often beckoned, much as it does in the fiction of Henry James and Edith Wharton, with the promise of cultural values that could transcend the vulgarity of American materialism. One might thus conceive of a culture irrevocably split between culture and process, drama and reality. Or one might argue, like Henry Adams in his *Education*, that the New World called for a new account of history, a new type of consciousness, or perhaps a new pragmatism that could order the increasing sense of chaos.

▶ Looking forward

And there were indeed those who found justifications for and challenges in the new society. These individuals did not idealize a bucolic past, nor apparently did they feel any sense of innocence betrayed. Rather, they saw factories and cities as the inevitable products of Progress. In terms of the American past it was relatively easy to justify industrialization and *laissez-faire* capitalism. The factory was merely the large-scale manifestation of industrial processes that had been going on in New England homes since the seventeenth century. It was said of Henry Ford that when he looked out of his office window he never saw the massive River Rouge plant, but only his machine shop in Greenfield village. Certainly machines to save time and cut costs were essential in a nation with a chronic shortage of labour. On the level of ideology there were few problems. The Puritan ethic with its stress on thrift, industry and frugality, its admonition to 'work for the night is coming', was as applicable to the industrialist Amos Lawrence in the nineteenth century as it had been to his agricultural forebears in the Massachusetts Bay Colony. The Jacksonian division between productive and non-productive classes may have cast aspersions on bankers and stockholders, but not on the honest industrialist. Alexander Hamilton, Matthew Carey and Henry Clay had an image of an industrialized America long before the Civil War. Even in the South, where rural and patriarchal values lingered the longest, ante-bellum proposals for industrial expansion were greeted with enthusiasm, albeit with little money. In the Gilded Age the movement to extend railroads and open cotton mills and iron foundries was carried forth on a wave of Southern nationalism and crusading rhetoric. The general American delight in statistics – agricultural, commercial, industrial – reflected the faith of a nation which identified its validity not in a hoary past but a bright future. Americans were by nature teleological in their thinking.

Social Darwinism reinforced the older American business and industrial ethos. Charles Darwin and Herbert Spencer offered a scientific rationale for a *laissez-faire* system based on competition, and flattery for those who survived the struggle for competitive existence. Most importantly, Spencer argued that social evolution was inevitable, and that its apogee was in Western industrial society. The Americans, Spencer stated, could 'reasonably look forward to a time when they will have produced a civilization grander than any the world has known'. Furthermore, Spencerians could invoke the 'Master' – as Andrew Carnegie called Spencer – to oppose any criticisms of the industrial system. Scientific 'laws' supported *laissez-faire* capitalism; to interfere with them would be harmful in the short term and absurd over the long run. Nor was Spencer's scheme at odds with the rise of big business. John D Rockefeller, half Spencerian, half Puritan divine, expressed this view in a Sunday School address:

> The growth of big business is merely the survival of the fittest . . .
> The American beauty rose can be produced in the splendor and
> fragrance which bring cheer to its beholder only by sacrificing the
> early buds which grow up around it. This is not an evil tendency
> in business. It is merely the working-out of a law of nature and
> a law of god.

'Not evil, but good', Carnegie declared, 'has come to the race from
the accumulation of wealth by those who have the ability and energy to
produce it.'

The critics of *laissez-faire* capitalism did not, with the exception of
Henry George, decry industrialism. In part this was because they were
soaked in Spencerian thought, and their criticisms of Spencer's conclusions were usually argued in terms of evolutionary premises. John R
Commons stated that 'I was brought up on Hoosierism, Republicanism,
Presbyterianism, and Spencerianism'. And Commons was not alone
in American intellectual circles. The economists and sociologists who
studied in Germany or at Johns Hopkins accepted evolution and with it
the concomitant view that the growth of industry was inevitable and desir-
able. Lester Ward contended that human evolution proved the validity of
co-operation rather than competition, and nowhere was this more true
than in advanced industrial states.

What the critics of *laissez-faire* capitalism wished to do was to measure
the effects of industrialism by moral considerations. And they were willing to advocate the use of the state not to destroy industry – few were
interested in William Morris's neo-Medievalism – but to use its powers to
ensure competition and soften the impact on those least able to survive
in the industrial jungle. Thus Edward Bellamy's *Looking Backward* (1887),
the most popular Gilded Age criticism of contemporary society, depicts a
good and humane future world which is both pastoral and intensely
industrial. Bellamy's readers could easily extrapolate his Boston of 2001
from potential tendencies of 1887. Perfection no longer was dependent
on a close harmony and communion with Nature. Right reason, a touch
of 'true' Christianity, and the rational organization of industry could
provide the good society and a higher form of mankind.

Evolutionary thought, in particular its concepts of inevitability, and
the realities of industrialization and urbanism, forced literary figures to
observe and analyse the world in a new way, and to discover new literary
forms in which the new dimensions of society could be expressed. Writers
were freed from the incubus of the past which was, in Spencerian terms
at least, meaningless. The contemporary scene was found in the spatial
dimensions of the city, the binding discipline of commercial or industrial
work, and all determined by forces over which the individual had little
control. Stephen Crane's *Maggie* in New York could no more prevent her
tragic fate than could Upton Sinclair's back-of-the-yards Lithuanians in

The Jungle of Chicago. Frank Norris's Grain Exchange and the working of the Southern Pacific Railroad in *The Octopus* (1901) and *The Pit* (1903) were locations in which the universal rules of competition and the struggle for existence prevailed. Its actors were puppets in some dimly perceived evolutionary plan. The naturalists seldom seriously question a society based on competition, one that produced mill hands and millionaires. They might consider it vulgar, as Dreiser and Samuel Fuller did, but it existed, and existence transcended moral judgments. Paul Dressler might have sung about the memories of 'new mown hay' along the banks of the Wabash, but his brother Theodore Dreiser had no such romantic notions. In Theodore's world there were no innocents, least of all in Indiana.

In many ways, industry was easier to justify and adjust to than was the city. The discipline imposed by the factory may have been alien to immigrants and Americans of rural origins, but the factory as such was not incompatible with America's past value system. And in Social Darwinism the large factory and monopoly capitalism had the sanction of Science and the aura of Progress. The literature of naturalism and realism found its roots and its defences in an industrial society. Although the city was a logical result of industrialization, it seemed a more alienating force – somehow less 'American' than the Carnegie Steel Works. Josiah Strong, writing in 1885, saw the city as a 'serious menace to our civilization'. It was filled with unassimilated foreigners and Roman Catholics, along with 'gamblers, thieves, saloon keepers and all the worse elements of society'. 'Here the sway of Mammon is widest and his worship the most constant eager.' In the city, where riches contrasted with dire poverty, governments were apt to be corrupt and thus the heresy of socialism was likely to find advocates.

The city impinged on people's consciousness more than the workplace, and the city contrasted vividly with real or imagined memories of a rural past. Where the factory and office were efficient and work was routinized, and to that extent acceptable, the city was filthy, ugly, chaotic and alienating. A girl from Emporia, Kansas, desperately lonely in Chicago, caught this sense of alienation:

> The city is like that. In all my work there had been the same lack
> of any personal touch. In all this city of three million souls I knew
> no one, cared for no one, was cared for by no one . . . I had read
> how the universe is composed of millions of stars whirling about.
> I looked up at the sky. I was just like that – an atom whirled about
> with three million other atoms, day after day, month after mouth,
> year after year.

There was no focus, no sense of community except what the individual might create out of his organizational ties: the lodge, ethnic saloon, trade union, fire company, political club, literary society, church.

By the turn of the century the bleak view of the city began to change. Progressive reformers became increasingly convinced that the city was politically redeemable, that corrupt bosses could be overthrown, that the city could be operated efficiently and humanely. The structure of city government, hitherto modelled on two-house legislatures, typical of state and national governments, could be transformed by the strong mayor system, or by introducing city manager or commission forms of government. Urban reformers declared that the city need not look like a treeless jungle, that parks, boulevards and recreation centres would provide breathing space and beauty to an urban population. While many reformers had an ambivalent view of the foreign-born, others, chiefly from the settlement houses, saw in the immigrant community values which were lacking in American natives. Then, too, there were millions who by 1910 were born in cities, and for whom there was no alternative living place; nor was there a rural past except as a folk memory passed down from an older generation.

The concept of the city as a distinct urban form, and as a positive and beneficial force, was reflected by the turn of the century in new physical appearances and in new ways of interpreting life in the metropolis. A remarkable group of engineer-architects – William LeBaron Jenny, Dankmar Adler, Daniel Burnham, John Wellborn Root, Louis Sullivan – created in the steel-girdered skyscraper a *city* architecture. The skyscraper evolved from technological advances and urban commercial motivations. Structural steel and the hydraulic and, later, electric elevator, allowed for an upward extension of buildings, and high land prices in central business districts made the skyscraper economically viable. The skyscraper presented a unique cityscape. Tall buildings – offices, factories and apartment houses – came to distinguish the town from the country. The city was now not merely the town overgrown, but physically a new creation. The skyscraper became the symbol of a triumphant urbanism.

Men who could change the skyline of American cities could also determine other aspects of its physical appearance. Throughout America, planners were stimulated by the World's Columbian Exposition of 1893 with its overall contribution of architecture, landscaping and lake-shore setting. Parks, parkways, recreational centres, were expanded or created in all major American cities. It seemed possible, as Daniel Burnham and Edward A Bennett remarked in their general plan for Chicago, for a city to 'be made an efficient instrument for providing all its people with the best possible conditions of living'. The concepts and plans which Burnham and others in America drew and put into practice was popularly called the 'City Beautiful' movement. The title itself indicates a new and positive conception of the city.

Settlement houses, starting with Chicago's Hull House in 1891, and numbering over 400 by 1915, became the locus for a new evaluation of the city. Settlement-house residents accepted the city as the basic context in which they lived. Their efforts to create a sense of community in the slums did not grow out of any desire to re-establish a rural or village society, but rather because community was a means of breaking down urban alienation. They argued that their experience showed that the city was capable of regeneration by reforms, example and community spirit.

Settlement-house workers usually stressed the 'scientific' character of their work, by which they meant that they developed a methodology for observing and studying the social and economic conditions of the city. Sociologists, in particular Robert E Park of the University of Chicago, developed a theory of urban ecology which assumed that cities lent themselves to scientific observation, that change – the life blood of sociology – could be charted, and that in the city human behaviour was as 'natural' as in a rural society. Although the Chicago school of urban sociology operated from environmental premises which stretched back to Jefferson, it denied that there were associations between environmental conditions and moral results. Park and other American urban sociologists rejected such categories as rural innocence and urban depravity.

In his autobiography, the progressive urban reformer, Frederick C Howe, writes of his conversion to a new conception of the city:

> The possibility of a free, orderly, and beautiful city became to me an absorbing passion. I had an architectonic vision of what a city might be. I saw it as a picture. It was not economy, efficiency, and business methods that interested me so much as a city planned, built, and conducted as a community enterprise. The city was the enthusiasm of my life. And I saw cities as social agencies that would make life easier for people, full of pleasure, beauty and opportunity.

Except in Whitman, or city booster literature, it would be rare to find such a fulsome view of urban life in the nineteenth century. By the time Howe was writing, the city need no longer represent sinful menace, but promise. In *Sister Carrie*, it lures like a magnet or a lover; in *The Jungle* it contains the political seeds of its own amelioration. And for the writers of the developing new arts movement that stirred the United States around 1912, when Progressivism seemed dominant, Woodrow Wilson was elected, radical and avant-garde causes abounded, and the impact of European modernism began to reach American shores, the city was experimental bohemia, dislodging the Puritanism of an old and confined America. When Sherwood Anderson in 1912 walked out of his paint factory in Ohio and moved to Chicago and the modern arts, he felt he was experiencing the transition of an entire generation, advancing, certainly, into the complexities of modern industrialism, but away from the confinements of the small town and the past. In any case, as the tentacles of railroad lines and, later, highways spread to the farthest reaches of the country, the old rural–urban distinctions began to collapse.

By the early Twenties, America was sure of its modern condition. Around this time, too, Professor Charles J Galpin of the University of Wisconsin was discovering 'rurban' areas where farm and town had developed a symbiotic relationship, so that the distinction of behaviour and value systems between them diminished. Certainly rural nostalgia, and appeals to the virtues of agrarian life, as well as to images of the city as Waste Land or Slough of Despond, persisted in American thought and art after the First Would War. But increasingly these struggles were focused in recognition of the complex power and pull of the modern city, or else they became defensive and cranky. Innocence, in so far as it was based on images of pioneers, noble yeoman and villagers, itself became either complex – as in Hemingway – or suburbanly sentimental. Factories and cities, and an acceptance of their life-styles and discipline, had created a new reality.

▶ For further reading

P Conn, *The Divided Mind: Ideology and Imagination in America, 1860–1920* (1983).

Herbert G Guttman, *Work, Culture and Society in Industrializing America: Essays in American Working-Class and Social History* (1976).

Alfred Kazin, *On Native Grounds: An Interpretation of Modern American Prose Literature* (1942).

T J J Lears, *No Place of Grace: Antimodernism and the Transformation of American Culture, 1880–1920* (1920).

Blake McKelvey, *The Urbanization of America, 1860–1915* (1963).

Robert H Wiebe, *The Search for Order, 1877–1920* (1967).

9 The Twenties

Jacqueline Fear-Segal and Helen McNeil

▶ What were the Twenties?

When the United States economy teetered and then crashed in the last months of 1929, 'The Twenties' became an entity for the first time, defined in retrospect. Initially the significance of the stock-market crash was not grasped; financiers looked confidently toward recovery. But, as the nation slid into depression and despair, with banks and factories closing, bread-lines lengthening, and one-quarter of the labour force seeking work, the year 1929 assumed a mythic quality. In 1931, F Scott Fitzgerald called the past decade of economic boom and high personality 'the Jazz Age', and Frederick Lewis Allen's sparkling book *Only Yesterday* characterized the eleven years from the end of the First World War to the stock-market crash as 'a distinct era in American history'. Recording the facts, fashions and follies which touched the daily lives of millions of Americans, Allen synthesized a now-familiar picture of the Twenties as an era of bootlegging and Babe Ruth, Fords and Flappers, Babbitts and Bohemians – an era which, in 1931, had already receded into the past, leaving Allen wondering 'What was to come in the nineteen-thirties?' In fact, the idea of 'the decade' as a principle of historical interpretation ignores the slow and uneven development of social and economic trends, and exaggerates superficial qualities and differences. Yet the Twenties did mark major, irreversible shifts in America's mood and style of life, matters whose importance was then being recognized for the first time.

After the First World War, it seemed to many that the pace of life in America greatly quickened, and that the War had drawn a barrier between generations. In *Middletown* (1929), their sociological study of Muncie, Indiana (a book that compares interestingly with Sinclair Lewis's fictional treatments of middle America, *Main Street* (1920) and *Babbitt* (1922)), Robert and Helen Lynd set out to chronicle the changes that had occurred in a representative Mid-Western city between 1890 and 1925. Acknowledging that 'any people are in a process of change', they did, however, assert that 'we today are probably living in one of the eras of greatest rapidity of change in the history of human institutions'. Many echoed their opinion, and generational oppositions and distinctions mattered greatly to the politics and discourse of the Twenties. Social changes under way for decades now had to be acknowledged. Considering the problem of cultural change, the anthropologist Ralph Linton observed:

> Even in the most progressive and forward-looking community, changes in culture produce some individual discomforts. At least some of the members of the group will develop nostalgic attitudes toward a past which appears rosy in the light of present difficulties. The more intense and widespread the discomfort due to change, the more widespread the attitudes are likely to be.

A struggle between progress and nostalgia seems strikingly central to the Twenties, a decade in which many Americans looked back with yearning to a past age which seemed simpler, morally surer, more pastoral, and less troubled. The singularity of the Twenties lies in the fact that it was a postwar, affluent decade when Americans confronted the onrush of the modern world with few distractions.

▶ War and postwar

In April 1917 the United States had entered the First World War in support of the Allied cause. Woodrow Wilson defined the war aims in moral terms: 'The world must be made safe for democracy. Its peace must be planted upon the tested foundations of political liberty.' In 1918, while war still raged, Wilson formulated his famous Fourteen Points, which outlined the need for a peaceful world and provided a 'guarantee' of continued peace through a 'general assembly of nations'. This League of Nations became the focus of hostility for the Republican Party as well as for other Americans opposed to the war or to Wilson. While on a speaking tour to win support for the League, the President suffered a debilitating stroke and the Senate rejected both the Treaty of Versailles and the League of Nations. When, in 1920, a small-time politician, Warren Gamaliel Harding from Marion, Ohio, was thrust forward as the Republican candidate. H L Mencken, who scourged the 'Booboisie' of the decade of 'normalcy', predicted that:

> the overwhelming majority of Americans are going to vote for him. They tire, after twenty years, of a steady diet of white protestations and black acts; they are weary of hearing high fallutin' and meaningless words . . . Today no sane American believes in any official statement of national policy, whether foreign or domestic . . . He wants a renaissance of honesty – even ordinary, celluloid, politician's honesty. Tired to death of intellectual charlatanry, he turns despairingly to honest imbecility.

The Progressive coalition, founded on a shared belief in reason and man's ability to build a better world, had been shattered. The reform impulse did not die, but it was fragmented. Issues of class and justice addressed by Progressive or Naturalist writers like Theodore Dreiser or Edgar Lee Masters simply felt dated. Meanwhile Americans suffered economic troubles: 4 million men from the armed services were suddenly demobilized; inflation spiralled, rising by a shocking 28 per cent in 1919–20 in New York City; farm prices fell, and continued to fall. There was also an alarmist psychological mood, described by William McAdoo as 'a strange poison in the air', which fostered hostility towards labour and radicals and resulted in riots and lynchings. After 1919, the ugly fervour of the Red Scare died down, but the unity of political vision which had characterized the Progressive period had gone.

The promise of unified cultural vision set out by the New England tradition had also long since dissipated, and in Europe a sense of rupture with the past and even with history had preceded the Great War. Eliot and Pound had already moved American poetry into modernism by 1914, and Imagism had been founded in 1912 by Pound, H D (Hilda Doolittle) and editor Harriet Monroe. The Armory Show (1913) had brought the innovation of French Cubism into American art; and Henry James in his later novels and Gertrude Stein in her prose experiments had begun a stylistic revolution which deeply affected American writing after 1913.

Literary and artistic modernism was an explicitly international movement; of the cultural innovators mentioned above, only Monroe was living in the United States, and all American 'moderns' interacted creatively with their European contemporaries.

The enormous achievements of the American novel in the Twenties were, of course, partly triggered by the war, which became a symbol for the cut-off from the past. For Fitzgerald, Hemingway, Dos Passos, Faulkner, and others, the literary modernism of the Twenties was the beginning of a new age. Yet for American writers the war as political, social and personal experience hardly seemed to have occurred at all. American postwar fiction was not marked, as in Europe, by a struggle to understand the relations between the war, state power, and capitalism. In American writing, the public arena of history was approached, if at all, through myth, sometimes overlaid with a naturalist determinism. American writers were struggling to understand the self and validate the role of the artist in language; these 'aesthetic' themes and problems of their relation to modern American society became fundamental artistic issues.

None of the important writers of the Twenties had actually served at the front except Hemingway, who was wounded while an ambulance driver in Italy, 'the picturesque front' of *A Farewell to Arms* (1929). Fitzgerald was at training camp in Alabama when the Armistice was signed; William Faulkner was learning to fly with the RCAF in Canada, not in France, as he liked to say later. For British authors the war meant the death of friends, even one's own death (Rupert Brooke, Wilfred Owen, Isaac Rosenberg); the hideous reality of trench warfare exposed official cant and either broke the survivors or marked them for life. But for Americans the war was more often a symbolic event: a chance to explore freedom, courage, and personal maturation. The impossibility of personal heroism turned the literary war into an incomplete, unreal experience, but one which released energies instead of crushing them.

The First World War thus gave a sense of impetus, power and discontent, even a feeling of generational uniqueness. But by mid-decade it had become one of the many events in American life in which something promised, some important event, had its fulfilment in meaning mysteriously withheld. In 'Echoes of the Jazz Age', Fitzgerald argued that he had succeeded with his first novel *This Side of Paradise* (1920) 'simply for telling people that he felt as they did, that something had to be done with all the nervous energy stored up and unexpended in the war'. In e e cummings's autobiographical experimental novel *The Enormous Room* (1922), ambulance driver Cummings paradoxically first feels free when he is imprisoned by the French military, who become the enemy in his private war: Cummings's language bursts into surreal vigour the moment the prison gates shut and he is let loose into 'the Delectable Mountain' of bizarre personalities. John Dos Passos's *Three Soldiers* (1921) shows the dehumanization of war with bitterness comparable to Robert Graves's *Good-bye to All That* (1929); but he went on to write the energetic urban collage of *Manhattan Transfer* (1925), a characteristic work of Twenties experiment. Almost inevitably, other war novels, such as Dos Passos's earlier *One Man's Initiation* (1920, complete version 1969), and William Faulkner's *Soldier's Pay* (1926), assimilate the war to the fictional model of the young man growing to manhood that was set for American literature by Stephen Crane's *The Red Badge of Courage* (1895), another convincingly realistic war novel written from imagination.

The most famous American war novel of them all, Hemingway's *A Farewell to Arms* (1929), appeared when the war was a decade in the past. Here the collapse of the Italian front confirms Frederic Henry's belief that effort is futile since 'they get you in the end'. However, the destructive symbolic rain that washes away Frederic's 'separate peace' falls mainly on the non-combatant Catherine Barkley, the English nurse who dies giving birth to Frederic's dead child, conquered not by war but by what the novel takes to be her body's biological fate. *A Farewell to Arms* remains a compelling mixture of compressed realism and ritualized dialogue, despite its misogynist tone and its rather less-noticed ambivalence about war itself. Like Byron in *Childe Harold*, Hemingway hates war for its stupidity, its sloppy arbitrariness, its slaughter of the good, but is attracted to it for its ability to make heroes who can display what Hemingway calls 'grace under pressure'. Vivid as it is, Hemingway's Great War exists to validate a nihilism already fixed by *The Sun Also Rises* (1926; published in Britain as

Fiesta), in many ways his true war novel. Hemingway's terse tale is set in an expatriate's Paris where the wounds of war have created what Gertrude Stein, Hemingway's stylistic mentor, called 'a lost generation' of men and women adrift in a chaotic hell of their own solipsism. In such a sterile age Jake Barnes, the cynically idealist hero who narrates the story, is appropriately impotent, like T S Eliot's Fisher King in *The Waste Land* (1922), who sits by 'the dull canal' of a postwar 'Unreal City' musing 'on the king my brother's wreck/and on the king my father's death before him'. Such images of impotence and alienation coloured much modernist American writing.

Some American writers expressed their alienation by moving to Europe, either briefly or for a lifetime. Twenties literary expatriatism, a phenomenon unequalled before or since, arose from disillusion with the puritanical and provincial limitations of home. In the nineteenth century, the Jamesian expatriate sought an older, richer culture. Twenties expatriates, many from the Mid-West, overshot New York and arrived in a Paris which was sufficiently bohemian, avant-garde, and sexually liberated to accommodate the most rebellious American. These alienated writers did not generally absorb French language or culture, unless, like photographer Man Ray and writer (later stockbroker) Matthew Josephson, they joined the Surrealists. They went, as Stein put it in *The Autobiography of Alice B Toklas* (1933), to be 'all alone with English and myself'; they went to be published by small presses (Stein, Hemingway, H D), to publish, and to edit small magazines. Or, like Hart Crane and (briefly) the Fitzgeralds, they joined a restless crowd of English-speaking cultural tourists, possibly reading Joyce's *Ulysses* at Sylvia Beach's bookshop, certainly drinking and living their sexually active lives (both straight and gay) at the favourable exchange rates brought about by the postwar superiority of the American economy, at a time when the United States, having become an economic creditor, was on its way to becoming a cultural one.

A postwar hunger for new styles of life and art went hand in hand with an anxious need to have these new sensations explained. If one sign of major literature is its ability to give meaning to the great social events of its age, then Sinclair Lewis's *Main Street* (1920) and Fitzgerald's *This Side of Paradise* (1920) are the major works through which the nation perceived its new sensations at the beginning of the Twenties. Both novels exposed American social patterns which their readers desperately needed to understand; a grateful public made them both best-sellers. *This Side of Paradise* was read as a chronicle of the young in revolt against convention, even though the very young Fitzgerald had clearly already read James Joyce's *Portrait of the Artist as a Young Man* (1917) with profit. Lewis's *Main Street* crystallized the shift of national values from rural to urban. For the heroine, Carol Kennicott, the city is 'good': complex, free and modern, but the petty, constrained middle-American society of Gopher Prairie finally grinds her down. As in Sherwood Anderson's poetic, psychological short stories, *Winesburg, Ohio* (1919), the only way to mature and escape Puritan repression is to flee to the city, preferably into the life of art. Black Americans, fleeing overt racial oppression, sought self-expression in the Northern cities. Regional fiction, often by and about women, was considered backward; today, however, Willa Cather's deservedly high reputation has been restored and Zora Neale Hurston's huge influence on later African-American women's writing keeps on growing.

By the Twenties, politicians and pulpits had lost credibility: literature, newspapers, and the burgeoning mass culture of popular magazines, radio, and the movies had to bear the weight of a new quest for social and personal models. Fitzgerald, Lewis, Dreiser and H L Mencken genuinely influenced their avid readers, but when the questions raised seemed too complex or the answers too shocking, the work was rejected. This pressure for the easy answer deepened the split between high culture and mass society.

▶ A fragmented culture

Literature can sometimes thrive on its own resources: it can appear perversely peripheral to contemporaries, yet in retrospect seem close to the heart of an era. In a changing society, some separation between literature and life is essential; literary attention to form can give an age a shape by which we can perceive what is happening to it. Symbolism and fragmentation were two such formal modes of the Twenties. American theatre, dominated by Eugene O'Neill, tried to shape social and psychological issues by what O'Neill called 'the touch of the poet': heightened language, expressionist staging, psychological plots, mythic allusions. In *The Emperor Jones* (1920), the black, vitalist hero reverts to a Freudian savagery under pressure; in *The Hairy Ape* (1922) class conflict is acted out through sexual conflict with Darwinian overtones; *Desire Under the Elms* (1924) sets a mythologized Oedipal struggle in New England. But it was above all modernist poetry that played the form-shattering and form-giving role. The cosmopolitan modernist strand of American poetry threatened the apparently less urbane native line. 'Others taunt me with . . . never seeing/Deeper down', wrote the New England poet Robert Frost as he defended his own fiercely independent regional classicism. Torn between the two strains, aspiring poet Hart Crane wrote from Cleveland, Ohio, in 1920 'there are still Rabelais, Villon, Apuleius and Eliot to snatch at occasionally . . . a small Gauguin I have on the wall, Japanese prints and Russian records'. Anything to blot out provincial Cleveland.

T S Eliot's *The Waste Land* (1922), probably the most important and influential American poem of the decade, has almost no American references. Its themes of impotence and loss are structured through accumulated shards of 'impersonal' myth and history, cultural fragments 'shored against my ruins'. Widely read during the Twenties as a summary of postwar disillusion, it now looks more like an intense, even personal outcry, its famous fragmentation a means of psychological, spiritual and stylistic investigation as well as an analogue for cultural decay. With his brilliant, uneven *Cantos* (1925), Eliot's friend Ezra Pound undertook his life work, a modernist epic that makes a positive Odyssean quest. But where Eliot's 'difficult' fragmentary references make a conservative ideological point about the fragmentation of Western tradition, Pound's eclectic collage of classical, oriental, Renaissance and contemporary imagery is meant to build towards what Pound called a 'paideuma' or culturally unified society, to be led by an enlightened ruler-patron – a line that he unhappily pursued to the extremes of anti-Semitism, fascism, and dictatorship, making Mussolini 'the Boss' of Canto XLI (1934).

William Carlos Williams commented sourly in the Preface to his surreal prose poem, *Kora In Hell* (1920), that a meeting on contemporary American poetry in Paris would find half the poems submitted in French or ancient Provençal. Like the 'Chicago Renaissance' poets, Edgar Lee Masters, Vachel Lindsay and Carl Sandburg, Williams wanted a specifically *American* modernist poetry. He attempted to make his 'Objectivist' short poems into tools of social change *and* literary experiments. 'The Red Wheelbarrow' insists that 'so much depends on' the way a particular red wheelbarrow looks; it is through small compositions of the real that we know ourselves.

Williams's short, strongly enjambed line, his later 'American measure', and his social commitment have made him a continuing influence on subsequent poetry. What Pound and Williams did share was a hope for a mature *and* an American literature. The critical perspectives of Edmund Wilson and the poetry of Wallace Stevens achieve this goal.

To be an American writer in the Twenties actually meant that one was free to embrace Europe or not, as one chose. Wilson showed in *Axel's Castle* (1931) that French symbolism had become the English-speaking modernism of a Joyce or Eliot. Stevens took care never to set foot in Europe; but his *Harmonium* (1923) expresses an almost Emersonian optimism about perception through the radiating ambiguous imagery of French symbolism: 'Poetry is the supreme fiction', replacing religion. For Stevens's Poundian *persona* Crispin, the hero of 'The Comedian as the Letter C', the American soil inspires first a 'green brag', then through 'disguised pronunciamento' yields a relation between the real and the imaginary which is always imperfect but always evolving. By the end of the decade, the modernist experiments of Stevens, Williams, Pound, Marianne Moore and Eliot had created a new American poetic – a poetic which fully explored the experience of language, even if its audience stayed small.

In American painting, the separation between Europeanized moderns and nativists took dramatic form in the Armory Show of 1913, where both

Cubists and the realist Ash-Can School were represented. Walter and Louise Arensberg's New York salon (1914–21) introduced European Dadaists like Marcel Duchamp and Francis Picabia to the American photographer Man Ray, the painters Charles Sheeler and Charles Demuth, the poets Amy Lowell and William Carlos Williams, and the socialist Max Eastman. The American painters influenced by Cubism and Dada celebrated the machine and the city, much as did Hart Crane in his modernist epic *The Bridge* (1930). Realist and regionalist painters like George W Bellows and Thomas Hart Benton went on working; Benton's mural cycle, 'American Historical Epic' (1919–26), suggests he is almost waiting for the Depression to bring realism back. It was, ironically, Benton's pupil Jackson Pollock who was finally to create a profoundly American abstract art owing nothing to this realist and national imagery.

Perhaps the most impressive American visual art of the Twenties was photography. It had behind it a strong avant-garde tradition, coming from Alfred Stieglitz's and Edward Steichen's '291' gallery and its successors. The experimental photo-journalism and advertising photography in mass-circulation magazines profoundly influenced popular taste. Margaret Bourke-White, Paul Strand, Berenice Abbott and Charles Sheeler, photographer as well as painter, abstracted machinery and skyscrapers into powerful angular forms whose stark presence and often ambiguous scale gave a critical edge that the European futurists never achieved. Other photographers – Ansel Adams, Edward Weston, Imogen Cunningham – and the painter Georgia O'Keefe made sharply focused, often highly sensual studies of wilderness, nudes, or individual objects that share something of the spirit of poetic 'objectivism' ('No ideas but in things', said William Carlos Williams).

▶ A divided society

Although the tensions and fragmentation of the Twenties were keenly felt, there was, superficially, a political and economic consensus. A journalist wrote in *Harper's Magazine*, in April 1929:

> When ten thousand widely scattered hearts are beating high with hopes of a rise in some favourite discovered overnight . . . When the whole country follows the same tips . . . finds comfort in the same reassuring signs that normalcy is here to stay, we know without doubt that this is a untied people.

But that earlier conflicts had continued to fester through the decade, despite the prosperity, was well demonstrated when Sacco and Vanzetti were executed in 1927. Convicted in 1921 after a payroll robbery in Massachusetts, Sacco and Vanzetti were both Italian immigrants and self-confessed anarchists. The evidence against them was regarded by many as inconclusive, and their cause attracted world attention. They were condemned to death after a group of Boston 'Wasps' (white Anglo-Saxon Protestants) refused a retrial. 'All right, we are two nations', John Dos Passos declared later in his synoptic novel *USA* (1938), writing about this divisive episode.

There was, of course, a Twenties radicalism, but it was mainly preoccupied with such matters as the Red Scare and the IWW (Industrial Workers of the World), with Sacco and Vanzetti's trial and with the implications of the Soviet Revolution, popularized by John Reed in *Ten Days That Shook the World* (1919). Magazines like *The Masses* (1911–18) and *The Liberator*, both edited by Max Eastman, and Michael Gold and Joseph Freeman's *The New Masses* moved on from a permissive experimental radicalism to a call for communist world revolution, even though, as the bourgeois expatriate Matthew Josephson said in 1928, 'the people vote for General Motors'. Scores of American political tourists visited Soviet Russia in the Twenties: Eastman, Freeman, Gold, Isadora Duncan, Lincoln Steffens, Senator Robert La Follette, John Dos Passos, Theodore Dreiser, e e cummings, Claude McKay. But their experiences had no effect on the American worker; nor did these radicals agree with one another. Eastman explored the post-Lenin struggles in *After Lenin Died* (1925) from a Trotskyite viewpoint; Freeman wrote off the Stalin–Trotsky clash in *An American Testament* (1938), and, like some leftists in the Twenties and many in the Thirties, saw the Communist Party as 'selfless, incorruptible'.

The Twenties are often represented as an era of materialist conservative retrenchment when politics were in abeyance. Throughout the decade, Republicans succeeded in winning a high proportion of the popular vote: 60.4 per cent in 1920, 54 per cent in 1924, 58.2 per cent in 1928. Yet, there was an underlying political strife, occasionally erupting into social strife, and perceivable in the struggles between the two major political parties. Within the Democratic Party, the heterogeneous remnants of the Wilson coalition, without direction or leadership, struggled against one another. Issues like prohibition highlighted the conflicts between the diverse dividing elements of American society. The Volstead Act of 1919, making the production and consumption of alcohol illegal, can be read as a progressive measure, based on a belief that social problems could be curbed by legislation; but it also reflected and deepened social divisions, as an older Protestant America sought to control a less tractable immigrant minority. Rifts within the Democratic Party became clear at the convention of 1924. Big-City Democrats supported the Irish Catholic Al Smith, a 'wet' and a product of a big-city machine, who demanded that the party condemn the Ku Klux Klan – a secret organization which terrorized blacks, Catholics and Jews, claiming it was fighting for 'Americanism', and working to 'win a return of power into the hands of the everyday, not highly cultured, not overly intellectualized, but entirely unspoilt and not de-Americanized, average citizen of the old stock'. Smith, when asked what he would do for the states west of the Mississippi, reportedly answered: 'Which are the states west of the Mississippi?' Rural Democrats thus backed William G McAdoo of Tennessee; in the end a compromise candidate, John W Davis, a Wall Street lawyer, was nominated on the 103rd ballot.

Four years later this conflict was re-enacted on the larger national stage. In the 1928 election Al Smith won the Democratic nomination, but lost the Presidency to the Republican Herbert Hoover. Analysing the impression of unity given by the election results, *Harper's Magazine* asked, 'What is the bond of union between a Pennsylvania manufacturer and an Iowa farmer?' and answered, 'Not interest certainly, nor political theory, but a common faith that God loves the typical American as he has been, and that what he has been he should continue to be.' This faith was to be painfully shattered by the Depression. The strife which immobilized the Democratic Party during the Twenties actually concealed a shift in political power which was to guarantee the party's success in the Thirties. In 1922 and after, the big cities, Republican for nearly three decades, went unwaveringly to the Democrats, and western states, already experiencing an agricultural depression, consistently sent radical Democrats to Congress. Even though during the Twenties it appeared that there was an unchallenged political consensus, the Republican majority was being progressively undermined throughout the decade.

If old stock and rural Americans were suspicious of Smith's New York East Side accent and big-city style, it was partly because they feared the political power of the first- and second-generation Americans who supported him. Demands for immigration restriction were by no means new to America; but in the Twenties, for the first time, the federal government began imposing rigid laws. Congressmen expressed their fears of ethnic changes occurring in society by passing the National Origins Act in 1924 (which based immigration to the United States on the proportion of residents of each nationality already resident in the country); more lowly Americans joined the reorganized Ku Klux Klan. However, the Klan was in decline by 1925 after the disgrace of its leaders, and superficially many of the schisms within society seemed to heal.

To describe political struggles as Dos Passos did in terms of 'them' against 'us' simplifies what was occurring in Twenties America. Mencken blamed the problems of the nation on rural Americans, who, 'abandoned for years to the tutelage of their pastors, have now gone so far into darkness that every light terrifies them and runs them amok'. He insisted: 'In the long run the cities of the United States will have to throw off the hegemony of these morons. They have run the country long enough and made it sufficiently ridiculous.' But the developing mass society of the Twenties was rooted in an industrial economy which reached deep into the countryside. A clear urban–rural division could no longer be made.

The year 1920 marked the symbolic moment when over 50 per cent of Americans were found by the census to be urban rather than rural (living in towns of over 2,500); by 1930 this figure had grown to 69 per cent. However, other less quantifiable developments were of greater significance. The automobile gave mobility to both country and city people, and the radio brought the same programmes into rural and urban homes alike. In 1926, the National Broadcasting Company, and the following year the Columbia Broadcasting Service, hooked together hundreds of local stations in national networks. If urbanites like Mencken felt threatened by rural America, farmers reciprocated these feelings. The Scopes Trial, held in Dayton, Tennessee, in 1925, was a staged event which dramatized the cultural dimensions of the Twenties. A young schoolteacher was brought to trial for teaching Darwin's laws of evolution; William Jennings Bryan, three times Democratic presidential candidate and champion of rural protestantism, confronted the agnostic Chicago lawyer, Clarence Darrow. Although it appeared that Bryan and his cause were the losers, and Bryan died a few days after the trial, there were many non-fundamentalist Americans who nevertheless felt ambivalent about the direction their new, technological and scientific society was taking. 'Science', wrote Joseph Wood Krutch in *The Modern Temper* in 1929, 'has always promised two things, not necessarily related – an increase first in our powers, second in our happiness or wisdom, and we have come to realize that it is the first and less important of the two promises which it has kept most abundantly.'

Meanwhile, blacks in the Twenties experienced an increase in pride without a corresponding increase in power. During and after the First World War, millions of blacks emigrated from the rural South to Northern urban centres. Detroit and Chicago offered industrial employment, and New York had a variety of trades, and the magnet of Harlem, even if black employment everywhere was subject to humiliating 'Jim Crow' practices. These urban blacks had a crucial impact on the nation's economy and cultural life. When Joseph 'King' Oliver's New Orleans Creole Jazz Band came to Chicago in 1920, a new era began, and jazz, swing and blues spread from the black South to become the essential music of the Twenties. The 'Harlem Renaissance' linked black themes with modernism. These black writers felt their contradictory position. As Countee Cullen wrote in *Color* (1925), 'Yet do I marvel at this curious thing/To make a poet black, and bid him sing!' Langston Hughes combined, in *The Weary Blues* (1926), a Whitmanesque free verse with jazz and blues rhythms; Jean Toomer published *Cane*, a finely styled short-story collection, in 1923; West-Indian-born Claude McKay wrote militant sonnets and the powerful autobiographical novel *Home to Harlem*. The problems were focused in Alain Locke's *The New Negro* (1925), an influential integrationist book that pleaded both for racial pride and white acceptance, and saw the Twenties as a 'coming of age' for black Americans. But if Locke was right about the new breadth of black writing and music, he was wrong about white American society: in the Twenties not even American radicals joined the black struggle for equality.

▶ The economy in the Twenties

In 1919, when Congress rejected Wilson's League of Nations, American foreign policy seemed to move decisively towards 'isolationism'. Domestic issues preoccupied the decade, and the world outside seemed a threat. Yet, paradoxically, 1919 was the moment when the United States emerged as the world's leading creditor nation. Now one of the largest producers and exporters of agricultural goods and one of the largest import markets, America's economic health and politics would have more direct effect on the world economic conditions than those of any other nation. If the decade ended with a loud economic crash which left no one unaffected, it opened with a silent transferral of economic power from which many benefited, although, in general, the rich remained rich and many of the poor remained poor. In 1922, after the brief postwar recession, the boom began. Three years later, an overwhelming majority of Americans were to agree with Calvin Coolidge that 'the business of America is business'. The city, not the railroad, was now the main stimulus to the economy; after 1922, the construction industry accounted for much of the Twenties boom. Visible symbols of corporate prestige were provided by the great skyscrapers of New York and Chicago. The technology of lifts, plate glass, concrete and steel girders had been available since Louis Sullivan's innovations in the 1890s, and typically American 'gothic' skyscrapers such as the Woolworth Building were prewar (1913), but the Twenties accelerated this upwards trend into a norm. A brightly coloured, machine-age exoticism became the high-capitalist Art Deco style, two of whose monuments are the Chrysler Building (Walter van Alen) and Radio City (Raymond Hood), John D Rockefeller's paean in stone to the communications industry which his Radio Corporation of America dominated. Architect Frank Lloyd Wright pioneered 'organic' modernism, but his thrice-rebuilt model home Taliesin and the stark International Style modernism of Eliel Saarinen's rejected design for the *Chicago Tribune* made less mass impact than pastiche styles such as surface classicism, 'Alhambra'-like movie palaces or suburban chalets. As cities expanded, automobile-orientated upper-middle-class suburbs appeared, their development often virtually uncontrolled, as in Zenith, the home of Sinclair Lewis's hero Babbitt. A good suburban home like Babbitt's cost ten times the average annual wage, and at the end of the decade a third of the population (mainly in the South and on farms) still lacked one or more of what were now considered basic amenities: a sound, dry structure, electricity, inside running water, bathtub, indoor toilet. Industry now manufactured new goods, some of them previously unknown and unimagined – radios, vacuum cleaners, electric irons, toasters, record players and, most important of all, the automobile – to transform the life-style of Americans. Consumer goods became foundation stones of the economy; with manufacturing output growing three times faster than population, the American economy had entered a new phase.

To market this new wave of nationally distributed, standardized brand-name consumer goods, advertising expenditure more than quadrupled in size from 1914 to 1929. It soon integrated itself into the popular tabloid press, women's magazines and radio. Within a decade, advertising developed from announcement to image-maker. Always depicting an idealized mean rather than the diverse reality of American life, advertising represented its products through such values as democracy, the family, bourgeois comfort and modernity itself. Negative values such as shame about the body or the insecurity of a mobile society were also used. Even women's suffrage could sell, as women, having gained the vote with the Nineteenth Amendment in 1920, could now 'vote' for Listerine mouthwash. Indebtedness, another corollary of consumerism, became respectable for the first time through automobile credit schemes; inflation was low and the prices of some goods had actually declined. The logic of the economy had shifted from saving to spending. 'We've spent close to $100 on our radio', said a worker's wife in Muncie, Indiana, quoted in *Middletown*: 'Where'd we get the money? Oh, out of our savings, like everybody else'.

Americans now enjoyed a higher standard of living than any other people. Yet technological developments transformed more than the economy; they also created new dreams and provided, for some at least, the means of fulfilling them vicariously. In 'Echoes of the Jazz Age', Fitzgerald recalled how

> In the spring of '27, something bright and alien flashed across the sky. A young Minnesotan who seemed to have had nothing to do with his generation did a heroic thing, and for a moment people set down their glasses in country clubs and speak-easies and thought of their best dreams.

Charles Lindbergh's solo flight across the Atlantic stirred the nation. Commentators have pointed out the dual nature of the popular celebration. Lindbergh was the living symbol of the young, independent American, unbound by organizations and public pressures. Yet, ironically, his achievement was made possible through the refinements of technology, organization and industrial finesse. Lindbergh himself gave equal credit to the plane, 'that wonderful motor', and President Coolidge expressed his pride 'that in every particular this silent partner represented American genius and industry'. The celebration of the great aviator showed the American people torn between conflicting interpretations of their own

experience. Committed to the ease, affluence and thrill of their technological age, they nevertheless mourned a simpler, purer, less frenetic past.

Abroad, American business organization was admired and envied. 'The
future of America is the future of the world', wrote Aldous Huxley in
1927, 'material circumstances are driving all nations along the path in
which America is going . . . speculating on the American future, we are
speculating on the future of civilized man.' In the factory the increased
rate of technological development meant that costs fell as productivity
rose. But as tasks were divided into their component parts, work became
repetitive and meaningless. 'Ye get the wages, but ye sell your soul at
Fords', complained one worker in the Detroit factory. 'You've worked like
a slave all day, and when ye get out yo're too tired to do anything.' In *The
Big Money* (1936), Dos Passos saw Ford spreading 'the Taylorized speedup
everywhere, reachunder, adjustwasher, screwdown bolt, shove in cotterpin,
reachunder, adjustwasher, screwdown bolt, reachunder adjust screwdown
reachunder adjust, until every ounce of life was sucked off into production and at night the workmen went home grey shaking husks'. As enterprises became larger, 'scientific' methods were increasingly employed to
control production and labour.

In the Twenties the Ivy League universities founded schools of business studies, training professionals to rationalize the work process and to
secure the consent and contentment of workers. This 'welfare capitalism', a confused combination of paternalistic reasoning and hard-headed
economic sense, was partially responsible for the staggering decline in
union membership: from 5 million in 1920 to 3.5 million in 1929. Many
workers were content, as the Lynds showed in *Middletown*, to enjoy the
material benefits of the age and let power be concentrated in the hands
of the employers. But the Crash of 1929 destroyed the belief in the
possibility of welfare capitalism: employers had made a commitment to
look after their workers which they had proved unable to fulfil.

The decline in the labour movement cannot be attributed entirely to
the new prosperity. The changing structure of American industry undercut
union membership. Several unionized industries – coal and New England
textiles – were 'sick' and the numerous new industries had no union
tradition. Also, the labour force was changing fast. Blacks had never been
welcomed in unions, nor women, who made up one-quarter of the
workforce, nor immigrants, still more concerned with adapting to life in
America. Unions kept their anachronistic craft orientation, even when an
increasing proportion of the workforce was unskilled. And despite the
reassurances that the interests of labour and capital were identical, no
previous era in the Supreme Court's history compared with the Twenties
in the number of statutes invalidated, most of them labour laws. Whatever
the diverse reasons for the weakening of the labour movement, Lincoln
Steffens pointed to the main one: 'big business was producing what the
Socialists held up as their goal: food, shelter, and clothing for all'.

▶ The role of gender

Changes in life-style and values were the most striking aspect of the Twenties. As affluence and mobility increased personal expectations without offering models for newly changed roles, American men and women experienced abrupt shifts in education, family structure and sexual behaviour.

Americans in general were marrying younger and having fewer children – bringing changes in roles and relationships within the household. One result of the declining birth-rate was that, in relation to the very young, the proportion of people in the 15–24 age group was growing larger; while the shift of the economy towards the service sector meant that more young people stayed in educational institutions. In 1920 only 32 per cent of the 10 to 17-year-olds were in high school; the figure was 51 per cent by the end of the decade. (There is an interesting parallel between the Twenties and Sixties in educational expansion coupled with a dominant 'youth culture'.) Education was now seen as a child's right, with every state enacting compulsory attendance laws by 1930; meanwhile child labour declined sharply (helped by the ending of child immigrant labour). These changes ricocheted back into the heart of the family, altering relations between parents and children. With school classes growing, children were increasingly divided by age; the authority of the family weakened, that of the peer-group increased. Experts, often self-appointed, moved into the gap left by the decline of mother's values. James Watson's *Behaviorism* (1925) advocated rigid 'scientific' stimulus–response patterns for infant care. By contrast, schools became far more 'child-centered'. The Lynds found that, for parents and children alike, school education was 'more valued as a symbol of things hoped for than for its specific content' and, as the school's function widened beyond the traditional '3 Rs', children engaged in a wide round of extra-curricular activities. Sports teams and social clubs ranked high in priority. When asked what made a girl eligible for a high-school club, a Middletown girl replied, 'the chief thing is if the boys like you and you can get them for the dances'. If the older generation decried the precocity and sexual mores of the young, changing family patterns, the automobile and the movies meant that over half the junior and senior boys and girls in Middletown marked 'true' in a questionnaire stating: 'Nine out of every ten boys and girls of high school age have "petting parties".' (In Fitzgerald's *This Side of Paradise*, Amory Blaine is behindhand when, already a sophomore at Princeton, he goes to 'that great current American phenomenon, the petting party'.) When prostitution declined dramatically during the Twenties, it was partly because of the efforts of anti-vice pressure groups, but it was also the case that a young man's regular girlfriend might well agree to pre-marital sex.

Even more striking, because more celebrated, was the changing image of women: the flapper was, and still is, one of the most compelling symbols of Twenties culture and society. Provocatively flaunting her bobbed hair, hiked skirt, cigarettes and bootleg liquor, she personified the 'new woman', different in spirit and shape from her Victorian mother. This seductive image led both men and women to equate sexual availability with personal freedom. However, in a society still overwhelmingly economically dominated by men and continuing a Victorian double standard, such freedom could prove a costly illusion for the woman. The sexually experienced woman was still unacceptably 'fast'. According to Henry Steele Commager, the Twenties saw the emancipation of women, begun in the 1890s, 'dramatised by the vote and guaranteed by birth control'. Commager is implicitly referring to real changes in sexual behaviour.

The spread of venereal disease during the First World War had broken down many taboos about male contraception, but female contraception faced an uphill battle. Margaret Sanger, convinced that only birth control could free poor women from the tyranny of ill-health and poverty, courted arrest under anti-vice laws. During the Twenties her American Birth Control League and other organizations succeeded in establishing numerous clinics; but Sanger's politics moved steadily to the right at the same time, towards the good-breeding theories of eugenics. While an astonishing 90 per cent of middle-class couples admitted to using some form of birth control by the end of the decade, with sex becoming a pleasure rather than a duty, poor women still often lacked access to contraception. Women's health as a whole improved, however, with the female death-rate for the first time lower than that for men.

Yet in important areas the situation of women in the Twenties was unchanged. An ex-flapper, writing in 1922, praised the flapper's potential:

> Watch her five years from now and then be thankful that she
> will be the mother of the next generation, with the hypocrisy,
> fluff and other 'hookum' worn entirely off. Her sharp points
> wear down remarkably well and leave a smooth polished surface.
> You'll be surprised at what a comfort that surface will be in the
> days to come!

So the 'fluff' and naughtiness are merely preparation for a woman's traditional role. H L Mencken likewise identified the flapper as a staunch Main Streeter: 'What she dreams of is not an infinitely brilliant husband, but an infinitely *solid* one, which is to say, one bound irretrievably to the claims of normalcy.' Statistics endorse this cynical view. Though more single women now worked and became an important reserve force in the economy, most married women gave their energy to home-making. Those in professions were blocked by prejudice, discriminatory pay practices, and (sometimes) a marriage bar. At the same time, home-making itself became professionalized in the Twenties, especially for the middle classes. Women's colleges like Radcliffe, Mount Holyoke and Smith, founded to provide female equivalents of Harvard and Yale, began to turn motherhood into a profession: Vassar created a School of Euthenics in 1924 to re-route 'education for women along the lines of their chief interests and responsibilities, motherhood and the home'. The flapper may have dispelled certain nineteenth-century taboos; but she did not represent a large change of role for women, marriage or the family, as one ex-feminist emphasized in 1926:

> In six years of married life I have gradually but surely descended from that blithe, enthusiastic, cocksure young person I was eight or ten years ago to the colorless, housewifely, dependent sort of female I used to picture so pathetically and graphically to my audiences – the kind of woman we must all have a chance not to be.

The marriage rate increased in the Twenties, but not as rapidly as divorce, which now ended one-sixth of all marriages (though mainly childless ones). As one 'Middletowner' explained:

> The main reason there are more divorces is that people are demanding more of life than they used to . . . In former times . . . they settled down to a life of hard work . . . and putting up with each other.

Others, though, demanded that the institution of marriage should adapt to changing times. More emphasis was put on emotional fulfilment, less on financial bonds; increasing numbers of people lived in large cities far from their parents; the private as well as the public dynamic of marriage changed. In 1927, Judge Ben Lindsey shocked respectable public opinion by advocating 'compassionate marriage', urging that with divorce and contraception made readily available, only the most suited need or should contemplate parenthood. And individual marriages that broke with traditional forms hit the headlines (like that of the novelist Fanny Hurst, who lived separately from her husband).

The American Twenties were the 'sex era', a time when the existence of an instinctive 'sex drive' in young people, especially women, gained wide social acceptance – an emphasis made reputable by Sigmund Freud, whose Clark University lectures in 1909 fostered a popular, optimistic version of psychoanalysis, which America absorbed with amazing speed. By 1915, psychoanalysis had displaced all other therapies and reached the women's journals; Mabel Dodge serialized her analysis in the Hearst Press. Popularized psychoanalysis meshed with the American belief in self-improvement; Freudian theories seemed a way to get rid of neurotic symptoms without analysing what they meant. 'Do you suffer from headaches, nausea, "neuralgia," paralysis, or any other mysterious disorder?' asked Max Eastman only semi-satirically in *Everybody's Magazine* (June 1915); if so, Freud could 'sink a shaft into the subconscious region and tap it of its mischievous elements'. The sexually hungry 'liberated' woman (Zelda Fitzgerald, Mabel Dodge (who, failing to win D H Lawrence from Frieda, married a 'primitive' Navajo Indian), Mae West, Elinor Glyn, Caresse Crosby) became a familiar stereotype; while sexually sophisticated women like Dorothy Parker, the Algonquin table wit, or bohemian poet Edna St Vincent Millay behaved more like the Hemingwayesque 'chap': defiantly tough outside, vulnerable underneath. Others, like poet and editor Marianne Moore, saw marriage as a stifling 'enterprise . . . requiring all one's criminal agility to avoid!' and duly avoided it, either through 'free love', celibacy or lesbianism (H D, Gertrude Stein).

The sexual revolution of the Twenties was supposed to belong to the women; but the first great literary erotic revolution was certainly male, and in America at least, it took the form of narcissism or the embattled male trying to protect himself from the sexually aggressive female. In Fitzgerald's *This Side of Paradise* (1920), sexual favours are still traded for social status, but the rules have changed to allow the narcissistic young to fall in love with the image of their own beautiful, daring selves. And in *The Great Gatsby* (1925), Gatsby's 'Platonic' self-image seeks a reflection in Daisy. So blinding is 'the colossal vitality of his illusion' that Gatsby never sees how Daisy lives only in response to men's images of her – and the stronger and more brutal the imprint, the more she likes it. Daisy is figuratively (and literally) a killer, like Nicole Diver in Fitzgerald's *Tender is the Night* (1934), whose victim is a very American psychoanalyst who thinks neurotics are nice weak creatures who *want* to be saved. In Hemingway the battle lines are even more firmly drawn. Jake Barnes's mysterious groin wound is a necessary defence against Lady Brett Ashley, whose life is determined by her sex drive. Jake and Brett love each other, but when he can't satisfy her sexually, she rejects him: 'It's my fault, Jake. It's the way I'm made.' Meanwhile the housewife learned from popular magazines and movies that unless she had 'It' (sex appeal), she could expect her husband to stray, and her husband saw himself depicted as a machine for making money; after courtship the picture is distinctly less rosy in American popular and high culture alike.

▶ Culture, mass and élite

The exploding mass culture of Twenties radio, film, and popular magazines marketed standardized behaviour models to populations with different backgrounds and needs, generating a new kind of conformity based on middle-class consumer values. In one of the more striking American partnerships of social perception and the profit-making impulse, Hollywood wholeheartedly exploited the flapper type in films such as *Flaming Youth* (1923), *It* (1927), and *Our Dancing Daughters* (1928). The flapper film was a product, packaged around a star, marketed by the studio in the controlled outlets of its nationwide theatre chains, and consumed by millions. Against the undoubted democratizing force of such mass imagery must be set the inadequacy that these commercial visions induced in the many who would never be able to buy the pleasures that Hollywood made them think they ought to have.

Ambivalence about the function of mass myth, and a conflict between production and art, were built into the Hollywood studio system. From about 1912, Hollywood had exploited its 'star system', whereby mythic types are created by the star and his or her imitators. Because photography always records a version of reality, every cinematic act is validated by the audience's knowledge that in some way this visual fantasy is also 'real', involving a real person like themselves. From the 'silly little saint' Mary Pickford to the impossibly sexy Latin lover Rudolph Valentino, the star image is always based in the body of a human actor: Hollywood myths of youth, success and glamour can thus seem 'true' in a way that the manifestly imaginary characterizations of novels can never be. When the human star contradicted the image, a high price was paid: baby-faced comedian Fatty Arbuckle's trial for a sex-orgy murder wrecked his career, even though he was acquitted.

The Hollywood star system still dominates world cinema – so completely that its cultural origin in American silent cinema is not always obvious. Yet the Hollywood-star type is a characteristic product of a society which is deeply mythical while pretending to be pragmatic, passive in its acceptance of mass consumption while considering itself active, and dedicated to the belief that the individual's life is entirely his own responsibility, whatever social conditions might be. The star images of the Twenties do not, however, provide a simple index of popular taste. Some 'star cycles' competed with others, or expressed urges only dimly articulated elsewhere. In the early Twenties, for instance, the All-American boy Douglas Fairbanks shared popularity with Valentino, and the virginal Pickford competed successfully with the 'vamp cycle' of Theda Bara, who was finished by 1920.

Techniques of classic Hollywood cinema such as parallel editing between two narratives, flashbacks and close-ups had already been developed before D W Griffith and his cameraman Billy Bitzer made *Birth of a Nation* (1915). During the Twenties these codified conventions became accepted as the language of cinema and are still used today. As an art form based upon the manipulation of fragments through montage (editing), cinema is arguably the modernism that broke through into the popular; it is also, in Hollywood institutional cinema, a corporate product which must pay its way. The Twenties saw a continuation of American silent comedy (Chaplin, Buster Keaton), much melodrama, various leaden spectacles (*The Ten Commandments*, 1923, *Ben-Hur*, 1926), and several socially and artistically powerful dramas, such as King Vidor's anti-war film *The Big Parade* (1925) or his expressionist indictment of urban life, *The Crowd* (1928). William Wellman's *Wings* (1927) used brilliant aerial photography in a

Hemingwayesque treatment of male comradeship under stress, and there was a rare artistic indulgence in *émigré* director Erich von Stroheim's ten-hour *Greed*. The arrival of sound in Warner Brothers' *The Jazz Singer* heralded the end of the expressive style of silent acting; the expense of sound technology meant smaller studios were driven out, and banking and corporate interests increasingly controlled the industry.

Mechanization – of society, of the arts – was an essential motif of the Twenties. In the mid-nineteenth century, social change was seen in evolutionary terms. But the generation of the Twenties could no longer equate change with progress. The American version of Oswald Spengler's 'decline of the West' theory was a mild pessimism mingled with quasi-religious awe of the machine. In Henry Adams's meditative memoir *The Education of Henry Adams* (1907, 1918), the dynamo has abolished history and replaced it by a continuous modernity. For Joseph Wood Krutch, and Van Wyck Brooks, as for Lewis Mumford, who praised the cold modern beauty of skyscrapers, mass production's insult to craftsmanship and intelligence made a not-entirely-coincidental parallel to the insult to the intelligence of their own older, cultured eastern group whose social and political dominance had passed on to the 'booboisie' – a shift from caste power to capital power already analysed in Thorstein Veblen's *Theory of the Leisure Class* (1899). To the extent that critics and creative artists (Hart Crane's *The Bridge*, O'Neill's *Dynamo*, many artists and photographers) were absorbed by *things*, by machine mysticism and the glamorous modern city, they were deflected from any analysis of the people ,and the investment capital that fuelled those machines and built those skyscrapers. This displacement from causes to results limited critical understanding, despite concerned descriptions of mass production's dehumanizing effects in Sherwood Anderson's *Poor White* (1920), John Dos Passos's *Forty-Second Parallel* (1930) and Charles Chaplin's savagely funny film *Modern Times* (1936), with its scenes of conveyor-belt madness and a Taylorized 'feeding machine' that goes berserk.

Cultural commentators in the Twenties usually took for granted a gap between immaterial culture and a materialist society, an assumption given weight by sociologist William Ogburn's influential theory of 'cultural lag'. According to Ogburn's *Social Change* (1922), material culture (houses, factories, raw materials, manufacturers) *always* surged ahead of non-material culture (customs, beliefs, institutions, governments):

> When the material conditions change, changes are occasioned in the adaptive culture. But these changes in the adaptive culture do not synchronize exactly with the change in the material culture. There is a lag which may last for varying lengths of time . . .

Not change itself was at fault, but a disharmony of change. Ogburn's theory located all change in technology, but in fact the changes were in the values which determined the use of existing techniques. In the Twenties, few Americans grasped the fact that ideology – as Max Weber has shown – influences change as much as technology. No new technology was needed to bring in the Ford conveyor belt or to 'Taylorize' the workforce.

Understanding of the ways in which the Twenties were indeed an age out of kilter was thus impeded by a belief in the inevitability of 'cultural lag'. Harold Stearn's *Civilization in America* (1921) glibly assumed that Americans should look to other countries for civilization, as the expatriates did. The well-publicized 'victory' of agnostic Clarence Darrow over fundamentalist William Jennings Bryan in the 1925 Scopes trial masked the fact that evolution no longer made sense as a model for society. Freud's sombre humanism became in America a technique for cleaning up the inner life to fit the outer world.

Yet the 'cultural lag' ceases to function when it is recognized that an age expresses itself by the form, as well as by the content, of art or writing. The Twenties saw three major works – Hart Crane's *The Bridge* (1930), William Faulkner's *The Sound and The Fury* (1929) and F Scott Fitzgerald's *The Great Gatsby* (1925) – which not only grasped the peculiar American mixture of pragmatism and illusion, but did so through an uncompromising literary modernism. All three works examine symbolism's dual role as carrier of multiple truths and as agent of delusion, so that symbolism becomes a means into social analysis as well as an example of artistic self-sufficiency. It is a critical cliché that American literature has no Dickens or Tolstoi, no great realist to sum up an age. But a symbolic or illusion-ridden society may well be served best by a mainly symbolic literature that uses technique and structure as well as subject matter to occupy the ideological ground between material things and the secret self.

Doubly alienated from his middle-class, Mid-West background by literary vocation and homosexuality, Hart Crane had a cautionary modernist career. He fled to New York bohemia; later to Paris and Mexico; a heavy drinker, in 1932 he committed suicide. His epic poem *The Bridge* was intended to be an American, optimistic, 'ecstatic' work opposing *The Waste Land*'s European 'pessimism'. It is structured by its central symbol, Brooklyn Bridge, whose 'inviolate curve' is meant to make technology transcendent, and raise the poet-visionary until all America can be comprehended by his myth ('and of thy curveship lend a myth to God'). Crane's balance between a fragmented lyric subjectivity and a public voice lasts as long as the bridge remains a generative symbol, loosening other symbols: rings, curves, flights, returns, the 'arc synoptic' and the 'hellish tunnels that rewind themselves'. The aim is ever-increasing, 'symphonic' resonance. The bridge is both the object of Crane's desire and his image for forging links of past and present, inner and outer. Where *The Bridge* falters is when Crane takes too literally his attempt at synthesis. As in Williams's *In the American Grain* (1925), Crane sees an American heroism – Columbus, Edgar Allan Poe, Emily Dickinson, Isadora Duncan – rejected by a venal society; yet he aims for epic confidence. The results are contradictory: the alienated, personal perceptions remain authentic, the effort at an all-embracing positive answer fails.

Beginning with *The Sound and The Fury* (1929), William Faulkner gave his native South an authentic voice which was also at the forefront of modernist experiment. In Faulkner's mythical Yoknapatawpha County, Mississippi, developed over more than a dozen novels, the tragedy – and tragicomedy – of the South was acted out in microcosm. Faulkner's command of the South's social and psychological past is all the more impressive since, in the Twenties. Southern historiography consisted of biography and legislative history, and Southern literature (with the exception of Kate Chopin and Ellen Glasgow) culpably ignored the realities of racial oppression and economic inertia which had made the South a separate, almost tribal, nation buried inside the Twenties' consumer society. Faulkner recast Southern history to bring out its murderous heritage (as in *Absalom, Absalom!*, 1936), but he was even more concerned to erase the myths which had blighted the South and to form powerful new mythic images which could lead to knowledge. *The Sound and The Fury* is written around its heroine, Caddy Compson – the familiar mythic Southern belle revised by Faulkner into images of defilement, loss, and Christian sacrifice. Caddy is known only in fragments, through the minds of the novel's four consecutive narrators. *The Sound and The Fury* begins daringly with the disjointed Joycean stream of consciousness of Caddy's idiot brother Benjy, for whom past and present are fused into an eternally repeating experience of love and loss: 'Caddy smelled like trees.' Then follow the absurdist, time-obsessed suicide Quentin Compson and the vicious 'modern' brother Jason, who thinks time is money and so loses both. The novel ends with the third-person 'objective' narrative of Dilsey, a saintly black mother-figure to the doomed white Compson family. Ironically, Dilsey is the novel's most highly mythicized figure, symbolizing the blacks, who understand and suffer beyond mere history: 'They endured.'

F Scott Fitzgerald's *The Great Gatsby* gave the Twenties what now seems its inevitable tragic hero in James Gatz, the Mid-Western boy who reads Ben Franklin and improves himself into Jay Gatsby, the brilliant hedonist whose tragic flaw is an outdated idealism. Had he loved money for its own sake, and not as a means to win Daisy Buchanan, Gatsby would have been a success, like Daisy's husband Tom, a racist, moneyed brute. But Gatsby must pay for his surreal glitter by a dark contract with the underworld of bootlegging and crooked stock deals. The rich world of suburban West Egg, with its fluttering women in white dresses like sails and the 'green light' of Daisy's dock, is linked with the money and excitement of New York by a waste land of cinders and cars, where the god-like face of Dr Eckleburg gazes balefully down from an advertising poster upon Tom's sexy, vulgar mistress Myrtle, who lives below. At this symbolic crossing-point between getting and spending, image and fact, Daisy crushes Myrtle while driving Gatsby's car, and he takes the blame, believing to the end in his inner image of an absolute love. Yet Daisy, like Twenties America, is simultaneously infinitely innocent and utterly, carelessly corrupt; the object of hopeless desire also for sale to the strongest bidder. In the novel's remarkable closing image, Gatsby's style of illusion is made the basis for all of America, from the moment that Dutch sailors gazed raptly at the 'green breast' of a new land awaiting despoilation.

The prosperity of the Twenties itself was rooted in unanalysed illusion about the availability of wealth. According to *Harper's Magazine*, there would be prizes for everyone:

> One thing that is quite new and definite is the proof that our modern industrial civilization is not going to the bow-wows . . . but is steadily growing more strongly and highly integrated, more stable, and more efficient, meaning thereby that the average livelihood is becoming surer . . . and that we may confidently look forward to a day when what we call poverty will be practically extinct.

Of course the day that came was the day of the stock-market crash, 29 October 1929, the beginning of the end of an era. From the economically obsessed perspective of Depression-era America, the excess and vividness of the Twenties seemed a phantasmagoric illusion. In the Thirties, the cultural expressions of the social trauma of boom and bust were divided between a hectic surrealism and social realism. The Thirties couldn't use the Twenties fusion of regional and personal, outer and inner, through highly styled mythologies.

Today, the 'usable past' of the Twenties seems to lie in the way it embraced the habit of change. It was the first consumer society. It was also the first era to express fully the contradictions which now seem inextricably part of modern life.

▶ For further reading

Frederick Lewis Allen, *Only Yesterday* (1931, various later edns).

Malcolm Bradbury and David Palmer (eds), *The American Novel in the Nineteen Twenties* (1971).

Stanley Coben, *Rebellion Against Victorianism: The Impetus for Cultural Change in 1920s America* (1991).

Malcolm Cowley, *Exile's Return* (1934, various later edns).

Ann Douglass, *Terrible Honesty: Mongrel Manhattan in the 1920s* (1996).

Elizabeth Ewen, *Channels of Desire: Mass Images and the Shaping of American Consciousness* (1982).

William E Leuchtenberg, *The Perils of Prosperity, 1914–1932* (1970).

Michael E Parrish, *America in Prosperity and Depression, 1920–1941* (1992).

10 The Thirties

Ralph Willett and John White

▶ The crisis of capitalism

It was the Great Crash of 1929 that ended the Twenties. Throughout that decade, stock prices had been rising so rapidly that they bore little relation to the earning power of corporations. Yet the Panic of 1929, when it came, was as much a crisis in American confidence as an economic phenomenon. Many factors were involved. President Hoover blamed worsening European conditions, but at home there were dangerous imbalances between agricultural and business incomes, irresponsible practices in the security markets, and structural weaknesses in the banking system. When trouble came, what J K Galbraith calls the 'generally poor state of economic intelligence' made many, including bankers and financiers, oblivious to the worsening situation: in November 1929 Henry Ford was declaring 'Things are better today than they were yesterday', and the President of the National Association of Manufacturers saw 'little on the horizon today to give us undue or great concern'. Until the eleventh hour, and beyond, Americans continued to express their faith in prosperity by stock-market investments. In September 1929 stock prices were 400 per cent over their 1924 level. But, on 24 October 1929, the market finally broke – to usher in a Depression that would deeply test the traditional American faith in economic progress, and redirect many American impulses.

The Wall Street crash now became a continuing and worsening catastrophe. From 1929 to 1933, *per capita* income dropped alarmingly, and unemployment, notably low in the Twenties, rose from 500,000 to 12 million. Most of the unemployed were without any kind of assistance, and were rapidly reduced to the primitive conditions of a pre-industrial society struck by natural disaster. Millions wandered the country in an abortive search for work. They fabricated, on the outskirts of cities and towns, shanty slums, ironically called 'Hoovervilles', and rode freight trains across country, risking death or injury, even climbing into refrigerated cars. Farmers, unable to meet mortgage payments or to afford coal, burned corn to keep warm, while millions were near starvation. The Commisioner of Charity in Salt Lake City reported adults and children without food or adequate clothing. A member of the Hoover administration seriously proposed that restaurants give the unemployed left-over food in return for work – a superfluous suggestion, for many were already reduced to eating garbage. Apple-sellers, soap-box orators, beggars, bread-lines and soup kitchens appeared in every city. In many instances, the employed were little better off. In December 1932, wages in a wide range of industries averaged from 20 to 30 cents an hour, and a quarter of the women working in Chicago earned less than 10 cents an hour. The economic indicators of unemployment are readily available; the human costs defy quantification.

To many, though, it appeared that the collapse would be short-term. Hoover announced in 1930 that the worst of the Depression was over: billboards appeared asking 'Wasn't the Depression Terrible?' Conservative newspapers ignored or played down economic conditions; *Fortune*'s famous attack, 'No One Has Starved (. . . which is not true)', did not appear until September 1932. Between 1929 and 1932, business and industry were united in their view that they wanted unemployment prevented, not treated with welfare programmes. They sought massive government loans to activate industry and regulate the economy, but in vain. Meanwhile the arts and popular culture were equally slow in reacting to the Depression. The glossy middle-class magazine *Vanity Fair* was more interested in prohibition than unemployment; radio copied the ostrich-like behaviour of the press. Yet the hard facts now began to penetrate. Kaufman and Ryskind's prize-winning musical *Of Thee I Sing* (1931) began to show growing public disillusionment with politicians. And Edward Dahlberg's *Bottom Dogs* (1930), a fictionalized autobiography, was among the first of a growing row of books that would now start to explore the 'lower depths' of working-class culture and deprivation. But perhaps the most potent images of the time were the dynamic yet elegant gangsters of the movies, their attraction being their temporary mastery over the urban environment which now seemed to so many oppressive, bewildering and defeating.

Vulnerability was not confined to the cities – or the North. In 1931, nine black youths were charged with the rape of two white girls on a freight train in Alabama. The 'Scottsboro case' had national repercussions: both the NAACP (National Association for the Advancement of Colored People) and the Communist Party became involved. But the event which most clearly showed the increasing gap between the authorities and the ordinary people was the savage dispersal of the Bonus Army in 1932. Over 21,000 First World War veterans marched on Washington to demand their war-service bonus; the majority, many with families, stayed in a huge Hooverville across the Potomac. Hoover complained, 'Their continued presence here will have a depressive effect on Wall Street', and, after a bonus man died in a skirmish, Hoover panicked. Tanks appeared in Pennsylvania Avenue; but the squatters on Anacostia Flats refused to move, and troops, led by General MacArthur on a white horse, attacked the ex-soldiers' camp with bayonets and tear gas, setting the shanties on fire. MacArthur denounced the marchers as revolutionary Reds; in fact, they were largely conservative men, with a tendency to beat up communists. Many returned home, but hundreds simply joined the jobless drifters who roamed aimlessly across America.

Hoover was not naturally inclined to panic. In *American Individualism* (1922), he had expounded his confident faith in the equality of opportunity and voluntarism: Americans could succeed by their own efforts, developing, in answer to a 'rising vision of service', a sense of community responsibility. In the event, Hoover's response to the Depression was a confused mixture of individualism and 'corporatism' (an economy comprising self-governing, collaborating, monopoly groups). He sponsored a series of White House meetings for large corporations to establish common industrial policies, and, in an effort to ameliorate hardship, used his executive powers to co-ordinate measures of *private* relief. It has been suggested that some of Hoover's policies during the early Depression anticipated the New Deal. Certainly, he approved the creation of the Reconstruction Finance Corporation (RFC) in 1932, a new government credit agency with which he hoped to supply working capital to private industry and local government. But Congress watered down these plans and his willingness to implement theoretical initiatives was constrained by political prejudice and a rigid belief in his own wisdom.

▶ Roosevelt and the New Deal

The Wall Street crash and the ensuing Depression had of course made a bitter mockery of Republican claims to be the 'party of prosperity'. Renominated by his party in 1932, Hoover faced a Democratic challenger with an illustrious name in American politics: Franklin Delano Roosevelt, a distant cousin of Theodore Roosevelt, and a former governor of New York. A landslide followed: Roosevelt received 427 electoral votes to Hoover's 59, and he promised the beleaguered country a 'New Deal'. A master politician, a shrewd manipulator, and a man of extraordinary physical energy (despite being crippled by poliomyelitis), Roosevelt took office with no clearly defined programme, pledged only to get the country moving again. In his first inaugural, Roosevelt warned Congress (and the country) of his intention to act quickly and decisively: 'I shall ask for broad Executive power to wage war against the emergency as great as the power that would be given to me if we were in fact invaded by a foreign foe.' The New Deal measures of recovery and reform indeed operated in and drew on an atmosphere of continuing crisis analogous to war. Between 1933 and 1938 more significant reform legislation was passed than during any other five-year period of American history. The disparate policies of the New Deal – devised and implemented by a carefully chosen group of advisers, often in violent disagreement with each other – were unified only by Roosevelt's commanding personality and strong leadership. As President, Roosevelt greatly expanded the powers of his office, and came to assume an executive role not unlike that of a British prime minister. A superb communicator, Roosevelt also dominated the mass media with his informal 'fire-side chats' to a national radio audience and spontaneous answers to reporters at press conferences. For the first time, the presidency became an institution directly in touch with all Americans, with Roosevelt as a hero to his admirers or simply 'that man in the White House' to his detractors.

After closing all banks for four days, and placing an embargo on the export of gold, silver and currency to protect US reserves, Roosevelt called the 73rd Congress into special session on 9 March 1933. From then until 16 June – the first Hundred Days of the New Deal – it enacted a mass of complex and sometimes inconsistent legislation at high speed. An Emergency Banking Act authorized the regulated re-opening of banks (2,000 were to remain permanently closed); the Federal Reserve Board was given stronger control over credit. An Economy Act cut the salaries of all federal employees, reduced veterans' pensions, reorganized government agencies. The Civilian Conservation Corps – a kind of domestic Peace Corps – was founded with a grant of $300 million to enrol 25,000 young men on relief. Since many people regarded the CCC as being primarily concerned with the planting of trees, it came to be known as 'Roosevelt's Tree Army'. Direct relief ($500 million) for states and municipalities was to be administered by the Federal Emergency Relief Administration; farming interests were served by the Farm Credit Administration. Bank deposits were secured by the Glass–Steagall Banking Act, which created the Federal Deposit Insurance Corporation. The National Industrial Recovery Act, the Agricultural Adjustment Act and the Tennessee Valley Act represented the early New Deal approach to the problems of industry, agriculture, conservation and community planning. Later, in 1935, the Social Security Act was a notable welfare-state measure, providing for a system of old-age retirement payments and fixed-period unemployment compensation. Much of this programme appeared to have been designed to maintain rather than to dismantle the capitalist system. But the proliferating relief agencies alarmed conservatives as much as they heartened their beneficiaries.

Activity was the hallmark of the New Deal, and H L Mencken observed of Roosevelt in 1934 that 'We have had so many presidents who were obvious numbskulls that it pleases everyone to contemplate one with an active cortex.' Not only did Roosevelt possess a very active cortex, but he attracted to Washington thousands of highly skilled people who staffed the new agencies and formulated policies and programmes. Roosevelt's 'Brain Trust' – a group of advisers assembled to provide ideas for the

1932 campaign and subsequent interregnum – included specialists in economics and law such as Raymond Moley, Rexford Tugwell, Adolf A Berle and Samuel Rosenman. Collectively and individually, they represented a return to progressivism, a new assertion of the belief that organized social intelligence and its proper application could effectively remould society. To its critics, the Brain Trust was composed of impractical academics, grown arrogant and publicity-conscious because of their sudden elevation to national prominence. They were, in fact, not only the architects and administrators of the New Deal, but Roosevelt's first line of defence against his opponents, often serving to deflect criticism from himself. The Brain Trust devised an 'alphabet soup' of agencies designed to reinvigorate the economy – the NRA, the AAA, the PWA, the CCC, the FSA, the TVA and many more – and constituted the central thrust of the 'first' New Deal.

The National Industrial Recovery Act of 1933, designed to revive industrial and business activity, created the National Recovery Administration (NRA), and was said by Roosevelt to represent 'a supreme effort to stabilize for all time the many factors which make for the prosperity of the nation'. With the Blue Eagle as its symbol, and General Hugh Johnson as its colourful administrator, the NRA was empowered to prescribe codes and standards of fair practice for industries and to punish violators. Johnson declared grandly that: 'When every American housewife understands that the Blue Eagle on everything she permits to come into her house is a symbol of its restoration to security, may God have mercy on any man or group of men who attempt to trifle with this bird.' The NIRA (National Industrial Recovery Act) was also designed to stabilize prices, spread employment, raise wages and provide emergency relief through the Public Works Administration (PWA). So industry was to be stimulated and labour protected – Section 7a of the NIRA authorized workers to organize and bargain on their own behalf. But businessmen dominated the NRA, and wrote its codes, often including unenforceable provisions. Many corporations, in fact, evaded the codes, and doubts about the constitutionality of the NRA Act encouraged evasion. In the event, the NRA was destroyed by a Supreme Court decision in 1935.

The Agricultural Adjustment Acts (AAA) of 1933 and 1938 were attempts to maintain farm prices by artificially induced scarcity, thereby laying down the basic lines of the present American approach to the problem of agricultural overproduction. In compensation for a restriction of output, farmers were offered benefit payments through a processing tax on certain farm products – cotton, wheat, corn, pigs, tobacco and rice. Because the 1933 farm season was well under way when the first AAA began operations, large-scale destruction was necessary to cut crop and livestock surpluses. The Secretary of Agriculture, Henry Wallace, reluctantly agreed to a proposal by farm leaders to forestall a glut in the hog market by slaughtering over 6 million piglets and 200,000 sows due to farrow. While 1 million pounds of salt pork were salvaged for families on relief, nine-tenths of the yield was inedible, and was thrown away. Again, faced with the prospect of a huge cotton crop in 1933, AAA agents went to the South to urge planters to uproot their cotton. For ploughing up 10 million acres, farmers received over $100 million in benefit payments. Cotton destruction and the slaughter of pigs fixed the image of the AAA vividly in the public mind, and it was widely believed that these were annual operations. In fact, almost all the actual destruction ended in 1933, and afterwards the AAA restricted yields in a more orderly fashion. The AAA received the active support of large farm organizations and brought benefits to most commercial farmers. But, in limiting acreage and encouraging technological innovation, the AAA forced sharecroppers off the land and did little to improve the conditions of farm labourers. Yet, as W R Brock notes, the AAA 'was successful in its immediate objective, it tied the farmers politically to the New Deal, it turned Jefferson's chosen people into foster children of the federal government, and it raised questions of the ethics of restricting production in a time of scarcity'. The Supreme Court took another view of the ethics of the AAA processing tax, and in 1936 declared the first Agricultural Adjustment Act invalid.

Among other New Deal agencies, the Resettlement Administration (RA), under Rexford Tugwell, attempted to remove farmers to better land and to provide low-paid workers with 'Greenbelt Towns' outside cities, where they could supplement their salaries by part-time farming. The three towns – near Washington DC, Cincinnati and Milwaukee – were to attract more European comment than any other project of the New Deal except the Tennessee Valley Authority (TVA). The RA was also the least discriminatory of New Deal agencies in its treatment of African-Americans, and was the only agency to set up group medical plans. In 1937 it became the Farm Security Administration (FSA), and, against the opposition of Southern conservatives, attempted to regulate the supply, hours and wages of migrant workers. But, lacking a strong political base, the FSA was starved of funds by its Congressional opponents, and its material achievements were limited.

The most imaginative, successful and dramatic of the early New Deal measures was the Tennessee Valley Act. Created in 1933, the TVA was designed to prevent floods in the area of the Tennessee River, and to provide cheap and plentiful electrical power. A great experiment in regional planning, the TVA was attacked by private power companies as 'creeping socialism', although its farm programme tended to benefit the more prosperous farmers. The TVA was to become the greatest producer of electric power in America, and a manufacturer of low-cost fertilizers. During the Second World War, the TVA provided power for aluminium and arms manufacture. Its successful operation proved that efficiency and social concern were possible in government-owned, non-profit-making organizations. With its emphasis on conservation and reclamation, the TVA implemented proposals urged by progressives since the Twenties.

Of all the New Deal agencies, the Works Progress Administration (WPA), under the direction of Harry Hopkins, did most to implement relief work on a massive scale. By 1939 it had provided employment for 8,500,000 people in activities ranging from highway building and construction work to slum clearance, rural rehabilitation and reafforestation, at a total cost of $11 billion. Although accused of inefficiency, waste, and political favouritism, the WPA stimulated private business during the Depression years and completed projects that individual states had been unable to subsidize. Yet the WPA, like other New Deal agencies, could only scratch the surface of unemployment and poverty. African-Americans gained some real benefits from the WPA – by 1940, there were 237,000 black workers involved in WPA projects – but black women were confined to indoor occupations (extremely limited) by this New Deal agency. A blues lyric of the period commented wryly on this situation:

I don't want no woman to sit around on her DBA.
Hell, I don't want no woman to sit around on her DBA
She got to bring me some kind of job – if it's working on the WPA

Falls in industrial production and agricultural prices challenged the New Deal in 1935–36 and new leaders and movements emerged to confront Roosevelt and diagnose the unhealthy economic situation.

In an era of European demagogues, America produced a few home-grown and unique examples. Senator Huey Long, the virtual dictator of Louisiana, promised to make 'every man a king' by the gospel of 'Share-Our-Wealth', a simple, sweeping programme to expropriate the wealth of the very rich and provide all families with a $5,000 homestead and an annual income around $2,500. Long's assassination in 1935 removed the threat, but Roosevelt confided to Tugwell that Long was one of the two most dangerous men in America, the other being General MacArthur. Other popular demagogues emerged, like Father Charles Coughlin, the radio-priest of WJR Detroit, and founder of the National Union for Social Justice, who delivered over the CBS network venomous, anti-Semitic broadcasts against the 'Drain Trust' and the 'Pagan Deal'. Panaceas were much in demand: from Long Beach, California, Dr Francis E Townsend started 'Townsend Clubs', demanding monthly payments of $200 for each unemployed person over sixty, appealing to millions who, he said, 'believe in the Bible, believe in God, cheer when the flag passes by, the Bible Belt solid Americans'. Such demagogues, like the hostility of the Supreme Court, the emerging power of labour, and the growing alignment in some intellectual quarters between Marxism and the American progressive creed, helped push Roosevelt left when he appealed to the American electorate in 1936.

▶ Moving left

There is no doubt that events from 1929 deeply damaged the Twenties'
faith that America was stabilizing itself as a commercial nation secure in
all its institutions, capable of reconstituting old faiths, able to leave the
economy to business, and politics to its supporters. The times called for a
renewal of the progressive impulse and the radical view, and intellectuals
who had felt alienated and displaced in the Twenties involved themselves
in the political urgencies of the Thirties. Many writers who had previously
devoted themselves to a religion of art, bohemianism and expatriation
now became politically active, moving leftward, reporting on national
agonies. Fifty-three writers and artists explicitly supported the Communist Party in 1932, and for much of the decade authors identified
themselves with the Left and the 'toiling masses'. The modernist impulse
certainly did not disappear; indeed its awareness of fragmentation now
seemed the more relevant. Some of Faulkner's best, most experimental
work belongs to the decade: in 1930 came *As I Lay Dying*, and two years
later *Light in August*, a deeply symbolist evocation of the racially divided
and historically disordered South, potentially reintegrated by the pregnant folk-heroine Lena Groves; in 1936 came *Absalom, Absalom!*, perhaps
Faulkner's masterpiece – an exploration, through several perspectives, of
the history of Thomas Sutpen's doomed project to found a plantation
dynasty in northern Mississippi. In most of Faulkner's writing the grim
circumstances of the contemporary South appear only obliquely, though
Sanctuary (1931) evokes in the character of Popeye a modern mechanized dementia; *The Wild Palms* (1939), remarkable for its counterpointed
double plot, explores a disorderly age; and the story 'Tall Men' (1941)
can be read as a conservative rejection of the New Deal and welfare
legislation. But Faulkner's continuing saga of Yoknapatawpha County
offers a longer and more complex historiography of a ceaselessly dis-
oriented South.

Hemingway tried more directly to treat the challenge of the times,
most notably in his journalism ('Who Murdered the Vets?', 1935); the
reports from Spain were collected in *By-line: Ernest Hemingway*. His novel
of the Spanish Civil War, *For Whom the Bell Tolls* (1940), has remarkable
moments, but the lyricism of its central love story, beyond which lies
Hemingway's familiar Twenties universe of waste and death, is uneasy.
Perhaps the writer from the Twenties who most succeeds in the transition
is Scott Fitzgerald, who in his 1936 essay 'The Crack-Up' linked the economic breakdown with his own psychic collapse, and saw both pointing
to a new kind of art. It was Hemingway who observed that Fitzgerald's
Tender Is the Night (1934) gets better and better in retrospect. A novel of
moral wisdom informed by a strong Marxist insight into the economic
determination of his moneyed characters, it traces Dick Diver's finally
unsuccessful attempt to hold together a demoralized leisure class from

collapsing into psychic decay and sexual disorder. In *The Last Tycoon* (1941), left unfinished on Fitzgerald's death in 1940, there is again a charismatic hero undernourished by an exhausting and exhausted society. Monroe Stahr, the Hollywood director, a tycoon in the original Japanese sense of a great prince, represents responsible authority, humane and imaginative. But he is trapped between Wall Street and communists, and Fitzgerald's notes for the book indicate he was to succumb to illness and corruption: a last dark image of the American dream.

However, possibly the most outstanding experimental enterprise that distinctively belongs to the Thirties – if one sets aside Thomas Wolfe's expansive self-recording through four novels, culminating in *You Can't Go Home Again* (1940) – is John Dos Passos's massive three-volume novel, *USA* (1930–36). It used montage and collage techniques to trace America from the turn of the century to the Sacco–Vanzetti case, when the nation becomes two nations. There are fictionalized narratives about the lives of individuals; stream-of-consciousness sections emanating from the author himself ('Camera Eye'); a documentary collage of newspaper headlines, popular song fragments, etc. ('Newsreel'); and 'Biographies' of various strategic real-life villains and heroes – from J P Morgan to Thorstein Veblen, who diagnosed 'the sabotage of production by business'. Dos Passos puts modernism's ends to radical purposes (like Eisenstein), showing how capitalism destroys entrepreneurs and radicals alike. But his attempt to bring back Whitman's spirit of 'storybook democracy' tends to work from surfaces; his characters in the end possess only mobility and appetites.

It was those appetites that Henry Miller turned into a Whitmanesque hunger for experience, nonconformity, vitalism, and an anti-puritan celebration of sex. His books were not, he said, novels; in fact they are surrealist acts claiming the rights of the artist while refusing to produce Art. Written from expatriate Paris, *Tropic of Cancer* (1934, Paris; banned in the US until 1961) is fictionalized autobiography evoking a cancerous world which sexuality both exposes and redeems; *Tropic of Capricorn* (1939, Paris) goes back into the 'air-conditioned nightmare' of American experience to evoke working-class Brooklyn life. Nathanael West, too, was briefly an expatriate, and certainly a surrealist. His *A Cool Million* (1934) is another key book of the Thirties, using the clichés of success literature to explore and mock the entire American dream of rags-to-riches. In addition, West warns of latent native fascism, and his novels constitute a savage and satirical attack on an America where, he says, 'violence is idiomatic' and apocalypse is the nightmarish conclusion for a society based on deception and characterized by a tawdry mass culture. His books are a sombre commentary on that culture; his characters are cartoons: *Miss Lonelyhearts* (1933) is told in the form of a comic strip, and *The Day of the Locust* (1939), set in the 'Dream Dump of Hollywood' and ending in the burning of Los Angeles, is modelled on a movie.

But if modernism and surrealism lasted during the Thirties, one of the literary effects of the decade was the emergence of a 'proletarian' literature, though mostly written by and for the middle classes. At best, as in Robert Cantwell's *The Land of Plenty* (1934), or in some of the journalism of Sherwood Anderson, James T Farrell, Malcolm Cowley and others, it took the form of a humane documentary realism. This is a central note in Thirties prose, but other parts of this writing were sentimental, melodramatic and, as the naturalist theme of the beast in man reappeared, excessively brutal. It reached grotesque proportions in the black comedy of Erskine Caldwell, whose *Tobacco Road* (1932) records the exhaustion of the land and the betrayal of Jefferson's agrarian dream as peasants are dispossessed by the banks. The technique is, however, sensationalist and the characters are demoralized, physically repulsive, and degenerate; their emotional inertia presages destruction and death. The book was a popular success, and Jack Kirkland's vulgarized play version (1933) ran on Broadway for over seven years. John Steinbeck contributed a 'strike' novel with *In Dubious Battle* (1936), where he identifies 'group-man' (the mob) as a savage, monolithic beast. Steinbeck's subject is not revolution, but transcendence as a biological way through crisis.

This is clear in his *The Grapes of Wrath* (1939), probably the decade's best-known novel, bringing together many of its central cultural assumptions: a nostalgia for the agrarian past, a documentary desire to record contemporary fact (soil-erosion, foreclosures, industrialized farming, Hoovervilles), a populist faith in 'the people', and an indignation against man-made suffering. The migrating Joads, moving westward from dustbowl Oklahoma, represent 'humanity' rather than 'the workers', and Steinbeck's naturalist analogies with resilient animals emphasize his commitment to stoicism and survival. The appalling conditions of rural life also provided the material for James Agee's *Let Us Now Praise Famous Men*, commissioned in 1936, though not published until 1941. About the lives of three poor Southern tenant-farming families, it is an experimental documentary. Agee's collage form integrates Walker Evans's photographs, quotations from Blake, and other items into a discontinuous text, thus challenging his own professed artlessness, designed to convey the simple dignity and beauty of his subjects.

Not surprisingly, the Thirties also saw a return to naturalist urban novel-writing, a notable example being James T Farrell's examination of Chicago's Irish lower-middle class in the trilogy *Studs Lonigan* (1932–35). His aim was to reveal the effects of 'spiritual poverty'; so he shows the Catholic Church reinforcing prejudice, while the alternative mass-culture provides only escapist fantasies. In the third novel, *Judgment Day*, the Depression completes the process of human decline; his health shattered by smoking and liquor, the jobless Studs drifts towards death, melancholic, still dreaming. The culminating book in this line is Richard Wright's *Native Son* (1940), a major novel about African-American experience in the Chicago slums, which combines naturalism and expressionist night-mare; its materials explore loss of identity, ghetto poverty, double murder and liberal explanations from a communist lawyer.

The pressure of events in the Thirties brought about a mood of change in all the art-forms, and a demand for literary relevance. So James T Farrell's sceptical reviews of proletarian books earned him the antagon-ism of Mike Gold who, on becoming editor of *New Masses* in 1928, had turned it into a revolutionary magazine dedicated to 'the workers' art'. From 1934 to 1949, the weekly *New Masses* printed such writers as Rukeyser, Lorca, Brecht, Caldwell and Dos Passos, and cartoons, drawings and political humour. Though inferior material was published, *New Masses* 'had a bead on the time, which went to its heart'. It was in the New York office of *New Masses* that the John Reed Club – named after the American radical intellectual and journalist who died in Russia just after the Rev-olution – was founded in October 1929, to disseminate and enact 'the principles and purposes of revolutionary art and literature'. Similar clubs sprang up throughout America: in 1934, the New York branch of the club sponsored a 'little magazine', *Partisan Review: A Bi-Monthly of Revolutionary Literature*, edited by Philip Rahv and William Phillips, an important guide to the intellectual evolution of the Thirties and the schismatic nature of radicalism. The first issue proclaimed its revolutionary stance and offered to combat 'the debilitating liberalism which at times seeps into our writers through the pressure of class-alien forces'. But it also made clear its re-sistance to 'sectarian theories and practices': a 'centrist' position opposed to *New Masses* 'leftism'. Despite absorbing the 'crude vigour' of Jack Conroy's *Anvil* in 1936, *Partisan Review* began to divide internally. In 1937 it was restructured with additional editors and took on an anti-Stalinist, pro-Trotskyist line (voiced at the second American Writers' Congress that year) while simultaneously making the innovations of modernist Euro-pean literature, rather than social realism, its focus. As Christopher Lasch has noted, this was a valuable reaction against the proletarian-literature campaign, but it was soon absorbed within the retreat from ideology and postwar 'realism'.

The social responsibility of writers was a much-argued theme of the Thirties, later to affect attitudes deeply in the Fifties. In poetry, two major events occurred in 1930: the publication of Hart Crane's lyrical celebra-tion of mythic America, *The Bridge*, and Ezra Pound's *A Draft of XXX Cantos*, part of his epic enterprise in combining image, vortex, ideogram and rhythmic line in a total spatial action. Pound went on to move to-wards Social Credit and support for Mussolini, his contribution to the politicization of poetry; in 1930, likewise, the Southern cultural aristo-crats who had produced in the Twenties the poetry magazine *The Fugitive* issued a significant statement of Eliotic and Southern agrarian values in *I'll Take My Stand*. But the most important poetic movement of the Thirties was the Objectivists, the group including Charles Reznikoff, George

Oppen, Carl Rakosi, Louis Zukofsky and William Carlos Williams. Their sympathies were to the Left, but they avoided the banalities of propaganda poetry, drawing attention to form and shape, to the poem as object or 'an organism with distinct characteristics' (Rakosi). In Williams's intense non-symbolic re-creations of direct experience can be found the group's most memorable and influential poetry. Other poets more directly criticized Depression America: Kenneth Patchen, also an important love poet, who would link up with the Beats in the 1950s; Muriel Rukeyser, whose *US 1* (1938) used items from the daily press to show what a social revolution should rectify; and Kenneth Fearing, who attacked bourgeois society with sharp irony through its noisy advertising and specious cinema dreams (see his *New and Selected Poems*, 1956).

In theatre, too, the radical note grew. Clifford Odets, a principal dramatist of the Group Theatre, founded to produce plays of 'social significance' in 1931, exposed Hollywood's escapist images, though the hard-boiled vernacular of *Awake and Sing!* (1935) and *Golden Boy* (1937) owes a debt to the movie language of Cagney and Bogart. No formal experimenter, Odets remains the theatre's leading analyst of the emotions and tensions of the lower-middle-class Thirties family. Eugene O'Neill, winner of the Nobel Prize in 1936, mitigated earlier expressionist methods in his drama of the Thirties: *Ah, Wilderness!* (1933) is a 'hazy daguerrotype of Irish family life' (Robert Brustein), calling up small-town life in 1906, but *The Iceman Cometh* (written 1939) looks to social derelicts whose home is the saloon. One consequence of the Depression was the Federal Theater Project, sponsored by the WPA (Works Progress Administration) to re-employ thousands of theatre workers. It was a national organization of theatre groups, organized by Hallie Flanagan, which by 1937 was playing to weekly audiences of over 350,000. Among its most successful ventures were the Negro theatre and the 'Living Newspaper' deriving from revolutionary workers' theatre in Europe. It used projections, statistics, announcements and short dramatic scenes: *One-Third of a Nation* (on housing) was the most popular production, but Joseph Losey's *Injunction Granted* (on labour history) was sharper and more inventive. Other projects included Marc Blitzstein's *The Cradle Will Rock*, a sharp political musical, and Sinclair Lewis's and John C Moffit's exposure of the risks of American fascism, *It Can't Happen Here* (1936). It was the radicalism of the project that provided the excuse for its closure by the House Un-American Activities Committee in 1939.

Federal support for the arts was an important stimulus at many levels in the Thirties. The plight of the rural working class permeates the photographs taken for the Resettlement Administration (1935–37) and the Farm Security Administration (1937–42): these pictures of dustbowl landscapes, timber-shacks and dispossessed families, taken by Walker Evans, Dorothea Lange and Russell Lee, constitute the best-known and most admired collection of its kind. A varied body of work (after 1937 a more heroic mood appeared), it records popular America and its folkloric expression and shows even disintegrating America as a place ingeniously patched and assembled. It can be argued, however, that the documentary movement suppressed more than it exposed. Paul Strand, another great photographer who also worked for the Resettlement Administration, assisted Pare Lorentz in making the film *The Plow that Broke the Plains* (1936). This and *The River* (1937) use music, dynamic editing and language to extraordinary effect to trace a history of land exploitation and ecological disaster. But since the New Deal films offered government policies as sufficient solutions, Strand and Leo Hurwitz broke away to form the radical group Frontier Films, whose most notable achievement was *Native Land* (1942), a condemnation of civil-rights violations and the oppression of unionists.

Painting too was restimulated. A key part of the programme of the 'American Scene Painters' – Thomas Hart Benton, John Steuart Curry and Grant Wood – was the populist expression of vanishing qualities of good neighbourliness, social order, hard work. (Thus the heroic Washington of Leutze's famous painting is contrasted with the complacent modern 'aristocrats' of Wood's 'Daughters of the Revolution', 1932.) The 'scene' they concerned themselves with mainly was the frontier or small town, often with irony, so that their political attitude defies easy definition. Previously sympathetic to the '291' movement and communism, Benton became a populist anti-modernist and anti-Marxist. There was also an urban regionalist tendency working close to poster art and political cartoon, though few of their melancholy paintings matched the power and ambition of the Mexican muralists Rivera and Orozco, who worked in the USA at this time, combining native arts, modernism and political expression. Painters employed by Federal or Treasury projects to decorate banks, schools and post offices drew on the themes of labour, agriculture and history. Stuart Davis, painting abstract images of urban life, achieved four major murals, but, as secretary of the American Artists' Congress, he managed little else. Indeed, his career raises the problematic issue of the times: the appropriate relationship between government and creation, politics and art.

▶ Popular culture

Like any other American industry, the cinema was seriously affected by the Depression. In 1932, box-office demand slumped to almost half the 1930 level; Paramount and Fox went bankrupt, and by the midsummer of 1933, 5,000 out of 16,000 movie theatres had closed down. Yet even in the early Thirties the cinema, capitalizing on the introduction of sound, was the cheapest and most appealing form of entertainment: for 10 cents, the unemployed bought escape, rest, warmth and even a night's sleep. By 1936 cinema was recovering again, and by 1939 there were an estimated

40 million regular movie-goers, amongst them Edward Hopper, arguably America's greatest modern painter. His cityscapes with their slanting 'film noir' light have been much admired by movie cameramen. For its part, Hollywood was creating a formulaic cinema of genres which yielded some memorable films but also contributed to an evasive conservatism. Movie-goers were sustained by the myth of opportunity, and few films actually dealt with the life-styles or problems of working-class Americans or with national politics and economics. In 1934, restraint was formalized by the Hays Code, which heavily censored sexuality and profanity, and required that sin and crime be shown only if ultimately punished. Many films thus engaged in nostalgia: Walt Disney's cartoons looked back to a sanitized small-town way of life; Shirley Temple offered an escape into the world of childhood; Empire films like Ford's *Wee Willie Winkie* (1937) and films set in Europe's past evoked old hierarchical societies.

But other films, often musicals and screwball comedies, did provide sardonic commentary on the Depression years, if without offering any real challenge to the status quo. Pro-democratic works boosted public morale and at the same time challenged the rising threat of fascism in Europe. The most popular supplier of inspiring liberal messages was Frank Capra. A Sicilian immigrant, he came to believe in the American Dream of which his own success story seemed undeniable proof: his comedies evoke the democratic myths and images of the American past. In *Mr Deeds Goes to Town* (1936), Longfellow Deeds visits Grant's tomb and praises the United States as the only country where a poor farm-boy could eventually be elected President; in *Mr Smith Goes to Washington* (1939), Jefferson Smith – played by James Stewart, who, like Gary Cooper, provided Capra with a lean, rangy, decent and dependable outdoors type – visits Lincoln's statue when he arrives in the capital. In these films, the simple and naïve triumph over the wicked and powerful; their emotional structure combines sentimental feeling for small-town life with populist resentment of the city and its cynical, corrupt leaders.

Like the populists, Capra was not anti-capitalist, but he distrusted the large-scale trust, and sided with the small businessman against banks and corporations. Despite his happy endings, however, he acknowledges the vulnerability of his heroes, and his belief in the 'little man' is complicated by a fear of mob-action. By contrast, John Ford's films are more con-cerned with the creation of a natural community, strong and resilient – the community of *Stagecoach* (1939), the extended family of *The Grapes of Wrath* (1940). His sympathies, too, are populist (so, in *Stagecoach*, civilized Easterners confront disreputable Westerners, the whore with the heart of gold, the drunken but humane doctor, the outlaw). His taste for the West is partly nostalgic, but also draws on the wish to show an embryonic society forming rituals and customs which give it value and stability. But the Thirties' major cinematic achievement fittingly appeared at the end of the decade. If *Gone With the Wind* (1939) represents the apotheosis of

production values, *Citizen Kane* (1941) was the height of Thirties' cinematic invention. An eclectic work, it fused elements of contemporary
popular culture (radio, newsreel, theatre) with modernist techniques of
montage. Kane's life is revealed gradually from different points of view;
old RKO sets and clips from earlier films form an equivalent to theatrical
and painterly techniques of collage. The film displays the advances in
cinema technique made in the decade, as well as Welles's youthful brash-
ness and enthusiasm.

Network radio was already established by 1928, but in the Thirties it
was to function as a unifying force and a popular antidote to the fragmentation of the times. Yet, with half its revenue coming from ten advertising agencies, it was effectively controlled by its 'sponsors'. Controversy
was rigorously avoided, most radio drama took place in a social vacuum,
and current events were kept in the background for much of the decade.
The networks filled the air with comedy and music, but it was the human
voice that made the most powerful impression – the apparently casual
but carefully planned fireside talks of Roosevelt, the harangues of Father
Coughlin and Huey Long, and, as war approached, the magnificent coverage of European events by Hans Von Kaltenborn and Ed Murrow for
CBS. The success of talking pictures, the rapid increase of radio ownership and, after the end of Prohibition in 1933, the spread of the jukebox,
all led to a massive spread in the dissemination and promotion of popular
music and records. The Thirties heard some of the best American songs
ever written: 'Night and Day', 'In the Still of the Night', 'Smoke Gets in
Your Eyes', for example. Jerome Kern, Cole Porter and George Gershwin
introduced remarkable harmonic and melodic innovations, though only
Gershwin caught the conditions of the age – above all in his opera *Porgy
and Bess* (1935), set in the poor black community of Charleston. In the
early Depression, songs like 'Life is Just a Bowl of Cherries' (1931) were
cheerful and optimistic, giving temporary relief from breadlines and
unemployment. But in 1932 one song, 'Brother, Can You Spare a Dime?',
caught the bitterness and bewilderment of the times, and sounds more
like Kurt Weill than Tin Pan Alley.

However, the detective novels of Dashiell Hammett and Raymond
Chandler plunged the reader into a brutal and disordered world closer
to the shabby urban environment of the dominant newspaper headlines,
and provided a writing close to the form of contemporary anxiety.
Hammett was no simple realist, as the eccentric villains and symbolic
black bird of *The Maltese Falcon* (1930) demonstrate. His hard-edged pared-
down style is the work of a craftsman, and, as Julian Symons claims, *The
Glass Key* (1931) bears comparison with any contemporaneous American
novel. Hammett's and Chandler's private-eye detectives fill out a vague
region somewhere between the criminal underworld on the one hand and
the society of money, power and dishonest cops on the other. Chandler's
Philip Marlowe indeed represents a vanishing ethical code, like the knight

in the Sternwood window panel (*The Big Sleep*, 1939), redeeming the drab, tacky world he encounters with versatile wisecracking. Yet his wry, sleazy style in turn neutralizes his aestheticism. And, though Hammett writes of labour–boss conflict in a company town in *Red Harvest* (1929), it now seems Chandler's Marlowe, lonely, vulnerable, edgy, who best evokes the mood of the decade.

There were other levels of realism in Thirties' writing. John O'Hara, writing of the underlying disturbances of middle-class life, is in fact one of the sharpest social historians of the decade. His *BUtterfield 8* (1935), set in the speakeasy life of New York, a decadent democracy of aspiring journalists and dope-pushing debutantes, generates a sense of instability through an ever-present consciousness of unemployment, gangsters and possibilities of revolution. And the instability of social arrangements also pervades his most assured novel, *Appointment in Samarra* (1934), set in a Gibbsville, Pennsylvania, where the surface of public behaviour veils alienation, neurosis, resentment and fear. Julian English's doom is set in motion by a heartless, competitive bourgeoisie; it is completed by his own inner uncertainty and self-destructiveness. O'Hara is a sophisticated writer, whose work appeared in the *New Yorker*, a magazine perhaps never quite as sophisticated as Ross, the first editor, and James Thurber, its distinguished humorist and cartoonist, liked to claim. Its pieces often worked on the tension between the naïve small town and the demanding big city, and Thurber himself created the characteristic *New Yorker* piece about the bewildered, anxious little man confused by the menacing and mechanized society. The mood of many stories – 'The Secret Life of Walter Mitty', 'The Remarkable Case of Mr Bruhl' – reflects the insecurity and tension of the age, the tug between old values and new threats, the struggles of the sex war, the uneasy principles of change, and the powerful images of the popular culture. Mitty's dreams belong in comic books; Mr Bruhl turns into a movie gangster. Thurber has a streak of Victorian puritanism; the conservative Ross regarded anything serious as 'grim stuff'. In fact, the Depression is only hinted at in the *New Yorker*; the 'realism' of its stories is disinfected, and the trivial often assiduously cultivated, while its advertising (vintage wines, movie cameras, jewellery from Tiffany's) surrounds the text with middle-class fantasies and asserts the permanence of consumer capitalism.

▶ The second New Deal

Renominated by the Democrats in 1936, Roosevelt faced the Republican contender, Alfred M Landon, former Governor of Kansas. Roosevelt stood firmly on the achievements of the New Deal, stressed his basic conservatism, and appealed directly to the electorate as the adversary of 'the old enemies of the peace – business and financial monopoly, speculation, class antagonism, sectionalism, war profiteering'. The result of what was virtually a plebiscite was an astounding victory for Roosevelt, who carried every state except Maine and Vermont, received 523 electoral votes to a mere 8 for Landon, and carried into power a Democratic majority in both Houses of Congress. The victory owed much to a highly efficient Democratic Party organization masterminded by James A Farley; the support of farmers, small businessmen and organized labour (the Congress of Industrial Organizations (CIO) under Lewis raised $1 million for the Democrats); and to the fact that 1936 was the high-point of recovery under the New Deal. But it was, above all, a personal triumph for Roosevelt, and an endorsement of the principles and policies of the 'first' New Deal. Roosevelt's campaign addresses, one reporter noted, resembled the 'friendly sermons of a bishop come to make his quadrennial diocesan call. Bishop Roosevelt reported on the excellent state of health enjoyed throughout his vast diocese, particularly as compared with the miserable state that had prevailed before he took high office.' His congregation agreed, and entrusted their material, if not spiritual, welfare to him for another four years.

With his landslide victory in 1936, Roosevelt continued to emphasize reform and 'security' rather than simply recovery. But in a 1935 decision, the Supreme Court had declared the NRA codes unconstitutional in delegating legislative power to the President to draft the codes; they were also an illegal intervention in intrastate affairs. Six months later the Court declared the AAA processing tax invalid. Those justices opposed to New Deal legislation enjoyed excellent health, and showed no signs of wishing to retire. In a constitutionally sound but crudely handled manœuvre, Roosevelt proposed to enlarge the Supreme Court from nine members to a maximum of fifteen, in the pretended interests of judicial efficiency. Congress resisted this 'court packing' bill, FDR lost Democratic and popular support, and the Republican opposition, enjoying his embarrassment, was rejuvenated. Yet during the Congressional fight, the Court surprisingly upheld the constitutionality of the Wagner Act by a margin of one vote – eliciting the quip 'a switch in time saved nine'. And by 1941, the Court had authorized sweeping regulatory power over all the nation's commerce and upheld the principal legislation of the New Deal. But Roosevelt's court-packing bid alarmed conservatives, destroyed the unity of the Democratic Party, and tarnished his reputation as an invincible leader; the episode also strengthened the bipartisan anti-New Deal coalition within Congress.

Before 1935, Roosevelt, although pro-labour, was decidedly anti-union, regarding labour as a dependent part of industry. But with the Supreme Court's decision on the NRA codes, the administration needed a new labour policy and with the National Labor Relations Act (Wagner Act), it committed itself belatedly to supporting unions that were independent of management. The dominance of company unions was at an end and any form of employer discrimination against members of a union was at an end. The introduction of minimum wages and maximum hours in 1938 was a landmark for women factory workers, most of whom were white. But as in much New Deal legislation, there were shortcomings: the Wagner Act did not protect the bargaining rights of public employees, workers in intrastate commerce, or service and agricultural workers.

The passing of the Wagner Act, however, did have a decisive and divisive effect on the labour movement. Led by John L Lewis, president of the United Mine Workers, a group of dissident unions left the craft-oriented American Federation of Labor (AFL) to reach skilled and semi-skilled workers in the mass-production industries. A new organization for labour – the CIO – was formed in 1935, but faced opposition both from the AFL and from employers in the unorganized industries. The CIO began its unionizing campaign when workers at a number of General Motors affiliates staged 'sit-down' strikes to gain recognition for their new union, the United Auto Workers (UAW). Ignoring court orders to leave the buildings, and repulsing police attacks, the auto workers achieved victory in February 1937, when General Motors capitulated to their demands. In March, US Steel signed a contract granting the Steel Workers' Organizing Committee recognition for its members, a wage rise, and a forty-hour week. By the end of 1937, the UAW had gained recognition from every car manufacturer but Ford, and other industrial giants had also recognized the right of their workers to form independent unions. The 'blue collar' revolution was not achieved without violence, most notably in the 'Memorial Day Massacre' (1937) outside Republic Steel's plant in Chicago, when police fired on steel strikers and their families, killing 7 and wounding over 100. At one stage in the steel dispute, an exasperated Roosevelt blamed labour and management alike for industrial unrest, and Democrats in Congress took opposing sides on the unionization issue. But Roosevelt's refusal to use force against the sit-downers, together with his attack on the Supreme Court, alienated many of the New Deal's middle-class supporters. With unemployment remaining high and a sharp business recession in 1937–38, the New Deal appeared to be running out of steam and ideas. But events in Europe were soon to provide another remedy for American unemployment, and also help to secure Roosevelt's re-election for a third term.

Even before the 1940 election, American attention was being increasingly drawn to European affairs. There is evidence to support the view that Roosevelt perceived the dangers of the German alliance with Italy and with Japan more acutely than did the British, French or Russians. On 5 October 1937, he warned a Chicago audience that Americans could no longer hope to escape from involvement in world events through illusory policies of 'isolation and neutrality'. Yet Roosevelt had never made firm commitments to Britain and France in the event of war, largely because of the strength of American isolationist sentiment, and he expressed relief at the news of the Munich settlement. However, Hitler's continuing territorial aggression, Nazi persecution of German Jews, and the new German arms programme brought a swift response from Roosevelt. He announced an expenditure of $300 million on American armaments, and in July 1939 informed Congress of measures 'short of war, but stronger and more effective than mere words'.

With the establishment of the Popular Front in 1935, fascism replaced capitalism as the principal enemy of the American Communist Party, and the fight for 'unity, democracy and peace' took precedence over the class struggle. Talk of revolution was discouraged, and by 1939 even 'progressive capitalists' (but not Trotskyists) were considered comrades in the struggle. Thus the Communist Party was able to attract thousands and to make inroads upon the middle classes and the unions. But although antifascism seemed to bind the Popular Front together, it remained relevant only until the Russian–German pact was signed. And while liberal support for the Loyalists in the Spanish Civil War was not, as Ezra Pound claimed, 'an emotional luxury to a gang of sap-headed dilettantes', those who joined the International Brigade were soon disillusioned by Communist Party intransigence and violence towards other groups of the Left.

In the late Thirties, the United States sought to rediscover its cultural heritage; the Popular Front played a significant part in this process, encouraging the fusion of populism and nationalism, and rejecting élitist 'intellectual' forms in favour of folk arts that represented 'the people'. The Communist Party sponsored a 'Why I Like America' contest and 'The Star-Spangled Banner' was sung along with 'The Internationale'. The deeply felt urge to rediscover America as an idea and to confront the nation and its cultural history was also fostered by the New Deal, especially the WPA, and by the documentary impulse. Yet the promotion of cultural nationalism served to underpin the capitalist hegemony of the period.

Broadway's offerings included Elmer Rice's liberal allegory, *American Landscape* (1938), and Kaufman and Hart's anti-fascist play, *The American Way* (1939). Mythic heroes within the democratic heritage (such as Mike Fink, Paul Bunyan and John Henry) were often evoked, and the more detailed revelations of the American Guide Series (compiled by The Federal Writers Project) displayed a USA not only white and middle class, but also black, Mexican, Indian, immigrant, and agricultural. Historically, this was not a nation devoted to the Protestant ethic, but 'a child-like, fanciful, compulsive, absent-minded people' (Robert Cantwell). Thus the historical novels which enjoyed a boom during the Depression were not simply a form of escapism. The past was plundered in the quest for needed values and for those memorable episodes which, as in *Gone With the Wind*, demonstrated the nation's ability to endure and survive.

Generally artists and intellectuals were aware of political events in Europe, and many responded passionately to the Spanish Civil War. Yet a

Gallup Poll in 1937 revealed that 94 per cent of Americans favoured a policy aimed at keeping the country out of foreign wars. Reflecting such views, the Neutrality Acts of 1935–37 prohibited American loans to belligerents, embargoed shiploads of arms or munitions, forbade American citizens to travel on the ships of belligerents, and prohibited the arming of American merchant vessels. Implicit in this legislation was the isolationist principle that the United States should refuse to distinguish between the respective moral claims of warring nations. With the German invasion of Czechoslovakia in 1939, Roosevelt (who had increasingly begun to criticize Nazi Germany in his messages to Congress and his fireside chats) asked for repeal of the 1936 Act. Congress refused but, following Hitler's invasion of Poland, restrictions were relaxed. In 1941, Congress approved the President's request for $7 billion for 'lend-lease', empowering him to lend or lease materials to any nation whose defence he regarded as necessary for the security of the United States, now the 'arsenal of democracy'. With the Japanese attack on the US naval base at Pearl Harbor, in December 1941, the United States declared war on Japan; three days later Germany and Italy declared war on the United States. American isolationism and American neutrality were destroyed at Pearl Harbor and, as Roosevelt later observed, 'Dr New Deal' had to make way for 'Dr Win-the-War'.

▶ What happened in the Thirties?

In simple terms, the New Deal operated to relieve suffering, and in most of America the spectre of starvation was removed. In addition, social security and unemployment insurance were introduced, and the provisions of the Wagner Act significantly extended the rights of workers. But the rise of industrial unionism meant that Big Labour – bureaucratic and corporate – joined Big Government and Big Business in a national triumvirate. So, under the state capitalism of the New Deal, unions contented themselves with the conservative goal of acquiring a share in the *expansion* of capitalism. There was at that time, however, no significant redistribution of wealth. Roosevelt, in 1936, praised his administration because it had 'saved the system of private profit and free enterprise'. It is hardly surprising that the most popular board game of the Thirties was 'Monopoly'.

New Deal reforms were of greatest benefit to the middle classes; migrant workers, tenant farmers and unskilled labourers were relatively neglected. Also, the New Deal failed to address itself to the problem of the caste system in the South. Yet, in many respects, the South was profoundly affected by the New Deal which brought unprecedented changes and modernization to Southern industry and agriculture. Again, traditional landlord/tenant relationships began to give way to the powers of the federal government and the alphabetical agencies. New Deal legislation reduced wage differentials between the Northern and Southern states, and encouraged greater political participation by Southern labour. On the other hand, FDR, dependent on Southern support in Congress, refused to support a federal anti-lynching bill, and African-Americans themselves had no roles in the planning or execution of NRA, TVA or AAA programmes. But, as Frank Freidel observes, although Roosevelt 'never sufficiently challenged southern traditions of white supremacy to create problems for himself . . . he did back economic changes to improve the lot of the underprivileged, white and black alike, which did lead to a change in the status of the Negro'. Southern white liberals were attracted to and inspired by New Deal idealism, and began, for the first time, to question the immutability and morality of racial segregation. However, by the late Thirties, conservative Southern politicians began to protest against the reforming tendencies of the New Deal and its threat to states rights, so that Southern loyalty to FDR and the Democratic Party began to falter. The inability of the New Deal to end the Depression – the credit is given to the Second World War – has now become a truism. Nevertheless, capitalism, under pressure, did demonstrate its resilience and even inventiveness, not least in the new automotive culture of highways, gas stations, drive-in restaurants, trailers and motels.

Though the impact of the Thirties was deep and lasting, the mood of the period remains elusive and contradictory. Some 'survivors' report a pervasive camaraderie; others recall the emergence of a predatory mentality. A sense of powerlessness and fatalism is often apparent, but Roosevelt clearly rekindled hope, and radical politics was at times a source of euphoria. One of the dominant emotions was fear – fear of others and fear of losing things, the latter instilling a desire for acquisition and for security. Both fears lay behind the affirmation of home and private life, reinforcing the traditional role of women. However, the authority of that role was strengthened by Depression conditions, and married women obtained work to supplement the family income. The increased visibility of women in politics was symbolized by Eleanor Roosevelt who worked tirelessly for social reform and sought federal jobs for women. Also prevalent was a feeling of personal guilt and shame, usually brought about by the humiliation of unemployment. Most Americans blamed themselves rather than Wall Street or the government. Bewilderment and shock, even a sense of imminent catastrophe, were widespread responses, and American nervousness was unequivocally demonstrated by the reaction to Orson Welles's radio adaptation of H G Wells's *The War of the Worlds* on 31 October 1938. For the previous month, the American radio audience had been bombarded with the news of the European crisis that had been temporarily halted by the Munich agreement. So conditioned to disaster was the public that the broadcast triggered a national panic. Traffic was blocked by fleeing citizens, and scientists rushed into the open to look for meteors.

Assisted by technological innovation, radio and cinema together constituted a powerful ideological apparatus, sustaining the myth of a mobile, classless society containing endless possibilities for success. The affluent suburban society of the Fifties ('The American Way') was already being advertised on roadside billboards in the late Thirties, while in New York the World's Fair (1939–40) simulated a streamlined and socially harmonious utopia. Increasingly, passive consumerism was to become characteristic of American leisure. But in the Thirties, people bravely continued to believe that the actions of individuals and groups could influence history. That belief would be successfully put to the test in the following decade when, in the words of one broadcaster, 'a distant fire rolled towards them'.

▶ For further reading

Anthony J Badger, *The New Deal: The Depression Years, 1933–1940* (1993).

Stephen W Baskerville and Ralph Willett (eds), *Nothing Else to Fear: New Perspectives on America in the Thirties* (1985).

Roger Biles, *The South and the New Deal* (1994).

Alan Brinkley, *Voices of Protest: Huey Long, Father Coughlin, and the Great Depression* (1982).

William Stott, *Documentary Expression and Thirties America* (1986).

David P Peeler, *Hope Among Us Yet: Social Criticism and Social Solace in Depression America* (1987).

T H Watkins, *The Great Depression: America in the 1930s* (1993).

11 War and Cold War

Howard Temperley and Malcolm Bradbury

▶ The age of anxiety

In 1947 W H Auden – the leading British poet of the 1930s, who had left for America in January 1939, a few months before war in Europe began, to settle in the USA (he became a citizen in 1946) – published his powerful, influential poem *The Age of Anxiety*. Auden was one of a stream of European intellectual *émigrés* who moved westward from the troubled, murderous European scene of the 1930s, starting with Hitler's rise in 1933. Their numbers included leading writers like Bertold Brecht, Thomas Mann and Vladimir Nabokov, composers and musicians like Igor Stravinsky, great modern architects like Mies van der Rohe, intellectuals like Herbert Marcuse. H Stuart Hughes called this move of modern artists and scholars from Europe into America's artistic and academic scene 'the most important cultural event . . . of the second quarter of the twentieth century', and it would have a transforming and cosmopolitanizing effect on American culture. It would prove a clear sign of a shift in the geographical location of intellectual power, away from Europe to America; its consequences continue to this day. With the *émigrés* came many of the fundamental ideas and techniques of the Modern movement in the arts, architecture, science; in time they changed the intellectual texture and architectural face of the land they turned to for refuge. Auden's poem, a 'baroque eclogue' set in a New York bar in wartime, itself transferred to the USA many of the gloomy, anxious ideas that disturbed European intellectual life in the interwar years. It speaks of troubled modern consciousness, the faithless world after the Death of God, dismaying materialism, anxious individualism, the general breakdown of the historical process.

Auden was not alone in seeing wartime and postwar America as a place where the existential anxieties of modern Europe found a second home. During the war and after it, the United States, released from the preoccupations of the Depression, had been affected by the historical tensions and troubling conflicts that had dominated the early twentieth century and brought crisis to Europe. After the Great Crash of 1929, economic problems had appeared intractible, democratic capitalist theories insufficient to solve them. Marxist ideas took an increased hold on

American social and political thought, particularly among intellectuals and artists. Entry into war – particularly the highly ideological war in Europe – intensified awareness of the international pressures and processes of modern history, and changed American attitudes further. Then the events of the war's end – the revelation of the Holocaust, the Nazi's genocidal slaughter of Jews and others; the successful completion of the Manhattan Project and the use of atom bombs against Japan; the terrible and ruinous disorder that prevailed right across the European continent, where great cities lay smashed and wartime survivors wandered and starved; the rising evidence of conflict and global rivalry with Stalin's Russia – increased the sense of world-historical change and a feeling of new exposure. In entering the war America found itself summoned to new responsibilities. With its end a new era in its history seemed to begin.

So the title of Auden's poem seems as good a name as we can find for the decades of the Forties and the Fifties, in which the United States went through some of the most profound changes in its modern history. The changes altered the national direction, transformed the economy, shifted the ideological temper, vastly expanded America's role in world affairs. This fundamental, abrupt transition had been foreseen by few. The USA entered the Forties an inward-looking nation, still obsessed by economic fears, social and ideological division, problems of finding an appropriate assertion of American identity and the American mission: themes that, as we have seen, preoccupied the Thirties. Events beyond America seemed a world away; the growing global turmoil took second place to America's own problems. The American army was nineteenth in size in the world (a little larger than Bulgaria's). One decade later all had changed. Voices speaking for the nation spoke in different language, about different issues, to a different world. American voices were not solely for national consumption. They spoke from and for a USA that was now a world superpower: the one outright victor from war, a nation with huge international responsibilities (some still to be clearly defined) that ranged through Europe, the Middle East, and the major war-zone of the Pacific. All were regions where American armies had seen action, regions where great responsibilities had either been inherited or assumed. Europe's nineteenth-century empires were in process of collapse. New revolutionary movements were developing, in Europe, Africa, India, above all in China. The USA held vast military might; its military administrations were responsible for Japan and much of Western Europe. War had powerfully revived the American economy, now maintained by an energetic new era of consumption. That unpinned a world economy in postwar chaos. As never before, American politicians now had to address themselves to major issues of political and economic responsibility that would affect the future shape of the world at large.

No longer were American anxieties predominantly economic. The war had, essentially, righted the American economy, for all the fears of renewed Depression that arose after 1945. The nation had pulled all its resources and technological energies together; in the postwar years it entered into a period of unprecedented general affluence which in time made the Depression seem a historical aberration. War and postwar boom created an all-American sense of unity and purpose, only reinforced by the need to accept global responsibilities. The age of internal conflict and ideological division seemed over, a future of limitless self-sustaining growth seemed to lie ahead, as long as the economy was effectively managed and world peace preserved. The 'free world's' market economy seemed entirely dependent on the American system; in turn it spread its influence and its markets widely through the world in a new age of 'Americanization'. Western economies were rescued, American-style democracy offered as model for new nations emerging from the chaos. Large segments of the world turned to the USA (though others turned to the USSR) to admire and if possible emulate its affluence, adopt its political systems, assimilate its culture. The task of uniting the nations fell heavily on Americans (the United Nations, formed as war ended, settled on New York for its permanent home in 1946). By 1950, when the Korean War started and the Cold War had begun in earnest, the difficulties were ever more apparent. By now Europe was remapped and divided, and the post-colonial era had produced a new order in Asia. Above all, Russia had risen to its long-predicted position of rivalry with America. In this world, America now represented one of the two essential principles of postwar modernization and development: the 'American way' of individualism, capitalism, mass consumerism, and democracy, which faced, and increasingly confronted, the 'Communist way' of collectivism, state-run economy, the one-party state.

No longer economic, American anxieties were now atomic. Now the Cold War is (more or less) over, a fair degree of global peace prevails, and many of the nations and societies that lay in ruins after 1945 have achieved a high degree of American-style affluence (and influence), it is not easy to recreate the sense of disorder and the fear that marked the postwar 'balance of terror'. The origins of the Cold War and who was chiefly responsible for the stand-off have been much contested by several generations of historians, and recent archive material from Russia and China has become available to answer at least some of the questions. One key question was whether the confrontation was always 'inevitable', as it appeared to many (like George F Kennan) in the years after 1945. Yet for a time it did seem that the two former rivals but recent wartime allies might settle their differences and find an accommodation. They had had a common enemy, in fascism, and an interest in reconstructing a new world order. But suspicions and hostilities soon resumed. Neither trusted the other; co-operation was diminishing by the war's end. American nuclear capability, the American occupation of Japan (to Russia a legitimate sphere of influence), fear of losing wartime gains in Europe fuelled

Stalin's near-paranoid suspicions. In turn American suspicions were fed as across Europe they encountered recurrent examples of Russian intransigence and brutality. The battleground nations of Central Europe were turned one by one into Russian satellites with puppet administrations; firm borders were drawn on the European map; in Greece, Italy and elsewhere communist aspirations were evident. Russia's blockade of Berlin in 1948 was a symptom of a growing tension scarcely contained. China went Communist in October 1949; by 1950 American troops were again engaged overseas, in Korea. Over all this was the shadow of the 'bomb': the nuclear cloud that brought the war in Japan to a sudden end in August 1945. Its awesome power was the greatest symbol of world unease, and Russia competed for possession in a tense atmosphere of distrust and espionage. By 1949 they were successfully testing their own weapon. By 1950 they announced themselves the second atomic power.

So the Japanese attack on Pearl Harbor on 7 December 1941 did not simply bring America into a world war many had hoped to avoid. It totally transformed American experience, precipitating the nation into new areas of consciousness and anxiety for which the preceding years had done nothing to prepare. American troops now went overseas in vast numbers, to new and unknown theatres of war, and saw action on a scale quite different from that of the First World War. Thanks to their powerful news media, Americans at home shared the wartime campaigns. When atomic bombs dropped on Hiroshima and Nagasaki, Americans found their nation possessed an unprecedented instrument of power and annihilation. Even then, few could foresee the way the hot war against Axis powers would not end entirely, but evolve into a cold war – 'war by other means' – against a former ally. Ideas of American identity – and un-American identity – were shaken; American life felt different and exposed in fresh ways to world forces. In this rapid sequence of transforming events we can find the beginning of 'the Fifties': that period of new affluence, cosmopolitanism, and Cold War anxiety, which roughly begins with the death of Franklin D Roosevelt, transformed from New Deal president to great world leader, in 1945, and continued through the Truman (1945–53) and Eisenhower (1953–1961) administrations that followed.

'The Fifties' now seems fixed in folklore as a conservative, bland, suburbanized time in modern American culture – a time when people began talking of an 'Age of Abundance', indeed of a post-political 'Age of Equilibrium'. It appears a time of optimism, consensus, great national pride – when American ascendancy grew and its influence spread American styles, commodities, trade, mass culture, artistic, scientific and technological achievements and democratic values widely through the world. Yet many internal tensions remained. Americans often felt threatened from without and within; spy scandals multiplied through the Fifties, historians spoke of a 'paranoid style' in American culture as political witch-hunting grew; there was a strong sense of conformity, provoking a mood of youthful rebellion. There were worries about foreign commitments, nostalgia for older ways of life being swept away by modern systems and urbanization. The role of the military, and national dependency on military spending, caused political anxiety. Affluence and social bureaucratization brought their own problems of alienation; there was a feeling of entering a new world of moral emptiness, individualized insecurity. Middle American, Norman Rockwell daily life seemed increasingly robbed of its certainties. War had brought new expectations about education and human rights; African-Americans were no longer content to accept their previous 'invisibility', other ethnic groups were demanding a better place in the sun. All this is part of the atmosphere of Auden's poem, and of much of the literature and art of the time, with its concern with existential anxieties and alienations. The Fifties may seem a stable period, but it bred many of the dissents and arguments that passed on into the Sixties, not least the dawning of the Beat Generation. The 'Age of Abundance' was indeed also the 'Age of Anxiety'.

To some degree the mood of the Fifties was born of a quarrel with the Thirties. Old political ideologies now seemed suspect, particularly those of the Left. In the McCarthy hearings the quarrel acquired the dimensions of a purge (Arthur Miller's timely play *The Crucible* appeared in 1953). But if the Fifties quarrelled with the Thirties, the Sixties would quarrel with the Fifties, seeing it as a period of repression, caution, political retreat. Eventually many of the political decisions taken from VJ (Victory in Japan) Day on would be questioned: to resist Communism, support European recovery through the Marshall Plan, organize a Western military alliance through NATO, intervene in foreign crises like the Korean War of 1950–53. To later critics the Truman–Eisenhower era seemed a time when progressive momentum was lost, American capitalism embarked on world domination, intellectuals and scientists betrayed their task by becoming tools of government. So postwar culture begat its 'counterculture', and the entire Cold War policy came under question, with substantial consequences for the later intervention in Vietnam. As has been noted, American historiography of the Cold War often tells us little about the war itself, and much about the American intellectual history of the 1960s and 1970s. Now at a reasonable distance, we can add to the new evidence over Soviet intentions the political situation of the time: a Russia massively devastated and in internal disorder; an America tempted to return to the isolationism of the 1920s; a world process that saw the disappearance of key players like Germany and Japan, and a collapse of nineteenth-century empires to which both Russia and the USA had to respond.

Still, the ideological questions that arise from the period from 1945 to the election of John F Kennedy in 1960 remain fundamental for understanding recent American history and experience. Was there a Communist threat to world stability; or did American inexperience and misjudgement bring a tense situation to the boil? Did the emergence of two competing world-empires show two opposite social and political orders were on a collision course, or were they moving in related directions, albeit starting out with different premises? Did America's Fifties 'new liberalism' – with its loss of progressive momentum, its will to bow to the claims of realism – weaken the nation politically, or was it simply part of that oscillation between conservatism and reforming radicalism that has been common in modern American politics? Was the 'new liberalism' – a term that has substantially shifted in meaning, but then referring to the post-ideological ideas of self-reforming Marxists and intellectuals who felt bloodied by recent history – what David Caute once called it, part of a machine for the suppression of the radical spirit in American life, or a way of responding to the recent age of totalitarianism and totalitarianism's continuing threat? What any account of Fifties politics must acknowledge is that all such choices were made under pressing conditions, in times which often seemed frightening and incomprehensible. They were made uncertainly in a period of great world changes and shifting spheres of influence, and shaped by fears of both an ideological and an economic return to the difficulties of the Thirties. Americans were faced with serious problems of deciding, as they so often had, whether to stay in their own sphere of influence, or assert a world role. They were unsure whether to seek alliances with any nation that would ally with them, or demand consent to their own values. Internal choices seemed no less difficult. Wasn't bland affluence better than economic instability? Should intellectuals, artists, radicals (those who felt most in dispute with the Fifties climate) reaffirm international radical allegiances, or defend a political order that globally defended democracy and liberalism, if sometimes by illiberal means?

Many Americans relished the new confidence history bestowed on the nation, and saw themselves in the forefront of modern progress (something many foreign visitors to the country after 1945 affirmed). Others read books like David Riesman's *The Lonely Crowd* (1950) – a famous anthropological reading of the 'joylessness' and anomie of life in a country pressured by, among other things, great political and military responsibilities – and felt theirs an age of intolerance and repression. The age of internationalism was also an age of often narrow nationalism, as many Americans, feeling themselves the custodians of basic democratic values, saw the need to reassert to themselves (and others) the values for which they felt they stood. Moreover, for intellectuals, the lessons of Auschwitz, Buchenwald and Babi Yar seemed plain, displaying the banality of evil, demanding an assessment of the totalitarian values that had blackened the age just past. So this was a time to reassess the political naïvetés of the recent past, a time of uncertain compromises and stoical acceptances. The works of bleaker modern thinkers (Kierkegaard, Heidegger, Buber, Niebuhr, Sartre, Camus) offered a vision of modern despair and absurdity. French existentialism, spread by Sartre, exerted powerful influence over the generation, and a 'tragic sense of life', perhaps even a return to faith, seemed more urgent than the radicalism of the Thirties.

This changed the flavour of the culture. In the creative arts of the postwar period we find a new quality of modern anxiety, a sense of extremity, that had never been so visible in the American imagination. It is in the more intimate expressions of culture – the accounts of conscience and consciousness given by intellectuals, artists, writers – that we usually find the dramas of an era most richly explored. Like postwar American life, postwar American writing, theatre and painting acquired a changed character. Though much American writing of the Thirties is radical in attitude, it largely affirmed Americanness, the spirit and soul of the people. Postwar literature is more ambiguous, portraying the new affluent and urbanized order with a vision closer to the disturbances of European modernism. Ideological sympathies gave way to what Lionel Trilling – who was in this book *The Liberal Imagination* (1950) one of the most interesting spokesmen of the era – called 'moral realism', and defined not as a clear sense of good and evil, but an awareness of good-and-evil. Not surprisingly, much of the best writing of the time came from writers who considered themselves 'survivors': Jewish writers who could identify directly with the six million victims of the Holocaust, who survived to speak for those who could not. Other writers, like J D Salinger, Norman Mailer, and Randall Jarrell, had experienced the barbarities of the war overseas. Others saw the underside of affluence, sensed unease and moral confusion; there was a fiction and a poetry of confessional unease and despair (John Berryman, Robert Lowell). Others displaced anxious fears into black humour, as in Terry Southern's famous screenplay for the film *Dr Strangelove: Or How to Stop Worrying and Love the Bomb*. Questioning the darker aspects of their own time, they pointed the way to Beat writing, and the criticisms of the 1960s. With its increased cosmopolitanism and its intensive analysis of a new way of American life, its enlarged sense of history, its growing confidence on the power of American literature to speak to a wider world, its concern with the problems of human need and human nature, American writing and American intellectual culture too began to find a bigger role in a wider world.

▶ The impact of war

The event that plunged the United States into the greatest change to affect the nation since the Great Crash of 1929 was, of course, the Japanese attack on Pearl Harbor on 7 December 1941. The United States was joined by Britain in its declaration of war on Japan on the following day, and on 11 December the United States and Germany and Italy went to war. As we have seen earlier, these events had been some time in the making, though national problems had largely concealed this from most

Americans. In Europe the political settlements made at Versailles after the First World War had been coming apart for many years. In 1933 the Nazis had risen to power in Germany, and in 1936 they occupied the Rhineland. Meanwhile the Neutrality Acts inhibited American responses, and the nation clearly had no wish to be involved. But with the annexation of Austria in 1938, the invasion of Czechoslovakia in March 1939 and the assault on Poland on 1 September 1939, which marked the outbreak of European hostilities, the American administration began increasingly to respond to European problems and assist the Allied cause. In the Far East, conflict between China and Japan had begun long before with the Japanese occupation of Manchuria in 1931, later broadening into a full-scale struggle for control of all of China. But it was not until the end of 1941 – by which time France had fallen, German tanks were rolling towards Moscow, and most of China and Indo-China were in Japanese hands – that America found herself, with a mixture of surprise and outrage, an involuntary belligerent.

What made the American people so surprised and angry was not just that Pearl Harbor came totally without warning and, as far as they could see, provocation: it was that nothing remotely like this had ever happened before. Ever since the founding of the Republic they had believed that their geography provided them with a barrier against potential aggressors, and though they had been involved in previous international conflicts they had always had a choice in the matter. But the Japanese assault on the US naval base at Pearl Harbor – and simultaneously on American forces in the Philippines, Guam and Midway Island – forced them into the international arena and the defence of their interests. Indeed the US Congress's declaration of war on 8 December was a recognition of a state of war that already existed. Yet though this declaration, followed three days later by Germany's and Italy's declarations of war on the United States, marked official American entry into the conflict, her actual involvement had started much earlier.

As was noted in the last chapter, American neutrality legislation during the Thirties had attempted to forestall American involvement in future conflict by preventing America giving assistance to belligerent powers, but many were opposed to these isolationist measures, including Roosevelt. He rightly saw that the legislation provided encouragement to potential aggressors while preventing their victims from looking to the United States for assistance. But there was little he could do without the support of public opinion – which was divided betweeen those who wanted Americans to attend to their own affairs and those who wanted an anti-fascist front. Once the European war had started, however, Roosevelt hastened to remove the Congressional restrictions with as much speed as public sentiment would allow. In November 1939 he repealed the arms embargo, authorizing 'cash and carry' exports to belligerents. In his State of the Union address of January 1941 he warned of the threat to American institutions, and of a situation 'unique in our history', and enunciated the idea of the 'Four Freedoms' in the face of a breakdown in the world balance of power, saying 'Every realist knows that the democratic way of life is at this very moment being directly assailed in every part of the world.' In March 1941 Congress approved his Lend-Lease Bill, which allowed the President to supply arms to countries whose defence was deemed vital to American interests. An initial appropriation of $7 billion was set aside for this purpose; eventually over $50 billion would be spent. Meanwhile secret staff talks were taking place between Britain and the United States to agree a common strategy in the event of American involvement. In August came the Atlantic Charter, drafted jointly by Roosevelt and Churchill, affirming the democratic principles on which it was hoped the postwar world would be built. More immediately, arrangements were made to create a defence zone east of Iceland and use US naval vessels to convoy American shipping.

At home, as Roosevelt emphasized in his State of the Union address, Americans had moved from peacetime to wartime production, and were pushing ahead with military preparations of their own. During 1941 munitions production trebled, and car-factories were being adapted for aircraft and armoured-vehicle production. For the first time in America there was peacetime conscription, and more than 16 million men registered for service. Already, then, the switch from peacetime to wartime arrangements, from isolationist to internationalist policies, was underway. If the assault on Pearl Harbor took Americans by surprise, it did not find them unprepared.

The war shocked Americans but it also changed their perspectives and above all their economy. The Japanese attack undercut the position of the 'America Firsters', strengthened those who called for an anti-fascist front, and meant that Roosevelt took the nation into war with the nation behind him. And an immediate effect of entry was to shift the economy into high gear – something the New Deal, for all its deficit spending, had failed to do. Between January and June 1942, the War Production Board, entrusted with the task of co-ordinating the national economic war efforts, placed orders for goods valued at more than $100 billion – more than the entire Gross National Product of 1940, and more than the military spending of all the other combatants combined. Among the targets the President set were 8 million tons of shipping, 60,000 planes, 45,000 tanks, and 20,000 anti-aircraft guns. In all, federal spending during the war amounted to $320 billion. What was most remarkable was that this production was achieved without any drastic cutback in civilian consumer spending. There was some rationing, but so enormous was America's latent productive capacity that her response to war consisted largely of superimposing her new military requirements on top of existing peacetime production. Indeed, the output of some luxury goods grew because of the increases in earning power created by the war economy.

Job opportunities boomed: those who – like the 'Okies' in John Steinbeck's *The Grapes of Wrath* (1939) – were still jobless when war started, were quickly recruited into the services or taken into expanding war industries. So were women, many of whom had never thought of working, but now found it gave them a new measure of prosperity and independence. And, though in the armed services as well as in some civilian occupations segregation continued, blacks prospered too.

The war, of course, produced much real suffering for Americans: 322,000 of them lost their lives in battle; more than double that number were wounded, and many more suffered in other ways. Yet, even when all the casualties were added together, the fact remains that, in a war that claimed upwards of 50 million dead, Americans fared better than most. This could be no consolation to those who took part in the death march from Bataan to Corregidor, or in the murderous jungle fighting at Guadalcanal, or in the Ardennes retreat. Yet it did mean overall that the experiences of American soldiers tended to be different from those of their Russian – and very different indeed from those of their German and Japanese – counterparts. Even in the first stages of conflict, Americans had little reason to fear that they would *lose* the war, let alone that they would see their cities occupied, or their Jews herded into gas chambers. For most Americans at home, and a good many serving abroad, the war brought compensations as well as hardships, and sometimes the former outweighed the latter. If contact with the military machine was shocking to some, others found the experience liberating, opening new opportunities that would be claimed in postwar life. Unlike the Great Depression, which brought misery to almost everyone, the Second World War was an event in which, J K Galbraith later claimed, 'a large number of people found pleasure in jobs they never expected to have, in responsibility they never expected to assume, in travel previously reserved for the rich, and in escape from worthy but routine lives'. Above all, the war dispelled the Depression, and America emerged from it the one outright victor, forced into an experience of world contacts which shaped its subsequent policies in directions far away from those of the Thirties.

The shift of mood is evident in intellectual and cultural life. During the Thirties, many intellectuals had been on the Left and aligned themselves with a radical future, usually mediating between American progressive radicalism and revolutionary internationalism. But the effectiveness of the New Deal, the revelations about Stalin's purges, and finally the signing of the Nazi–Soviet Pact in 1939 weakened communist sympathies. In a spectacular defection from the Party after the Pact was signed, the writer Granville Hicks noted: 'However much strength and influence the Communist Party has lost remains to be seen, but it is my belief that the events of the last few weeks have largely destroyed its effectiveness [in America].' With the coming of war, writers who had been Left in the Thirties now became loyal war-correspondents attached to the cause of

252 Introduction to American Studies

American democracy: John Steinbeck in Africa and Europe, John Dos Passos in the Pacific, Ernest Hemingway in France (where he had to be restrained from combat, and took pride in having liberated the Paris Ritz). Around this time, too, a number of major writers from the experimental Twenties and political Thirties died: Thomas Wolfe in 1938, Scott Fitzgerald and Nathanael West in 1940, Sherwood Anderson in 1941, Gertrude Stein just after the end of the hostilities. As in the First World War, a new generation seemed to emerge from the war experience itself. With books like John Hersey's *A Bell for Adano* (1944), John Horne Burn's *The Gallery* (1947), Irwin Shaw's *The Young Lions* (1948), Norman Mailer's *The Naked and the Dead* (1948), James Gould Cozzen's *Guard of Honour* (1948), Herman Wouk's *The Caine Mutiny* (1951), and James Jones's *From Here to Eternity* (1951), the war novel again flourished. But, like the war novels after the First World War, they also marked the changing mood of the times. Malcolm Cowley has noted that the post-First World War writers went in not for disillusion so much as rebellion, and tried out elaborate technical experiments: the post-Second World War writers wrote of despair and disillusion, yet often used conservative technical forms. Their themes were the dark discovery of European ruination, of historical waste, political anxiety, and the threat of totalitarianism, which they found not only posed by the enemy but within the military system itself. Norman Mailer's *The Naked and the Dead* (1948), the best of these works, explores the impotence of liberalism and foresees a new fascist potential released in the psychic and social world by war: 'You can consider the army as a preview of the future', says his General Cummings.

Perhaps the best book about the dislocations of war is by a writer who did not see the battlefields. In 1944 Saul Bellow, a Jewish writer from *Partisan Review* circles, published *Dangling Man*, a novel about Joseph, who had been a communist in the Thirties, but now lives in a dead, modern, wartime Chicago, awaiting induction into the army. Politics and human and romantic relations have failed him; he moves into solitude, irritable enclosure. A marginal man, he nevertheless notes that 'we have history to answer to', and sets himself the task of defining a humanist world view: 'He asked himself a question I still would like answered, namely "How should a good man live; what ought he to do?"' he says, considering his past self. Joseph's is a modern existential dilemma – he exists without an essence in a non-reflecting, hostile world. What resolves it is the arrival of his induction papers. His final cry – 'Hurray for regular hours! And for supervision of the spirit! Long live regimentation!' – is an ambiguous resolution, a testament to loss and gain: the deprivation of the solitary realm of the free spirit, the acquisition of enforced community and historical attachment. In its very ambiguity, *Dangling Man* is a notably modern novel. Its roots lie in the dark literature of European modernism, especially that concerned with romantic deprivation and historical disorder (Kafka, Dostoevsky, Sartre). It is a breakaway from the pastoral nostalgia or the epical American ambition that shaped many novels a generation before, a recognition of the contingent modern city, the struggle of individual and community, the wasting of self. It is also – in a period when the Jewish voice both cosmopolitanized and darkened American thought – a Jewish novel, seeking a ceremonial of life in a bleak world. Joseph's stoical acceptance of the system in its inadequacy is a bleak parable that would resound through much postwar American writing, as writers divided between agonizing fears and liberal desires, struggling with Reinhold Niebuhr's warning that liberal moralism could not cope with the 'ultimately religious problem of the evil in man'.

▶ The Truman years 1945–52

Thus it was an uneasy, changing, morally bloodied nation that, after Roosevelt's death in April 1945, President Harry S Truman led through the last months of war and into the uncomfortable peace after 14 August, after the dropping of two atomic bombs on Japan. Americans had no wish to return to the economic disasters of the Thirties nor to the unpreparedness and the chaotic international politics of the interwar years. Though the bomb, the Holocaust, the tactics of the Russians in Eastern Europe all raised shadows over the future, the central fear haunting Americans at home was that the end of hostilities would mean a return to Depression. The great boom of the war years, which had raised the nation's Gross National Product by over 60 per cent in real terms between 1939 and 1945, was so plainly the product of the war economy that it was hard to see how it could continue when military spending was cut. Yet Americans wanted the rewards of peace; there were 12 million returning veterans to be absorbed into the labour force. Severe strikes hit the nation in 1946, and inflation took off again. Distrustful of Truman's capacity to manage these issues, the nation elected a Republican Congress, the first since 1931, that proved highly critical of Truman's Democratic administration. Yet the fears were groundless. Although federal spending was slashed by almost 60 per cent, from $98 billion in 1945 to $39 billion in 1947, the actual fall in GNP was less than 10 per cent, and within the next three years this shortfall was made up by growth in the domestic sector. Unemployment rose briefly from its all-time low of 1.2 per cent in 1944 to 3.9 per cent in 1946, but dropped to 3.4 per cent in 1948. By the early Fifties, the promises were that American society was evolving into a new kind of mass society based on exponential economic growth and more or less general abundance.

How was this managed? Partly it was through government planning of the economy, in part based on continued defence needs. For, though by European standards America was far from being a 'welfare state', Truman saw that there was no going back on the New Deal. Returning veterans were treated with generosity through the GI Bill, with grants on leaving service, low interest loans for acquiring farms, businesses or new homes, and educational subsidies on such a scale that they fuelled a rapid expansion of higher education, in turn bringing an increasing sophistication, a higher level of scientific, technological and cultural activity, and an enlarged academic élite, into the culture. More important, economically, was the demand for new consumer goods that had built up over the preceding five years, when, despite general prosperity, production for civilian consumption had not kept up with spending power. So now articles that had been scarce or unavailable (cars, refrigerators, radios) needed replacing, while a whole new range of consumer goods (electric clothes dryers, television sets, air conditioners, synthetic fabrics) came on to the market thanks to mass-production techniques and new, often war-derived, technologies.

Construction boomed: by the late Forties, commercial and industrial building was at more than double the level of the Thirties. Firms ploughed back high proportions of profits into research and development, reflecting growing confidence; American business, freed of the demands of the war economy, turned its enormous energies and resources into creating a consumer society that would soon inspire fascination and envy around the world. The stark contrast between American affluence and European poverty became clear; America was the only nation to emerge from the war with her plant intact and her economy strengthened. In 1949, American *per capita* income was double that of Britain, three times that of France, five times that of Germany, seven times that of Russia. With only 6 per cent of the world's population, America consumed 40 per cent of the world's energy, had 60 per cent of its motor vehicles, 70 per cent of its telephones, 80 per cent of its refrigerators, and nearly 100 per cent of its television sets. Americans, who had dreamt throughout the Depression of recapturing the prosperity of the Twenties, found themselves by 1950 with a *per capita* income 44 per cent above that of 1929. It was the American economic miracle: no other nation had ever been so rich.

But American consciousness of good fortune was tempered by a newly awakened sense of international vulnerability. Pearl Harbor had shown that the Pacific and Atlantic Oceans no longer provided effective barriers against aggressors. It also demonstrated the dangers of hiding away from world responsibilities while major crises developed. During the war, the lesson had already been drawn that the United States must henceforth play an active part in world affairs if issues were to be settled before they reached crisis proportions. It seemed clear that the origins of the Second World War lay in the economic collapse of the Thirties and the consequent rise of the dictators. If prosperity were assured, and international disagreements thrashed out in public, the chance of world peace would be greatly increased. One spectacular convert from isolationism was Senator Arthur Vandenberg, who announced in 1945: 'I want a new dignity and a new authority for international law. I think American self-interest requires it.' The instrument that many Americans looked to was the newly established United Nations, which held its inaugural meeting in San Francisco in April 1945. It was in many ways an American product, reflecting American assumptions about the efficacy of free discussion as the best mode of resolving differences, and depended on the willingness of members to abide by majority decisions. American foreign policy was now based in principle on a new universalist approach, a rejection of the old sphere-of-influence politics of the interwar years. In retrospect, it now appears that much of the idealism the Americans invested in the UN was a product of their inexperience in world affairs, but at the time it appeared to provide an American-style model for the future.

What immediately alarmed Americans was the behaviour of the Soviet Union. During the war, disagreements between the two powers had been largely concealed from the public, and there was something of a honeymoon period as postwar politics evolved. However, over the next years conflict quickly became open and bitter, especially over the question of the 'satellite' countries of Eastern Europe. What the Soviet Union hoped to achieve in these years will remain mysterious until Russian archives are fully opened; but it is plain that the Russians had drawn quite different lessons from the Second World War from those Americans had drawn. Their losses had been incomparably greater: for every American killed some 50 Russians had died, and vast areas of the country had been devastated. For the second time in a generation, German armies had swept east; there was little to suggest that such invasions were the product of economic dislocation, nor that an international debating chamber could prevent recurrence. Moreover, as Marxists, Russians were committed to an inexorable interpretation of history that saw socialism and capitalism locked in a life-and-death struggle. The establishment of socialism was justified in the satellite countries by historical world-purpose as well as by security.

The Americans were at first prepared to recognize considerable Russian rights in Eastern Europe in exchange for advantages elsewhere. But, as the Red Army remained in Eastern Europe, democratic regimes began to fall, and the satellite-state system evolved, American policy, committed to the principles of political and economic liberalism, found itself increasingly at odds with the Soviets. To those liberals who regretted their earlier failure to see the fascist threat, what was happening now in Poland, Czechoslovakia and Hungary was all too like Hitler's adventures of a decade earlier. Did the Soviet Union, too, intend to move west and establish throughout Europe satellite states and puppet governments? If so, there was little except American power to stop her: all the Russians needed to reach the Channel ports, went a saying of the day, was boots. In retrospect, it is clear that much that was menacing and conspiratorial in Russian behaviour could as readily be seen as signs of weakness. But it was hard for Americans not to feel that history was repeating itself, and there were reasons – even good liberal reasons – why a Truman administration should exploit such fears. With a Republican Congress attacking humanitarian programmes for financing development overseas, Truman could readily defend them on the grounds that they were necessary to fight encroaching communism.

By 1947, the philosophies of containment and confrontation were well evolved. In 1946, Churchill had seen an 'iron curtain' coming down on Europe. In 1947, the term 'Cold War' was coined. In 1949 came the Hiss case (involving Thirties espionage), the news that China had gone communist, and the acquisition, through espionage, of the atomic bomb by the Russians. By 1950, American troops were again in action, this time in Korea. This period was the 'crucial decade' that transformed the nation. In intellectual circles, events had brought many to the position of rejecting their Thirties political attachments to the Left, and taking up positions of 'liberalism' or 'neo-conservatism'. That was partly based on the feeling of the failure of radical-revolutionary principles, as evidenced by events in Eastern Europe, hard to distinguish from the fate of those nations under Nazism, and also on a rejection of American progressive innocence, as intellectuals, bloodied in war and doubtful that history was working in humanity's favour, sought to recover an adequate modern humanism. Time and again the issues of the Thirties, the era of communism, which, as the title of one key book of the period had it, was 'The God That Failed', demanded replay. Older intellectuals looked to their pasts, as did Trilling in his interesting novel *The Middle of the Journey* (1947), which portrays radical hopes turning to conspiracy and intransigence, and 'imperious and bitter refusal to consent to the conditioned nature of human existence', in that era of politics and history. Here and elsewhere, Trilling defined a new kind of liberalism that recognized the dangers of Utopianism and of attachment to History, acknowledged the variousness and complexity of reality, and sought the realization of that complexity not in politics but literature. Other intellectuals attempted to reconstitute the 'conservative' principles they saw underlying American life – what Peter Viereck in *Conservatism Revisited* (1947) called 'the permanent beneath the flux.' Hence there was a turn towards myth, religion and classicism in a good many of the writings of the time.

These intellectual developments help explain one of the stranger phenomena of the times: the fear of communist subversion at home. It is easy to see why intellectuals might now feel more fully reconciled with their society, and why Russian behaviour inspired American apprehension. It is harder to understand why, when capitalism was proving so triumphantly successful and few spoke on behalf of the adversary position, people should feel their society was internally threatened – though a crucial factor, of course, was the knowledge of the betrayal of atomic secrets, which generated an atmosphere of suspicion. Even stranger was the cast of characters constituting the threat: Hollywood scriptwriters, New York intellectuals, Ivy League and other professors and academics not usually thought of as having the power to do much harm outside their own families. According to Joseph McCarthy, the Republican Senator from Wisconsin who gave his name to the 'witch-hunting' phenomenon that now arose, it was 'the enemies from within', 'the bright young men who are born with silver spoons in their mouths', who were responsible for sapping America's strength in a new war that could not end 'except by victory or death for this civilisation'.

Like most influential political movements, McCarthyism was made up of many strands. It rose partly from party politics: some Republicans found in the subtle link that was drawn between communism, left-wing politics, the New Deal and subversion an admirable weapon for attacking the Truman administration. Partly it reflected the resentment and frustration of those – lower-class Catholics, rural mid-westerners, the new middle classes advanced by affluence but uncertain of their status – who feared intellectual change, and had grounds for envying the groups identified by McCarthy as 'parlor pinks' and 'egg-heads'. Whether McCarthy himself had strong convictions is questionable. The evidence points towards his being a shrewd opportunist who had simply chosen to exploit a prevailing mood deriving from the new challenges facing America and traditional anti-intellectual suspicions. McCarthyism reflected the ambiguity felt by Americans about their international role, revealed their doubts, their traditionalism, their desire for moral assurance. It also indicated that to do much that was unfamiliar – finance the Marshall Plan, which set European industry on its feet again, aid the UN, make generous gifts to developing countries – Americans needed to persuade themselves they were indeed 'at war'. They had to draw on reserves of moralism, persuading themselves the struggle was not just between America and the Soviet Union, but good and evil, right-thinking and wrong-thinking. In so far as American leaders did encourage this mood and the apocalyptic fears that ran through the times, they were, as events would prove, storing up trouble for themselves in the future.

In general, however, Americans could look round with a sense of achievement and success as they surveyed their society and world-role. Intellectuals, though, had stronger doubts about the kind of materialism and conformity that was emerging – though they too seemed not entirely unhappy with a nation that had emerged from economic disaster, defeated Nazism, expanded education, opened new welfare programmes, and encouraged the spread of American culture abroad. American freedom might be imperfect, but it was still, preciously, freedom, as many *émigrés* understood. In a famous 1952 symposium in the magazine *Partisan Review* – originally founded as a Marxist publication in the 1930s, and an important mouthpiece for New York intellectuals – a group of writers and thinkers of broadly radical persuasion contributed on the theme

'Our Country and Our Culture'. Recalling the history of American literary dissent – expatriation in the 1920s, Marxism in the 1930s – they expressed broadly positive opinions. New Deal aims had been largely fulfilled; the GI Bill had opened universities to a new generation; intellectuals in America could even feel closer to power and influence than before. Not all agreed. Norman Mailer sniffed a new flavour of militaristic totalitarianism in American culture. Irving Howe complained in an essay 'The Age of Conformity':

> Far from creating and subsidizing unrest, capitalism in its most recent stage has found an honored place for the intellectuals; and the intellectuals, far from thinking of themselves as a desperate 'opposition,' have been enjoying a return to the bosom of the nation . . . We have all, even the handful who still try to retain a glower of criticism, become responsible and moderate. And tame.

Preparing the way for the Sixties critique, Howe saw an intellectual sector won over by mental weariness and increased financial opportunities, withdrawing from 'the bloodied arena of historical action and choice', failing to create a counter-politics to confront the Eisenhower mood. He attacked the 'new liberal' intellectual, preferring the radical or bohemian avant-gardeists whom he saw as the true culture-makers of the prewar years. The results were, he said, clear. Experimentalism had died. 'Moral musings' were the order of the day, and the avant-garde artist had been replaced by the drab professional critic, devoted to tradition, orthodoxy, abstract formalism.

In retrospect the gloom seems unnecessary. This was the era when New York became a major centre of painting (Abstract Expressionism, etc.) and some of the greatest postwar writers emerged: Saul Bellow, Norman Mailer, John Updike, James Baldwin, J D Salinger, Carson McCullers, Robert Lowell, and more. The experimental radicalism of Pound, Eliot, Stein, Williams, or Faulkner might have faded (though nearly all these continued to write), and formalism did have its day. But there were major strong poets with a tense confessional energy as well as a formal sense of verse: Robert Lowell published *Lord Weary's Castle* (1946) and *Poems 1938–1949* (1950), Delmore Schwartz *Vaudeville for a Princess* (1950), John Berryman *The Dispossessed* (1948), Theodore Roethke *The Lost Son* (1950). Since the Agrarians Southern fiction had been associated with formalism; but the work of 'Southern Gothic' writers like Eudora Welty (*Delta Wedding*, 1946), Carson McCullers (*The Heart Is a Lonely Hunter*, 1940; *Member of the Wedding*, 1946), Truman Capote (*Other Voices, Other Rooms*, 1948) and Flannery O'Connor (*Wise Blood*, 1952) showed a strong sense of disturbed evil and psychic displacement – and Gothic was revived as a central mode of American fiction. There was the theatre of Tennessee Williams, also intensely Southern, and Arthur Miller, which dominated Broadway in a high moment in the late 1940s and 1950s.

While it may be true that, as one critic puts it, 'the issues of ambiguity and paradox had suddenly taken on a new moral prestige, and politics thus became a gesture in the direction of "the tragic sense of life"', this was to the advantage of literature. As political argument diminished, creative energy rose – not least in writers from the Thirties for whom the loosening of ideology and proletarian realism opened up new energy of vision.

Many writers important after 1945 had begun their careers in the Thirties: Richard Wright, Saul Bellow, Eudora Welty, Robert Lowell, Tennessee Williams and Arthur Miller. The two last had worked in peoples' theatre in the Depression, then made their way on Broadway after 1945. Williams's *The Glass Menagerie* opened there in 1945, followed by *A Streetcar Named Desire* in 1947. Each depicted a 'decadent' (implicitly gay) American South, and the dreams and fantasies of troubled, emotionally fragile people. Williams said he dealt with a displacement and panic that became emblematic of the times. Arthur Miller, one of America's greatest postwar writers, published a fine radical novel, *Focus*, in 1945, dealing with anti-Semitism in New York, before taking Broadway with *All My Sons* (1947), directed by Elia Kazan. About the conflict between American idealism and materialism, it concerns a wartime entrepreneur whose commercial opportunism in supplying defective parts for aero-engines brings about the death of his airman son. The theme – the conflict between dog-eat-dog mentality and higher standards of human worth and dignity – is at the centre of his finest, most famous play, *Death of a Salesman* (1949), also directed on Broadway by Kazan. The story of Willy Loman and his foolish lost dreams was, Miller said, 'a dream arising out of a reality'; the poetry of Miller's half-realistic theatre has always been apparent. In 1953 came *The Crucible*, later rewritten as a major film, about the Salem witch-trials of the 1690s; it was no less a comment on a time when, Miller said, 'any man who is not reactionary in his views is open to a charge of alliance with the Red hell'. Miller himself was: in 1957 he appeared before the House Un-American Activities Committee. Refusing to name former associates, he was convicted of contempt by Congress the next year, and pardoned a year later.

Miller's theme – the conflict between inner dignity and outward conformity ('How can a man make of the outside world a home?') – was repeated through much of the writing of the Forties and Fifties, less as a political than a psychological and moral issue. The sense of fragmentation and exile shows in the work of the best poets; Lowell's *Lord Weary's Castle* is the work of a poet who mixes formal achievement and containment with an intense, fragile inner experience; the same is true of Berryman and Schwartz, one of whose volumes is titled *In Dreams Begin Responsibilities*. Similarly in much of the best fiction the problem of reconciling the moral with the social world forms a key theme. Bellow's *Dangling Man* (1944) had shown the anxieties of the individual driven underground in wartime; *The Victim* (1947), set (like Miller's *Focus*) in a naturalistic and hostile New York during a heatwave, is about the Darwinian competition that threatens the Jewish hero, Asa Leventhal. Finally he is forced to ask about his own social responsibilities to others, above all to an unattractive gentile called Allbee, in whose misfortunes he played an unintended part. Bellow would become one of the great postwar writers, and a Nobel prizewinner. Likewise J D Salinger explored the conflict between squalor and human compassion in his book of stories *For Esme – With Love and Squalor* (1953). His most powerful book, on a similar theme, is *The Catcher in the Rye* (1951), which became a kind of student bible for the postwar generation. The young Holden Caulfield is a modern Huck Finn, trying to maintain his innocence and responsibility toward others in a collapsing, corrupted adult world; finally he falls into a psychic breakdown that would prove typical of Salinger's heroes and heroines.

Literature gives us a bleak, often critical portrait of the America of the postwar years, filled with intimations of moral unease if not moral collapse, and suggestions of totalitarian threat. Mailer had shown totalitarianism deep inside the wartime military machine in *The Naked and the Dead*. In *The Barbary Shore* (1951), his most overtly political novel, he considers the failure of liberal and progressive sentiment in the age of modern American power. A new wave of African-American as well as Jewish writers explored the sensibility of exposure of the self and alienation of the spirit – above all Ralph Ellison in *Invisible Man* (1952), the story of a man rendered 'invisible' by his skin colour who can have no sense of social presence or identity, though this is less a protest novel than a novel of modern existentialism. In fact the broad spirit of postwar fiction was one of an experimental neo-realism, in which defeated selves and anxious inner identities confront a hostile society. But other tendencies were afoot. Postwar American fiction was indeed returning to the Gothic, the surreal, the modern grotesque. John Hawkes's two novels of the squalid terror of wartime and its aftermath – *The Cannibal* (1949), set in wartime Germany, and *The Beetle Leg* (1951), in wartime Britain – are full of dream-images and Gothic imaginings, reminding us the Gothic tradition has always been a powerful source of American fiction. And, though these books relate to the Southern Gothic revival, they also point the way to post-modernist experiments to come.

▶ The Eisenhower years 1953–60

Yet is seemed that when, in 1952, Americans dismissed Adlai Stevenson and chose General Dwight D Eisenhower as the first Republican president since Hoover, the conservative vein in American culture now dominated the nation. Certainly there was nothing in the platform on which he was elected to suggest that his administration would take a more relaxed view of Communism, abroad or at home. His running mate Richard M Nixon, who had first made his name on the House Un-American Activities Committee, indicated that there would be no let-up in the drive to root suspected subversives out of government service; Eisenhower himself promised an audience at Billings, Montana, a month before the election: 'We will find the pinks, we will find the Communists, we will find the disloyal.' Nor was his choice of John Foster Dulles as Secretary of State reassuring to those who hoped for a reduction in Cold War tensions. Dulles was committed to a Manichaean view of the world; he had been highly critical of Democratic 'no win' policies, and referred repeatedly during the campaign, as adviser on foreign policy, to 'the liberation of captive peoples' and the possibility of 'roll back'. The voters had no doubt that an Eisenhower administration would be against any 'softness' on Communism. Yet, from the beginning, Republican rhetoric and policies were at odds. 'I will go to Korea', Eisenhower promised in the campaign; what, though, he intended to do there was not to practise 'roll back' but to find a mutually agreeable way of ending a struggle that had gone on too long. In any case, the aggressiveness in foreign-policy statements conflicted with other promises, to cut taxes and balance the budget. If the government was going to do more, it would have to do it with less.

Much the same was true in domestic policy. Eisenhower believed that the Democrats had encroached too much on the legislative powers of Congress; it was not part of the presidential role to engage in unseemly legislative tussles, still less to assume an active part in the management of the economy. Business was best left in private hands; the Democrats had been altogether too interventionist, driving inflation up to unacceptable levels (70 per cent on the Consumer Price Index under Truman) by deficit financing and Welfareism. Eisenhower saw his responsibility as being to preserve the value of the dollar and give private enterprise freedom to develop. Thus, for the first time since the Twenties, the United States had a president who believed in maintaining an appearance of masterly inactivity. On the occasions when he did take the initiative, it was as often as not to *prevent* things happening: he vetoed public-works bills, community housing legislation, anti-pollution measures. Yet there is no doubt that in Eisenhower the American people found a president admirably suited to the mood of the times. It was, some critics argued, a case of the bland leading the bland. But most felt that, after thirty years of crisis, Americans deserved a little time to enjoy their material comforts and take stock of their position: a period of 'equilibrium'.

Eisenhower's equilibrium worked. The American economy continued to expand. Some years were better than others: GNP actually dropped during 1953–54 and again during 1957–58, but what was lost then was more than made up in other years: expansion during the decade averaged some 3 per cent a year overall. It was less than the growth rate of some other nations, notably Germany, Japan and – a fact that caused unease, especially after the firing of *Sputnik* in 1957 – the USSR; but, as Americans reminded themselves, these countries started from much lower base lines. In average income per head, as in roads, factories and accumulated capital assets, no other country could compare with the USA. It was America that set the style in everything from building construction to hula-hoops. The modern consumer society was, in a sense, her invention; and where she led, others eagerly followed. The new high-rise buildings springing up from the rubble in London, Paris and Tokyo looked, and sometimes were, American. So were the music and entertainment young people in those cities danced to, listened to, or watched. Every summer, hordes of Americans poured through the airports of Europe, much as their ancestors had poured through the Cumberland Gap, often carrying such novel pieces of latter-day equipment as air-travel bags, king-size cigarettes, disposable paper handkerchieves, and expensive-looking cameras, signs of the richer life across the Atlantic. Most astonishing of all, there was no indication where it would all end. Now well into their second decade of growth, it seemed clear that Keynesian economics worked and that, barring some incredible act of government folly, another Great Depression was inconceivable. Public-opinion surveys indicated that fewer Americans now expected a major depression ahead than expected a major war – though, following the death of Stalin in 1953, and the more liberal policies of Khrushchev, even that fear receded somewhat. The idea that gasoline might cease to flow or other resources run out occurred to virtually no one. Looking forward to the Sixties, the editors of *Fortune* magazine noted that there were 'cogent reasons for expecting that output per man-hour will advance at least as fast during the next decade as it has over the last one'. Some of this increase would be absorbed by defence and there would be need for additional investment. But, they concluded, 'for the US as a whole the price of growth will be magnificently easy to bear; the economic pie will expand so enormously that almost everybody can get a substantially bigger cut'.

The society of abundance was so novel that it called for analysis, and the Fifties was an era of sociological revival; 'value-free' sociology seemed the best instrument for recording and analysing the new order. Indeed, some thought that sociology was taking over alike from politics and the novel, offering large-scale explanations that became – as with the Kinsey report on American male sexuality in 1948 – part of the folklore. After all, never had a people possessed so much in worldly goods, or apparently been so troubled in spirit on that account. In a succession of best-sellers, Vance Packard recounted the consumer society's problems. *The Hidden Persuaders* (1957) showed how Americans were manipulated by advertising men; *The Status Seekers* (1959) how they struggled to establish themselves in their own and others' estimations; *The Pyramid Climbers* (1962) how anguish reached even the executive suite. The managerial élite, no doubt because they epitomized the Fifties' idea of success, received more than their share of attention: like the Brooks Brothers suits they were credited with wearing, they represented a distinctive blend of glamour and sobriety. Yet, as film-makers, novelists and sociologists pointed out, their lot was not entirely a happy one. If it was true, said William H Whyte in *The Organization Man* (1956), that they enjoyed many privileges through running the big private and public organizations that increasingly dominated a more and more corporational America, it was also true that to a large degree these organizations also ran them – putting them through batteries of psychological tests, monitoring their family lives, fostering an attitude of conforming mediocrity. The giant modern corporations were quite unlike the monster trusts of the past. The robber barons had gone. But control over those who served the corporations had not lessened, thanks to modern management techniques and psychological screening processes. Indeed, said C Wright Mills in a study of the rising service class, *White Collar* (1951), becoming part of the non-manual labour force meant not only selling one's work but also one's personality. The employee subscribing to the organization ethic was more a slave than the old factory worker, who at least knew when he was being exploited.

The blandness and artificial coherence of the consumer society disturbed many. J K Galbraith saw, in a book that named the whole phenomenon, *The Affluent Society* (1958), a price for private affluence in public squalor: the prices paid in the shops did not represent the full cost of articles to the consumer, who paid an added premium in the form of unsafe cities, congested highways, polluted rivers, devastated countryside. But Galbraith also suggested the difficulties in arriving at a critique: in a new world of expanding production, old assumptions born in a world of scarcity did not apply. Others extended that point: indeed, in *The Lonely Crowd* (1950), the sociologist David Riesman had suggested that affluence and consumer culture were generating a new character type. Riesman divided mankind into three categories: the tradition-directed, found in those parts of the world untouched by industrialization; the inner-directed, found most commonly in those cultures which had begun to experience more rapid change; and the other-directed, living in cultures where change was so rapid that members looked for guidance and values not to ancestors or even parents but to their peers. The inner-directed tended to be job-minded and concerned with resource exploitation; the other-directed were 'people-minded', moving freely from role to role, sensitive to the needs of others, reflecting the fact that in a consumer society the major problem was no longer production but handling other people. And in *People of Plenty: Economic Abundance and the American Character* (1954), David M Potter pointed out that material abundance of one kind or another had marked American experience from the earliest days of settlement, and played an important part in the formation of American character and expectations. In general, there emerged from these studies a portrait of a new America, rescued from Depression anxieties, changed in life-style and opportunity. It was egalitarian, other-directed, consumerized, suburbanized, a compound of traditional individualism and Welfareism, with an embourgeoisified working class, a large expansion in service functions, a managerial élite, a corporate order, and large opportunities for personal mobility and opportunity. It was, in short, a prototypical affluent modern mass society.

Yet the problem of consent, conformity and conservation preoccupied many. One problem was to define the discourse of dissent. Not all intellectuals were content with their culture. In 1955 Herbert Marcuse (a European *émigré* from the Frankfurt School, which moved to Columbia in the Thirties) began, with *Eros and Civilization,* a row of latter-day studies from a Freudian-cum-Marxist viewpoint which portrayed affluent capitalist society as socially and psychically repressive. The same romantic-therapeutic view, found in Wilhelm Reich and others of reformist Freudian persuasion, became popular during a decade in which the questions of conformity versus alienation, rationality versus sexuality, conservatism versus romanticism, were widely debated. In 1958 William Barrett published *Irrational Man,* a stoically existentialist study of modern absurdity which noted the temptations of indulgent romanticism. In 1959 Norman O Brown published, in *Life Against Death,* a psycho-historical account of the coerciveness of modern industrialism, offering the alternative of a permissive non-capitalist 'polymorphous perversity' which might relieve civilization's discontents. What Philip Rieff called the 'triumph of the therapeutic' was becoming a dominant factor of American life; even Marx had to be taken with a twist of Freud. Beyond the therapeutic critique there were more structural accusations. C Wright Mills, in *The Power Elite* (1956), saw the United States as a militarized society run by a 'military-industrial complex'. In *The Sociological Imagination* (1959), influenced by the British New Left, he attacked the neutral, value-free approach of American sociology, demanding a radicalized version of the sociological imagination which would give men a sense of 'social relativity and the transforming power of history'. Despite the Eisenhower equilibrium, the romanticization of anarchic unreason, the insistence that a conflict rather than a consensus model of society was necessary, were central themes of the Fifties. Among certain intellectuals and writers, as well as among many of the affluent young, the issues of the Sixties – social and sexual repression, minorities, race, poverty, the military-industrial complex, the politics of global interference – were already alive.

▶ Writing in the Fifties

Despite the gloomy prophecies that were to come from critical observers in the years after the war, when it seemed that the arts were not to enjoy a fine flowering comparable to that which followed the First World War, the achievement of the writers, dramatists and artists of the years after 1945 was in time to prove a remarkable one. By the end of the Fifties America seemed to have established on the world scene a generation of writers and artists who were commensurate with, though often critical of, the new influence of America in the world. It had major novelists in Saul Bellow (awarded the Nobel Prize for Literature in 1976) and Norman Mailer, major playwrights in Tennessee Williams and Arthur Miller, a great poet in Robert Lowell. The Fifties was a period when a good deal of artistic activity seemed to find its centre in the United States. Painters like Jackson Pollock and Robert Motherwell established New York as the centre of Abstract Expressionism, and other important late Modern and Post-modern movements developed there throughout the decade and into the Sixties. The very look of the American urban skyline showed that the Modern spirit in architecture had fulfilled itself in a postwar merger of neo-European theory and American technology. Likewise the intellectual and artistic *émigrés* of Europe united with their American contemporaries to produce a new intellectual mood. If during the Twenties Americans had seemed important figures in the new arts of Europe, now they seemed to be the major custodians.

In American fiction the Fifties were a particularly vigorous period, when, in addition to Bellow, Mailer, Salinger, and Ellison, many other major figures – Bernard Malamud, Philip Roth, John Updike, Eudora Welty, Carson McCullers, Truman Capote, Mary McCarthy, Gore Vidal, James Baldwin and even the ex-Russian author Vladimir Nabokov, who would have so much influence on the following generation – came to dominate the scene. Compared with the high experimentalism of the Twenties the tone of this fiction seemed more sombre and muted, more disposed to follow the tradition of realism. If the sociological imagination was one way of exploring the new age, so was what Lionel Trilling in 1950 called 'the liberal imagination'. He meant the term both politically and as an awareness of variety and plurality. That variousness he looked to the novel to provide, arguing that the novel form had always mediated romantic individualism and social reality, and concerned itself with 'the hum and buzz of culture'. Realism did enjoy a revival in the Fifties, and this fact is often used to distinguish the novelists of the Fifties from the more flamboyantly experimental and playful generation that followed after, the 'Post-modernists'. Yet it was a qualified realism, for in the new America both realism and liberal humanism were under strain. If, as Trilling says, the novel endeavours to reconcile the history of individual lives with the public world of society, we can see that the reconciliations of much of this fiction were imperfect. The troubled portrait of modern consciousness evolving in psychology, philosophy, and sociology is present in this fiction. Frequently the self is visibly in retreat from society, oppressed by it if not in protest against it. As Irving Howe, who now acknowledged there was a significant development in postwar fiction, said, it was a fiction of a mass society, in which writers found it hard to acknowledge any valid form of social unity and value in the 'relatively comfortable, half welfare and half garrison society in which the population grows passive, indifferent, and atomized'. Thus fiction was increasingly dealing with the metaphysical distance between self and community; it was growing more grotesque and, as he put it, 'post-modern'.

Howe's is a useful generalization, for little of this writing resembles the social realism of the nineteenth-century novel. It tends to deal with a world of estrangement, to see the world existentially, as a place of solitude, and it was to move from realism to surrealism, fact to formalism, social density to therapeutic myth. The mythic and romance dimension was always strong in the American novel, but in many of these writers it takes on a distinctive modern sense of dislocation. As critics have noted, there are marked tendencies in this period of fiction to portray society as a naturalistic and deterministic process external to the individual, and depict heroes who are anxious and alienated, mixtures of the rebel and the victim. Saul Bellow's novels during the Fifties show some of these developments. *The Adventures of Augie March* (1953) and *Henderson the Rain King* (1959) seek to depart from the tighter form of Bellow's two novels of the Forties, and are about expansive heroes whose attempt to break 'the spirit's sleep' takes them away from and beyond society, into nature and metaphysics. Augie March leaves a naturalist Chicago for Mexico; Henderson goes to an imaginary Africa in the quest for self-discovery and to find a human standard away from the American social world. Myth plays an important part in Bernard Malamud's *The Natural* (1952), which uses the world of baseball to tell a version of the legend of the quest for the Holy Grail. Malamud's work is illuminated by the vigorous surrealism of the Jewish tradition, though he too writes naturalistically, as in *The Assistant* (1957), the story of a small-time Italian hoodlum who, affected by the saintliness of a poor Jewish storekeeper, becomes an 'imaginary Jew' and enters a metaphysically enriched world as a result. Philip Roth's *Goodbye, Columbus* (1959) questions the metaphysical largeness of Jewish culture, portraying a bland, suburban Jewishness, but other stories appeal to larger moral needs. In the African-American novels of Ralph Ellison (*Invisible Man*, 1952), Richard Wright (*The Outsider*, 1953) and James Baldwin (*Go Tell It On the Mountain*, 1953), the life of black suffering acquires a similar generalized, ethical dignity. On one hand we may read in these novels, and those of Salinger, John Cheever, J P Donleavy and Vladimir Nabokov (*Lolita*, 1955), a feeling of the dissolution of a rewarding and ethically valid social world, so forcing the self into retreat, and generating nihilism, absurdism, and formalism. Yet on the other hand political force remains. History is real, and while it is inhabited by those processes and the disinheritance we associate with mass society and modern urban-technological life, it is also the place in which we seek our normal rotundity.

Art hungers for a substance in reality; absurdism must balance with realism, formalism with morality. Bellow, Salinger, Malamud, Nabokov, and, at the end of the decade, Updike and Roth represent the best fiction of the Fifties. In their work the struggle between the purified wholeness of art and the claim of ordinary reality continues to be seriously enacted, generating a humanist force.

But more romantic gestures of alienation were on offer. The term 'Beat' was associated mostly with the Sixties; it was, though, a phenomenon of the Fifties. John Clellon Holmes claimed to have used the word as early as 1952 in his jazz novel *Go*. Jack Kerouac made use of it with ironic purpose, defining both a sense of defeat and the spirit of 'beatitude' felt by the truly free spirit, attuned both to Buddhism and the improvised rhythms of jazz. Kerouac's novel *On the Road* – a great map of underground, transcontinental America – appeared, sensationally, in 1957, and the term 'beatnik' (liked with Sputnik) was born. But Kerouac had finished the book – part of a sequence of freewheeling books about transient, mobile American counter-culture, written in 'spontaneous bop-prosody' – by about 1950, and the journeyings of this novel of unending American motion come from that time. Here Salinger's fragile mysticism turns to outright disaffiliation and easy-riding defiance; in other books in the sequence – *The Dharma Bums* (1958), *The Subterraneans* (1959) – Kerouac linked this with a philosophical justification from Oriental mysticism. In 1955 Kerouac's Greenwich Village friend, the poet Allen Ginsberg, went to the Bay area, and there met other West Coast poets of like mind. In October he gave the famous reading at the Six Gallery in San Francisco, linked to Lawrence Ferlinghetti's City Lights Bookstore, and presented his poem, *Howl*, perhaps the most famous single statement of the Beat Generation:

> I saw the best minds of my generation destroyed by madness,
> starving hysterical naked,
> dragging themselves through the negro streets at dawn looking for
> an angry fix
> angelheaded hipsters burning for the ancient heavenly connection
> to the starry dynamo in the machinery of night,
> who poverty and tatters and hollow-eyed and high sat up smoking
> in the supernatural darkness of cold-water flats floating across
> the tops of cities contemplating jazz . . .

Published by City Lights in 1957, *Howl* – a night-poem written in a kind of enraged Whitmanesquese beat – was an anarchic cry for freedom and independence, a howl of rage against the 'wasted' Eisenhower years, perceived as a destructive nightmare in which the best minds wandered unfixed (in every sense). It was less a poem than a clarion-cry to a whole sector of the disaffiliated: the young, the displaced, the gay, the black, the disenchanted. It displayed its own freewheeling, performance-oriented art-style, but it was just as much a life-style: jazz, drugs, sexual freedom, psychedelic experiment, street-talk, urban speed, the bohemian camp of the cold-water flats on the tops of the big American cities where the angel-headed hipsters met. 'Beat' became a cultural statement, taken up by the media, pushed by *Time* magazine. Its significance quickly spread beyond the names of the poets (Ginsberg, Gregory Corso, Peter Orlovsky, Gary Snyder, Lawrence Ferlinghetti, Diane di Prima) or novelists (Kerouac, John Clellon Holmes, William S Burroughs) associated with it. It made the arts seem once again a centre of bohemian action, cultural and behavioural revolution; it marked a changed attitude to writing, painting, music – but also to confession, spontaneity, improvisation. It emphasized free forms, chance connections, loose structures, easy meetings, cultural mixing, letting it happen, hanging loose. If the Fifties were square, it was hip – as Norman Mailer emphasized in his essay 'The White Negro' (1957), where he portrayed the figure of the 'hipster' as a revolutionary against a totalitarian social order:

> One is Hip or one is Square (the alternative which each new
> generation is beginning to feel), one is a rebel or one conforms,
> one is a frontiersman in the Wild West of American night life, or
> else a Square cell, trapped in the totalitarian tissues of American
> society, doomed willy-nilly to conform if one is to succeed.

It was Easy Rider versus the Man in the Gray Flannel Suit, Elvis Presley versus the Baptist Minister. And as movie heroes like Marlon Brando (*The Wild One*, 1953; *On the Waterfront*, 1954) and James Dean (*Rebel Without A Cause*, 1955) showed, it all tapped into a youthfully rebellious mood in popular culture.

'Beat', always on the road, extended its geographical boundaries too – to Mexico, Tangiers, Paris. Here the expatriate William Burroughs was writing his realistic drugs novel *Junkie* (1957) and the experimental *The Naked Lunch* (published in Paris, 1959), which used the 'cut up, fold in method of Bryon Gysin' to explore in a scattered, collage-like, surreal text the horrors of modern technological society, and the ambiguous solace of drug-based alternatives. Burroughs liked to see his book as a Swiftian satire on the repressive forces of a militarized age, which harmed both mind and sexuality. In fact the book has an ambiguous perspective, an engaged excitement with the repressive cruelties it seems to reject. That ambiguity would reappear in a good deal of the satirical, embittered, black humour writing of the next decade, with its bitter portraits of technological society and militaristic sensibility, its anti-humanistic fantasy about the sexual opportunities of the same technological world. Still, the novel – Burroughs's most interesting – is a remarkable act of invention, as well as a move back toward the surrealist avant-gardeism present in American life and art from the 1920s. Banned in America till the middle

Sixties, it pointed to a new claim to freedom of expression and behaviour that would push into the next decade, and form a powerful counter-cultural spirit, born equally of artistic experiment and political opposition. It was the product of many of the oppositions, resentments, and experiments that had surged during the Fifties – some of them radical reactions to political conservatism, some artistic experiment with loose, open, improvised, popular form. But both of these trends worked toward a revolt in expression and consciousness that was evident in the decade. Not surprisingly, they were seized on by the media as an important aspect of contemporary American culture.

Thus by 1959, as the Eisenhower era closed, there were clear signs the Fifties were in revolt against themselves. 1959 saw publication of Robert Lowell's most powerful, confessional book of poems, *Life Studies.* The confessional mode was also apparent in the work of a significant new generation of women poets: Sylvia Plath published her first volume *The Colossus and Other Poems* in 1960, and Ann Sexton, who studied with Lowell, her *To Bedlam and Part Way Back* in the same year, followed by *All My Pretty Ones* in 1962. In 1959 the radical West Coast poet Gary Snyder published *Riprap*, going well beyond 'Beat' into a distinctive subjective exploration of history and legend. The Black Mountain poets grew increasingly important. In 1959 three poets associated with the group published important volumes: Robert Creeley brought out *A Form of Women*, Robert Duncan his *Selected Poems*, and Denise Levertov her *With Eyes at the Back of Our Heads.* These were followed a year later by *The Distances* by Charles Olson, perhaps the most significant figure in the group. The work of the poets of the 'New York School' of Frank O'Hara (*Meditations in an Emergency*, 1957), John Ashbery (*Some Trees*, 1956) and Kenneth Koch (*Ko*, 1959) began to flourish, emphasizing an art of 'surfaces, play, process, improvisation, chance'.

They were linked with the Abstract Expressionist painters – Jackson Pollock, William de Kooning, Robert Motherwell and others – who increasingly represented the powerful, internationally important direction of new, avant-garde American painting. They in turn were linked with the development of the 'happening' – a kind of multi-media evolution from the successful poetry and poetry-and-jazz readings of the Fifties, which had brought a revival of bohemianism in Greenwich Village and San Francisco, and increasingly networked the nation. In 1959 the painter Allan Kaprow staged his 'living painting', '18 Happenings in 6 Parts', a collage of events which drew on the spirit of Neo-Dada and the ideas of the Black Mountain musician and composer John Cage. The arts were growing more collective and communitarian; they were also emphasizing the random, the provisional, the instantaneous, the improvised. The same trends were developing across music, painting, film – as in the work of Andy Warhol, whose play with American stereotypes and use of multi-media helped establish the flamboyant culture of Pop Art. Theatre moved in the same direction. By 1959 Living Theatre, using open improvisational techniques, staged *The Connection*, Jack Gelber's play on drug addiction. Similar groups like the Arts Theatre were already opening the way to the Off-Broadway and Off-Off-Broadway experimental theatre boom of the Sixties. Even on Broadway itself, Lorraine Hansberry's play *A Raisin in the Sun* promised the start of a new era in Black Theatre, an old dream of the Harlem Renaissance. By the latter half of the Fifties, many of the events, movements and happenings we associate with the Sixties had already happened.

The fact was that, by the later 1950s, America had taken on a distinctive postwar character. It showed in the confident energy of its cars – tailed-finned and chrome-plated – in the spread of domestic labour-saving pos-sessions, in the millions of new TV sets that were part of the process of development of a collective mass-culture, in the miles of suburban housing that displayed a fresh, car-borne, out-of-town way to live. It showed in the great changes taking place in American urban architecture – of which a supreme example was the slim cuboid Seagram Building in New York, designed by Mies van der Rohe and Philip Johnson (1955–58), the shape of many things to come. The familiar image of the Fifties is social contentment, and that is true by comparison with the mood of the decades that followed. In 1960, the political scientist Daniel Bell pub-lished a noted book, *The End of Ideology: On the Exhaustion of Political Ideas in the Fifties*. He argued that affluent mass society had so successfully united the Real and the Utopian for most Americans that 'the ideological age has ended'. However, he added, the situation seemed to create a restless yearning, for the ideology and radicalism they somehow felt should be there. Bell was both right and wrong. The Fifties was a time when the forces of progressive radicalism and conservatism, millenarian desire and satisfaction, seemed to merge, when present responsibilities seemed more appealing than long-term social dreams. It was a time of adaptation to a new kind of America. Yet in many of its doubts, dissents and disenchantments, particularly among young people born after the War, lay the seeds of the change that came in the Sixties. The decade to follow was partly an extension of its options and its national and international tensions; and partly a time of revolt.

▶ For further reading

Daniel Bell, *The End of Ideology: On the Exhaustion of Political Ideas in the 1950s* (1961).
Malcolm Bradbury, *The Modern American Novel* (rev. edn, 1992).
John Diggins, *The Proud Decades, 1941–1960* (1989).
John L Gaddis, *The United States and the Cold War* (1992).

Warren W Kimball, *The Juggler: Franklin Roosevelt as Wartime Statesman* (1991).

Richard Rhodes, *Dark Sun: The Making of the Hydrogen Bomb* (1995).

Tony Tanner, *City of Words: American Fiction, 1950–1970* (1971).

Helen Vendler (ed.), *The Harvard Book of Contemporary American Poetry* (1985).

The Sixties and Seventies

Daniel Snowman and Malcolm Bradbury

'We stand today on the edge of a new frontier... a frontier of unknown opportunities and perils... I am asking each of you to be pioneers on that New Frontier.'

John F Kennedy, 1960

'We have come through a long period of turmoil and doubt, but we have once again found our moral course, and with a new spirit we are striving to express our best instincts to the rest of the world... For the first time in a generation, we are not haunted by a major international crisis or by domestic turmoil.'

Jimmy Carter, 1978

▶ When were the Sixties?

Historians like to divide the past into conveniently labelled eras. People at the time were unaware they lived in 'The Dark Ages' or 'The Renaissance', but scholars tell us they did. The division of our past into centuries is less arbitrary, but even then the historian's tidy packaging can impose too rigid a shape on what is essentially fluid. The *real* history of many centuries indeed often seems to begin some fifteen years or so after the official inaugural date. Luther set the Reformation in motion in 1517; the Thirty Years War began in 1618; the rule of the Stuarts ended in 1718, and the age of Louis XIV a year later; the Napoleonic Wars finished in 1815. As for the fundamental turning point of our own century, that was not in 1900 but in the First World War of 1914–18. Yet more seductive is history by decade. In thinking of the evolution of modern America, it becomes convenient to think of the Twenties as heedless, the Thirties as the era of Depression, the Forties as the time of war and reconstruction, the Fifties as the age of conformity and affluence. As we have already seen, these images are usually more complicated, the dates do not fit neatly, and our reading of the decades varies in ways that often more closely resemble the cycles of taste and fashion than of considered historical judgment.

In the history of the United States after the Second World War, the Sixties have a special significance. Daniel Bell's announcement in 1960 of 'the end of ideology' suggested that the politics that had shaped ideas and events over the first half of the twentieth century were no longer relevant to the improved social conditions and greater historical realism of the second half. The notion that an ideologically radical and often revolutionary fervour would sweep through American life a few years later seemed absurd. Yet anti-war protests, urban riots, black militancy and a revolt of youth against their elders were soon to create insurrectionary situations that also spread to Europe and for a time persuaded many that a major change in the political and social order of the West was impending. An International New Left had formed, and in a few short years become so vocal that to those of Utopian persuasion it began to appear that the revolutionary millennium might be within sight. These expectations were encouraged by the postwar economic boom, increasing personal affluence, particularly among young people, and the rising expectations these engendered. To many Americans it appeared that the long radical history of the United States, a nation founded on revolutionary principles, was now coming to its fulfilment, and the future of the capitalist system itself was in doubt. The war in Vietnam was one source of outrage and protest, as young people were drafted to fight on foreign soil for a suspect cause; black civil rights was another. Major social changes were demanded and, though the more extreme demands of the time were never satisfied, much change occurred. Postwar political life took on a new direction, and many serious observers believed that the American way had been challenged and transformed for good.

To some then, the ending of ideology that had seemed in prospect in the cold grey light of the Fifties had been reversed, and politics came first. The American radical tradition which went back to the Revolution itself, the New England reformers, and the progressive movement of the early twentieth century had come to its peak, aided by the ideas of the New Left of Europe. For a few, like Leslie Fiedler and Charles Reich, a whole new order of consciousness was coming into being, marking the end of the philosophical ideas that had dominated Western thought since the Renaissance, reconciling mind to body and individual to body politic, inaugurating the birth of a millennial new America. To others, like Irving Howe, in a brilliant article on 'The New York Intellectuals' in the key year of 1968, it was the manifestation of a shallow and hedonistic radicalism incompatible with a 'high civilization', a betrayal of the radical tradition. It was an age of new theories, new arts, new consciousness. It was also a time of demographic explosion, of youth revolt, when the numbers of young people in the population were vastly increased. To some it represented the breakthrough into a new, unauthoritarian era of modern thought, cool, unrepressive, hedonistic, innovatory, a moral, erotic and intellectual millennium; to others it was a period of the collapse of fundamental social and moral values, a time of serious damage that only return to traditional moral and religious virtues could redeem.

But whatever the new spirit was, it did not neatly attach itself to the actual decade of the Sixties. As usual, the reality was nowhere near as tidy as the label. For instance, those who like to regard the Sixties as a period of conflict neatly sandwiched between two 'quiet' decades have some difficulty in accommodating to the fact that, as we have seen, the heyday of the 'Beat' movement occurred in the Fifties – which was when the counter-culture began, the rock scene exploded, and Marlon Brando's leather-jacketed image of the radical outsider and Norman Mailer's image of the hipster were created. Equally, it is important to recognize that the national mood that followed the assassination of President Kennedy in 1963 produced a nationwide emotional consensus rare in American history. Even in the dramatic year of 1968 – the year that saw the assassinations of Martin Luther King and Robert F Kennedy, massive student protests on and off the campuses, the rise of violent action, the brutal confrontations that accompanied the rowdy Democratic National Convention in Chicago, when the police faced protesters with frank violence – the outcome was the election of the Republican candidate Richard M Nixon to office. For most people most of the time the general business of America continued in a familiar and orderly way. Most planes took off and landed on schedule, most classrooms held normal classes, most politicians and soldiers in Vietnam continued doing what they were officially expected to do. Indeed the biggest protest against the Vietnam War occurred not during the Sixties, but in May 1971, while perhaps the major period of national reassessment occurred not during the era of protest itself but following the fall of South Vietnam to the Communists in 1975.

The American Sixties were not *uniformly* rebellious – any more than the Fifties were *uniformly* conservative, or the Seventies *uniformly* quiescent. And even if decades, like centuries, can be thought of as starting a little late – so that we date the 'real' Sixties from, say, 1964 to the Watergate scandals of 1974 – the contrasts still do not quite work. Perhaps the most powerful grassroots protest against the way the nation's powerbrokers functioned was the reduction of property taxes initiated in California on a popular referendum in 1978, leading the way to the politics of the Reagan era. As this suggests, American change came often from the Right as well as the Left, and one legacy of the Sixties might well be considered the rise of the Radical Right of the Eighties, just as the heir to the 'hippie' seems to be the 'yuppie'. Several different transformations were taking place simultaneously. The notion that the Sixties was the period when the United States moved into the hands of the 'New Left', generating a radical and irrevocable change, was not to survive the following decade. Like many famous revolutionary moments, the events of the Chicago convention or of the March on the Pentagon have taken on the flavour of folklore rather than become clearcut elements of an ongoing process. The part they played seems very different from what the participants intended, and the pattern of accommodation and readjustment that followed was quite as remarkable as the protest itself.

Today 'the Sixties' may probably best be regarded as less a term to describe the state of the nation over a decade than a catchword for a state of mind – youth-oriented, radical, counter-cultural, easy-riding, committed to New Left ideology, minority rights, black consciousness, drugs, rock music, psychedelic experiences, sexual experiment, protest and dissent. There is no doubt that American life over the Sixties and Seventies experienced a shift in tone. It began with a period of extended optimism that was shattered by the hammer blows of the assassinations of the two Kennedy brothers and that of Martin Luther King, troubled by the campus and more importantly black urban riots, rocked by the catastrophe of Vietnam. It was followed by a gradual, muted return to a more stable if also more low-key national life. The political system went through new trauma, the status of the presidency was weakened, personal problems gradually came to take precedence over public ones, and concern about the quality of the physical environment, the reconstruction of inner cities, the diminishing role of America in an expanding world economy, and the growth of new technologies became more important than the spectacular political issues that dominated for a time.

In all the arts, in the development of American culture, there was a similar cycle. There was an optimistic radical phase, which started in the Fifties, when both in high and popular culture – this was a time when the two came to seem indistinguishable – an experimental or avant-garde mood flourished. There were festivals, happenings, performance events, multi-media shows, great participatory spectacles like Woodstock and Altamont, which brought back something of the folk solidarity apparent in the Thirties. (Bob Dylan's hero was Woodie Guthrie, and the protest song of Dylan and Joan Baez reconstructed an old tradition in the world of rock and psychedelics.) The late Fifties saw a multiplication of cultural activity, attendant on the growing wealth and social excitement of a younger population. Theatre groups flourished, venues multiplied, the arts seemed to interact in a fresh way with American life. Poverty programmes supported theatre, the Civil Rights movement brought special interest groups into many forms of cultural activity, the Ford Foundation assisted theatres and authors. Many of the arts, like much of the protest, came from the campus. Many arts took on the dimension of protest, so that they became part of what came to be called the 'counter-culture'. Unlike the avant-garde of the past, it had a strongly popular air, and merged with the rising youth culture.

This too had its heyday in the Sixties, but then began to subdivide, following the paths of particular interest groups, and often growing more subjective and private. By the Seventies the books that celebrated drugs, rock and the 'Greening of America' were replaced by books that dealt with inner fulfilment, life passages, ageing, feminism. The merger of avant-garde and popular art had turned into 'Post-modernism'. In the rapid self-historicization of American society, the Sixties had quickly turned into an image, an object of nostalgia even. In fact it was vastly more than that, for there is a strong case for saying that the oscillations that took place between the Fifties and the Seventies have done much to shape the direction of American experience, American culture, American choices, American history, for the second half of the twentieth century. So how do such foreshortened images reveal and suggest the actual experience of a great nation over the years from Kennedy to Reagan? And why did its history take the forms and directions that it did?

▶ The Kennedy era

There can be no doubt that, when John F Kennedy was elected President of the United States in 1960, a new mood was growing. On 20 January 1961 Kennedy took office, and with his inauguration came an expectation of great change. It was not that a majority of American citizens had voted for him, or were convinced that he was the best person to chart the course the nation should follow. In the presidential election the previous November, 49.6 per cent had cast their vote for the rival candidate – Richard M Nixon, Eisenhower's Vice-President, who would have to wait until the end of the decade to take his seat in the Oval Office. Kennedy himself received only 49.7 per cent of the votes cast, and so became the fourteenth president to be elected on a minority ballot. Many who might traditionally have been expected to support a Democratic candidate disliked Kennedy so much that they voted for his Republican opponent. Many, especially in the South, distrusted him for his 'airs and graces', unearned personal wealth, his relation to the Boston Kennedy dynasty, intellectual arrogance, preference for big government, apparently casual liberalism (and especially, for Southerners, in the crucial issue of race, which would dominate the decade), and his Catholicism.

Kennedy was the youngest president ever elected, and represented a new political generation that had scarcely known the Depression and had grown up since the war. He belonged firmly to the postwar political generation for whom the issues of the day came less from wartime than peacetime, and looked less to the American past than the American future, and he made his impact with his vigour and incisive intelligence. Moreover the authority of his office quickly worked its traditional magic, and even sceptics were impressed as they heard him set the tone of his administration in his Inaugural Address:

> Let the word go forth from this time and place, to friend and
> foe alike, that the torch has been passed to a new generation of

Americans, born in this century, tempered by war, disciplined by a hard and bitter peace, proud of our ancient heritage, and unwilling to witness or permit the slow undoing of those human rights to which this nation has always been committed, and to which we are committed today at home and around the world.

Let every nation know, whether it wish us well or ill, that we will pay any price, bear any burden, meet any hardship, support any friend, oppose any foe in order to assure the survival and success of liberty . . .

These were stirring words for stirring times, though few roused by them knew where they might lead: to the moon, to the elimination of poverty and disease, or to the Third World War?

Kennedy's appeal to the modern generation and the younger style of his presidency not only attracted new groups but reflected new attitudes and forces in American life. His America was a nation of 180 million, a large and growing number of whom were white suburbanites living comfortably on the outskirts of great metropolitan areas and engaged in an increasingly white-collar and service-orientated economy. By 1960, nine out of every ten American families owned a television set and nearly three-fifths a car. Average family income was well over $6,000 per annum, which meant close to $2,000 for every man, woman and child in the country – an increase of nearly 50 per cent since 1950, a decade during which inflation had raised most prices by only about 15 per cent. Not only were Americans better off than ever before; there were also far more of them than previously. The most significant fact about American society in 1960, alongside its unprecedented wealth, was the startling population increase that had begun to make itself felt. During the Fifties, the US population had risen by a massive 18.5 per cent, a figure unmatched since the great waves of immigration prior to the First World War. Even more significant was the age-profile by 1960. Much of the increase in the previous decade had been due to a high birth-rate (25 per 1,000 population compared with 18 per 1,000 in the mid-Thirties), while medical advances had prolonged average life-expectancy from 60 years in 1930 to 70 years in 1960 – so that by the time of Kennedy's inauguration, as much as 45 per cent of the population was either under 18 or over 65, too young or too old to pull its full economic weight. These economic and demographic tendencies were to have a major influence upon the history of modern America; their effects will be evident in much that is contained in the following pages.

There were other important factors: for instance, the ways in which America's wealth and its population were distributed. There is no doubt that the nation as a whole was enjoying a period of substantial prosperity as the legacy of the Eisenhower era. America's gross national product had gone up from $285 billion in 1950 to over $500 billion in 1960 at an annual growth rate of some 3 per cent, and all indicators seemed on their inexorable way upward. However, families in the bottom 20 per cent of the income bracket were still, in 1960, earning only 4.9 per cent of all income, while those in the top 20 per cent were earning 42 per cent. There were other uneven patterns. While the American population as a whole was rising rapidly, certain areas of the country (the big, new sprawling cities of the South and West like Houston, Phoenix and San Diego) were growing fast, while older East Coast cities like Washington, New York, and Philadelphia – particularly their downtown areas – were experiencing a net *loss* of population as people moved south, west, or to the suburbs. Everywhere in the nation, suburbia was growing fast and was largely white. Meanwhile, the decaying inner-city areas of the North tended to attract blacks moving up from the rural South, or Puerto Ricans and others from the Caribbean. New arrivals often found themselves trapped in squalid ghettos, in a climate of urban neglect and social deprivation, cut off from the general affluence. Millions of other Americans, white as well as black, were caught in pockets of apparently ineradicable poverty in America's rural hinterland: fruitpickers in California and Florida, strip miners in the hills of eastern Kentucky, black sharecroppers in Mississippi, white smallholders in Iowa. As the ranks of those too young or too old to work continued inexorably to swell, so did the discrepancy between those who stood to gain from the nation's wealth and those who felt excluded.

If the basis for some of the tensions of the latter Sixties was already established, hope and expectancy still tended to take precedence over rumblings of discontent. In foreign affairs, most Americans seemed for the moment to take a cautiously sanguine attitude. The later Fifties had been a period of relatively unproductive diplomacy, as the anti-communist alliance-building of John Foster Dulles gave way to the gentler diplomacy of Secretary of State Christian A Herter and the genial globe-trotting of a well-intentioned but largely ineffective President Eisenhower. Eisenhower's last years in office had been marked by several setbacks – notably the breakdown of the East–West summit in Paris as Khrushchev made Eisenhower look foolish over the issue of US spy planes, and the cancellation of a presidential trip to Japan on the grounds that Eisenhower's safety could not be guaranteed. As Kennedy ran for the presidency, he made much of the apparent weaknesses of the Eisenhower administration's foreign policy, and some of his most telling points in the televised debates with his opponent, Vice-President Nixon, were in this area. Kennedy's 'New Frontier' thus included the promise of a fresh approach to foreign as well as to domestic policy (though he was singularly vague as to details); it was to America's approach to world affairs his Inaugural Address was largely devoted. With the Cold War still at its height, Kennedy's sparkling but sometimes abrasive rhetoric suggested a new and tough activism towards the Russians ('We will pay any price, bear any burden, meet any hardship, support any friend, oppose any foe'). In the early days of his administration, he was at pains to suggest that he had a carefully considered global strategy, and he talked of his hopes for Western European unity, for a new alliance for progress between the USA and its hemispheric neighbours, and for various other American-backed policies that would regain the initiative he saw as having fallen into the hands of the Communist bloc.

In talking this way, Kennedy was expressing a widely prevalent American mood. Americans were worried about their country's 'loss of purpose' and the supposed subordination of genuine national goals to gods of plenty and materialism. Books appeared with titles like *What Ivan Knows and Johnny Doesn't*, reflecting the fear that the Russians were catching up with American scientific research and military skills and hardware. The *Sputnik* launch in 1957 had dismayed the scientific and educational establishments, and Khrushchev's mixture of sabre-rattling and comedy left most Americans uneasy, remembering his ambiguous phrase: 'We shall bury you!' Though the McCarthyite witch-hunts against domestic 'subversives' had largely disappeared, many still felt that domestic communists were conspiring to erode all America stood for, and there was widespread conviction that the Russians, and their supposed puppets the Chinese, were being allowed to get away with too much: it was time America cleared its head, got off its backside, and stood up to them.

Thus, both at home and abroad, the United States at the time of Kennedy's inauguration was a country of enormous capacities, anxious to take further its great achievements, yet apprehensive lest the chinks in its confidence show through. This was a time of brave new rhetoric accompanied by an undercurrent of self-doubt, of certainties expressed uncertainly, of promises rather than fulfilments, of transition rather than direction. America in the early Sixties showed unmistakable signs of being on the move, but whether for good or ill no one could say with confidence.

The ambiguities of public policy and rhetoric were reflected in intellectual life and the arts. To many, Kennedy seemed the first cultured president America had had since the war – a young, vigorous, intellectually alert figure who surrounded himself with an enlightened 'Camelot' court. The Sixties began, not with signs of schism between the worlds of art and power, but with signs of reconciliation. Poets and musicians were welcomed at the White House; Robert Frost celebrated Kennedy's inauguration; to younger writers, the path between culture and government, scarcely trodden during the previous decade, seemed to be reopening. Time would show this new rapport was more apparent than real, that the cult of intellectual withdrawal from the political world that began to stir in the Fifties – the decade of Allen Ginsberg's *Howl* and Norman Mailer's 'hipster' – represented the deeper current of the times. But for a while not only Stravinsky, Casals and Frost but also Lowell, Bernstein and Mailer himself were drawn by Kennedy's style, power and energy. Mailer even published a collection of essays, *The Presidential Papers* (1963), in which he explored his own identification with Kennedy; in 1965, in *An American Dream*, he fictionalized this, making his violent, purgative hero a friend of Kennedy, and plunging into fantasies of power, violence and radical vitalism by means of which Mailer – and his hero – hoped the nation's conscious-ness might be revivified. For Mailer, Kennedy had become by the time of his assassination an ambiguous symbol of political possibility in an age caught between creative and cancerous growth; still, for a moment, the 'hipster' or 'white negro' saw himself in office – and he was later to enter the world of real politics by running for Mayor of New York.

This fable of the possible reconciliation of art and power runs as a fanciful possibility through much modern American writing; it appears in many novels, by, for instance, Gore Vidal, Philip Roth, Saul Bellow and Joseph Heller, all of whom paint heroes who seek to minimize the charac-teristic alienation of the modern artist and allow him some place in the national counsels. The Camelot era seemed to permit the imagination, perhaps even the artist himself or herself, to take this chance. So, as Morris Dickstein rightly notes (*Gates of Eden: American Culture in the Sixties*, 1977), a good deal of the writing of the early Sixties shares the Kennedy spirit in its fascination with a newly imperial, globally engrossed, inter-nationalized and historically mobile America: 'Grandiose and experi-mental in form, these books partook of some of the imperial buoyancy of the Kennedy years. But their vision sometimes had a bleak, dead-end character that belied any official optimism.'

Certainly the problem of the relationship between self and society, individual and politics that had so preoccupied the Fifties did not go away in the early Sixties. 'The American writer in the middle of the twentieth century had his hands full in trying to understand, describe, and then make *credible* much of the American reality', wrote Philip Roth in an influential essay in 1961, listing some recent horrors. 'The actuality is continually outdoing our talents, and the culture tosses up figures almost daily that are the envy of any novelist.' 'The power of public life has become so threatening that private life cannot maintain the pretence of its importance', wrote Saul Bellow in a 1963 essay where he looked at recent novels – among them John Updike's *Rabbit, Run* (1960), J F Pow-ers' *Morte d'Urban* (1962), Bruce J Friedman's *Stern* (1962) and Philip Roth's *Letting Go* (1962) – and observed they tended to divide the world up between a chaotic, fleeing self and a disordered society in which his-torical process was plot and conspiracy, so forcing modern man to 'hoard his spiritual valuables'. Bellow criticized the tendency, but his own fine novel of the early Sixties, *Herzog* (1964), shows his hero retreating into madness in the face of the mass of modern urban America, even if he manages an ambiguous reconciliation at the end. Other books showed a similar drift. Joseph Heller's absurdist war novel *Catch-22* (1961) displays a world in which no cause or purpose is rational. John Barth's *The End of the Road* (1961) offers a character who is 'weatherless' and inert before reality ('In a sense, I am Jacob Horner', is the book's first line). Kurt Vonnegut's *Mother Night* (1961) returns to war time and shows the spy Howard Campbell committing 'the crime of the times' by serving evil too openly and good too secretly; Vonnegut's bittersweet despair shifts into science fiction in *Cat's Cradle* (1963), about 'Bokonism', a soporific religion of 'harmless untruths'. In *The New Yorker* J D Salinger told tales of his sensitive wise children, the Glass family, in the sequences *Franny and Zooey* (1961) and *Raise High the Roofbeam, Carpenters, and Seymour* (1963), taking the whizz-kids closer to a fragile Zen mystical salvation, and the author himself toward an extended literary silence. Meanwhile Ken Kesey's *One Flew Over the Cuckoo's Nest* (1962) chose to explore the social order from the critical standpoint of the madhouse.

The early Sixties was a remarkable period for new fiction, and produced one clear classic: Thomas Pynchon's first novel, *V* (1963), a vast work of zany experiment and arcane learning. The mad unstructured present – the world of the Whole Sick Crew – is set against an historical past, American and European. There is a quest for a mysterious cipher (woman), 'V', but no significant history or order can be constructed. When the mind looks back for the plot of history, it is left teetering, in a state of entropy. There was a new sense of experiment, and a deep fascination with the power and games of fictions: influenced, undoubtedly, by Vladimir Nabokov – whose erotic and experimental *Lolita*, published in Paris in 1955, was now released to American readers, followed by *Pale Fire* in 1962 – and the Argentinian story-writer Jorge Luis Borges. Poetry, too, was experimental, developing from the new groupings of the late Fifties: the Beats, Black Mountain, the New York School. 1960 was a key year. The Beats extended not just their influence but their range: there was Ginberg's moving *Kaddish*, Gregory Corso's *Minutes to Go*, written with William S Burroughs and Bryon Gysin, Gary Snyder's *Myths and Texts*, and Denise Levertov's *Jacob's Ladder*, followed next year by Ferlinghetti's *Starting from San Francisco*. From Black Mountain, Charles Olson's extended *Maximus Poems* (1960) suggested a new poetic language of epical intent was in formation. In 1959, at the close of what he punningly called 'the tranquil-lized Fifties', Robert Lowell published his *Life Studies*, beginning a new confessional mood that passed to Sylvia Plath and Anne Sexton, who became major poets over the Sixties. The 'New York School' produced Frank O'Hara's *Second Avenue* (1960), followed by John Ashbery's key collection *The Tennis Court Oath*. 1960 also saw important books of poetry by Galway Kinnell and James Dickey.

There was a general feeling that a new age of American poetry was beginning, comparable to the Twenties, and many readings and a vogue for poetry-and-jazz events gave it performance and popularity. In theatre there was even more excitement. New theatre groups that had developed over the late Fifties now began exploring both the agit-prop and the poetic dimensions of drama with new intensity. They found a fine playwright in Edward Albee, who soon challenged the domination of Arthur Miller and Tennessee Williams both on Broadway and off it. His *The Zoo Story* (1959) was an hallucinatory image from a modern America where, as the play told us, not everything was 'peachy keen'. Other plays, notably *The American Dream* (1961), mocked the American psyche and the folksy American spirit, and the bleakly comic *Who's Afraid of Virginia Woolf?* (1962), showing the illusions that sustain a hostile marriage, and the slow destruction that led toward a new sense of reality, was surely the best single play of the decade. American theatre was now reacting to the fresh realities of stagecraft introduced by the international theatre of Beckett, Ionesco, and other absurdists, new theoreticians like Antonin Artaud (Theatre of Cruelty) and Grotowski, new notions of 'method' acting and performance from Konstantin Stanislavsky and the Actors' Studio. Important experimental companies formed; once experimental Off-Broadway gave ground to even more experimental Off-Off-Broadway. In 1959 the San Francisco Mime Troupe formed, and other key groups like Performance Theater, Open Theater and the Living Theater worked with open stage, improvisation, audience involvement, the happening. The Living Theater's production of Kenneth Brown's *The Brig* (1962) – half-improvised, absurdist, indebted to theatre of cruelty – marked an era where, like Pirandello in the Twenties, companies staged not fully crafted works but 'plays in the making'.

In similar ways, the art scene was changing too, with a wave of movements – Abstract Expressionism, Pop Art, Op Art, Action Art – which signalled to many that the heart of the modern avant-garde experiment had shifted from its traditional home in Paris to New York. In 1962 the Sidney Janis Gallery held an exhibition, 'New Realists', which signalled the collective emergence of 'Pop Art'. The work of painters like Roy Lichtenstein, Claes Oldenburg, Jim Dine, Richard Estes, Larry Rivers, Robert Indiana, Jasper Johns, Robert Motherwell and Andy Warhol exploited stereotypes, billboard advertising, the comic strip, brand logos, even the American flag: the core iconography of American life. In these works it is hard to know whether commercial and national imagery is being mocked or venerated, whether the art object was a put-down or a put-on. Pop Art deconstructed, and reconstructed. Warhol in particular declared the open availability of all materials, a total freedom of form. He expanded art's methods far beyond the canvas – directing improvised films, creating nightclub entertainment (the Velvet Underground), turning himself into a celebrity filmstar. At his Philadelphia retrospective in 1965, the crowds were so great for his celebrity appearance that many of the exhibits themselves had to be removed.

Over the Fifties, many doleful commentators had warned that the rise of mass culture marked the end of the arts. The Sixties showed it was different; media and arts could come into a single warm, even radical embrace. New trends and tendencies drew big audiences – just like radical protest music – if sung by the right voices. The Sixties thus began with rich artistic and avant-garde promises, developed from underground or minority trends from the supposedly 'tranquillized Fifties'. The realistic, formalistic aspects of Fifties art and writing were challenged; open form was better than closed. If the Fifties insisted on the moral solemnity of individual genius, the Sixties emphasized collective improvisation, spontaneous event, open confession, the magic moment of impermanence. The Fifties tried to fix the sign and secure the frame in which art was created; the Sixties sought to break free of frames and stress the multivalence of any act, event, performance. Fifties writing was often about the self in hiding from the power of society; Sixties writing questioned society directly, and was ready to challenge or deface the American dream. In many respects this amounted to an avant-garde renewal, a return to the bohemian experimentalism of the Twenties. In other ways it was different: more open, freewheeling, more American, more populist, more contemporary, far less concerned with questions of history, quality or morality.

In fact history generally appeared in the form of some vast exterior threat or system (as in *V.*, or *The American Dream*), or simply as a fiction open to re-invention. As Philip Roth said, contemporary history's recent absurdities seemed so great it resembled fantasy, and the writer or artist had to go to new lengths to embrace it. Realism was now an encumbrance; reality, said Nabokov in *Lolita*, was a word that meant nothing except in quotes. Hence writing became increasingly aware of its fictive or its improvised nature, as in the work of new authors like Richard Brautigan or Gilbert Sorrentino. Even those writers who dealt with history or social and political facts demanded their fictive freedom. The result was a Hyper-Realism in fiction and journalism that closely resembled Pop Art in painting. Truman Capote coined the term 'nonfiction novel' to describe his book *In Cold Blood* (1966), the story of a real murder which took place in rural Kansas, for which two killers went to the electric chair. Capote made it novel-like by constructing it as a literary allegory of a middle America violated by malign intruders (a later similar 'report' turned out to be a less factual report than the author's invention). The 'New Journalism' of Tom Wolfe, Hunter S Thompson, Seymour Krim, Joan Didion and many more changed the look of the magazines and newspapers, emphasizing the performance of journalism, not its objectivity. Journalists were part of the fear-and-loathing scene itself, extremists of prose. Their aim, said Wolfe, was to have 'the whole crazed obscene uproarious Mammon-faced drug-soaked mau-mau lust-oozing Sixties in America all to themselves'. Wolfe was as good as his novel word, flamboyantly writing up the various culture-heroes of the Sixties in *The Kandy-Kolored Tangerine-Flake Streamline Baby* (1965), looking at Ken Kesey's Merry Pranksters and other psychedelic scene-setters in *The Electric Kool-Aid Acid*

Test (1968). Wolfe claimed that the baroque inventiveness of the New Journalism was finally putting the novel out of business, a proposition he later challenged himself by writing a large-scale New York novel from the age of Eighties greed, *The Bonfire of the Vanities* (1988).

To this day the thrust of the Sixties stays ambiguous. On the one hand, a mood of cultural revolt was in the air, fed by an almost anti-American rage against the conformities of the Fifties, the Cold War politics that heated the Sixties, the Vietnam War, the lack of social justice and civil rights for several 'minorities', including women. On the other, this was a great age of American style – self-conscious, experimental, energetic, youthful, satirical. It sang out through the art, the music (Bob Dylan's album *The Freewheelin' Bob Dylan* appeared in 1963), the theatrical performance, the satirical nightclub shows of Tom Lehrer, Mort Sahl, Lennie Bruce. It found its most visible communal expression at the decade's end at the Woodstock Rock Festival, which drew 400,000 young people together in 1969. The new openness could lead in many directions. Some of its artistic effort (John Cage in music, John O'Hara in poetry) was avant-garde, a radical experiment with form and expression. Some (Richard Brautigan in fiction, Andy Warhol in painting) was populist. Some was deeply rebellious and political, an agit-prop art pursuing specific political goals – like the work of Amiri Baraka, formerly LeRoi Jones, the black activist writer who wrote the radical play *Dutchman* (1964), campaigned for Black Nationalism, and changed his name following his conversion to Islam in 1965. Many campaigns and causes produced radical voices – liberal reform, civil rights, gay rights, and, very importantly, feminism, which found a new energy over the Sixties (Betty Friedan's *The Feminine Mystique* appeared in 1963). At some moments art and politics seemed to pull willingly together, at others they split apart. The Kennedy years – like the Kennedys themselves – may look very different, even more dubious, in retrospect. At the time they appeared to open a huge new sense of possibility. As the Sixties started, it seemed, in the arts as well as society, that – as Kennedy said – things were 'moving again'.

▶ The Johnson years

There are no effects entirely without causes, and the events of history, however, haphazard and unexpected some may seem at the time, generally take their place when seen in retrospect as part of a continuing pattern of development. Even the most jarring discontinuity – like the totally unanticipated murder of the vigorous young President Kennedy by Lee Harvey Oswald in Dallas in November 1963 – can come to seem part of the warp and woof of the times in which it occurred. In perspective, Kennedy's assassination can be regarded as a watershed in American history. It may seem fanciful to suggest that the shot that killed the President also inflicted grave wounds upon the country's traditional optimism. The optimism of America goes back far earlier than the presidency of Kennedy, and was deeply rooted in the whole history of white American civilization, with its notion that nothing was impossible if you tried hard enough. Nevertheless, there can be little doubt that America before Dallas tended to display greater confidence than it would after, and that the 'New Frontier' belief that all problems were susceptible to rational solutions grew harder to sustain once the Prince had gone. Under Kennedy, it was widely assumed that domestic conflict could be minimized by the provision of more money and better education, that international conflict could be contained by the firm assertion of America's military commitments. Soon after his death, such assumptions began to go sour as the appalling destructiveness of the urban riots of the mid-Sixties and of the Vietnam War etched their way into the national consciousness. When Kennedy had assumed the presidency, Robert Frost spoke of a 'golden age/Of which this noonday's the beginning hour'. Ten years later, a leading historian and political scientist, Andrew Hacker, could write that 'America's history as a nation has reached its end.'

The Kennedy presidency and the way it ended provided a kind of psychic watershed for the nation. Nevertheless, the seeds of the disaffection and discord that so notoriously characterized the later Sixties were sown long before the tragedy of Dallas. While the assassination provided an opportunity for people to bewail their nation's failures, it was neither the prime cause nor the first occasion for their doing so. Many signs of what was to come were already there just under the surface of the aggressively conformist, largely acquiescent, wealthy, middle-class America of the Fifties. The unease had already displayed itself in the growth of the Beat movement, the racial struggles that had occurred in places like Montgomery and Little Rock, the popularity among young people of symbols of revolt like James Dean and Elvis Presley, the radical theorizing of social observers like C Wright Mills. As the excitement and promise of the early Sixties moved towards the tragedy of Dallas, American life was already infused with a spirit of protest – the protest of poets who abhorred the culture of materialism, African-Americans whose patient opposition to institutionalized racism was close to boiling point, students and other young people who, initially through satire or rock or black humour and then through politics, came to realize the depth of their opposition to the standards and values in which they had been raised. The young, the black and the 'unwashed' – all had been largely impotent in 1960. All were to some extent revitalized by the rhetoric of the 'New Frontier'; all felt the end of the Kennedy era left them with important unfinished business to complete.

For a season after the death of John F Kennedy, harmony seemed to reign. The nation grieved for its fallen leader and instinctively closed ranks. Political squabbles were held in abeyance, social conflict seemed of secondary importance. The new President, Lyndon B Johnson, building upon the foundations Kennedy had begun and appealing to the memory of his departed predecessor, skilfully exploited the consensus to erect the scaffolding of what he hoped would become a major edifice of social reform. Within months of becoming President, LBJ managed to get a major new Civil Rights Bill and a tax reform through Congress. In November 1964, he was triumphantly returned in his own right to the presidency, and plunged himself and his administration into a whirlwind of reformist activity. Proposals emanating from the White House dealt with medical care for the aged, education, housing, immigration, urban and rural development, crime, black voting rights and much else. Nothing like it had been seen since the first hundred days of the New Deal back in 1933 and, although Johnson, unlike Roosevelt, did not have a Depression to use as a political spur with which to goad the Congress, much of what he called his 'Great Society' programme successfully passed into law.

Alongside this burst of activity, though, were other developments that proved more representative of the directions America would take. The Civil Rights movement had grown more militant and assertive since the days of Montgomery and Little Rock. Still predominantly Southern-based, largely Christian-inspired, strictly law-abiding, optimistically integrationist in its aims, it had none the less shifted tactics. Instead of merely boycotting segregated facilities, black and white activists began to use them – sitting side by side together on buses and at lunch counters. By 1963, massive confrontations occurred in several Southern cities between civil rights workers and local white officialdom, and in August a rally of a quarter of a million people in Washington DC heard Martin Luther King, the movement's greatest leader, talk of his dream of a multi-racial society. The optimism of the Civil Rights movement did not last long beyond 1963. The next year, 1,000 Northern students, most of them white, went South to help black voter-registration campaigns. Many of the civil rights workers were harassed by local whites and three were killed, while, back North, Harlem erupted in a spasm of destructive violence in a pattern that was to prove the wave of things to come. Later in 1964, as Lyndon Johnson was building up his coalition of electoral support, students at the Berkeley campus of the University of California formed a Free Speech Movement (FSM) to protest against the refusal of the university administration to let them use land adjacent to the campus for recruitment drives for various political clubs and groups. The FSM, greatly aided by the inept over-reaction of the administration, burgeoned into a major campus revolt and, in time, helped to fuel the worldwide student protest movement of the later Sixties.

In 1964 the greatest issue of all, the Vietnam War, was still scarcely perceptible. That summer, LBJ persuaded Congress, in response to what we now know to be a largely stage-managed incident in the Gulf of Tonkin off North Vietnam, to give him almost unlimited powers of war. At first he appeared to use them with discretion and in his election campaign that autumn talked plausibly about what he saw as the Communist threat from North Vietnam against the non-communist South, while pouring scorn on the hawkish policies of his Republican opponent, Barry M Goldwater. Returned to office, Johnson began to outstrip anything that Goldwater had proposed, pouring American troops into Vietnam, bombing the North (just when its capital, Hanoi, was hosting the new Soviet premier Alexei Kosygin), and committing America's global prestige and armed might to a massive land war 12,000 miles from Washington on the basis of a largely inaccurate reading of the forces involved. To Johnson and his advisers, North Vietnam was a Communist puppet-state entirely beholden to the Russians. In fact its leaders had for twenty years been united in their determination to rid their whole country, South as well as North, of foreign influences – whether Japanese, French, Russian or American.

At first, Johnson's Vietnam venture seemed too remote and not sufficiently brutal or unsuccessful to arouse passionate domestic criticism. But as the war absorbed more and more of the administration's time and the nation's money, as LBJ's 'Great Society' and 'War on Poverty' began to take a back seat, as stories began to filter back of the fruitless death and devastation being caused in Vietnam, people in America – particularly young African-Americans and students politicized by their own protest movements – came to oppose what was being done in their country's name. As the war continued and the voracious requirements of the American military effort required the draft to creep gradually up the social scale so that the sons of the wealthy, white upper-middle class began to find their lives at risk, opposition to the war became not only more vociferous but also more respectable, better organized, better financed, better argued. By 1967, millions of ordinary Americans felt personally bruised by what their nation was doing, and took to the streets in protest. Civil rights leaders like Martin Luther King, writers like Robert Lowell and Norman Mailer, academics like Noam Chomsky and Robert Jay Lifton, the paediatrician Benjamin Spock – all joined together to denounce the war. America, said some of their more radical followers, was a racist society that would never rain napalm on white populations. Others claimed it was run by a ruthless 'military-industrial complex', to whom profits were more important than lives. America's political leaders, most protesters agreed, rode roughshod over all the individualistic and libertarian principles in whose name the republic had been founded.

By the end of 1967, the optimistic visions of the early Sixties had almost entirely eroded. The conflicts and insecurities of America in the early years of the decade, submerged under the uplifting rhetoric of the Kennedy era, now bubbled through to the surface as it seemed clear that all attempts to deal with them – the 'New Frontier', the 'Great Society', the Civil Rights movement – had invariably promised more than they could deliver. The black ghettos were aflame every summer, the campuses every autumn, Vietnam every day of the week. As 1967 gave way to 1968, sane people predicted apocalypse.

▶ Culture and counter-culture

'If You're Lost You've Come To The Right Place!' said the slogan on the besieged campus of Columbia University in the spring of 1968. It might have served as a text for the nation that year. In February, the North Vietnamese, supposedly wilting under a constant barrage of American might, launched a new offensive so devastating as to undermine the entire US position. Prior to this 'Tet offensive', American opinion had stood behind the war; from now a majority opposed American involvement. A month after Tet, Johnson announced that he would not run for a second term as president. He had had enough.

In April Martin Luther King was murdered in Tennessee and African-Americans in many parts of the country – including the vicinity of the White House – went on a furious spree of arson and looting. In early June, Robert F Kennedy, the most exciting political figure in the country, the one man who might have had the chance of achieving the White House *and* a vision of what to do once there, was shot dead in Los Angeles. When the Democrats met in Chicago in August for their nominating convention, the proceedings were upstaged by the tremendous wave of protest that swept through the streets, as demonstrators of every hue found themselves in pitched battle with the city's armed police. By the end of 1968, it seemed to many that there were two distinct American societies existing side by side – an 'official' America that had just elected as president that throwback to yesteryear, Richard M Nixon; and a 'counter-culture' of hippies, yippies, political activists, angry blacks, alienated youngsters, disenchanted parents. And though 'official' America tried to function as it always had, it seemed that much of the time it was having to *re*-act to the initiatives of the counter-culture.

The counter-culture, a loose amalgam of forces united by their sense of opposition to officialdom, represented many varied, often mutually contradictory strains. Some emphasized the importance of 'life-style' and tried to shock by ostentatiously making love, consuming illegal drugs in public, wearing their hair unconventionally long if men, their skirts unconventially short if women. Others were more concerned with political issues and would (for instance) urge young men to burn their draft cards or help draft-resisters escape to Canada or Sweden. To the 'life-style' people, reality seemed so intractable they were tempted to let fantasy take its place – hence the vogue for hallucinogenic drugs or huge posters in 'day-glo' colours that 'breathed', or massively amplified rock concerts where new heights of love or destruction seemed equally possible. To the politically active, reality was an oppressive system of ideologies and institutions built up by the misguided liberalism of the early Sixties. Armed with the cultural critique of C Wright Mills, Norman O Brown and Herbert Marcuse, the 'New Left' argued the nothing less than a fundamental overhaul of Western capitalist society could save America from itself.

The counter-culture thus included both a 'soft' and a 'hard' element, people who looked to Zen Buddhism for solutions and others who looked in the direction of the gun, hippies who talked of love and revolutionaries who spoke of the overthrow of society, some 'turned on' by the gentleness of the Beatles, others who preferred the progressive snarl of the Rolling Stones. But through these and other contradictions ran a single line. The counter-culture in all its manifestations was imaginative rather than intellectual, expressive rather than analytical, interested in trying new types of experience rather than improving old ones. Its language was scatological and apocalyptic, its politics radical. It cared even more about feeling than doing, more about the authenticity of personal experience than its communicability to others. It was a culture that encouraged styles and images to be constantly remodelled and that offered in every boutique new versions of self and society.

In this atmosphere, a much more mobile, kinetic, politically activist sensibility infused the arts of the later Sixties. The liberal model of the artist as a figure integrated into and expressing his culture was replaced by that of the artist as a provisional consciousness transforming that culture. No longer did America's principal writers dream of reconciliations with political power. Many thinkers in the later Sixties saw an end of Kennedy-style liberal humanism and the dawn of a new phase of radical sensibility. Saul Bellow records this confrontation in *Mr Sammler's Planet* (1970), a bleak novel that sees in modern history two systems of force, one humane, the other barbaric, moving forward in competition for modern consciousness. The instinct in the late Sixties leaned towards the barbaric; it was common at the time to talk as if the entire structure of past art and civilization had been overthrown by a new, non-reverential art of immediacy and spontaneity, rejecting concern with form or standards, there to serve protest and revolution. In fact the record now looks rather different. One of the striking features of the late Sixties is its eclecticism, its willingness to generate plural styles without necessary synthesis. And the styles, in painting and elsewhere, are enormously varied, moving between political activism and high experimentalism and formalism. None the less, a new cultural climate – a post-modern one – was forming.

As the Sixties developed, the sense of historical pressure on style increased, and writers changed in manner. J D Salinger followed the Glass family of his later stories into a mystical silence. Mailer displaced American neuroses from the battlefield to the homeland in *Why Are We in Vietnam?* (1967). John Updike opened the delicate world of his middle-class couples to historical disturbance, following on Kennedy's assassination, and the search for salvation by sexuality in *Couples* (1968). Philip Roth left his formalism behind and took up the confessional mode in *Portnoy's Complaint* (1969), an address from the psychiatrist's couch. John Barth, in *Lost in the Funhouse: Fiction for Print, Tape, Live Voice* (1968), attempted a set of experimental texts for a McLuhanite world; the pieces dwell on their own fictionality in the manner of Borges and Nabokov. History may have seemed in acceleration in 1966–68, but fiction was growing increasingly concerned with its own business. In *Snow White* (1967), Donald Barthelme offered to replace the traditional novel or fable with the materials for a random collage into which meaning could not be structured. Among other confusions, the book included a questionnaire for the reader; 'Do you feel,' it asks, 'that the creation of new modes of hysteria is a viable undertaking for the artist today? Yes ( ) No ( ).' Richard Gilman, reviewing the book, saw it as the art of a new reality:

> open-ended, provisional, characterized by suspended judgments, by disbelief in hierarchies, by mistrust of solutions, denouements and completions, by self-consciousness issuing in tremendous earnestness but also in far-ranging mockery...

The fluid, unstructured reality that Gilman describes came to be called 'Post-modernism'. The term embraces much, in writing, architecture, life-style. In the novel it meant not only Barth and Barthelme but also the work of John Hawkes, William Gass, Thomas Pynchon (who followed *V* with *The Crying of Lot 49* in 1966), Richard Brautigan (whose *Trout Fishing in America*, 1967, gently and radically evokes a world of mechanism and its magical alternatives), and Ronald Sukenick, who produced in 1969 the aptly titled *The Death of the Novel and Other Stories*, in which he notes: 'The contemporary writer – the writer who is acutely in touch with the life of which he is a part – is forced to start from scratch: Reality doesn't exist. God was the omniscient author, but he died: now no one knows the plot....' Politically committed fiction did exist in the later Sixties, most notably, and understandably, in the work of African-American writers. Here too the experimental note showed itself, most memorably in the surreal world of Ishmael Reed (*The Free-Lance Pallbearers*, 1967) which explores new uses, so important to the era, of 'fictiveness' and fantasy.

Poetry and drama, performance arts for the times, revealed more inclination to commitment. Yet the same processes are evident: we can see a move towards a theatre of revolt and confrontation, but also towards experimentation, fantasy and abstraction. Sometimes both came together: the Sixties was an era of unexpected aesthetic mixtures – high art and popular art, one medium and another, collectivization and privatization, synchronicity and structure, social protest and surrealism. Marshall McLuhan was the Sixties' guru, and his image of a global village of multiple, inter-secting forms predominates: the media were the message. Poetry may have howled protests from poets like Allen Ginsberg, Allen de Loach and Ed Saunders; it also explored form, myth, legend, with the work of Gary Snyder, Ed Dorn and Galway Kinnell. In the theatre there was a mingling of socially radical and experimentally surreal forms – in, for example, the Living Theatre's four-hour *Paradise Now* (1968) (called by one critic 'a wet dream in a cold universe', with audience participation, collective nudity, and anarchic appeal to universal innocence), the work of Joseph Chaikins's Open Theater or the La Mamma Troupe. A playwright like LeRoi Jones (Amiri Baraka) might move from a formal poetry to his play *Dutchman* (1964), a fable of the violent relationship of black and white, and into the Harlem Black Arts Theater, with its Marxist roots and rejection of white audiences. Others reversed this momentum; Edward Albee moved from the psycho-social conflicts of *The Zoo Story* to the minimalism and abstrac-tion of *Box-Mao-Box* (1968), a post-modern commentary on a world in which politics becomes just one available discourse.

The strength of the culture of the Sixties, which survived far more influentially than its political ideas, lay in its enormous eclecticism. The sense of living through a period of avant-garde opportunity created a wide variety of forms, a strong sense of invention and innovation. It brought very disparate arts and means of expression together, from free abstract painting (Rauschenberg, de Kooning) to graffiti. When Marshall McLuhan celebrated the global village because of the number of exten-sions of self it offered, he touched on the ambiguity of the revolt. It incorporated much against which it appeared to protest, and was remark-ably inclusive. It functioned as psychic release rather than political move-ment, was an expression of the desire for radical style rather than radical content. It claimed that it despised and rejected 'reality', yet – in, say, Warhol's pop paintings – re-created realism within its forms of fantasy. Its art-forms were provisional, seemed to disappear in the moment of cre-ation, yet they became a tradition or lineage. Though many spoke of the political and revolutionary purposes of the new arts, they found them-selves amid the classic ambiguities that belong to all avant-gardes: art is rarely a direct spur to action and reform. Precisely because of this we can see a clear continuity between the artistic and stylistic developments of the Sixties and the arts of the more sober Seventies. Even the most pro-visional arts can transcend the environment in which they are made – if they are good enough.

▶ The Nixon years

If the year 1968 saw the high point of the counter-culture, it also saw the election to the presidency of Richard M Nixon – a man whose appeal was directed chiefly to what came to be known as 'Middle America', and whose political links with the Fifties (he was Eisenhower's Vice-President) were strong. For all the publicity and drama associated with the radical spirit, traditional American values remained influential. To many Americans, a vote for Nixon was a vote for return to normality – to the Puritan ethic of thrift and hard and honest work, respect for parents and elders, a *laissez-faire* economy and the maintenance of American prestige. In practical terms, this was assumed to mean that the Nixon administration would know how to end political protest, ghetto and campus violence, anti-war demonstrations, the collapse into disorder, the slide towards what many saw as communism. Certainly the next few years would see the weakening and gradual fading away of many of the more extreme types of protest – though the supposed return to virtue had its price.

For the change over the following years, the Nixon administration – which early showed its expertise in cracking heads and arresting protesters, and later graduated to more sensational methods of undercutting political opposition – claimed much of the credit. Even observers unsympathetic to the administration felt that the advent of a genuinely right-wing government helped steer left-wing protest off the streets and back into its traditional institutional home, the Democratic Party. However, this kind of analysis misreads the influence political leadership can normally exert on a society. Great social movements do not rise and fall as the result of a change of party at the top; both are visible expressions of deeper historical forces. The counter-culture of the late Sixties and the administration of Richard Nixon had one thing at least in common: an arc-like history stretching over a five- or six-year period. The constituent elements in the counter-culture came together in the mid-Sixties, reached their peak of visibility, and audibility, in 1967 or 1968, and largely dispersed, regrouped or declined by the early Seventies. Nixon was elected to the presidency in November 1968, re-elected four years later, and left office in disgrace in August 1974. The two arcs thus intersect in the late Sixties and early Seventies. To understand the relation between them, it is necessary to consider the underlying social trends against which they occurred.

An important clue lies in the nation's vital statistics. The American birth-rate, so high after the war and reaching 25 per 1000 of population in 1955, had been declining ever since; the death-rate remained largely constant. One consequence was that, as each year passed, the overall population increase in the United States was occurring at a decelerating pace. Between 1960 and 1965 the annual rate of population increase averaged 1.5 per cent; over the next five years it had dropped to 1.1 per cent. A further consequence was that a slightly healthier ratio was developing between the number of those in the earning bracket and those too old or too young to earn. In 1960, out of every 1000 Americans, 357 were seventeen years old or less; by 1970 the figure had gone down to 342. The orange was sliding down the neck of the ostrich; by the Seventies, the postwar 'baby boom' had begun to enter the workforce and, in general, take on the responsibilites of young adulthood. Some of the pressure was thus lifted off the schools, colleges and youth groups that had often been the reluctant locus of tension in the Sixties. One reason why the size and frequency of youthful protests and demonstrations tended to lessen in the Seventies may have been that the sheer numerical prominence of young people in the population as a whole had somewhat diminished.

Also important were changes in the economic climate. In many ways the US economy was strong and healthy, and continued to be so. It was certainly, in the literal sense, delivering the goods. The American gross national product continued to rise (from \$503 billion in 1960 to \$974 billion in 1970) and so did individual and annual earnings. Personal savings rose over the Sixties from a total of \$17 billion to over \$56 billion, an average annual increase of a colossal 12.7 per cent. But there is another side to the story. If GNP rose during the Sixties by 4.6 per cent per annum, most of the economies with which the USA might reasonably be compared – Belgium, France, West Germany, Norway, Italy – were doing well or better, while Japan was streets ahead (though Britain was bringing up the rear). Inflation in the USA was worse during the later Sixties than in most countries in Western Europe (and Canada) while throughout the decade the US dollar lost its consumer purchasing power to the tune of some 2.7 per cent per annum. Above all, America's annual balance of payments was fluctuating dangerously, and showed signs – soon to be all too accurately verified – of tumbling into by far the largest deficit in US history.

The reasons for the huge balance-of-payments deficits of the Seventies were complex: the last stages of the Vietnam War form part of the story and so – particularly after 1973 – did America's vast bill for oil imports. In addition, the once high productivity of American industry slumped badly in the late Sixties, so domestic output was not able to keep up with demand. Though Americans continued to enjoy the world's highest standard of living, there were tell-tale signs by the late Sixties of some of the economic problems that would face them in the next two decades. These removed the economic safety net which in the affluent Sixties had helped to give the young, the black, the transient, and the angry the confidence to challenge the system and run the risk of losing. The harsh fact was that, as the economic situation became tighter, many American students, blacks and political and cultural outsiders came to attach greater importance to obtaining their meal ticket (a college certificate, a good reference, a job, a bank loan) than to fighting for great causes or against the establishment. As one radical leader of the Sixties put it a few years later 'You can't make a revolution if you have to make a living!'

Demographic and economic statistics help to suggest some of the underlying influences on social and political behaviour as the Sixties came to an end. The new social quiescence had other correlates as well. As middle- and upper-middle-class Americans continued to move out of city centres – a process which the urban riots of the later Sixties both stimulated and reflected – the increase in the crime rate in cities went down somewhat (though any comfort derived had to be balanced against the acceleration of crime in suburbia). In the matter of black rights, figures from the South showed massive gains in African-American voter registration and job and educational opportunities (Jimmy Carter, the first President elected from the Deep South for over a century, could not have won without a sizeable black vote from the South). Health care, too, was greatly improved over the Sixties and, for those at the bottom of the social heap, expenditure on the federal government's food-stamps pro- gramme rose by over 400 per cent. Thus, the young, the black and the physically deprived had had part of the foundations of their discontent cut from under them, partly by the sheer passage of time and the broad currents of change that it had effected, partly as a result of deliberate social or political action.

However, while it is important to consider such trends when seeking reasons for the change in atmosphere in America in the late Sixties and early Seventies, it would be foolish to ignore more obvious explanations. One reason why there was less political protest in the Seventies was that to many there actually seemed to be less to protest about. Though import- ant problems remained unsolved, it is arguable that the most blatant dom- estic evils – extreme institutionalized racial discrimination, for instance – had been alleviated by the point-counter-point of protest and legisla- tion of the Sixties. Similarly, while the mindless death and destruction in South-east Asia, and domestic protest against it, continued throughout Nixon's first term, it was nevertheless clear that his administration was, however deviously, trying to disengage from that part of the world. When it finally agreed to do so, in early 1973, the most contentious single issue dividing Americans was removed from public controversy.

Not only was there less to protest about in the Seventies. Somehow it seemed more of an effort. The rise and fall of the counter-culture, like that of Ancient Rome, seems almost to have been subject to a natural life- cycle: full of brave feats of daring at the beginning, brilliantly innovative in mid-course, merely going through the motions towards the end. Eventu- ally, as one former leader of the Black Panthers donned a shirt and tie and ran for Mayor of Oakland and another found Christ, as the founder of the radical student group SDS ran for a seat in the US Senate and another took up a post in an insurance company, their younger brothers and sisters all over the country no longer had the heart to set up the barricades against 'official' America. It had been done; it had achieved some objectives and failed in others; who had the energy to try all over again? Many still talked of radical revolution and the need to overhaul the fundamental infrastructure of society, made clenched fists, wore jeans and long hair. But gradually these things became vestigial symbols of a revolt that had lost its head of steam, gestures of defiance the new society of the Seventies found it could accommodate without much trouble. The new radicalisms of the new decade – women's rights, gay rights, gray rights, the ecology movement – adopted their own characteristic styles and tactics. By the mid-Seventies new issues prevailed. It had become clear that neither the confrontation politics of the counter-culture nor its gentler 'life-style' wing any longer constituted a serious threat to those who upheld more traditional values, that a *modus vivendi* of sorts had been worked out between them.

▶ Watergate

The new *modus vivendi* was not simply a return to the life that the up-heavals of the Sixties had subverted – though the rhetoric of the Nixon administration sometimes suggested as much. On the contrary, the Seventies developed a unique, characteristic tone – for which the Nixon adminis-tration and its scandals were partly responsible. Politically, the decade was dominated to a degree unmatched since the Twenties by the issue of integrity in government; one must go back to the 1860s to find a period when the relationship between President and Congress was as acrimoni-ous – and Congress as assertive – as in the last year of Nixon's presidency. The presidency had been growing in power *vis-à-vis* Congress for many years, and there was no issue associated with Nixon's tenure of office – the impounding of Congressionally approved funds, the using of federal agencies as a means of putting pressure on political opponents, the pros-ecuting and widening of an undeclared war, attempts to 'manage' the news, the undermining of political opposition by 'dirty tricks' – which had not fuelled fires of criticism against previous presidents. But in the scale and consistency with which it resorted to these and similar opera-tions, and in the absence of any national crisis by which they might have been justified, the Nixon administration brought to a head American fears of the 'imperial presidency'.

The boil was finally lanced by Watergate. It was Watergate – merely the name of a building complex in Washington which housed the head-quarters of the Democratic National Committee whose offices were burgled one night in June 1972 – that became the symbol of the political chicanery and illegality for which the Nixon White House came to stand; Watergate that gave the mid-Seventies its major issue; Watergate that, in 1974, brought about the first presidential abdication in American history; Watergate that was to give the Seventies a political colouring all its own.

It is possible to argue – Nixon himself did – that the Watergate issue obscured the significance of his administration's achievement. 'I have done some stupid things', Nixon could acknowledge to David Frost in a television interview two and a half years after leaving office, 'particularly the pip-squeak Watergate thing; but I did the big things rather well.' The 'big things' Nixon had principally in mind were his government's achievements in international affairs. Not only was America's involvement in Vietnam at last brought to an end as a result of the efforts of the Nixon administration; but, through his visit to China in February 1972 and his signature of the first Strategic Arms Limitation Treaty (SALT) in Moscow a few months later, Nixon could with some legitimacy claim to be, with Henry A Kissinger, the architect of a new order in world affairs. Given such an achievement, Nixon and his defenders might, in the court of history, argue the sheer pettiness of the Watergate incident – in which, after all, nobody died, nobody's livelihood or reputation was unjustly or irrevocably destroyed, at the end of which the normal constitutional processes of America were seen to be functioning with renewed authority. It could also be argued that the Watergate improprieties were the activities of underlings whose zeal outweighed their judgment, whom Nixon sought to protect out of a misplaced sense of loyalty. Against such a view the prosecution might go as follows: if Nixon knew about the Watergate events and similar 'dirty tricks' activities he was a criminal, and if not he was dangerously ill-informed; however 'pip-squeak' Watergate was when measured against the great crimes of history, it so transfixed the American people and the wider world as revelation after revelation tumbled out in 1973 and 1974 that for more than a year US government business virtually stood still and no serious domestic or foreign policies could be pursued; Nixon, by his appointments and by the tone he set, brought the US government into disrepute and seriously alienated the American people from their elected leaders and the political process itself.

The memory of Watergate has remained a potent force in American politics, invoked whenever presidential wrongdoing was suspected, as during the Congressional 'Irangate' hearings of 1987. The repercussions of the Nixon administration were more profoundly felt on the domestic front, where he failed, than in foreign policy, where he appeared to succeed, though even here subsequent events cast doubts on the nature of his achievement. The *rapprochement* with China took seven more years to reach the point of mutual recognition, and China's new acceptability in the world arose more out of modification in its own policies than out of US initiatives. As for American relations with the Soviet Union, the signing of SALT I in 1972 did not substantially improve the atmosphere between the two superpowers over the years that followed. Soviet provocation over human rights and in central and southern Africa increased in the mid-Seventies, partly as a direct response to the impediments upon presidential action imposed by Congress in the post-Watergate atmosphere. So, while many of the international initiatives of the Nixon era were bold and imaginative, they cannot be said to have revolutionized world affairs in quite the way Nixon apologists might wish to claim.

As for the domestic front, the Watergate legacy was everywhere to be seen. Congress reasserted its power *vis-à-vis* that of the President to the point that even a Democratic president with an enormous nominal majority in both Houses found, in the later Seventies, he had the greatest difficulty in getting his proposals passed. The issue of integrity in government was a recurring refrain throughout the post-Watergate years, and a number of public figures were forced from office through the revelation of financial or sexual peccadilloes. 'Investigative journalists' from Maine to California tried to dig into the doings of publicly appointed officials in the hope of unearthing – as had Bob Woodward and Carl Bernstein of the *Washington Post* – their own Watergate scandal. Finally, to prevent future Watergate-style traumas, the American electors voted into office at national, state and local level a series of honest, honourable, well-meaning but often colourless leaders throughout much of the rest of the Seventies. The times required a rest from recent upheavals. Not just because of what it had done in office but because Americans wanted to prevent such things from being done again, the Nixon administration played an important part in creating the tone and quality of political life in the Carter years that followed.

▶ The post-Nixon Seventies

The new tone of the post-Nixon Seventies – less confrontation, less public drama, more emphasis on personal integrity and local self-help – was found not just in politics but in broader currents of national life. No longer were the great issues engaging politicians, columnists, academics, writers and citizens at large the major national and international injustices of the Sixties. Gone were the colossal military and economic aid to other countries, the huge federal expenditure on space research, the great expansion in schools, highways, and building programmes. Emphasis was on matters more directly affecting the individual: prices at a time of inflation and unemployment; sexual equality in a male-dominated society; the state of the physical environment in a country whose vast resources for the first time looked finite. Palpable inequities such as racial and sexual discrimination came to be regarded less as national issues than as questions for local and individual action. Tension did arise, demonstrations were held. The bussing of children to desegregate schools produced fierce controversy; so did the Bakke case, which was brought (and eventually won) by a white man who objected to being refused admission to a medical school that admitted blacks with lower qualifications. Some of the demands of the women's and gay liberation groups, produced powerful support in some quarters, occasional demonstrations were held to display solidarity. By and large, however, the activists of the Seventies were more disposed than their equivalents a decade earlier to fight battles at a local or even personal level.

Many of the nation's official leaders, too, stressed how little central government could do and how much self-help could achieve at a time when government budgets had to be severly scrutinized, and approved rhetoric stressed not how much was being spent but how little. Small, in the words of a book title that became a political slogan, is beautiful. Vast projects and the politics of confrontation might have seemed necessary if the North wanted to desegregate the South, or if a Johnson or a Nixon were to be overthrown as a result of nationwide popular pressure. But if you wanted to make sure that local air or water was kept clean, that your local neighbourhood school did not fire homosexual teachers, less histrionic measures seemed appropriate. The Seventies were more *muted* than the Sixties.

The mood of the Seventies is harder to describe and analyse than that of the Sixties, because its nature was to eschew the oversimplifications so popular during the earlier period. In the Sixties Americans often found it easy to define the big issues and identify 'goodies' and 'baddies', causes and solutions; in the Seventies people were more inclined to stress their doubts and inability to see clearly how best to deal with the problems that faced them. 'Your strength', said President Carter in his Inaugural Address in 1977, so far away in tone from Kennedy's 1961 Inaugural, 'can compensate for my weakness, and your wisdom can help to minimize my mistakes.' Doubt and bafflement were expressed as often as conviction. The USA had come through a series of damaging experiences, and for the first time Americans commonly expressed uncertainty about their nation's capacity to cope adequately with the problems it faced. The old optimism was by no means gone; but on it had been grafted a realization that not all problems could be easily solved, that some could hardly even be defined with confidence.

Such uncertainties helped give the Seventies – a decade affected by oil crisis, the Iran hostage crisis, double-digit inflation and growing de-industrialization – a character all their own. After the radical attempts during the Sixties to face down the establishment or confront world political problems, many turned back toward the spirit that had long dominated American society and character: individualism and self-fulfillment. As outward certainties shattered and ideologies died, the times seemed ripe for new pathways into self-exploration and issues of identity. In his influential book *The Culture of Narcissism: American Life in an Age of Diminishing Expectations* (1978), the cultural commentator Christopher Lasch noted a significant move away from political and social issues toward 'narcissism', a fascination with self, image and role, with personal and inter-personal performance on the stage of everyday life: who am I, what are my needs, what is my relationship with the larger universe? Such questions were no novelty in a rich post-immigrant society so much concerned with self-definition and self-analysis; however, they took on a more obsessive and sometimes even a more cosmic form in the Seventies. The emphasis was less on relationship to or revolt against the ghetto, the campus, the stifling mood of bourgeois or Fifties America. In fact the Sixties 'revolution' had basically been a bourgeois and affluent revolt, made out of many different strands and a multiplicity of claims for 'liberation'. The Seventies dissolved into its own separate concerns and interests, which were often with bodily, life-style or 'new age' preoccupations – with gurus and new religions, encounter groups, physical, psychic and spiritual health, knowing and using your own mind and body, exploring your personal relationships. The themes sounded through the Seventies in different ways. Popular writings of the decade included neo-philosophical studies like Robert M Pirsig's *Zen and the Art of Motorcycle Maintenance* (1974), psychosocial works like Erving Goffman's *The Presentation of Self in Everyday Life* (1969), but equally populist advice books like *Passages* or *I'm OK, You're OK*, the work of the mystic guru Carlos Castenada, the propaganda of cults like Scientology and the Moonies. Some of this was serious, some profound, some purely commercial, some quite bogus. An endless stream of popular psychology, para-psychology, astrology and life-style issues fascinated the ever expanding media.

For Lasch and other cultural commentators (many of them French), this was the 'post-modern' spirit, a term that was now used far more inclusively, to describe a non-ideological age, concerned with style over substance, devoted to life-style issues and image-making – a culture of rising hyper-reality, of pluralism, cultural eclecticism, irony and pastiche. In 1976, the year of the Bicentennial of the Revolution, which provoked considerable soul-searching, Saul Bellow was awarded the Nobel Prize for Literature, the first postwar American writer to receive it. The year before this he published his large novel *Humboldt's Gift*, a book of contrasts, about the high-reaching, postwar, late modernist writer-thinker Humboldt, who is contrasted with his younger acolyte Charlie Citrine, who understands he is simply making a 'comic end-run' late in a glutted, technological, materialist century. Philip Roth's fictional heroes grew ever more anxious, confessional, concerned with the triumph (or lack of it) of the therapeutic (*My Life As a Man*, 1974; *The Professor of Desire*, 1977). Works of psychological fantasy flourished, releasing surreal energies and an art of estrangement – Jerzy Kosinski's *Blind Date* (1977), John Hawkes's *The Passion Artist* (1979) – and fiction seemed to take place less in some 'real world' than inside the authorial imagination. The 'post-modern' spirit now incorporated many writers: Hawkes, Kosinski, Robert Coover (*The Public Burning*, 1977), Donald Barthelme, John Barth (*Letters*, 1979), but above all Thomas Pynchon, whose *Gravity's Rainbow* (1973), a massive and mysterious text set around the 'random' V-2 bombings of London in the Second World War, came to be considered the post-modern classic. Much of this writing displays the narcissism, therapeutic self-questioning, and doubt about the authenticity of society and the self which ran through the wider culture. Irony, parody, mocking quotation, 'retro', were very important voices for the Seventies. They found a newly important place in film, in the work of Robert Altman, Woody Allen, Mel Brooks. They shaped the new architecture in the age of the shed and the cabriole-topped office block; in 1972 the architects Robert Venturi, D Scott-Brown and S Izenour published their *Learning from Las Vegas*, an influential bible of new or post-modern architecture. A media- and image-led culture, increasingly turned toward development of satellite communication and the potential of the computer, was becoming ever more engrossed in itself, and in its own fantastic inventions, self-inventions and celebrities.

Paradoxically, the new concerns with selfhood and image reached into social and political issues of great importance. One crucial aspect was the rise of feminism. It was called the Women's Liberation Movement when it started in the Sixties, mainly as a series of loosely coalescent groups with their own influential texts – Betty Friedan's *The Feminine Mystique* (1963), Kate Millett's *Sexual Politics* (1970) – and tactics, over issues of female independence such as equal opportunities and abortion, often drawn from the civil rights campaigns. But if sexual freedom had been increasingly accepted during the Sixties, by the Seventies the issue was sexual politics. The impact of feminism grew greater, reshaping legislation, significantly changing gender and familial relations. Its effects were apparent in literature (and literary theory). Many widely read works of serious fiction appeared from women writers in the Seventies: Erica Jong's *Fear of Flying* (1973), Judith Rossner's *Looking for Mr Goodbar* (1975), Lisa Alther's *Kinflicks* (1976), Sarah Davidson's *Loose Change* (1977), Marilyn French's *The Women's Room* (1978) – works that were concerned not just with female self-empowerment but changed, franker notions of female sexuality. As we have already seen, during the Seventies there were also notable works by African-American women writers – above all Toni Morrison and Alice Walker – as well as women from other ethnicities, like Amy Tan and Maxine Hong Kingston. Male fiction – Philip Roth's novels, John Irving's *The World According to Garp* (1978) – reflected the transformation. And if public acceptance not just of female independence but female sexuality grew, the same was true of gay experience. Gays and lesbians too presented themselves as a minority denied equal opportunities, and again their experience was expressed in a new literature; the frank work of gay writers like Edmund White became known in the decade. Sexuality was in general more easily accepted in the Seventies than before; and the social statistics, along with the far more openly sexual and erotic books and films of the period, show young people in the Seventies were likely to be more widely sexually experienced than previous generations. Compared with their now-ageing Sixties predecessors, they were also far less inclined to use sex as a weapon of shock; to the Seventies it was 'quality' and 'authenticity' that mattered.

These were watchwords of the decade; the emphasis on personal rather than social criteria was applied not just to matters of personal self-understanding (that is the theme of Pirsig's book) but to the physical environment. Issues about the state of the planet, the air we breathe, the water we drink, the food we eat, took on new importance, and a consumerist and ecological movement flourished. This was not new; Ralph Nader had raised consumer protection issues in the Sixties, challenging the big corporations over unsafe cars and chemicalized food, and Rachel Carson had foreseen the pollution of the planet at large. By the Seventies even the corporations Nader attacked were concerning themselves with protection of resources and quality of life. With this came the awareness that not all social problems were subject to political or quantitative solutions. Housing programmes or welfare payments might solve public problems, but there was also an issue about the quality of urban life and environment. The emphasis on single issues, the stress on the authentic and the personal, had another meaning. It marked a movement away from the radicalism of the Sixties, and was often a way of amending or challenging its reforms and programmes. Egalitarian schooling was questioned (by James Coleman and Christopher Jencks). In an inflationary era with growing budget deficits, Keynsian economics were challenged by the new monetarists, led by Milton Friedman, and interventionist foreign policies disturbed almost everyone.

As in the Twenties, a time of major changes in culture and life-style was also a time cautious in politics and inward-looking in viewpoint. Now intellectuals began to speak of a 'New Conservatism' – and that included many who had been radical or liberal-left in the Sixties. The great prophecies about the 'permanent revolution' of American life had proved, at least in the short term, palpably absurd, and many of the Great Society reform and welfare programmes were simply not working. Meantime there was a visible process of reconstruction taking place, for instance in the downtown areas of cities, as commercial enterprises refashioned deteriorating urban and industrial environments and brought growth into the economy. Now it was service and hi-tech industries that became the major sector, and a great information revolution based on satellite and chip technologies was taking place. Movement of population from the old industrial East toward the 'Sunbelt' shifted the balance and mood of the nation, concentrating growth toward the South and West. The American way now seemed to be for Americans to go their own way, and that was through self-enhancement and self-fulfillment.

The collapsed authority of the presidency – following first the resignation of Vice-President Spiro Agnew for bribe-taking, then the spectacular impeachment and resignation of Nixon himself – showed small sign of recovery. Gerald Ford (whom Nixon appointed as Agnew's successor) served out the remainder of the Nixon term. But, though honest and hardworking, he proved an uncharismatic figure, and remarkably accident-prone

– not least in his decision to pardon Nixon for whatever crimes he might or might not have committed while in office. In 1976 Jimmy Carter, a relatively unknown Southerner, became President on a wave of Democratic euphoria. He soon discovered that, while Americans may have thought they were finished with the age of the 'imperial presidency', they did not warm to what they regarded as impotent leadership. Despite occasional successes, notably the brokering of peace between Egypt and Israel, Carter was frequently criticized for seeming to respond to events, rather than shape them. This, many thought, was evident in his handling of the energy and oil crisis, his weak response to the growth of Soviet military power, above all his humiliating failure to secure the release of US hostages in Iran. All seemed unhappy portents of American decline; and what Americans now yearned for – as it would prove – was a humane, dedicated, unassuming leader who would walk tall, give reassurance, evoke an historic sense of national pride and rugged individualism. This could of course only be a movie actor; as the next decade began Ronald Reagan, former Governor of California, and a firm champion of conservative causes, won presidential office.

So, over the course of one decade, America turned decisively from left to right – with great consequences for late modern development and Western and, as it turned out, Cold War history. The era of the counter-culture aged and expired, almost as quickly as it had been suddenly born; the postwar mood was over, lost in the glitz of a new consumerism. Yet the 'New Conservatism' that grew in the Seventies and steered the Eighties incorporated many aspects of the radicalism of the Sixties. Old ends were achieved, if under new banners. It could even be claimed the quiescent mood of the Seventies was due not to the counter-culture's defeats but to its considerable victories. The conflict over civil rights had faded, many American cities had black mayors, the role of 'minorities' changed, the USA seemed less likely to get embroiled in another foreign war like Vietnam. Self-enhancement might have taken over from revolutionary transformation, the yuppie from the hippie, the baby-boomer from the love-child. But many heterodoxies from the Sixties became orthodoxies of the Seventies. Did the Sixties shape the Seventies, or was it just absorbed by them? As decades continue to recycle each other, the question stays open. But Seventies culture is probably best seen as the fusion of two cultures – the radical and the conservative – that had clashed bitterly in the Sixties; and in this it manifests a characteristic and recurrent pattern in American history.

Historians tend to emphasize the discontinuities of history – its revolutions, ideological conflicts, wars and famines, the rise and fall of dynasties and hegemonies. Social scientists tend to emphasize the character of human behaviour at specific, fixed moments of time. Both tell us much about the nature of history, culture and society, but often say little about what most people do in most historical circumstances: eat, sleep, dress and undress, make a living, plan finances, rear children, worry about sickness and death, have a nice, or a nasty, day. Often the arts and popular culture, and today the media's endless serial, tell us a good deal more about these things. If we set both together, we see how hard it is to measure the balance between trends, conflicting interest groups and significant ideological transformations and the millions of local experiences that form daily life. Even the Cuban missile crisis of 1962, the assassination of Kennedy a year later, the first moon landing of 1969, the Watergate crisis or the disillusionment in Vietnam probably mean rather less to ordinary Americans than the shift from monochrome to colour TV, the replacement of stockings by tights (or pantyhose), the availability of the contraceptive pill. Such questions raise a more fundamental one: how do we know what was significant to the people of a huge, diverse transcontinental society? The answers depend on who does the asking. A pollster might find an answer in 'inflation', 'race relations', or 'the economy', a psychologist in 'sexual inadequacy' or 'childrearing'. While one historian considering Seventies Americans might see them chiefly preoccupied by the energy crisis and the weakness of the dollar, another might judge their great preoccupation was with consumer possibilities and the growth of shopping malls. A 'multi-disciplinary' view is meant to link both: not just the public realm but the informal aspects of experience and the close detail of the culture. What such an approach helps suggest is the extraordinary variety of American society, its sharp changes of direction, its regular generational transformations and ethnic regroupings, its capacity for self-criticism, and its ability to hold – or attempt to hold – widest variations of idea, belief and value, and even sustain its energy and its optimism, through the most troubled times.

▶ For further reading

Carl Bernstein and Robert Woodward, *All the President's Men* (1974).
William Chafe, *The Unfinished Journey: America Since World War II* (1995).
Morris Dickstein, *Gates of Eden: American Culture in the Sixties* (1977).
George Herring, *America's Longest War* (1985).
Michael Katz, *The Undeserving Poor: From the War on Poverty to the War on Welfare* (1989).
Christopher Lasch, *The Culture of Narcissism: American Life in an Age of Diminishing Expectations* (1978).
Charles Morris, *A Time of Passion* (1984).

13 The Eighties

Richard H King

As we have seen, historians perennially warn us that to think in terms of decades risks serious distortion of the past. In the United States, where presidential elections coincide with a change in decades every twenty years, it is particularly tempting to suppose that a shift in control of the presidency indicates a transformation in the mood of the country in general. Illusory though such assumptions often are, some decades *do* seem to possess a unity of tenor and tone, a common ethos. The Eighties will undoubtedly come to be seen as Ronald Reagan's decade, and his presence on the national scene interpreted as symptomatic of some deep shift in American life.

The immediate question to ask is: what does Ronald Reagan stand for in the history of the country and the culture? In *Reagan's America* (1987), Gary Wills suggested that because Reagan's adult life spans the period from the Thirties through the Eighties, he has seemed to encompass a widely shared sense of the American experience over the last half-century. White Americans have subliminally tracked him across the decades as he moved from Main Street ('How will it play in Peoria?' was the touchstone of Nixon's political advisors; Reagan provided the answer) to the Hollywood Babylon to the corridors of national political power on the Potomac. His ideological itinerary took him from mild rebelliousness as a student to a moderate New Deal stance to anti-Communist spokesman for American business to right-wing governor and then to President. As Wills asserts: 'He is a durable daylight "bundle of meanings" . . . one must explore the different Americas of which he is made. . . . We make the connections. It is our movie.'

What lent Reagan so much appeal was that through it all he seemed to remain the same modest, decent guy. Success neither spoiled nor changed him. Harsh critics likened him to a celluloid illustration of the old Bourbon mentality which never learned nor forgot anything. But that mistook the nature of Reagan's conservatism, since it was grounded in a patently mythical version of the past, organized around selective amnesia. Its coherence was only tenuously rooted in reality.

Wills's analysis also suggested that Reagan somehow harmonized, if temporarily, two mutually exclusive American ideals – a belief in American uniqueness, innocence and simplicity, an essentially backward-looking self-conception, *and* a commitment to a future of technological growth and sophistication. Reagan's career was furthered by the three great innovations in mass communications in this century – radio, film and television; yet that career was also devoted to traditional American values rooted in the experience of heartland America.

Still, Reagan's rise to political prominence was not inevitable, nor was his tenure in office the unalloyed triumph it initially seemed to be. In what follows I would like to concentrate on three areas of concern. First, I want to trace the competing versions of the recent past offered by liberal and conservative Americans, for they tell us much about the political and cultural divisions in Eighties America. Then I would like to focus on some of the crucial public issues of the decade, including the Reagan presidency itself. Finally, I want to discuss some recent attempts to imagine the shape and development of American culture in the Eighties.

▶ From the Sixties to the Eighties

Every political position and cultural stance is informed by a vision of history. Which comes first – the politics or the historical vision, the facts of experience or their interpretation – is a central issue in contemporary thought. But however the theoretical case is argued, Ronald Reagan's election to the presidency in 1980 was reflected in, and shaped by, two quite contradictory understandings of American history between roughly 1960 and 1980. Paradoxically, those of the 'conservative' persuasion read the history of the twenty-year period in an essentially optimistic way, as a triumph of the old America and its informing virtues ('America is back'); while those on the 'liberal-left', historically associated with visions of progress and increasing enlightenment, found themselves brooding openly about a 'malaise' abroad in the society and a decline into 'narcissism'.

To be more specific, in the early Eighties the liberal left (for these purposes a cultural as well as political category) saw the Sixties as the golden age of political and cultural change. Mainstream liberals remembered the efforts of the Kennedy–Johnson administrations to eradicate poverty and guarantee black civil rights, while presiding over an economy of low inflation and unemployment and a high growth rate. The future was Keynesian and it worked. Many younger people were indelibly marked by the civil rights movement, particularly Martin Luther King's vision of a 'beloved community', joined the insurgency of the New Left, and embraced the counter-culture's pristine vision of a society of peace and love.

The fall from grace, the snake in the garden, was 'The War', which for the generation of the Sixties referred to Vietnam rather than the Second World War. Civil rights turned into black power; the New Left declined into a small faction called Weathermen (people); the counter-culture failed to last. 1968 was the fateful year. The assassinations of Martin Luther King and Robert Kennedy, followed by the débâcle at the Democratic Convention in Chicago, sealed the fate of political and cultural insurgency and were paralleled in more extreme form in Paris and Prague. When it was all over, American liberalism's *bête noire*, the man liberals loved to hate, Richard Nixon, was President.

After that the liberal-left version of American history had its ups and downs, but the overall story was one of decline. Though Great Society social legislation had continuing effects and the Burger Court failed to fulfil the dire predictions of liberals, particularly in areas affecting women; though liberals 'got theirs back' with Watergate, no little consolation after the continuing duplicity over Vietnam and a hardening of cultural and racial attitudes; and though black people made significant political gains in the South during the Seventies, this was all a holding action against the rising tide of political and cultural conservatism.

Jimmy Carter's presidency personified the straitened conditions of American liberalism, in particular its shrinking popularity and loss of momentum. Activism seemed increasingly unattractive to the 'Me' generation, while Carter's attempt to bring the 'imperial presidency' to bay foundered on a mixture of good intentions, feeble implementation and establishment distrust of Carter, the outsider. One of the most decent and intelligent men to become President, Carter entered office committed to transcending the old Cold War issues, aligning the US more sympathetically with Third World liberation struggles, encouraging human rights and bringing the arms race under control. He left it with an unratified Salt II Treaty, after the Soviet invasion of Afghanistan and American humiliation in Iran. Indeed in the last years of his term, Carter significantly increased defence expenditures and became increasingly wary of support for insurgents in Central America.

Thus, by the end of the Seventies, the liberal left seemed bereft of energy and ideas. Inflation was rampant as unemployment grew. The Keynesian future no longer worked. Where Nixon's energy crisis came early in his second term (and then was overshadowed by Watergate), Carter's came late in his term and symbolized American vulnerability in a hostile and unappreciative world. In the campaign of 1980 Ronald Reagan promised something different, and the American people believed him.

But if the liberal account was one of decline-and-fall, the American Right's story was one of rags-to-riches. Indeed, for much of the burgeoning Religious Right and the New Right generally, the triumph of Reagan was hard to explain by their pessimistic, even apocalyptic indictment of the (post-)modernist decadence of American society. Reagan's victory represented the culmination of a growing reaction in the Seventies against liberalism's insistence on big government and social welfare spending, its tendency to side with the criminal not the victim, with the protester not the law-abiding citizen. Cultural freedom seemed to lead to sexual experimentation and promiscuity, which in turn led to the decline of the family and rising rates of illegitimacy and abortion. In general liberalism was charged with encouraging the hegemony of 'secular humanism' and hostility to law and order.

In the New Right's version of recent American history, Barry Goldwater, who had introduced many of these themes in his resoundingly unsuccessful campaign for President in 1964, was a voice crying in the wilderness; yet in retrospect his campaign had presaged the advent of Reagan. Richard Nixon had never been entirely trusted by the right wing of the Republican Party (or anyone else); and so his two presidential victories came as cold comfort to Reaganites, as did the Nixon–Kissinger policy of *détente* in the early Seventies. Indeed to the New Right, both *détente* and the winding down of 'the war' were symptomatic of an establishment consensus uniting the mainstreams of both political parties. In the political night, all cats looked grey. If that were not bad enough, for many on the Right, including a good number of former radical intellectuals become neo-conservatives, Carter's foreign policy seemed to appease the Soviets and spinelessly refuse to defend American interests and ideals against terrorism. It was McGovernism with a Southern accent.

Finally, then, according to both Left and Right versions of recent American history, the election of Reagan in 1980 was not just an important political phenomenon. In much the way that the Fifties had seemed a repudiation of the Thirties, the Eighties would finish off the Sixties and all its works. The end of political liberalism and cultural experimentation seemed in sight. A kind of counter-revolution promised to usher in a new political and cultural order. With Reaganism the conservative *Kulturkampf* had been successful.

▶ Economics and politics in the Eighties

For many Americans, the promise of American life has always been an economic one. For that reason faltering economic performance casts doubt on the viability of the American dream. Moreover, though the debate over the relative merits of capitalism and socialism was practically non-existent in American politics or among American intellectuals after the Sixties, many Americans in the Eighties came to feel anxious about the superiority of American capitalism and wondered if it were still the wave of the future.

In the Fifties and early Sixties, the major economic issue had been growth and productivity in the American economy as compared with the socialist, state-managed economy of the Soviet Union. In the Eighties the debate still concerned growth and productivity, but now the question was why the Japanese economy was outperforming that of the US? Some of the answers pointed to self-inflicted weaknesses involving both labour and management and ultimately to the decline of the American work ethic and to the triumph of the culture of post-industrial capitalism.

This worry about productivity, as well as about inflation and unemployment, antedated Ronald Reagan's accession to the Oval Office. But under the leadership from one-time Congressman and director of OMB (Office of Management and Budget), David Stockman, the Reagan administration set about instituting a capitalist revolution of sorts. According to Stockman's supply-side economics, the answer was neither to balance the budget by cutting spending and raising interest rates nor to stimulate the economy by increasing government spending. Rather, the answer was to maintain high interest rates and cut government spending, but also to cut taxes and stop worrying about balancing the budget. At one stroke, financial resources tied up in government programmes would be released for investment in the private sector; the pork-barrel projects of Congress would be cut to the bone, if not abolished; and the cultural values of autonomy and independence encouraged. The market would sort matters out.

The result was that the Reagan administration did get an economic recovery, and was returned overwhelmingly to office in 1984. But the recovery owed more to a form of 'military Keynesianism' than to supply-side economics. For Stockman discovered that there was no mandate for a supply-side revolution, even among Republicans in Congress. While two tax cuts were instituted and some welfare and entitlement programmes were abolished or trimmed, it was not politically feasible to enact massive cuts in areas such as social security and medicare/medicaid. Furthermore, not only were significant cuts not possible in the area of defence spending, but appropriations there increased drastically. Thus recovery was accompanied by a staggering increase in America's national debt, which grew from approximately $1 trillion when Reagan assumed office to almost $3 trillion in the final year of his administration. Americans were consuming more than they earned. Related to this was the overvaluation of the dollar and continuing high interest rates which sucked in foreign capital and placed American manufacturing and agricultural interests at a disadvantage in international trade. The result was foreign penetration of the American economy and a massive trade deficit. At the beginning of Reagan's stewardship the United States was the world's largest creditor nation, by its end the world's largest debtor. Yet the US dollar remained the principal medium of exchange in international trade and enormous sums were held by foreign banks. The United States was the leader *and* prisoner of the world economic order it ostensibly presided over.

Liberal economists spent the decade searching for alternatives to Reaganomics. Many, like Lester Thorow, focused on the need to increase productivity through innovative management practices and the development of a greater hi-tech capability based on the Japanese example. No liberals laboured under the illusion that market forces alone could reduce America's debt structure or bring the dollar into a healthy relation to other world currencies. But as the decade drew to a close, no new theoretical paradigm had emerged among liberal economists to describe or explain what had happened and what was likely to happen in the future.

Moreover, for many on the Left, the persistence of poverty in the midst of economic growth was the overwhelming failure of the economy. Here, as elsewhere, the debate between liberals and conservatives was as much cultural as it was economic. Of seminal influence was Charles Murray's *Losing Ground* (1984) which stood to the Reagan administration's attitudes towards poverty as Michael Harrington's *The Other America* (1962) had to earlier Kennedy–Johnson efforts to eradicate poverty. Shorn of qualification and complexity, Murray's basic thesis was that the persistence of poverty, including the emergence of an 'underclass', had been exacerbated by the social welfare programmes initiated during the Sixties. In short the War on Poverty had created the casualties it sought to avoid. Overall, Murray focused on the values – attitudes towards self, family and work – which hindered the able-bodied from working. To break this culture of dependence, it was necessary to cut back radically on certain accepted government programmes and closely to examine liberal pieties. It was not the victims so much as the programmes that created the victims that were at fault. 'Billions for equal opportunity, not one cent for equal outcome', Murray proclaimed.

Murray's analysis was controversial to say the least; and when combined with a faith in the capacity of market forces to revitalize the economy, it provided the intellectual rationale for Reagan efforts to undermine the welfare state. Though subjected to a barrage of strong and often effective criticism, it did force the Left to confront the problems the welfare state might be creating rather than solving, and to admit that one dimension of poverty was cultural and psychological. The dominant response of Murray's critics was that, for all the inadequacies of the social welfare programmes, the rising number of poor people had more to do with long-term patterns of black migration to northern urban areas; de-industrialization and the decline in creation of traditional blue-collar jobs; the increasing need both for highly skilled service and hi-tech positions and for low-paying positions in unskilled service industries (e.g. the fast-food sector); the flooding of American markets by cheap foreign goods; and the performance of the economy in general. The best cure for poverty was still an economy which created new jobs.

Indeed the gap between rich and poor in America, already wider than in most industrial countries, continued to widen during the Eighties. Furthermore the growth in the percentage of children born out of wedlock, particularly among the black population, the persisting high rates of unemployment among black males, especially black youth, a growing disparity between the black middle and lower classes, and the resulting growth of female-headed households among the poor – all pointed to a set of problems which seemed insoluble in the terms in which the Reagan administration was used to thinking or the American population was used to supporting.

Until the the Iran–Contra story broke in 1987, *the* domestic political story of the decade was the persisting popularity of Ronald Reagan and the resurgence of a Republican Party. The resulting questions posed by political analysts were obvious: were the Republicans becoming the majority party? – i.e. was the New Deal coalition finally finished – and the related, though not necessarily identical, question: was there a fundamental shift to the right among the electorate? Finally, could Ronald Reagan transfer his popularity to his Republican successor, his Vice-President, George Bush, as it turned out.

The answer on realignment was not clear at the time. Undoubtedly Reagan victories of 1980 and 1984 indicated the readiness of former Democratic voters in the historic South and the 'Southern Rim' and among all classes and among most ethnic groups, except for Jews and blacks, to vote Republican. That is, the GOP widened its base of potential support and at the same time got massive infusions of money from newer 'Sunbelt' industries such as oil, aerospace and petrochemicals. In the words of one analyst, the controlling sector of the GOP had become 'Easy Street', i.e. the new millionaires and the newly affluent, while former bastions of Republican loyalty on 'Main Street' and 'Wall Street' were placed in a subordinate position. Ideologically this meant that the Republican Party had moved considerably to the right by the Eighties, while becoming considerably more prosperous and better organized. Beyond that, it seemed to feed on an endemic hostility to established political, social and cultural institutions.

Considerable evidence indicated, however, that in the Eighties dealignment rather than realignment was (and is) the major tendency at work in the political culture. Party affiliation of any sort had become exceedingly shaky; and the fact that both Jimmy Carter and Ronald Reagan ran as 'outsiders' meant that their support could not necessarily be translated into firm party loyalty or consistent voting behaviour. Voters continued the pattern that emerged after the Second World War of splitting their vote between the parties at the local, state and national levels as well as in presidential elections.

Indeed polling data in the early and mid-Eighties indicated that on specific issues the American voters not only had not bought the entire Reagan ideological packet, but that, except for military spending, they generally favoured the existing programmes of the liberal 'welfare state'. Americans seemed to be 'ideologically conservative but pragmatically liberal'. This suggested that the 1980 vote was as much against Carter as for Reagan, while in 1984, in the midst of economic recovery, people voted their pocketbooks, at least in the presidential election. When one also considers that the Democrats received the overwhelming support of poor people, but that a lower percentage of the poor actually voted, that the politicization of the Religious Right redounded to the benefit of the Republicans, and then takes into account the mysterious, but real, appeal of Reagan to the electorate, then a provisional, if confusing, profile of the ideological alignments and party 'loyalties' in the American politics of the late Eighties begins to emerge.

Besides the issues of party affiliation and ideological tendency, one other issue emerged for discussion in the Eighties – the method of choosing presidential candidates and its implications for performance in office. To some observers, it had become clear that, given the length and cost of presidential campaigns, the qualities needed to become a candidate had only a tangential connection with the qualities needed to be President. (Heightened scrutiny of candidates' personal morality forced Democratic candidate Gary Hart to withdraw from the contest.) Cut loose from party loyalty or experience in national politics, a Jimmy Carter seemed a better campaigner than President and Ronald Reagan more in symbolic than actual control of the office. Finally, the cost of running an effective campaign meant that, though the process seemed more 'democratic' than selection of candidates by party regulars and stage-managed conventions, it made the candidates and the parties highly dependent financially on corporate interests for their survival.

Ronald Reagan came to office as a spokesman for right-wing anti-Communism and pledged to revive America's sense of pride which had been so wounded in Iran. Vietnam was to be 'left behind' and America should resume its role as leader of the free world without apology. Specifically the Reagan wing of the party wanted to nullify what was left of *détente*, claiming, at least initially, not to be bound by the unratified Salt II treaty with the Soviet Union.

More generally the Seventies and Eighties saw a marked reorientation of foreign policy, stimulated by economic and strategic interests, towards Latin America and the Pacific Rim. Indeed one reflection of this increasing turn to the South and East was the burgeoning percentage of the American population from the Caribbean and Central America as well as from the Far East and South-east Asia. From those points where American political and military power had been most obviously engaged – Cuba, Nicaragua and El Salvador, Korea, Vietnam, the Philippines, and Japan – America saw refugees, immigrants and students flow into the country, making it much less a 'European' country.

In the wake of the Iran–Contra affair, many conservative commentators blamed the administration's difficulties in conducting a coherent foreign policy on the nagging interference of Congress. Yet for most of Reagan's tenure, his policies were subject to much less scrutiny from Congress than his predecessor's had been. Indeed a certain pattern began emerging: Congress and the American people would support quick military interventions, e.g. the invasion of Grenada, the bombing raid on Libya, even stationing small contingents of troops in Lebanon. But if a policy seemed to threaten long-range military engagement, Congress and the people tended to rein the administration in – e.g. opposition to support for the Contra forces in Nicaragua, and to the President's SDI (Star Wars) project. Where the interests or strong sympathies of certain segments of the American population were involved – e.g. Israel and South Africa – the President either gave up attempting much of anything, as in the former case, or in the latter suffered a major foreign policy defeat when Congress overrode his veto and approved sanctions against South Africa.

Historians have already begun debating where prime responsibility for ending the Cold War lies. Defenders of Reagan point to the decision to proceed with deployment of Cruise and Pershing missiles in the early Eighties along with the President's insistence on developing the SDI programme as crucial in pressuring the Soviets. Others argue that the re-emergence of the peace movement in Europe and its emergence (as the nuclear freeze movement) in America put popular pressure on both sides to rethink certain basic issues of Cold War rivalry. Finally, many contend that the fortuitous accession of Mikhail Gorbachev to power in the Soviet Union was the single most crucial factor in leading to the end of the Cold War.

The implication of the Iran–Contra affair, reinforced by subsequent Congressional findings, was that President Reagan was only fitfully in touch with major policy debates within his administration, and that he had only the most rudimentary grasp of the issues involved. The resulting leadership vacuum allowed what Theodore Draper called a 'junta' directed by CIA director William Casey and NSC advisers Robert McFarlane and John Poindexter, along with their subaltern, Oliver North, to initiate policies which contradicted the stated policy concerning treating with Iran and with terrorists and violated Congressional legislation prohibiting military aid to Contra forces in Nicaragua.

Ironically, Reagan's hemispheric policy was so obsessed with Nicaragua that, for many Americans, Vietnam was called to mind rather than forgotten. Another irony was that an earlier Iranian fiasco had helped bring down the Carter administration. A final irony was that in 1987, the year of the bicentennial of the Constitution, Reagan's nominee for a seat on the Court, Judge Robert Bork, succumbed to almost unprecedented ideological opposition, while the tactics used to implement Reagan's foreign policy raised questions about the constitutional powers of the presidency and its relations with Congress.

But was Ronald Reagan's foreign policy a break with the past, or was it fundamentally in keeping with the broad sweep of postwar American foreign policy? Centrists of both parties criticized its bellicose pronouncements and nationalistic posturing. Yet while Jimmy Carter's foreign policy had been pushed from the left towards the centre, Reagan, against his earlier judgment, was pulled towards the centre from the right. This suggested that no American President could work a fundamental change in American foreign policy. On this view the Reagan foreign policy was no aberration but fell within the broad outlines of the containment policy which had historically mandated interventionist policies of all sorts. In sum, American foreign policy was, so this line of reasoning went, devoted not to freedom or self-determination but to the perpetuation of the American *imperium*. No better proof of this existed than President Bush's decision to raise a massive force against Iraq's Saddam Hussein in early 1991.

▶ Culture and society

America has always been resistant to sweeping characterization. Yet throughout its history, observers have confidently claimed to have captured the spirit of the place and the people. All generalizations about the state of American society and culture seem true and false, while all remedies for the country's problems seem self-contradictory. For instance, one perennial critique of American life stresses the way homogenizing, nationalizing and rationalizing tendencies threaten diversity and freedom. Analysts from Erich Fromm and David Riesman in the Fifties through Philip Rieff and Herbert Marcuse in the Sixties to Christopher Lasch and Allan Bloom in the Seventies and Eighties, have reacted strongly against what has been called 'post-modern' or 'post-industrial' society.

The complexities and contradictions begin to abound when one remembers that it is often leftist social and cultural critics who most fear such tendencies. Yet these allegedly pernicious social and cultural trends are the direct result, or at least the by-products, of the kinds of advances in science and technology, the growth of activist government and the democratization of education and consumption that the Left has always supported. On the other hand, conservative cultural and social critics are most often heard bemoaning the lack of cultural coherence and authority, the low level of educational achievement, the decline of social cohesion and the absence of a politics of civility. Yet to imagine the inauguration of an ordered society and a culture of authority, these conservative critics would have to consider a centralization of political and cultural authority of unprecedented magnitude, a move which would involve radical restrictions on immigration, imposition of a national educational system and probably the radical restructuring of America's advanced capitalist economy. The revival of a strong civic culture and a politics of the public interest might likewise involve radical transformations in the relationship between politics and special interests uncongenial to the Left and to the Right. Jeremiads come easy to American cultural critics and to critics of

American culture; the answers much less so. The conservative Philip Rieff's idea of the 'triumph of the therapeutic' was the great precursor of leftist critic Christopher Lasch's ideas of the 'culture of narcissism' and the 'minimal self' which were so influential in the Seventies and Eighties. Yet neither man has offered much, if anything, by way of remedy for what allegedly ailed the culture.

In fact, certain social and cultural developments of the Eighties cast doubt on the big generalizations proffered by thinkers such as Lasch on the Left and Allan Bloom on the Right. By the end of the decade, America had seen an incredible growth in cultural diversity largely explained by mass immigration, as mentioned, from Central and South America and from Asia. Where New York had once been the classic immigrant city, the Eighties saw Los Angeles emerge as the site of what came to be called 'multiculturalism'. Phrases like 'cultural difference' and the 'politics of difference' were bandied about. One of the most interesting developments by the end of the decade was the emergence of a cadre of African-American public intellectuals (on the Left and the Right) who raised issues of racial and cultural politics to public awareness for the first time, perhaps, since the early 1970s. Left-wing groups jettisoned large ideological visions for more concrete programmes. The 'New Social Movements', which included racial and ethnic groups, the women's movement, gays and lesbians and environmentalists, were the main vehicles for progressive change. Indeed, at this level of politics, the United States pointed the way to the future for the European Left which was still having difficulty coming to terms with issues of race and ethnicity.

The 1980s also witnessed the emergence of a post-modern plague – AIDS, not only in the United States but in Europe, Africa and Asia – to join the other post-modern nemesis of drugs. Originally, and wrongly, seen as affecting only gays and drug users, the danger of AIDS only gradually became clear to the public at large. For cultural conservatives, AIDS seemed to demonstrate that sexual freedom could only have pernicious individual and social effects. For the increasingly important gay communities in several American cities, AIDS also came as a deep shock and a challenge to basic practices. Indeed, the women's movement had already begun to seriously question whether the sexual revolution had been all that beneficial to women. Overall, what had begun as a vision of a sexually non-repressive society in the 1960s had been thoroughly commercialized by the 1980s.

This diversity of values created problems; and the Eighties, again, began looking like a mirror-image of the Sixties. Where the counter-culture and the New Left were the carriers of cultural and political change in that decade, the fundamentalists and the New Right championed cultural and political change in the Eighties. They upset liberal-leftist assumptions about the nature of 'post-modern' moral and spiritual life, and demanded that the political agenda encompass all sorts of 'cultural' issues which the

Centre and Left were uneasy about including in political discussion. Where once the New Left and the Civil Rights Movement raised the 'moral' issue in politics, it was now the New Right; where once a Christian minister, Martin Luther King, stood at the head of a movement for social and cultural change, it was now Jerry Falwell and Pat Robertson (and other televangelists) who threatened to shake the political foundations. Indeed this pattern suggests that the oft-remarked absence of ideological politics in America may be due to the displacement of ideological fervour into religious sectarianism which then can become political.

What linked the two counter-cultural movements was their ambivalence towards the world that had produced the technology upon which they were so dependent. (And rightly so, since what the media create and encourage to overreach, they also destroy.) Furthermore the last three decades suggest that the function of the diverse religious, ethnic and radical groupings Americans tend to divide into was to protect their members against the immediate onslaught of post-industrial society and post-modern culture. These 'post-' phenomena generate what they also try to destroy.

But conservative social critics in the 1980s posed hard questions for the advocates of diversity – where does the coherence come from? Is there an invisible cultural hand which regulates these matters? Are there political or social values, as opposed to skills, that Americans should adhere to? One lesson to draw from the defeat of the Equal Rights Amendment was that pluralism can be a problem rather than a solution, that there is no easy way for so many disparate groups to live in one society with much degree of success, that social and cultural coherence are not self-generated.

Indeed a dominant impression gleaned from Frances Fitzgerald's *Cities on a Hill* (1986) was that to secede from mainstream society in order to establish communities based on age, sexual preference, or religious commitment can be intellectually and morally impoverishing. Fitzgerald noted the truncated 'moral imagination' of members of Jerry Falwell's church community in Lynchburg, Virginia. Yet something similar could be said of the other communities she investigated. The gay community in San Francisco was highly biased towards white, middle-class professional males; the Florida retirement community was politically, religiously and racially homogeneous, while the latter-day hippie commune of Rajneeshpuram in Oregon acted with arrogance and insensitivity towards its neighbours, was educationally and racially homogeneous and yet beset by internal factions. In fact all these groups seemed bent on escaping rather than affirming social and cultural pluralism.

It is difficult to say whether all this confirmed Christopher Lasch's much-discussed characterization of American culture as 'narcissistic'. Professional and even family ties did seem suprisingly weak and intergroup relationships bland and formulaic, in the communities Fitzgerald studied.

Among Falwell supporters, as well as among members of the Oregon commune, there were principles and passions aplenty. But even there the brittle and tenuous nature of the commitment was striking. In general there was a certain lack of density and texture in the communities canvassed by Fitzgerald. Yet what Lasch condemned and Fitzgerald anatomized may represent the emergence of a new type of society which demands a different sort of loyalty to spouse, offspring, job, community or country.

Meanwhile the influential study *Habits of the Heart* (1985) by sociologist Robert Bellah and a number of colleagues provided yet another window on contemporary American experience. Like other social and cultural critics of America, past and present, Bellah *et al.* were intrigued by the way Americans worked out a balance between private and public, individual and community allegiances. What they arrived at, however, was neither Lasch's monolith of one-dimensionality – perhaps because they actually interviewed Americans – nor the fractured diversity suggested by the anxious characters in Fitzgerald's book.

The American society presented in *Habits of the Heart*, far from being the shallow, rootless place it so often appears to be, was one informed by three separate traditions. The biblical tradition, which stresses the obligations and duties of the self to the community and families, was to be found at work not only among the white fundamentalists and evangelicals, but also among native-born blacks and new immigrants from Spanish-speaking societies. A second tradition – which they name 'republican' – valued political activism and community participation as crucial for self-definition and for the good of the community. Interestingly Bellah and his associates noted that, though Americans are less tied to permanent political organizations such as trade unions or political parties than Europeans, this republican tradition of participation is in many ways stronger in America than Europe. Finally Bellah and his colleagues identified a third tradition – the one every outside observer thinks best characterizes America – the tradition of individualism. According to them, this tradition takes two forms: the utilitarian form which sees self-promotion as instrumental for success in the world, and expressive individualism which values self-expression, independent of any specific economic or social goal.

One conclusion to draw from this brief review of Eighties social and cultural analysis is that the enduring tension in the American experience between homogenization and dispersal, between uniformity and diversity, persisted well into the decade. This tension provided an element of continuity not only in the American experience but also in the various accounts of it, from de Tocqueville to the present. Indeed, the American debate over the nature of modernism and post-modernism was the uniformity versus diversity debate in a new guise. It suggested a similar question must be asked of American culture as was posed about American politics – did the Sixties mark the time when America entered the post-modern era and the distinctions between high and mass culture, fiction and non-fiction, art and non-art were rendered meaningless? And did the Eighties see the completion of that process?

This brings us back to the phenomenon of 'Ronald Reagan'. What happened to conventional thinking about the links between present and past when the President was a man from the traditional heartland of small-town America, transmuted by advanced technological means into an actor of a certain recognizable nature, 'Ronald Reagan'. From this 'persona' he articulated an idealized version of the past, while his public career was devoted to the expansion of the most revolutionary force in modern times – capitalism. His words say one thing, the music another. 'Ronald Reagan' suggests the puzzle of the simulacrum which Fredric Jameson has identified as central to the post-modern experience – what is the original and what is the copy?

▶ Coda: American Studies

The years since the mid-Sixties have not been entirely kind to American Studies. Attacked in that decade as enshrining a consensus approach to American culture while neglecting minorities and marginal groups, it was also challenged in American and British universities by the emergence of other 'Studies' – African, Russian, Black, Women's, to name but a few. As of the late Eighties two coexisting versions of American Studies seemed to exist. On the 'strong' view, American Studies was more than inter-disciplinary: it was an 'interdiscipline'. From this perspective, what was important about American culture and all its manifestations, from Bruce Springsteen through Michael Jackson to Noam Chomsky and Kate Millett, from the literary idea of 'innocence' to the political concept of 'rights', was the way in which each manifests a quality called 'Americanness'. This was the concept that the founders of American Studies attempted to formulate, and it is still an idea worth pursuing. For it is as important to understand how American culture incorporates its various marginalized and dissenting groups and normalizes their 'otherness'. Thus this 'strong' idea of American Studies was by no means necessarily conformist or celebratory of American culture.

What it did, however, imply was that America was not only different, but also unique; that its problems differed in kind from those that plague most of the rest of humanity; or, if that was too extreme, they assumed a radically different form. How, for example, America deals with post-industrial developments or with its tortured history of racial oppression has little relevance to the experience of other societies or cultures.

Those holding a 'weak' conception of American Studies saw it more as an institutional site for studying American phenomena. If generalizations were to be made, it was more likely that black Americans share more with each other and with other formerly oppressed people than they did with white Americans. What is interesting about Willa Cather, for example, is not the way her writing manifests 'American' themes *per se*; rather it would be the extent to which she worked in a realist vein or the problems she had dealing with the representation of men and women. To take another example: What is important about pragmatism is not the ways in which it is typically American, but its theory of knowledge, its conception of action, its political implications.

In this view 'Americanness' became only one among several relevant descriptions. Anybody – sociologists, literary critics, historians, political theorists – can do American Studies simply by locating him or herself within an appropriate institution or by offering the excuse that the topic studied has something to do with America. More generally, the study of American culture in all its manifestations is of interest in so far as it suggests, portends or subtends regions of thought, action and experience that other cultures have undergone or will undergo. If America is different, it is not uniquely blessed (or cursed) in any larger sense. There are always family resemblances to be drawn, lessons to be learned and imparted, between American and non-American phenomena.

But if these were two broad ways of thinking about American Studies, there did seem to be an emerging consensus among Americanists of all stripes around something that looked like a method. This consensus was a legacy of the political and cultural dissidence of the Sixties and was articulated by academics, most of whom came to intellectual maturity during that decade. Though not necessarily leftist in all its implications, its intellectual forebears and shaping influences were social theorists such as Antonio Gramsci, Raymond Williams, Georg Lukács and the Frankfurt School with an admixture, albeit highly diluted, of French Post-Structuralism, particularly from Michel Foucault, and of the contextual hermeneutics of Quentin Skinner.

As a way of historicizing ideas, genres, texts, movements, and events, this approach questioned hard and fast distinctions between literature and non-fictional modes of discourse, high and mass culture, canonical and non-canonical works, and more generally the academic emphasis upon white not black, male not female and occasionally heterosexual not homosexual. In addition the distinctions between literary history and intellectual history, literary criticism and philosophy became less than crucial. Aesthetic judgments or judgments of intrinsic value of all sorts were suspended. Rather it was the function of ideas and texts that became of prime interest. In other words the new consensus was about the power of culture and the culture of power as they related to the resistance of subcultures and the subcultures of resistance. Its keyword was 'hegemony'.

As with all methodological and theoretical models, this hegemonic approach also had its problematic areas. The first concerned its suspicion – to the point of rejection – of canonical, generic, intellectual and literary hierarchies. Useful as a corrective, the problem is that such suspicion is often selectively and unevenly applied. Most of the leading texts, thinkers and ideas remain in place; no one suggested removing *Moby-Dick* from the canon. Indeed, while several traditional distinctions were elided, there was a counter-tendency to consider women's writing or black literature as radically different in generic foundations and thematic concerns from (allegedly) dominant white male writing. What at first seemed to be descriptive categories easily ended up as normative entities.

A second objection, one John Diggins voiced, was that certain texts and ideas do in fact transcend their context of origin or reception. If so, then American cultural studies needed a way to talk about this, beyond positing some mystical canonical committee that enforces ideological hegemony. When Martin Luther King read Thoreau, he experienced *On Civil Disobedience* as a moral and political inspiration, not as a contextualized text. Different as the two men and their circumstances were, King not only understood but also responded to the power of Thoreau's work. It is dangerously easy to treat works as symptoms or as reflections of their contexts, while condescending to them and to the power they have exerted on their readers. Put another way, this new orthodoxy lacked a theory of influence.

Third, the new orthodoxy had an insufficiently complex view of the dominant culture and tended, as mentioned already in connection with writing, to erect a spurious distinction between the dominant culture and the various subcultures. It was the strength of the concept of hegemony, as Jackson Lears has asserted, that it allows for counter-hegemonies and resistance to the dominant culture. Yet this is not quite the same as noting that the dominant culture, at least the dominant American culture, can be used, as Sacvan Bercovitch observed, against itself. The notion of natural rights and law so often turned to conservative purposes was, between the Revolution and the Civil War, and then during the Civil Rights struggle, a powerful lever for change. Freedom has had many meanings in the American political culture, and not all of them were ideological covers for possessive individualism and *laissez-faire* capitalism.

Lastly, the new orthodoxy was drawn to the notion that power is the universal solvent of human action and thought. But this was metaphysics masquerading as realism, cynicism passing for radicalism. At the very least, the notion of power had to be unpacked and historicized. Furthermore, to equate politics with power and domination was to confuse a part for the whole, and to neglect the various historical meanings of the experience of politics and its importance for challenging the dominant ideology or culture.

▶ For further reading

Allan Bloom, *The Closing of the American Mind* (1987).
Stephen Connor, *Postmodernist Culture: An Introduction to Theories of the Contemporary* (1989).
Thomas B Edsall with Mary D Edsall, *Chain Reaction: The Impact of Race, Rights and Taxes on American Politics* (1992).
E J Dionne, *Why Americans Hate Politics* (1992).
Charles Murray, *Losing Ground: American Social Policy 1950–1980* (1984).
Gary Wills, *Reagan's America: Innocents at Home* (1997).

14 The United States after Reagan

Richard Crockatt and Allan Lloyd Smith

▶ Into the 1990s

It has been said that the early postwar presidents stood 'in the shadow of FDR', such was the influence of Roosevelt's terms of office on public life in the United States. A comparable case can be made that presidents George Bush and Bill Clinton stood 'in the shadow of Ronald Reagan'. While it is true that nothing on the scale of the Great Depression of the 1930s or the Second World War occurred to shape Reagan's presidency as they did Roosevelt's, Reagan did preside over a decade of fundamental change in political, social and cultural life. The sense that the Reagan years represented an important divide in the American experience is reinforced by the international upheaval of the end of the Cold War, which began during his second term and was carried through during the Bush presidency.

Reagan's ambition in the domestic field was nothing less than the reversal of liberal public policy and social values which had their roots in the Democratic Party tradition of Franklin Roosevelt, John Kennedy, and Lyndon Johnson. Liberalism was more than a political trend; it was regarded by its opponents as a cluster of well-intentioned but dangerously permissive social values, promoted by a highly educated élite which had become firmly entrenched in culture and public life during the 1960s. Liberalism, in the eyes of its opponents, meant big government, a reduction in individual freedom and responsibility, and an absence of clear moral values. All that was wrong with American life, from violence in the streets to drug abuse and the decay of the family, could be traced to the misguided and ultimately un-American values of an intellectualized élite. According to the conservatives, the worst of the liberals' mistakes, manifest originally in Roosevelt's New Deal but taken to new heights in Kennedy's New Frontier and Johnson's Great Society, was to believe that government was the solution to social problems. Government, said Ronald Reagan in his inaugural address, was not the solution; government was the problem.

Part of Reagan's legacy to his successors was a shift in the American political spectrum towards the right. This was, however, only half of the story. The 'Reagan revolution' was only partly carried through, whether one looks at economic, governmental, social or cultural values. Reagan had promised to reduce the budget deficit as part of the drive to get government off the backs of the people. But while he had slashed government expenditure in some areas, predominantly welfare programmes, he increased it in other areas such as defence, leading to an upward rather than a downward spiral in the deficit. Though Reagan succeeded in being re-elected by a substantial margin in 1984 (the first two-term President since Eisenhower in the 1950s), he was not able to convert that success into a major political realignment. The Republicans held the Senate for one term in the 1980s but failed to gain the House of Representatives. Finally, Reagan's supporters had looked to him to check or reverse liberal policies in race relations, abortion, public observance of religion and other social fields, but by the end of the 1980s their goals had been only partly attained.

The truth was that conservatism came up against the power of institutional inertia where it did not meet outright opposition – but it also came up against contradictions within its own philosophy and practice. One in particular helped to shape the world of his successors. While Reaganism was identified with conservative social and moral values, and more specifically with the revival of religion, the key economic developments of the Reagan years – the deregulation of business and the astonishingly swift introduction of information technology – were nothing short of revolutionary in their effects. They helped to change patterns of employment, career expectations, consumption, and many other aspects of social life. The Reagan legacy was thus deeply contradictory: a society in the throes of rapid modernization which sought to retain its moral roots in an older, simpler America. In the 1990s, the chief institutions of American life, from the power centres of Washington, the cities and localities to the media and the organs of popular culture, expressed this central contradiction.

A further defining characteristic of post-Reagan America was a deepening scepticism about politics and politicians. The general cause must lie in the failure of the liberal tradition of big government to deliver what it promised: stable economic growth and social justice. More particularly, declining public confidence in the presidency and the Federal Government had roots in Vietnam and Watergate, and Reagan himself inherited a weakened institution. He managed to arrest the decline and even produce a rise in public trust in the Federal Government which was continued for a while under George Bush, due in large part to the rallying effect of the Gulf War in 1991. The election year of 1992, however, saw a sharp drop in the percentage of those who trusted the Federal Government from around 45 per cent to 21 per cent. (For comparison it is worth noting that at the time of Kennedy's death exactly thirty years earlier the figure had stood at 76 per cent. During the Reagan presidency it never exceeded 50 per cent.)

According to some observers, such figures were symptomatic of a more pervasive decline in the faith of Americans in their democratic institutions. In the 1980s and 1990s the percentage of eligible voters going to the polls in presidential elections hovered around 50 per cent, while in mid-term congressional elections the figure was around 35 per cent. 'At a time', wrote E J Dionne in a book entitled *Why Americans Hate Politics* (1991), 'when the people of Poland, Hungary, and Czechoslovakia are experiencing the excitement of self-government, Americans view politics with boredom and detachment.' Americans, continued the same author, were exhibiting nothing less than a 'flight from public life', the effect of which was to destroy 'a sense of community and common purpose'. The most extreme manifestation of alienation from government and public life was the activity of survivalist and militia groups which cultivated armed isolation from the mainstream in the conviction that America's vital tradition of republicanism and limited government had been betrayed. The bombing of the Federal building in Oklahoma City in 1995 with the deaths of 113 people was the most dramatic and destructive demonstration of this rejectionist frame of mind. Undoubtedly the militia groups represented an extremist and marginal position, but it was noticeable that such groups invoked core American values of individual liberty and limited government in voicing their alienation from modern America.

While there are varied explanations for these developments, certain conclusions appear incontrovertible. First, a substantial minority of Americans were sufficiently disenchanted with public life that it did not matter to them whether their voice was heard. Since voting correlates highly with class, race, education and occupation – the poor and least educated among ethnic and racial minorities being least likely to vote – it would appear that talk of an 'underclass' in the United States may have had some validity. Second, presidents since Jimmy Carter (1977–81) sought to dissociate themselves from the Washington establishment and present themselves as outsiders. To that extent they exploited public cynicism about politics and politicians and thereby arguably reinforced it, no one more effectively than Ronald Reagan whose entire purpose was to urge the incapacity of government to solve economic and social problems. To a degree, Americans have always been suspicious of the people they have elected to rule over them – a feature of democracy which had been noted and deplored in the 1830s by Alexis de Tocqueville – the difference in the 1990s being the capacity of the news media to shape the ways in which public officials presented themselves.

In part for technological reasons, the news media were quicker to exploit a lead, more intrusive, and more integrally involved in the mediation of political information to the public than at any time in the past. One has only to consider CNN's instantaneous coverage of the Gulf War to confirm this last point. CNN proved able to supply information more quickly than governments could acquire it from their own sources. More generally, television came to dominate the presentation of the political process, placing a premium on the dramatic and the sensational, on personality and style, and exposing political leaders to unprecedented levels of scrutiny. If Reagan managed to turn such increased exposure to his advantage, enabling him to weather even such storms as the Iran–Contra scandal, his immediate successor, George Bush, was much less successful. Despite his effective conduct of the Gulf War, he was unable to convince the American people that he stood for anything definite and failed to secure re-election in 1992. After a poor start, Clinton learned quickly but was nevertheless dogged by scandals, both financial and sexual, which undermined his efforts to maintain a truly presidential image.

At the outset of the 1990s, therefore, American public life was characterized by deep ambivalence. Conservatism had made a bid for dominance but had achieved only partial success. Americans continued to expect much of their leaders but were at the same time reluctant to give them much credence or power. American public ideology continued to be highly idealistic and apparently consensual, but large sections of the population were dissociated from it. American society showed deep divisions along the lines of class, race, gender, and social values.

▶ The politics of deadlock

Nothing better illustrates the complex and contradictory state of politics in the 1990s than the party political battle at national level. Clinton's election in 1992 brought the Democrats back into the presidency after a long gap and, in addition, during his first Congressional session (1993–95) both houses of Congress contained Democratic majorities. In the Congressional elections of 1994, however, Republican majorities were returned for both houses, a result which was repeated in 1996 when Clinton won re-election to a second presidential term. Of course, a party split between Congress and the presidency was nothing new. With rare exceptions, Republican presidents since the Second World War had been faced by Democratic majorities in both houses (the exceptions were the 1953–55 session under Eisenhower, when both houses were Republican, and the 1981–83 session under Reagan when the Senate was Republican). Furthermore, since voting in Congress follows party lines less strictly than in parliamentary systems such as the UK, a party split between the executive and legislative branches did not necessarily mean deadlock.

Nevertheless, the situation in the mid-1990s was unusual in a number of respects. Firstly, it took place during a Democratic presidency, the only comparison being the Congressional elections of 1946 when Truman was

President, and to that extent it represented a sharp divergence from the postwar norm. The Republican victories in the congressional elections of 1994, coming two years into Clinton's first term, seemed a particularly pointed popular commentary on his performance to date. Secondly, a substantial number of the Congressmen elected in 1994 were new members and most of those were Republicans. As such they possessed a considerable *esprit de corps* and shared a broadly conservative agenda, thus tending to emphasize party lines within Congress and to complicate Clinton's task in gaining support for his legislative plans. Thirdly, the sense of a revivified Republicanism was associated with a spirit of resolve within Congress as a whole to recover the initiative in the legislative process from the presidency. The Speaker of the House of Representatives in the newly elected Congress, Newt Gingrich, expressed this ambition most clearly in his 'contract with America', at the core of which was a deficit reduction plan involving cuts in a variety of government programmes, in a bid to seize the moral and political highground from the President. It was a measure of the confused nature of national politics in the mid-1990s, and of the prevailing distrust of politicians referred to earlier, that Republican efforts to obstruct President Clinton's budget proposals in Congress should have backfired when, in the absence of appropriate legislation, government workers went unpaid and national parks were closed. It did not enhance Gingrich's public image when within eighteen months of assuming office as Speaker he was mired in a financial scandal which came close to destroying him politically. As it was, he survived this blow but at considerable cost to his credibility and power.

Clinton's legislative achievements were as mixed as this brief profile of national politics might suggest. His early plan for a radical overhaul of health-care, which had been a major plank of his 1992 election campaign, came to little. The most dramatic piece of domestic legislation to emerge during his first term was a welfare reform bill which was initiated by Congress rather than the presidency, Clinton's own proposals having been rejected as insufficiently radical. The new bill limited the period of eligibility for welfare, tied welfare to a willingness to work, and axed such programmes as Aid to Families with Dependent Children (AFDC), originated in Roosevelt's New Deal, and Food Stamps. Fears that this legislation would create a new army of destitute Americans when it came into force in early 1997 were not borne out in the first few months, though evidence of the full effects of this radical measure was not immediately clear. In this and other fields, such as crime control and drug abuse, such success as Clinton achieved resulted from meeting Congress more than half way, which is to say by trimming his sails to the conservative wind. More generally, Clinton and the Democrats sought to neutralize the opposition by adopting many of their policies and attitudes, including the central Republican plank of 'family values', in an effort to live down the permissive image associated with the Democrats stemming from the 1960s.

In fact, Clinton had begun to move in this direction well before the Congressional elections of 1994; indeed his election in 1992 owed much to his self-presentation as a 'New Democrat' who had shed much of the legacy of his 'tax and spend' Democratic predecessors.

In doing so, he was responding not merely to the increasingly conservative climate but to a profound shift in the social basis of the voting population. The old Democratic core constituency of ethnic working-class voters had for some years been fragmenting, as the old 'smoke-stack' industries of the industrial North-east died, the centre of gravity of American industry moved west and south, and the emphasis in the economy as a whole shifted to high-tech and service industries employing largely non-union labour. Blacks still voted overwhelmingly for the Democrats (91 per cent in 1992) as did a majority of Hispanics (61 per cent), but, E J Dionne noted, 'now everything conspires against group solidarity'. The new jobs in the service industries promoted 'individualism', while 'the decline of the small town and the old urban enclaves and the rise of new suburbs, exurbs, and condominium developments further weaken social solidarity'. In the new politics, he concluded, 'each voter is studied and appealed to as an individual'. Among black voters too, despite their historic commitment since the 1930s to the Democratic Party, there was a small but vocal minority which questioned the old liberal collectivist panaceas. The New Democrats, like New Labour in Great Britain in the 1990s, were responding to changed social conditions as well as the political agenda of their opponents.

▶ Economy and society

If political conditions were such that President Clinton did not have scope for the kind of changes which would match the rhetoric he employed in his election campaigns, the economy did considerably better than he could have dared to hope, and certainly helped to ensure his re-election in 1996. The 1990s did not begin well. After the Reagan boom of the middle 1980s, the stock market crash of 1987 exposed vulnerabilities in the American economy, above all rapidly rising budget deficits and a growing foreign trade imbalance. In the late 1980s the United States became a net debtor nation after over sixty years as a creditor, fuelling public preoccupation with the theme of American decline. Bush's years in office (1989–93) coincided with a downturn in the global economy, and his method of dealing with the government's increasing indebtedness, which was to raise taxes, not only lost him credibility with many of those who elected him but ran directly counter to his famous campaign promise of 'READ MY LIPS! NO NEW TAXES'. Clinton benefited from global economic recovery but also from policies which worked both politically and economically. Soon after he came into office he chose to reduce government spending rather than (as some of his advisers recommended) increase borrowing to stimulate the economy. In 1995 he undertook with Congress to aim for a balanced budget by the year 2002, thereby, as one commentator noted, breaking 'a generation's expectation that Democrats were fiscally irresponsible'. After the beginning of recovery in 1993, the American economy grew steadily, with low inflation and low unemployment, far outstripping Japan's growth rate and regaining its position as the world's leading car-maker.

The general economic picture does not, however, tell the whole story. It obscures the fact that prosperity was anything but evenly distributed. Large pockets of economic and social disadvantage persisted, casting doubt on the efficacy of both liberal and conservative approaches to social policy. The liberal, big-government approach had long been under attack and had few defenders; the conservative, *laissez-faire* approach was increasingly in the ascendancy but had yet to prove itself in terms of results. Significantly, the new orthodoxy of the 1990s, as measured, for example, by the new welfare bill, seemed remarkably close to the remedy proposed by Charles Murray in his 1984 book, *Losing Ground*: namely, that the welfare system should be dismantled. Murray's book was reissued in 1994 with a new preface which claimed his original thesis – that government welfare programmes create poverty rather than removing it – had been fully vindicated. In any event, in the 1990s, social problems were not by and large regarded as being amenable to solution by government. The most obvious instances were the gradual retreat from affirmative action in race relations in a sequence of US Supreme Court decisions during the 1990s, the erosion of Federal protection of abortion rights as established by the Supreme Court in the 1973 *Roe* v. *Wade* decision, and the efforts by a number of states to withdraw guarantees of civil rights to gays and lesbians.

In the field of race relations, as in others, the evidence suggested a complex picture of considerable progress in some areas combined with a persistence of underlying problems of discrimination and disadvantage. Statistics showed that by the mid-1990s middle-class African-Americans were closing the income gap with their white counterparts, that home ownership was rising, the black teenage birth-rate was falling, the number of young blacks being murdered was declining, and high school completion rates had reached those of whites. On the other hand, black rates of unemployment, teenage parenthood, drug addiction, and death by violence still remained disproportionately high. Most significantly, a detailed survey published in 1997 found an alarming and growing 'skills gap' between young black and white Americans. Employment opportunities and long-term earning potential were affected not so much by years of schooling as by the level of skills acquired. The evidence was that between 1988 and 1994 in reading, maths and science the racial gap had increased in each of these subjects by a full year, reversing an improving trend from the 1960s. While no definitive explanations have been offered, the figures confirm that, despite progress for many African-Americans, the issue of race remained intractable.

In the 1990s it also remained highly visible. On the night of 29 April 1992, the black area of Los Angeles erupted in a riot which killed thirteen people and left hundreds of buildings burning. It was sparked by the acquittal of four policeman for the beating of Rodney King, an event which had been caught on video and widely shown on television. In the days after the Los Angeles riot, demonstrations followed in cities all over the United States. Three years later, the long-running trial of football and media star O J Simpson for murder showed that race was the inescapable prism through which the public interpreted such events. Reactions to Simpson's acquittal for murder showed a nation divided along racial lines. Perhaps it was not surprising, given the erosion of public support for remedial race relations measures and the re-emergence (or re-legitimation) of traditional social values, that there should have been renewed speculation about the racial basis of intelligence. The same Charles Murray who wrote *Losing Ground* co-authored *The Bell Curve* (1994) which revived the kind of biogenetic thinking characteristic of periods of social conservatism.

The histories of gender and race issues demonstrate a number of parallels. Feminists and civil rights activists share the goal of achieving equality of rights, political representation and economic opportunity, and draw on some of the same arguments and ideological sources. Government policies since the mid-1960s have shown a broadly similar pattern in the fields of civil and women's rights: the activism of the late 1960s and 1970s giving way to a degree of retrenchment in the 1980s and 1990s. In a widely read book, *Backlash*, published in 1991, Susan Faludi saw a profound 'backlash' against the gains achieved by women. Anti-feminism, she maintained, had taken a firm hold on American culture. Arguably, however, the pattern in women's issues was not unlike that for African-Americans. Tangible gains in some areas were offset by losses in others. Politically, women were increasingly visible both as successful candidates for elective office and as a factor in voting in presidential elections. Women more than doubled their numbers in statewide elective offices between 1975 and 1993, constituting over 20 per cent of state elective officials in 1993. At the federal level, the rate of increase was similar, though numbers were lower, around 10 per cent. Most striking in the presidential elections of the 1990s was the gender disparity in votes for Democratic and Republican candidates, suggesting that the women's vote had become a highly significant independent factor which future candidates would ignore at their peril. On the other hand, anti-feminist views became more publicly acceptable in many quarters, bearing out Faludi's theme of backlash. It would seem that broad acceptance of the case for equality for women coexisted with fears in some quarters that it threatened the social fabric. One is confronted in this field, as in others, by evidence reflecting the existence of contradictory impulses in American society, or, perhaps more accurately, its fragmented nature.

Observers have developed a number of terms and images to describe this peculiar combination of unity and diversity. The shift from 'melting pot' to 'salad bowl' and now 'multiculturalism' reflected a progressive waning of the confidence that there was a fundamental social consensus. To older divisions deriving from ethnicity, race and religion have been added gender, sexual orientation and life-style. Indeed the term multi-culturalism itself, as it emerged in the late 1980s and 1990s, became ideo-logically charged, setting advocates of a new, experimental morality which celebrated new forms of diversity against defenders of traditional con-cepts of morality and social order. The battle over 'political correctness', which was fought out primarily in education, brought this debate into sharp focus. Were newly introduced speech codes at some universities, outlawing various forms of discriminatory language, manifestations of a new tolerance or did they impose absurd restrictions on individual self-expression? Did the requirement at some universities that all students take a course in non-Western culture represent a new openness or a politically loaded violation of academic freedom? Did the attack on the Western literary canon represent a welcome departure from a stultifying and poli-tically repressive diet of works by dead white males or was it an act of cultural vandalism? While many tried to avoid the polarized thinking implicit in these questions, there was no disguising the fact that these and similar debates exposed deep fissures in American society.

▶ America and the world

The one certain thing which can be said about the ending of the Cold War is that it confounded the expectations of virtually all observers, ex-pert and non-expert alike. In November 1989 that great symbol of the Cold War, the Berlin Wall, was pulled down. The people of Eastern Europe took to the streets and after a generation of repression took politics into their own hands. Within two years the Soviet Union itself had collapsed. Neither the way it happened nor its effects were foreseen – nor indeed easily foreseeable. Much debate took place over whether Reagan's hard-line policies had forced the Soviet Union into submission by increasing the pace and cost of the arms race to a level at which the Soviet Union could not compete. According to this view, Star Wars (the Strategic Defense Initiative) brought the Soviet Union to its knees. Others claim that inter-nal factors such as economic stagnation, the decay of communist ideo-logy, generational change, and the advent of new leadership in 1985 caused the collapse of communism in the Soviet Union and Eastern Europe. Doubtless all these pressures played a part. Above all, perhaps, the grow-ing recognition of the Soviet bloc's comparative economic and cultural disadvantage with respect to the West undermined the claim that communism was the wave of the future.

During the Cold War the communist threat had been the United States' consuming foreign policy interest. Its removal virtually at a stroke did not, however, automatically resolve America's foreign policy dilemmas. In the field of nuclear weapons, for example, while the United States and Russia agreed on substantial reductions and on ending the targeting of each other's cities and weapons sites, nuclear instability remained a source of high anxiety. Proliferation of nuclear weapons to other countries and the security of fissile material in the Soviet Union and its successor states replaced superpower competition as the chief threat. Nor did the end of the Cold War produce the massive financial 'peace dividend' anticipated by many optimists. True, the United States was able to cut the defense budget by approximately 20 per cent and substantially reduce the level of its forces in Europe. As a percentage of gross domestic product the defence budget was now smaller than at any time since 1940. Nevertheless, as the sole remaining world-class military power, with levels of defence expenditure equal to those of the next ten nations combined, the United States found in the years after 1989 that there were still demanding calls on its military power.

The overriding challenge posed by the end of the Cold War, however, was to the United States' conception of its national interest and hence to its judgement about when or if to intervene overseas. During the Cold War the priority of containing communism had simplified such decision-making. With the removal of the communist threat the United States was forced to respond to each situation on its merits, which meant formulating durable and consistent principles to guide policy. In 1991 President Bush announced the advent of a 'New World Order', a somewhat vague notion which registered little more than an aspiration to American leadership in an uncertain world. It is best seen as a justification for the intervention to end the Iraqi invasion of Kuwait. The intervention combined American military supremacy with international co-operation in the form of a broad coalition of powers under the aegis of the United Nations. The New World Order did not outlive the Gulf War, not least because the coalition was a fragile structure which endured only until the immediate task in hand was completed. Though such a UN-endorsed coalition would have been inconceivable during the Cold War (because the superpowers routinely employed the Security Council veto power against each other), it did not become a model for subsequent interventions, so the problem of providing a rationale for American foreign policy remained.

The Clinton administration's answer was 'enlargement', a substitute for the old policy of containment, by means of which he hoped to appeal to the public's idealism and its self-interest. Concerned to discourage any tendency towards isolationism, which appeared to be an option with the disappearance of the Soviet threat, he insisted that enlargement was necessary for domestic as well as foreign reasons. The health of the American economy and the flourishing of the democratic system depended on an expansion of the 'world's free community of market democracies'. Many of the Clinton administration's foreign policy measures can be seen in this light, a good example being the establishment in 1993 of the North American Free Trade Agreement (NAFTA) with Canada and Mexico. However, such a general principle could hardly of itself supply policy criteria in every case, and the record is one of hit and miss, especially early in the Clinton administration. The intervention in Somalia also in 1993 brought neither stability in Somalia nor consensus in the United States, with the result that American troops were withdrawn early the next year. Perhaps because of doubts about whether the US public would endorse further interventions in faraway places, the United States was slow to respond to the crises in Bosnia and Rwanda.

The Clinton administration was more consistent and more successful in its long-standing sphere of interest in Europe. There the issue was how NATO, originally devised to contain the Soviet threat, might develop as a Europe-wide security organization. Discussions about NATO enlargement led in 1997 to an agreement to include Hungary, Poland and the Czech Republic as members by 1999. A suspicious Russia, seeing in this process a threat to its own security, was mollified by assurances that it would be consulted at every stage. One important consequence of the enlargement agreement was that it cemented the American commitment to Europe at a time when, given the absence of a Soviet threat, many believed it could be reduced.

Opinions vary about how successful the Clinton administration was in developing consistent policies. What is clear is that a policy of enlargement, which had powerful advocates in the foreign policy establishment, was forced to run the gauntlet of a revived isolationism in sections of American public opinion. On balance, the record suggested that Clinton was winning his argument that prosperity at home depended upon a policy of enlargement abroad.

▶ The information revolution

As American society moves toward the end of the twentieth century, analysts in the USA and abroad are still seeking to define what makes its distinctive – though ever more world-pervasive – character. The French philosopher Jean Baudrillard in his *America* (1986) read the country as 'a utopia which has acted from the very beginning as though it were already achieved. Everything here is real and pragmatic, and yet it is all the stuff of dreams too.' He sees its present cultural mixture as 'post-modern', as does the American Marxist Fredric Jameson, in his study *Postmodernism: Or the Cultural Logic of Late Capitalism* (1991). Jameson sees society as being in an affluent and consumerist stage of late capitalism, living beyond the struggles of modernity. It is a world where the main agents are the market, the media, and the international corporation, the central participants the professional and managerial classes of an age of new wealth, new variety, and growing gentrification. Jameson offers a vivid account of America as a largely urban, highly corporate, pluralistic and dynamic society. It is a society of highrise office blocks and great shopping malls built in eclectic styles, renegotiating the relationship between history and space. It is a highly technological society full of speeding messages, drawing its entertainment, and to a lesser extent its news, from a great web of media on multi-channelled systems. It is shaped by new physics and biology, and by the service industry stage of post-industrial development. It is a society of enormous interactivity: of peoples, groups, ideologies, images, styles, and technical systems. It functions spatially, moving freely between one reality and another, and is also a 'depthless' culture, discontinuous with the past. It has little sense of 'real' history, and draws on history largely as nostalgia. As the cultural analyst Christopher Lasch was one of the first to point out (in *The Culture of Narcissism*, 1978) it sees the self not as a solid subject formed by individual experience, but rather a bundle of shifting images, styles and identities. Perhaps as a consequence, it is a culture addicted to personal therapy, as people seek to rediscover a sense of wholeness and meaning in their lives, and yet equally addicted to a virtual world of public icons, television and movie stars, and soap operas, and the realm of the 'simulacrum', Baudrillard's term for the imitation of the real which no longer bears substantial relation to any original. Yet if it is increasingly a Disneyfied culture, as outside observers think, the Disney world makes dollars; the fantasy is in this sense real. The massive expansion in personal access to life-transforming technology signalled by the explosion in use of personal computing but also by the enormous intensification of the penetration of technology into the life of the individual seems to be changing the very basis of the relationship with 'the real'.

While the nation was founded on a utopian model, it was also founded for the most pressing practical reasons, and these twin thrusts still explain much of what occurred in the 1990s. The land of the free is dedicated to freedom of speech, freedom of information, and, not least, the free local telephone call. Cold War anxieties concerning the stability of communication systems led to the development of a decentralized communications network which would not be vulnerable to nuclear attack; this much can be explained by military strategy. But, utopianly, the ensuing network was opened up, first to academic computer users, and then to all comers (hence the importance of free telephone calls), allowing the rapid expansion of the virtual world, the World Wide Web. Marshall McLuhan's global village now existed in interactive form as opposed to the earlier centralized and unidirectional shape created by television and radio.

As the Internet grew, funded by academic institutions and then by subscribers to online services, it raised new issues concerning regulation, in respect of security and censorship. On the Web, 'how to' manuals on bomb making, survivalism, militarist and racist propaganda became freely available, along with pornography and talk groups devoted to every conceivable issue. The commercial desire to ensure encrypted transactions to make the new medium suitable for financial exchange ran up against a governmental determination to retain the ability to decode messages; conversely, the desire of many concerned parents and fundamentalist groups to remove pornography came up against the American commitment to free speech. President Clinton spoke up firmly in favour of freedom in this respect, which made further regulation unlikely, at least for the time being. Business interests scrambled to take up commanding positions in the virtual realm but, initially, enjoyed little return from their considerable investments as the Net served primarily as an information provider rather than a market place. Cheaply produced mass circulation 'set-top' boxes for televisions seemed likely to enable greater business use of the Internet and to reduce the gap between the haves and the have-nots in information access. It is perhaps foreseeable that the American empire will in the end be a virtual empire, like the eventual legacy of the Greeks and Romans, not an empire of trade but of customs and mores, law and knowledge.

But what difference will the new medium and the concomitant explosion in personal computer use really make in the US culture? As a new means of communication, it has arguably less effect than the invention of the telegraph and the telephone; as an information provider it could be compared to the enormous changes made by radio, film and television. The potential of the Internet for interactive communication in politics and marketing will doubtless accelerate already existing trends towards the inclusion of detailed feedback mechanisms. At the same time it early on demonstrated a capacity to create online communities, whether of militia groups, extremist theorists, or simply hobbyists newly able to connect up with distant sympathisers. The inbuilt leaning of this new medium towards virtuality was perhaps its most significant aspect. Users of the network often signed in with false identities, with alternative gender or other invented characteristics. It was widely used for complicated fantasy play, in games and interpersonal transactions. Novelists like Robert Coover and John Updike created interactive fictions on the Web in the late Nineties and it promised the possibility of fully interactive engagements with film narratives. A new realm of freely accessible images from libraries built up by media corporations like Sony allowed a wider availability of art works, and a good deal of art was also created using computer technology. That same technology offered the possibility of image manipulation and was connected with the explosion of virtual imaging in other media, especially film. Oliver Stone's film *JFK* spliced imaginary footage together with shots of Kennedy's assassination; *Forrest Gump* used similar techniques although in a less provocative manner. This capacity to re-envisage the past in terms just as convincing as 'authentic' film foot-age, like the ability to adjust photographic images invisibly, coincides with a widespread interest in 'revisionist' history, through which, especially in the post-modern culture, competing versions can coexist, indeed even *should* coexist, on the grounds that truth is local, provisional, and relative (although paradoxically not less 'true' for that, only more self-consciously allowing for inevitable distortions).

Most blockbuster films of the Nineties appealed to audiences who had become sophisticated consumers of the culture of the spectacle, who had, that is, a strongly ironic sense of the nature of representation. It must also be acknowledged that some viewers might not have been too sophisticated to believe in abduction by UFOs, for example, and the extent to which the culture became itself a virtual experience might be judged by Vice-President Dan Quayle's political attack on Ms Murphy Brown, a fictional single mother in a TV show (21 May 1992). Like Thomas Pynchon's tubal addicts in his novel *Vineland*, the reality of the media could come to seem more real than anything else. Don DeLillo's pro-phetic novel *White Noise* concerned itself early with such issues, describing the 'most photographed barn in America', and the way that the televi-sion's background commentary interpenetrates the life of the family. Bend-ing over his sleeping child to hear what words she is uttering, 'words that seemed to have a ritual meaning, part of a verbal spell or ecstatic chant', the father hears '*Toyota Celica*'. Another significant Nineties exercise in virtuality came from Disney Enterprise itself, the building of *Celebration*, a brand new (and very exclusive) town based on nostalgic Americana style, with strict rules for community participation and correct behaviour. Appeal-ing to the same yearning for a vanished and possibly imaginary America, Hans Magnus Enzenberger's arguments about the need to build com-munity structures that would inhibit crime and reduce welfare depen-dency found favour in the liberal press and even with the President.

The Internet is itself, in some respects, a model of 'post-modern' culture in its decentralized structure and open access, whereby any par-ticipant can be at once consumer and producer, reader and publisher; its resistance to overarching controls or 'grand narratives'; its anarchic end-less particularity, and its jumbling together of disparate interests and images past and present. In these respects it is opposed to the essentially 'modernist' projects of centrally controlled and passively consumed tele-vision, film or radio. The subject's position in this medium is not predeter-mined but experientially developed. And the very fact of its non-existence, in the material sense, keys it with the increasing 'virtuality' of a culture dominated by the consumption of 'dematerialized' goods: film and video, consumer electronics, and software for business, entertainment and educa-tion purposes. The possibilities of a *machina sapiens* and its complement, the cyber-body, became a dominant theme in Nineties popular and even academic culture. In the novels of William Gibson, Pat Cadigan, and other 'cyber' novelists (initially but inaccurately called cyber-punk) the interface between man and machine becomes confused; Gibson investigates the 'Matrix' that the Internet might become, and the modifications of the humans who connect themselves into it; Cadigan explores the schizophrenic avenues of a world in which memories might be for sale, or stolen, and identities bought wholesale as cloned personalities. But not all visions of the cybernetic future were pessimistic. An interpretation of the usefulness of such ideas for feminism by Donna Haraway ('A Manifesto for Cyborgs') received much attention, especially in the academic community. The *Terminator* films pointed to a future in which the network becomes dominant and acts against humanity, but also articulated other cyborg themes. The Terminator itself, although not human, is a better father than any human one could be, according to the mother of the boy who is to save the humans from a machine-engendered apocalypse.

Exploiting a growing public fascination with otherworld possibilities as the millennium approached, Hollywood produced SciFi fantasies in large numbers: *Mars Attacks!*, *Independence Day*, *Men in Black*, to list just a few. The television equivalent, of course, was the popular programme, *The X Files*. Alien-abduction fantasies and a belief in UFOs were observed in increasing numbers among the otherwise apparently sane. In 1997 one spectacular West Coast cult called Heaven's Gate headed for a new extraterrestrial life by mass suicide. Despite the death of all its members, it quickly started up again with a new page on the Internet. Elvis Presley, however, did not make his widely expected personal appearance for the 1997 twentieth anniversary of his death.

▶ Film, post-modernism and popular culture

Post-modern culture is extremely difficult to 'read'. Contemporary aesthetics embrace discontinuity and intertextuality; the art object is frequently a self-referential pastiche of other objects, and there is no agreed way in which its meaning can be interpreted. In the culture at large the plethora of communication channels, including broadcast, cable and satellite, and the concommitant fragmentation of audiences able to choose what they receive – whether in newspapers, television, or other media – mean that quite disparate assessments of the dominant cultural concerns are almost inevitable. But in so far as there is an arena where the culture 'talks to itself' of its desires and its anxieties, the relatively uncensored expression of film (as opposed to the more controlled and self-inhibited media of newspapers and television, or the minority audiences of theatre and other arts) offers the best insight into the deeper movements in contemporary society. American films are multiply authored – which is to

say that an 'auteurist' analysis of the director's vision is usually inappropriate – and they are addressed to a multiple audience, which means that
they usually do not locate themselves in relation to any particular group
or interest within the society but attempt to capture the widest possible
range of consumers. The continuing international importance of American
film (a major exporting industry which makes up to 90 per cent of the
world's movies), and the new role of video marketing and merchandizing
tie-ins, which often produce more profit than box office sales, only increases these pressures. In consequence, popular films offer rich but
often self-contradictory reading possibilities.

As Joseph Natoli explains in *Hauntings: Popular Film and American
Culture, 1900–1992* (1994):

> Since popularity is a market issue, and profits are not undermined
> by paradoxes but can instead thrive on them, the popular film
> adheres to the market's own consumption of paradoxes. Further, in
> pursuing its profits both in the places where the common culture is
> being cemented and in those places where it is being haunted, the
> market itself displays a paradoxical nature. Popular film is just
> following right along.

It is no longer possible simply to ask, as one might of 'classic' Hollywood film – or even Broadway theatre – what is the meaning of the text
in relation to the culture in which it is produced and consumed. There
are likely to be multiple meanings and references, some of them coherent, some quite contradictory. Timothy Corrigan proposes the category
of 'illegible films', films that resist legibility and interpretation, and 'whose
fragmented mobility mirrors the technological and cultural conditions
that spawned them'. For example, *Basic Instinct* offered a psychotic picture of lesbian sexuality, which was duly protested by lesbians and feminists, while at the same time it offered a 'haunting', to use Natoli's term,
because the 'undecidability of the ending makes the whole film undecid-
able' and moreover the film created the image of a new woman 'exceeding
what we are able to say about her', and could thus be seen as empowering
even by lesbian viewers.

Popular film in the Eighties and Nineties continued to exploit conventional classical Hollywood narrative techniques but increasingly began to
twist, subvert, or parody them. In the work of David Lynch and Quentin
Tarantino, conventional narrative was subverted by elliptical interconnec-
tions, parallel narratives, exaggerated psychoanalytical resonances, and
humorous deconstructions of audience expectations: an Oedipal trajec-
tory sinisterly burlesqued in Lynch's *Blue Velvet*; an atrocious murder treated
as comedy in Tarantino's *Pulp Fiction*. In these films the most viable interpretative technique seems to be to 'read' them not so much in terms of
their ultimate import as for what they seem to have had to say about
whichever cultural urgencies appear within the overall frame. Concerns

about the pervading violence of the dreamlife, whether of individuals or, more nostalgically, a whole town, are at play in Lynch's work; the accidentality of psychotic violence and the discontinuity of individuals in Tarantino's. Fredric Jameson commented that such films 'show a collective unconscious in the process of trying to identify its own present at the same time that they illuminate the failure of this attempt, which seems to reduce itself to the recombination of various stereotypes of the past'. Even when the Nineties popular films appeared to offer a clearer message, almost forcing a reading on us, as in *Pretty Woman, Working Girl, Born on the Fourth of July*, or *JFK*, the inbuilt spin of paradox makes that reading precarious. *Pretty Woman's* Cinderella plot allowed for the rise of a hooker, not through virtue but through shopping (and fucking, in the popular adage). *Working Girl* showed how a woman could make it up the corporate ladder – by undermining her female boss from hell, lying (when necessary), and playing up to the paternalism of the real (male) bosses. *Born on the Fourth of July* showed how a boy growing up under Kennedy could become a patriot in the Vietnam War, and then a wounded anti-war spokesman – but by putting the blame on mom personalized the view of the conflict and its roots. *JFK*, the most politically committed of these, signed up to a highly controversial conspiracy thesis of Kennedy's assassination with a naïveté that brought its own evidence into question.

Looking at the *contents* of the frame, rather than the overt arguments of these films, however, it would seem that the Reaganite insistence on economic success by fair means or foul came under some sceptical scrutiny. *Wall Street* provided a particularly interesting example as a film that effectively celebrated the Reagan–Bush ethos (greed is good, proclaims corporate raider Gordon Gecko in a speech to shareholders, greed is what works) while ostensibly articulating resistance to its consequences, as eventually the tyro capitalist Bud Fox sees the light, turns against Gecko, and follows the lead of his union organizer father in a nostalgic tribute to the rule of law and John Ford's America. *Pretty Woman's* subplot also addressed the ethics of corporate raiding, as did *Working Girl* and an acerbic investigation of the takeover ethos, *Other People's Money*. Thus one of the – surely unforeseen – effects of Reaganite nostalgia was to focus the spotlight on Eighties and Nineties business practises as the popular culture attempted to reconcile a new financial rapacity with old Populist shibboleths.

Gender, sexuality, and race generated yet more paradoxes in such films as *Thelma and Louise, My Own Private Idaho, Do the Right Thing, The Accused* and *The Color Purple*. Women who reject domesticity struggle with male condescension and violence; their Bonnie and Clyde adventures lead them into the 'wild zone' of feminist articulation; they end either at the bottom of the Grand Canyon, or in the realm of the Imaginary. Some commercially successful movies began to offer new visions of powerful women, partly as a result of the impact of Sigourney Weaver in the *Aliens* series, showing tough women like Jodie Foster taking responsibility for themselves in *The Accused* and *The Silence of the Lambs*, Linda Hamilton in *Terminator 2*, or Gina Davis in *The Long Kiss Goodnight*. Gay film also entered the mainstream with *My Own Private Idaho*, *Philadephia*, and *Desert Hearts*. But lesbian homosexuality was represented as only a passing aberration in *The Color Purple* adaptation by Spielberg despite the fact that female homosexuality was so important a part of Alice Walker's novel. Spike Lee's *Do the Right Thing* posed Malcolm X's radical activism against Martin Luther King's message of peaceful protest, and concluded with a gesture which could be read as either inciting or defusing a race riot. That film, like the later *Falling Down*, acknowledged the complexity of racial tensions; not only between black and white, but between Korean, Italian, Latino and Jewish-Americans, as was highlighted in Tom Wolfe's novel and subsequent film, *The Bonfire of the Vanities* (1988). Wolfe's fictional mayor of New York fulminates:

> It's the Third World down there! Puerto Ricans, West Indians,
> Haitians, Dominicans, Cubans, Columbians, Hondurans, Koreans,
> Chinese, Thais, Vietnamese, Ecuadorians, Panamanians, Filipinos,
> Albanians, Senegalese, and Afro-Americans! Go visit the
> frontiers, you gutless wonders! Morningside Heights, St
> Nicholas Park, Washington Heights, Fort Tryon – *por qué pagar más!*
> The Bronx – the Bronx is finished for you!'

In his vision, neither the melting pot nor the salad bowl model remains at all plausible.

Largely due to Spike Lee's success, new opportunities were given to black directors, like John Singleton, who directed *Boyz'n the Hood*, but the Hollywood interest remained strictly commercial: even Lee had to organize alternative funding from friends when he went over the tight budget allowed for *Malcolm X*. Lee's early success was due to his film, *She's Gotta Have It*, which appealed to both black and white audiences. Such 'crossover' possibilities were also evident in popular music, when large numbers of white suburban teenagers came to appreciate the violent and frequently sexist lyrics of inner-city black music, 'gangsta rap'.

In the Nineties post-feminism became a widely used term, indicating on the one hand that real achievements in gender equality had been gained, and on the other an impatience with what had become widely perceived as a stridency of feminist discourse (in, for example, Andrea Dworkin's widely reported view that all men are rapists). Susan Faludi's 1991 book *Backlash* documented how such arguments might be used to reverse the gains that women had made, and to imply that no more need be done, and Tania Modleski in *Feminism Without Women* (also 1991) pointed out subversions of feminist thought by both male sympathizers and antagonists, to the extent that essential principles were lost to sight in the new feminism. The role changes of Hillary Clinton, as she moved from feminist authority to a more domestic image, offered some pointers to the pressures at work in this arena, as did numerous arguments about date rape and the widespread publicity given to David Mamet's play about the complexities of sexual harassment in a university setting, *Oleanna*, in which a male lecturer is victimized. The movement from feminist courses to gender studies in universities suggested a widening but perhaps also at the same time a weakening of the impetus that had initiated these new areas of study. In popular film too 'backlash' was prominently visible. *Fatal Attraction* had demonized the independent working woman; *Baby Boomer* showed the path to true happiness and success to be a country retreat with the right man and a new career making commercially successful infant food.

One important film of the early Nineties, *Falling Down*, highlighted the marginalization of the once dominant white male group. No longer employed by the post-Cold War Californian weapons industry, its protagonist stumbles through a Western landscape that is no longer his, using increasingly deadly weapons, towards a wife who has rejected him and his eventual death in a traditional shoot out – armed now only with a water pistol. 'I'm the bad guy?' he asks incredulously. Bad (white) guys were identified as psychotics in the serial killer fixation that gripped the nation in the Nineties, from the urbane (cannibal) Hannibal Lecter in *Silence of the Lambs* to the psychotic multiple murderers of *Red Dragon, Amerika, Henry: Portrait of a Serial Killer*, and *Seven*. Statistics showed an increase in real-life serial killers (or at least their identification), and did seem to suggest that white, even educated and middle-class, men might be unusually prevalent in that notorious group. Books about them similarly were written by white males: Thomas Harris, whose *Red Dragon* and *Silence of the Lambs* inaugurated the series, and Bret Easton Ellis, whose disturbing novel about a Wall Street psychopath, *American Psycho*, did not find a brave enough film producer. Ellis had previously offered a novel detailing the alienation of wealthy American kids, *Less Than Zero*, which began: 'People are afraid to merge on freeways in Los Angeles', and ended, after a devastating investigation of laid-back anomie, snuff movies and other atrocities, with the Hemingwayesque young observer saying: 'These images stayed with me even after I left the city. Images so violent and malicious that they seemed to be my only point of reference for a long time afterwards.' Even some less controversial presentations of white American youth, such as the films *River's Edge, Dazed and Confused, Clerks, Reality Bites, Mall Rats*, or *Slackers*, presented an alienated, bored, and remarkably unaffective youth culture, in keeping with the worst anticipations of such theorists as Christopher Lasch.

Bill Clinton responding to a widespread attack on gay rights, inaugurated his presidency with a damaging reversal of election pledges on gays in the military. Some states, notably Colorado, enacted measures to prevent the extension of equal rights legislation to homosexuals. The AIDs epidemic, which did particular damage to gays and was often therefore considered a gay disease, provided fuel for prejudice. New drug 'cocktails' offered more effective treatment but opened an even wider gap between those who could afford such expensive remedies and those sufferers – primarily black, and poor – who could not. There were also fears that the success of the new drugs might divert attention from research into finding a more substantial cure for the illness. But on balance, the decade saw an increasing acceptance of homosexuality in the mainstream culture, and it is significant in assessing the overall climate of the decade that the Colorado anti-gay legislation was declared unconstitutional in 1994 by a Federal court. A new openness about sexual preference was signalled by events such as the 'coming out' of celebrity figures including the 'Ellen' of the TV show. Talk shows developed comparably open conversations about personal and social issues, among them domestic abuse, drug addiction, and such highly controversial issues as 'recovered memory' syndrome in accounts of child abuse.

▶ The culture of nostalgia

Reagan's appeal to Americans had played upon a nostalgia for that utopian vision of what the United States might have been, but it might be added that, as Herman Melville prophesied, the Union 'spins *against* the way it drives'. While Reagan, and to an extent his successors Bush and Clinton, played to the mythic gallery, the forces of capital were freed further to threaten the very values that were publicly promoted: community, responsibility, family life. In the Eighties, and continuing in the Nineties, the free market overwhelmed all other values, and with the added threat of globalized competition it found little articulate opposition. In this respect Clinton largely adopted his predecessor's agenda. Quite how the free market ideal might be squared with a conservative belief in family solidarity, restriction of abortion rights, or the corrosive effects of promiscuity or gay life-styles is a question that has puzzled many commentators. To take simple examples, the high spending potential of gay people attracted specifically targeted advertising, and neither the market nor governmental initiatives did anything actually to promote family life in practical terms.

As part of the nostalgic appeal to an earlier and supposedly more decent America, the Nineties decade opened with a concerted assault on what many deemed to be pornography in the arts. Reagan had tried this ten years earlier, without much success, but in 1989 Senator Jesse Helms led a campaign against the federal funding of works that he and pressure groups such as the American Family Association considered 'indecent or obscene', choosing photographers Robert Mapplethorpe and Andres Serrano, who had both exhibited in exhibitions funded by the National

Endowment for the Arts (NEA), as particularly offensive examples. An amended version of Helms's bill eventually passed. This prohibited federal funding of 'obscene' art, which was defined as prurient to the 'average person', depicting 'in a patently offensive way, sexual conduct' and, as a whole, lacking 'serious artistic, political, or scientific value'. Homoeroticism and even 'individuals engaged in sex acts' were among the list of proscribed representations, along with the more predictable condemnation of sado-masochism or the exploitation of children. Defenders of artistic freedom were pleased to have won, by virtue of the 'serious . . . value' clause, a compromise that would make obscenity convictions difficult to achieve. But concern remained that charging arts administrators to avoid funding work which might be considered obscene according to such a wide definition would deny funding to any artist who aroused controversy. The reality of this threat became clear when in March 1990 Senator Helms complained that the new ban had been violated by grants given to 'three acknowledged lesbian writers'. President Bush spoke out against such censorship, adding, however, that he was himself 'deeply offended by some of the filth that I see into which federal money has gone'. The controversy did much damage to the notion of freedom of expression in the arts and was considered by many a 'sex panic'. Late in the decade, a sexually explicit remake of the film *Lolita* ran into a new hesitancy on the part of the gatekeepers of the culture when it failed to find distributors, causing its star, Jeremy Irons, to compare censorship in the US with that in China. Yet paradoxically this was also a time when Americans had unprecedented access to pornographic materials on the Internet and in the form of adult videos (rented at a rate of over 100 million each year).

Fiction also dealt with the nostalgia for an older America seen in political and cultural life, albeit sometimes obliquely, and by no means in a politically conservative way. Cormac McCarthy's popular *All the Pretty Horses*, a Faulknerian story of growing up in the early part of the century, appealed to the persistent mythos of American innocence bloodied in the encounter with other cultures. Nicholas Evans's bestseller *The Horse-Whisperer* and Robert Waller's *The Bridges of Madison County* explored related terrain in a sentimental but immensely popular vogue. Richard Ford's *The Sportswriter* and *Independence Day* considered the difficulties of remoralizing the demoralized American male in the new conditions, with an implicit nostalgia for a time when issues looked a little simpler. On balance, the Nineties appeared to be a time of widespread male anxiety, partly because of changes in gender attitudes and the increase in female work opportunities, and partly because of economic shifts towards more casual and part-time employment, especially damaging to blue-collar workers, but also affecting middle-class male self-confidence. Some of these issues were rehearsed in the so-called 'dirty realist' writings of Raymond Carver, Richard Ford and Tobias Wolff, among others, of the immediately preceding period. Avoiding such issues, while also dealing in male onto-logical insecurity, Paul Auster drew on the period of American Romanti-cism of Emerson and Thoreau, but crossed it with a nostalgia for tough-guy crime fiction in his *New York Trilogy*. Auster explored the landscapes of an earlier America in *Moon Palace*, and wrote a Twain-like fable of growing up in an older America in *Mr Vertigo*. This too is nostalgic, in some respects. But Auster's nostalgia is rigorously deconstructed, an assemblage of frag-ments or wraiths from the past which no longer seem to make sense in the present.

Among others concerned to remap the American past were Louise Erdrich, whose *Love Medicine* and *Tracks* offered a disconcerting view of American Indian experience. Toni Morrison, best known for her novels *Sula, Song of Solomon* and *Beloved*, pursued a nostalgic thread in *Jazz*, and also provided a powerful examination of the ways in which black Ameri-can experience could be seen to inflect white writing in her critical study of American literature, *Playing in the Dark*. Novelists Amy Tan (*The Joy Luck Club*) and Maxine Hong Kingston (*China Men*) reappraised the cul-tural legacy of Chinese-Americans. In film, the Quincentennary of Colum-bus's voyage produced revisionist versions in both *Christopher Columbus: The Discovery* and *1492*. In a similar vein, Kevin Costner's *Dances With Wolves* attempted a romantic version of the Indian experience, while Clint Eastwood's *The Unforgiven* worked around the question of how the west-ern past is encapsulated in unreliable – and unforgivable – narratives. Martin Scorcese continued in *Goodfellas* the retrospective analysis of the criminal shadow of 'legitimate' business begun by Coppola's *Godfather* films, whereas Tarantino and Lynch contrastingly explored a new and far less motivated violence in *Reservoir Dogs* and *Wild At Heart*. As opposed to the organized crime sagas of previous American legend, these reflected on such breakdown of order and purpose as was seen in contemporary 'wilding', the random violence of gangs and the new crime of drive-by killing ('depraved indifference to human life' in the words of a new crimi-nal law definition), in a way that seems to reflect the eclipse of earlier 'master narratives' in a randomized, fragmented, pluralist culture.

It would seem, then, that the fragmentations and pluralism fostered by the free market solution to all problems and the absence of a coercive homogeneity allowed by the collapse of the Cold War standoff could be seen as much in the cultural life of the Nineties as in the decade's politi-cal and economic shifts. An interest in more tentative and provisional solutions as opposed to all-encompassing answers was demonstrated in a movement among theorists towards post-modern openness and accept-ance of limited answers, away from grand syntheses or master-narratives and towards ideas like philosopher Richard Rorty's new pragmatic em-phasis on contingency and irony. Yet at the same time as intellectuals embraced a new uncertainty, it became apparent that the commercial aspects of the arts world were being determined by the same powerful tendencies towards consolidation and integrated marketing that directed business. Master narratives remained identifiable in the form of intensifying market pressures, the importance of public relations, publicity, and high profile self-presentation, whether of artists, media personalities, or the cultural products themselves.

▶ Towards the millenium and beyond

Thus, as the millennium approached, the United States presented a not unfamiliar mixture of self-confidence and anxiety. After the dire predictions of economic decline in the 1980s there seemed grounds for confidence in the 1990s that the United States was regaining economic strength and stability. In the late 1990s, it seemed rather to be the 'tiger' economies of Asia which were experiencing strains. In the field of foreign affairs, despite the persistence of crises in many parts of the world, few Americans doubted that the end of the Cold War represented a vindication of American values and of the policies pursued for over forty years. Some political scientists might regret the passing of the 'stable Cold War system', but there is little indication that this view was shared by most Americans. If some commentators exaggerated America's power in the claim that the world was now 'unipolar', it was nevertheless the case that American power and influence was remarkably uncontested. This applied particularly in the field of popular culture where Americanization continued its relentless progress, from films to Coca Cola, and was reflected in the increasing use worldwide of the American (English) language itself.

It would be uncharacteristic, however, of the United States to rest content with signs of progress. Though to the outside world American culture often appears complacent, uniform, even homogeneous, internally it expresses a restless vitality born of ethnic, religious, and regional diversity, the energetic pursuit of wealth and happiness, the persistence of extremes of wealth and poverty, and a political culture which alerts individuals and social groups to threats, real or imagined, to their rights and social status. The demise of the Communist threat allowed such energies to attach themselves to new targets. Family values have perhaps replaced anti-communism as the defining issue of the Right, but other forms of fundamentalism – religious, political, cultural – vie with each other in the marketplace of values which is the contemporary United States. In some respects, American culture in the 1990s recalled that of the 1920s with its kaleidoscopic social tensions following in the train of the 'Great Crusade' of the First World War. For all the manifest forces for change in the United States, there remained profound currents of continuity.

▶ **For further reading**

Timothy Corrigan, *Cinema Without Walls: Movies and Culture After Vietnam* (1991).

Michael Cox, *US Foreign Policy After the Cold War: Superpower Without a Mission?* (1995).

Philip John Davies (ed.), *An American Quarter Century: US Politics from Vietnam to Clinton* (1995).

E J Dionne, *Why Americans Hate Politics* (1991).

Frederic Jameson, *Postmodernism: Or the Cultural Logic of Late Capitalism* (1991).

Joseph Natoli, *Hauntings: Popular Film and American Culture, 1990–1992* (1994).

Maps

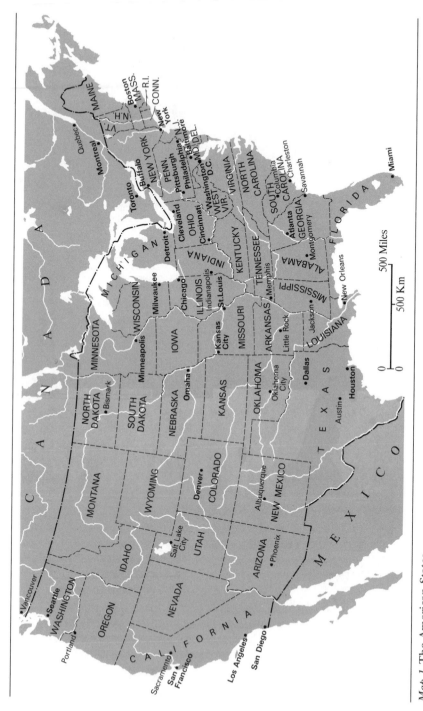

Map 1 The American States

Map 2 The original thirteen colonies

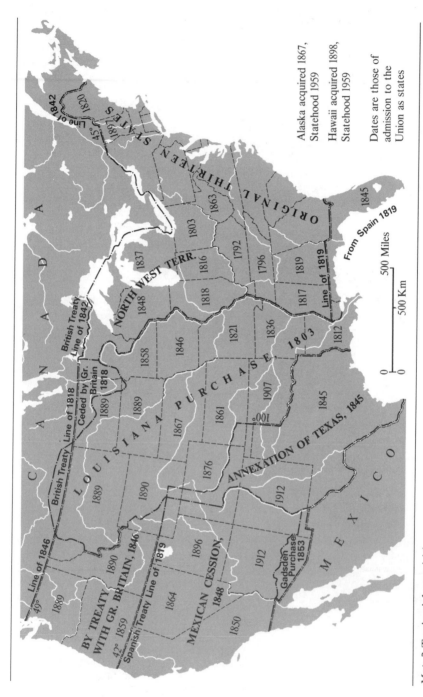

Map 3 Territorial acquisitions

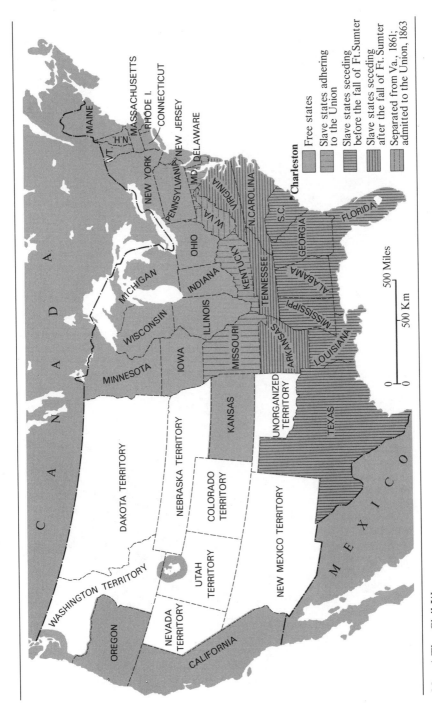

Map 4 The Civil War

Legend:
- Free states
- Slave states adhering to the Union
- Slave states seceding before the fall of Ft. Sumter
- Slave states seceding after the fall of Ft. Sumter
- Separated from Va., 1861; admitted to the Union, 1863

500 Miles

500 Km

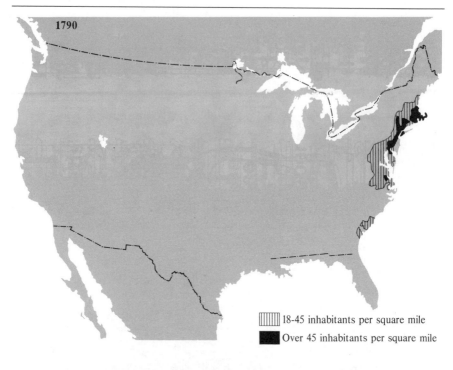

|||||| 18-45 inhabitants per square mile

■ Over 45 inhabitants per square mile

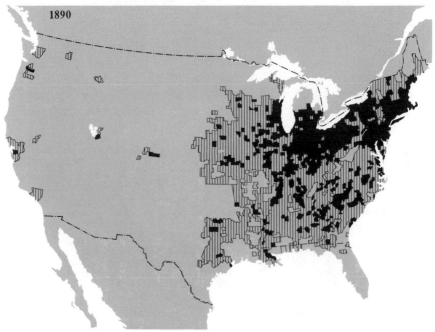

Map 5 Population expansion, 1790 to 1940

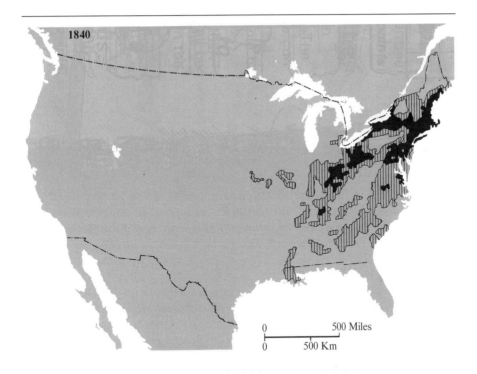

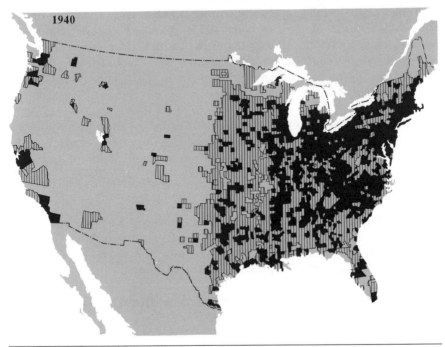

Notes on the contributors

C W E BIGSBY is Professor of American Studies at the University of East Anglia. He has written numerous books on aspects of American culture, including *The Second Black Renaissance* (1980), a three-volume *Critical Introduction to 20th Century American Drama* (1982–85), and *Modern American Drama 1940–1990* (1992).

CHRISTINE BOLT is Professor of American History at the University of Kent. She is the author of numerous books on American racial and social issues including, most recently, *The Women's Movement in the United States and Britain from the 1790s to the 1920s (1993)* and *Feminist Ferment (1995)*.

MALCOLM BRADBURY is Emeritus Professor of American Studies at the University of East Anglia, and a well-known novelist, critic and screenwriter. His novels include *The History Man* (1975), *Rates of Exchange* (1983), and *Doctor Criminale* (1992). Among his works on American subjects are *The Modern American Novel* (1992), *From Puritanism to Postmodernism: A History of American Literature* (1994), and *Dangerous Pilgrimages: Trans-Atlantic Mythologies and the Novel* (1995).

R A BURCHELL is Director of the Eccles Centre for American Studies at the British Library and Emeritus Professor of American Studies at the University of Manchester. His publications include *Westward Expansion* (1974), *The San Francisco Irish, 1848–1888* (1979), and *The End of Anglo-America* (1991).

ELLMAN CRASNOW was until recently Lecturer in English and American Literature at the University of East Anglia. He has published articles on American literature, literary theory and modernism and has produced an edited edition of Walt Whitman's *Leaves of Grass*.

RICHARD CROCKATT is Reader in American History at the University of East Anglia. His publications include *The United States and the Cold War 1941–1953* (1989), *The Fifty Years War: The United States and the Soviet Union in World Politics 1941–1991* (1995), and articles on American intellectual history.

JACQUELINE FEAR-SEGAL is Lecturer in American History at the University of East Anglia. Her main work is on Native American history, but she has also written on autobiography, race, education and multiculturalism.

RICHARD GRAY is Professor of American Literature at the University of Essex and Editor of the *Journal of American Studies*. His books include *The Literature of Memory: Modern Writers of the American South* (1977); *Writing the South: Ideas of an American Region* (1986), and *The Life of William Faulkner: A Critical Biography* (1994).

PHILIP HAFFENDEN was until recently Reader in American History at the University of Southampton. His publications include *New England in the English Nation, 1689–1713* (1974), as well as essays and articles on colonial North America.

ERIC HOMBERGER is Reader in American Literature at the University of East Anglia. His recent books include *Scenes from the Life of a City: Corruption and Conscience in Old New York* (1994), *The Historical Atlas of Old New York* (1994), and *The Penguin Historical Atlas of North America* (1995).

ANDREW HOOK is Bradley Professor of English Literature at the University of Glasgow. His publications include *Scotland and America 1750–1835* (1975) and *American Literature in Context 1865–1900* (1983), as well as articles on Anglo-American literary relations.

RICHARD H KING is Professor of American Intellectual History at the University of Nottingham. He is the author of *The Party of Eros* (1972), *A Southern Renaissance* (1980), and *Civil Rights and the Idea of Freedom* (1992).

A ROBERT LEE is currently Professor of American Literature at Nihon University, Tokyo. His most recent books include *The Beat Generation Writers* (1996) and *Designs of Blackness: Mappings in the Literature of Afro-America* (1997).

BRIAN LEE is Emeritus Professor of American Studies at the University of Nottingham. His publications include *The Novels of Henry James: A Study of Culture and Consciousness* (1978) and *American Fiction 1865–1940* (1967), as well as numerous essays on American literature and film.

ALLAN LLOYD SMITH is Senior Lecturer in American Studies at the University of East Anglia. He is the author of *The Analysis of Motives: Early American Psychology and Fiction* (1980), *Eve Tempted: Sexuality and Writing in Hawthorn's Fiction* (1987), and *Uncanny American Literature* (1994).

HELEN McNEIL was until recently Lecturer in American Literature at the University of East Anglia. Her critical study of *Emily Dickinson* appeared in 1986 and she has published widely on the topics of women and modernism.

PETER MARSHALL is Emeritus Professor of American History and Institutions at the University of Manchester. His publications are primarily concerned with aspects of Revolutionary and early national history.

EDWARD RANSON lectures in History at the University of Aberdeen. He is the author of various articles on early-twentieth-century American politics and military affairs.

ROBERT C REINDERS was a Senior Lecturer in American Studies at the University of Nottingham. He is now retired and lives in Milwaukee, Wisconsin. He was Executive Editor of *The Dictionary of World History* (1973) and is the author of *End of an Era: New Orleans 1850–1860* (1973), as well as of numerous articles on slavery and the anti-slavery movement.

DANIEL SNOWMAN was until recently the BBC's Chief Producer, Features (Radio), and before that taught Politics and American Studies at the University of Sussex. His books include *America Since 1920* (1968 and subsequent editions), and *Kissing Cousins: An Interpretation of British and American Culture, 1945–1975* (1977).

HOWARD TEMPERLEY is Emeritus Professor of American Studies at the University of East Anglia. His publications include *British Antislavery 1833–1870* (1970) and *White Dreams Black Africa: The Antislavery Expedition to the Niger 1841–1842* (1991), and articles on various aspects of American, Canadian and British history.

ROGER THOMPSON is Professor of American Studies at the University of East Anglia. Among his recent publications are *Sex in Middlesex: Popular Mores in a Massachusetts County 1649–1699* (1986) and *Mobility and Migration: East Anglian Founders of New England 1629–1640* (1994).

IAN WALKER is Senior Lecturer in American Literature at the University of Manchester. His publications include *Edgar Allan Poe: The Critical Heritage* (1986).

JOHN WHITE is Reader in American History at the University of Hull. His publications include *Black Leadership in America: From Booker T Washington to Jesse Jackson* (1990) and *Martin Luther King Jr and the Civil Rights Movement in America* (1991).

RALPH WILLETT is Senior Fellow at the University of Hull where, for many years, he taught American Studies. In 1985 he co-edited *Nothing Else to Fear: New Perspectives on America in the Thirties*. He is also the author of *The Naked City: Urban Crime Fiction in the USA* (1996).

Index

Note: reference is made to authors by name but not to their works by title.